A RIGHTS-BASED INTER-LEGAL APPROACH TO ARTIFICIAL INTELLIGENCE

How can European public law effectively address the profound rights challenges posed by AI systems?

This groundbreaking book delves into this pressing question by critically analysing the limitations of current regulatory frameworks, including the Artificial Intelligence Act, the General Data Protection Regulation, and European human rights law. Drawing on leading judgments from the European Court of Human Rights and the Court of Justice of the European Union, the book explores real-world case studies of AI systems employed by public authorities, highlighting their impact on fundamental rights.

Arguing that the EU's risk-based regulation approach falls short in protecting fundamental and human rights, the author introduces a compelling alternative: a rights-based inter-legal approach grounded in the theory of inter-legality. This innovative framework emphasises the 'publicness' and 'inter-systemic' nature of AI, advocating for a lifecycle perspective – from design to deployment and beyond.

Rich with legal insights and practical methodology, this book presents a three-step adjudication model to integrate the inter-legal approach into European legal practice, paving the way for a more robust protection of fundamental principles, rules and rights in the AI era. Essential reading for scholars, policymakers and practitioners, this work redefines how Europe can lead the charge in responsible AI regulation.

A Rights-Based Inter-Legal Approach to Artificial Intelligence

Elif Biber

•HART•
OXFORD • LONDON • NEW YORK • NEW DELHI • SYDNEY

HART PUBLISHING

Bloomsbury Publishing Plc

Kemp House, Chawley Park, Cumnor Hill, Oxford, OX2 9PH, UK

1385 Broadway, New York, NY 10018, USA

Bloomsbury Publishing Ireland Limited, 29 Earlsfort Terrace, Dublin 2, D02 AY28, Ireland

HART PUBLISHING, the Hart/Stag logo, BLOOMSBURY and the Diana logo are trademarks of Bloomsbury Publishing Plc

First published in Great Britain 2026

A catalogue record for this book is available from the British Library.

A catalogue record for this book is available from the Library of Congress.

ISBN: HB: 978-1-50997-901-1
ePDF: 978-1-50997-903-5
ePub: 978-1-50997-902-8

Typeset by Compuscript Ltd, Shannon

For product safety related questions contact productsafety@bloomsbury.com

To find out more about our authors and books visit www.hartpublishing.co.uk. Here you will find extracts, author information, details of forthcoming events and the option to sign up for our newsletters.

ACKNOWLEDGEMENTS

'Dear, dear! How queer everything is today! And yesterday things went on just as usual. I wonder if I've been changed in the night? Let me think: was I the same when I got up this morning? I almost think I can remember feeling a little different. But if I'm not the same, the next question is, Who in the world am I?',[1] wrote Lewis Carroll in 1865. Alice's bewilderment as the world around her shifted speaks to the same profound questions we face in the age of artificial intelligence. Yesterday, the world felt familiar; today, it feels transformed. As we encounter machines that think, speak, and even create alongside with us, we, too, find ourselves asking, who are we in relation to these new intelligences? This book seeks to navigate that Wonderland through the lens of law, drawing on my doctoral thesis, and to map a landscape at once strange, unsettling, and profoundly inspiring.

My intellectual home throughout this journey has been the vibrant academic community in Pisa at the Scuola Superiore Sant'Anna. Among many, I owe particular thanks to my supervisor Gianluigi Palombella, whose generous engagement and scholarly support pushed me to refine my arguments and broaden my perspective. His guidance was invaluable in helping me identify and articulate the core questions of my research. Thanks to our exchanges, I came to appreciate that the most fundamental questions are often the most difficult to grasp, yet they also offer the greatest potential for substantive and meaningful intellectual development. I am also deeply grateful to the Center for Inter-Legality at the Scuola, which quickly became an inspiring scholarly forum. The numerous conferences, workshops, and seminars hosted there profoundly enriched my understanding of the theory of inter-legality and fostered meaningful dialogue with many leading scholars.

I am also indebted to Giuseppe Martinico, whose support and guidance throughout my PhD journey were of great help and encouragement. I wish, as well, to thank Sofia Ranchordás and Damiano Canale, whose thoughtful comments and suggestions helped me sharpen and improve the arguments developed in this book.

My time in Pisa was made truly home-like by my dear friends Marianna Capasso, Guilherme Pratti, Kamilla Galicz, and Stefano Porfido. Their companionship, encouragement, and the vibrant conversations we shared were a constant

[1] L Carroll, *Alice's Adventures in Wonderland*, first published in 1865 (A BookVirtual Digital Edition v.1.2, November 2000) 19.

source of vital joy, sustaining me through the most rigorous stretches of this work. Their unwavering presence, especially, was invaluable, easing the isolation and challenges presented by the COVID-19 crisis and ensuring that this period remained one of meaningful connection.

I also wish to thank the Digital Constitutionalist team in Florence, with whom many enriching exchanges have taken place at the European University Institute, and in particular to Giovanni De Gregorio, for his valuable friendship.

Over time, a second academic home has welcomed me at the University of Luxembourg, where I have benefited greatly from a stimulating and supportive environment. I am especially grateful to Herwig C. H. Hofmann, whose insightful guidance and encouragement have been invaluable in bringing this work to fruition.

The concluding stages of this book were significantly enriched by a brief, but highly productive visiting period at the Oxford Institute for Ethics in AI. My sincere thanks go to the Institute's dedicated team for their hospitality and intellectual generosity. The challenging and insightful discussions shared at the Institute offered insights that proved invaluable in bringing this work to its conclusion.

I would also like to sincerely thank the library staff at the Luxembourg Centre for European Law of the University of Luxembourg. Their warm smiles, quick responses, and constant willingness to provide the books I needed were incredibly helpful and truly appreciated.

I am especially thankful, as well, to my long-time friends Mimi Shishkova and Margaret Kurkoski, who have been like sisters to me for many years. Their enduring presence in my life has been a source of strength, reminding me always of the value of friendship beyond academia.

I would also like to express my deep gratitude to the Hart Publishing team, and in particular to Verity Stuart and Sinead Moloney, for their consistent support and guidance throughout the publication process. Their excellence and professionalism were essential in shaping this book.

Finally, my deepest gratitude goes to my family, whose constant love and support have sustained me throughout this journey. Above all, I owe a special thank you to my mother, whose unwavering care, patience, and strength have been my anchor. Her presence has given me the courage to face challenges, and the comfort of knowing I was never alone on this path.

Elif Biber
Luxembourg, November 2025

CONTENTS

ABBREVIATIONS

AG	Advocate General
AI	Artificial Intelligence
AI Act	Artificial Intelligence Act
BVerfG	Bundesverfassungsgericht
CAHAI	Ad Hoc Committee on Artificial Intelligence
CAP	conformity assessment procedures
CCTV	closed-circuit television
CFI	Court of First Instance
CJEU	Court of Justice of the European Union
CoE	Council of Europe
COMPAS	Correctional Offender Management Profiling for Alternative Sanctions
EC	European Commission
ECHR	European Convention on Human Rights
ECtHR	European Court of Human Rights
EGTAI	Ethics Guidelines for Trustworthy Artificial Intelligence
EPO	European Patent Office
EU	European Union
EU Charter	Charter of Fundamental Rights of the European Union
FRA	European Union Agency for Fundamental Rights
GDPR	General Data Protection Regulation
HLEGAI	High-Level Expert Group on Artificial Intelligence
ICCPR	International Covenant on Civil and Political Rights
ICP	Intelligent Control Platform

IEEE	Institute of Electrical and Electronics Engineers
ISPs	Internet service providers
LLMs	large language models
ML	machine learning
OECD	Organization for Economic Co-operation and Development
OECD.AI	OECD Artificial Intelligence Policy Observatory
Report I	'Getting the Future Right: Artificial Intelligence and Fundamental Rights' (FRA)
Report II	'AI Watch: Artificial Intelligence in Public Services' (EC)
RPA	Robotic Process Automation
Schrems I	CJEU, *Maximillian Schrems v Data Protection Commissioner*, C- 362/14
Schrems II	CJEU, *Data Commissioner v Facebook Ireland Ltd*, Maximillian Schrems, C-311/18
TEU	Treaty on European Union
TFEU	Treaty on the Functioning of the European Union
2022 Report	AI Watch: European Landscape on the Use of Artificial Intelligence by the Public Sector (EC)
UDBHR	Universal Declaration on Bioethics and Human Rights
UN	United Nations
UNESCO	United Nations Educational, Scientific and Cultural Organization
UNSC	United Nations Security Council
WBG	World Bank Group
WHO	World Health Organization

LIST OF FIGURES AND TABLES

LEADING DOCUMENTS ON ARTIFICIAL INTELLIGENCE AND LEGAL INSTRUMENTS

Annex II, 'Case Studies Description' in L Tangi et al, *AI Watch: European Landscape on the Use of Artificial Intelligence by the Public Sector* (Publications Office of the European Union, 2022), EUR 31088 EN, doi.org/10.2760/39336. available at unfccc.int/files/essential_background/background_publications_htmlpdf/application/pdf/conveng.pdf (accessed 13 July 2023).

Charter of Fundamental Rights of the European Union [2012] OJ C326/391.

Communications Decency Act 1996, 47 USC § 230(c)(1).

Consolidated Version of the Treaty on European Union [2012] OJ C 326/13.

Convention for the Protection of Human Rights and Dignity of the Human Being with regard to the Application of Biology and Medicine (ETS No 164, 'Oviedo Convention').

Convention for the Protection of Individuals with regard to Automatic Processing of Personal Data (opened for signature 28 January 1981, ETS No 108) (Council of Europe).

Convention on Cybercrime (ETS No 185, 'Budapest Convention').

Convention on the Elaboration of a European Pharmacopeia (ETS No 50)).

Council of Europe, 'Guide on Article 1 of the European Convention on Human Rights', updated on 31 December 2020, available at echr.coe.int/documents/guide_art_1_eng.pdf (accessed on 13 July 2023).

——, Ad Hoc Committee on Artificial Intelligence (CAHAI), 'Feasibility Study' (17 December 2020), 4, available at rm.coe.int/cahai-2020-23-final-eng-feasibility-study-/1680a0c6da (accessed 1 September 2021).

Council of the European Union, 'Progress on Combatting Hate Speech Online through the EU Code of Conduct 2016–2019', 12522/19 (2019).

Directive 2000/31/EC of the European Parliament and of the Council of 8 June 2000 on certain legal aspects of information society services, in particular electronic commerce, in the Internal Market (Directive on electronic commerce) [2000] OJ L178/1.

Directive 2006/24/EC of the European Parliament and of the Council of 15 March 2006 on the retention of data generated or processed in connection with the provision of publicly available electronic communications services or of public communications networks and amending Directive 2002/58/EC, [2006] OJ L 105/54.

European Commission, 'A Union of Equality: EU Anti-Racism Action Plan 2020–2025', COM (2020) 565 final, 18 September 2020.

——, AI Watch – Artificial Intelligence in public services: Overview of the use and impact of AI in public services in the EU', Science for Policy Report (2020), available at publications.jrc.ec.europa.eu/repository/handle/JRC120399 (accessed 1 September 2021).

——, 'Annex to the Communication to the Commission Approval of the Content of the Draft Communication from the Commission – Commission Guidelines on Prohibited Artificial Intelligence Practices established by Regulation (EU) 2024/1689 AI Act' (4 February 2025) ('Guidelines on Prohibited AI Practices').

——, 'Communication – Artificial Intelligence for Europe' (2018).

——, 'Communication – Building Trust in Human-Centric Artificial Intelligence' (2019).

——, 'Communication: Establishing a European Declaration on Digital Rights and Principles for the Digital Decade', COM (2022) 27 final, 26 January 2022 (Brussels).
——, 'Communication from the Commission, Commission Guidelines on the definition of an artificial intelligence system established by Regulation (EU) 2024/1689' (AI Act), C(2025) 5053 final, 29 July 2025.
——, 'Communication on Artificial Intelligence for Europe', COM(2018) 237 final, 25 April 2018.
——, 'Communication on Establishing a European Declaration on Digital Rights and Principles for the Digital Decade', COM(2022) 27 final, 26 January 2022, 1.
——, 'Definition of AI: Main Capabilities and Disciplines', developed for the purpose of the AI HLEG's Deliverables (8 April 2019), available at ec.europa.eu/digital-single-market/en/news/definition-artificial-intelligence-main-capabilities-and-scientific-disciplines (accessed 1 September 2021), 1.
——, 'Ethics Guidelines for Trustworthy AI', High-Level Expert Group on Artificial Intelligence (HLEG-AI), 8 April 2019, available at op.europa.eu/en/publication-detail/-/publication/d3988569-0434-11ea-8c1f-01aa75ed71a1 (accessed 1 September 2021).
——, 'Europe's Strategy for Data' (2020).
——, 'European Declaration on Digital Rights and Principles for the Digital Decade', COM (2022) 28 final, 26 January 2022 (Brussels).
——, 'New European Interoperability Framework: Promoting Seamless Services and Data Flows for European Public Administrations' (2017), available at ec.europa.eu/isa2/sites/default/files/eif_brochure_final.pdf (accessed 1 September 2021).
——, 'On Measures to Effectively Tackle Illegal Content Online' C(2018) 1177 final.
——, 'Online Platforms and the Digital Single Market: Opportunities and Challenges for Europe' COM (2016) 288 final.
——, 'Report on the Safety and Liability Implications of Artificial Intelligence, the Internet of Things and Robotics' (2020).
——, 'Shaping Europe's Digital Future' (2020).
——, 'Shaping the digital transformation in Europe' (Communications Networks, Content & Technology, September 2020), available at digital-strategy.ec.europa.eu/en/news/commission-publishes-analysis-macro-economic-potential-digital-transformation-independent (accessed 1 September 2021).
——, 'Statement on Artificial Intelligence, Robotics and Autonomous Systems' (2018).
——, 'Tackling Illegal Content Online: Towards an Enhanced Responsibility of Online Platforms' COM (2017) 555 final.
——, 'The "Blue Guide" on the Implementation of EU Product Rules 2016', available at ec.europa.eu/docsroom/documents/18027/ (accessed 13 July 2023).
——, 'White Paper on Artificial Intelligence: A European Approach to Excellence and Trust' (Brussels, 19 February 2020) COM(2020) 65 final, available at ec.europa.eu/info/publications/white-paper-artificial-intelligence-european-approach-excellence-and-trust_en (accessed 1 September 2021).
European Commission, HLEG-AI, 'A Definition of AI' (2018).
——, *Draft Ethics Guidelines for Trustworthy AI* (2018).
——, 'Ethics Guidelines for Trustworthy AI' (2019), available at aepd.es/sites/default/files/2019-12/ai-ethics-guidelines.pdf (accessed 13 July 2023).
——, 'Policy and Investment Recommendations for Trustworthy AI' (2019), available at europarl.europa.eu/italy/resource/static/files/import/intelligenza_artificiale_30_aprile/ai-hleg_policy-and-investment-recommendations.pdf (accessed 13 July 2023).
European Commission for Democracy through Law (Venice Commission), 'Report on the Rule of Law' (adopted at the 86th plenary session, Venice, 25–26 March 2011, rapporteurs: P van Dijk, G Haller, J Jowell and K Tuori), available at venice.coe.int/WebForms/pages/?p=02_Rule_of_law&lang=EN (accessed 1 September 2021).
European Convention for the Protection of Human Rights and Fundamental Freedoms' (opened for signature 4 November 1950, entered into force 3 September 1953) 213 UNTS 221.

European Council, 'European Council meeting (19 October 2017) – Conclusions', EUCO 14/17 (2017), 8, available at consilium.europa.eu/media/21620/19-euco-final-conclusions-en.pdf (accessed 1 September 2021).

European Court of Human Rights (ECtHR), 'Extra-territorial Jurisdiction of States Parties to the European Convention on Human Rights' (2018) European Court of Human Rights Press Unit, July, available at echr.coe.int/documents/fs_extra-territorial_jurisdiction_eng.pdf (last accessed on 13 July 2023).

——, 'Mass Surveillance – Factsheet', Press Unit, May 2021, available at echr.coe.int/documents/fs_mass_surveillance_eng.pdf (last accessed on 19 May 2021).

European Data Protection Supervisor, 'Strategy for Union institutions, offices, bodies and agencies to comply with the "Schrems II" ruling', 29 October 2020, available at edps.europa.eu/data-protection/our-work/publications/papers/strategy-union-institutions-offices-bodies-and_en (accessed 1 September 2021).

European Digital Rights (EDRi), 'Technological Testing Ground: Migration Management Experiments and Reflections from the Ground Up' (2020), 16, available at edri.org/our-work/european-court-supports-transparency-in-risky-eu-border-tech-experiments/ (accessed 1 September 2021).

——, 'The Slide from "Self-Regulation" to Corporate Censorship' (2011), available at edri.org/files/EDRI_selfreg_final_20110124.pdf accessed on 13 September 2023.

——, 'Use Cases: Impermissible AI and Fundamental Rights Breaches' (2020), available at edri.org/wp-content/uploads/2021/06/Case-studies-Impermissible-AI-biometrics-September-2020.pdf (accessed 1 September 2021).

European Parliament, 'Civil and Military Drones: Navigating a Disruptive and Dynamic Technological Ecosystem' (2019), available at europarl.europa.eu/RegData/etudes/BRIE/2019/642230/EPRS_BRI(2019)642230_EN.pdf (accessed 13 July 2023).

——, 'Civil Law Rules on Robotics, Resolution of 16 February 2017 with recommendations to the Commission on Civil Law Rules on Robotics' (2015/2103(INL)) available at europarl.europa.eu/doceo/document/TA-8-2017-0051_EN.pdf.

——, 'Draft Report on Civil Law Rules and Robotics' (2016), available at europarl.europa.eu/doceo/document/JURI-PR-582443_EN.pdf (accessed 1 September 2021).

——, 'Report on Civil Law Rules and Robotics' (2017).

——, 'Resolution of 20 January 2021 on artificial intelligence: questions of interpretation and application of international law in so far as the EU is affected in the areas of civil and military uses and of state authority outside the scope of criminal justice' (2020/2013(INI)).

——, 'The US Surveillance Programmes and Their Impact on EU Citizens' Fundamental Rights' (2013), available at op.europa.eu/en/publication-detail/-/publication/0a3aa9b5-1fe9-4f85-aaae-cc515408cf97 (accessed 1 September 2021).

FRA, 'European Enterprise Survey on the Use of Technologies Based on Artificial Intelligence' (2020), available at op.europa.eu/en/publication-detail/-/publication/f089bbae-f0b0-11ea-991b-01aa75ed71a1#:~:text=The%20survey%20reached%20a%20total,have%20adopted%20at%20least%20two (accessed 1 September 2021).

FRA, 'Getting the Future Right: Artificial Intelligence and Fundamental Rights' (2020), available at fra.europa.eu/en/publication/2020/artificial-intelligence-and-fundamental-rights (accessed on 23 October 2021).

Gesetz über den Bundesnachrichtendienst (BNDG) of 20 December 1990.

Inter-American Court of Human Rights, *Advisory Opinion on the Environment and Human Rights* (2017) OC-23/17, 15 November, Series A No 23, § 104(h).

Machinery Directive 2006/42/EC of the European Parliament and of the Council of 17 May 2006 on machinery, and amending Directive 95/16/EC (recast) (Text with EEA relevance) OJ L 157, 9.6.2006, pp. 24–28.

Medical Devices Regulation 2017/745 of the European Parliament and of the Council of 5 April 2017 on medical devices, amending Directive 2001/83/EC, Regulation (EC) No 178/2002 and Regulation

(EC) No 1223/2009 and repealing Council Directives 90/385/EEC and 93/42/EEC (Text with EEA relevance) OJ L 117, 5.5.2017, pp. 1–175.

OECD, 'Global Information Infrastructure and Global Information Society (GII-GIS): Statement of Policy Recommendations Made by the ICCP Committee' (1996) OECD Digital Economy Papers No 18, OECD Publishing, Paris, doi:10.1787/237382063227 (accessed 1 September 2021).

——, 'Glossary of Statistical Terms: Social Benefits Definitions', available at stats.oecd.org/glossary/detail.asp?ID=2480 (accessed 1 September 2021).

OHCHR, 'Report on the Right to Privacy in the Digital Age' (2014), available at ohchr.org/en/calls-for-input/reports/2018/report-right-privacy-digital-age (accessed 13 July 2023).

Proposal for a Regulation of the European Parliament and of the Council laying down harmonised rules on artificial intelligence (Artificial Intelligence Act) and amending certain Union legislative acts, COM (2021) 206 final, 2021/0106 (COD), 21 April 2021 (Brussels).

Regulation (EC) No 765/2008 of the European Parliament and of the Council of 9 July 2008, available at eur-lex.europa.eu/legal-content/EN/TXT/PDF/?uri=CELEX:32008R0765&from=EN (accessed 13 July 2023).

Regulation (EU) 2016/679 of the European Parliament and of the Council of 27 April 2016 on the protection of natural persons with regard to the processing of personal data and on the free movement of such data, and repealing Directive 95/46/EC (General Data Protection Regulation), [2016] OJ L 119/1.

Regulation (EU) 2021/1767 of the European Parliament and of the Council amending Regulation (EC) No 1367/2006 on the application of the provisions of the Aarhus Convention on Access to Information, Public Participation in Decision-Making and Access to Justice in Environmental Matters to Community Institutions and Bodies, PE-CONS 63/21, 5 October 2021, available at data.consilium.europa.eu/doc/document/PE-63-2021-INIT/en/pdf (accessed 13 July 2023).

Regulation (EU) 2024/1689 of the European Parliament and of the Council of 13 June 2024 laying down harmonised rules on artificial intelligence and amending Regulations (EC) No 300/2008, (EU) No 167/2013, (EU) No 168/2013, (EU) 2018/858, (EU) 2018/1139 and (EU) 2019/2144 and Directives 2014/90/EU, (EU) 2016/797 and (EU) 2020/1828 (Artificial Intelligence Act), OJ L 1689, 12 July 2024.

Section 702 of the Foreign Intelligence Surveillance Act (FISA), Executive Order (EO) 12333, and Presidential Policy Directive (PPD)-28.

Tangi, L et al. *AI Watch: European Landscape on the Use of Artificial Intelligence by the Public Sector* (Publications Office of the European Union, 2022), EUR 31088 EN, doi.org/10.2760/39336.

Toy Safety Directive (2009/48/EC of the European Parliament and of the Council of 18 June 2009 on the safety of toys (Text with EEA relevance) OJ L 170, 30.6.2009, pp. 1–37.

United Nations Framework Convention on Climate Change (opened for signature 9 May 1992, entered into force 21 March 1994) 1771 UNTS 107.

LIST OF JUDICIAL CASES

Advocate General Pikamäe, Opinion in Case C-634/21, *OQ v Land Hesse*, with SCHUFA Holding AG as an intervening party, delivered on 16 March 2023, ECLI:EU:C:2023:220, available at curia.europa.eu/juris/document/document.jsf?docid=271343&doclang=en (accessed 13 February 2024).
Basu v Germany App no 215/19 (ECtHR, 18 October 2022).
BVerfG (Judgment of the Second Senate of 05 May 2020 – 2 BvR 859/15 -, §§ 1-237).
——, 20 April 2016, 1 BvR 966/09 – 1 BvR 1140/09; BVerfG 14 July 1999, 1 BvR 2226/94 – 1 BvR 2420/95 – 1 BvR 2437/95.
——, Case 1 BvR 2835/17, judgment of 19 May 2020.
CaseC-131/12 *Google Spain SL and Google Inc v Agencia Española de Protección de Datos (AEPD) and Mario Costeja González* [2014] ECLI:EU:C:2014:317, 13 May 2014.
Case T-13/99 *Pfizer Animal Health SA v Council of the European Union* [2002] ECR II-3305.
CJEU, Case 26/62, *Van Gend en Loos*, ECLI:EU:C:1963:1.
——, Case 6/64, *Costa v ENEL*, ECLI:EU:C:1964:66.
——, Case C-131/12, *Google Spain SL and Google Inc. v. Agencia Española de Protección de Datos (AEPD) and Mario Costeja González*, judgment of 13 May 2014, (*Google Spain*).
——, Case C-154/21, *RW v Österreichische Post AG*, EU:C:2023:3.
——, Case C-293/12, *Digital Rights Ireland Ltd v Minister for Communications, Marine and Natural Resources and Others*, judgment of 8 April 2014 *(Digital Rights Ireland)*.
——, Case C-311/18, *Data Protection Commissioner v Facebook Ireland Ltd and Maximillian Schrems (Schrems II)*, judgment of 16 July 2020.
——, Case C-362/14, *Maximillian Schrems v Data Protection Commissioner (Schrems I)*, judgment of 6 October 2015.
——, Case T-158/19, *Breyer v REA*, judgment of 15 December 2021.
——, 'Fact Sheet' of the CJEU on the 'protection of personal data' published in July 2020, available at curia.europa.eu/jcms/upload/docs/application/pdf/2018-10/fiche_thematique_-_donnees_personnelles_-_en.pdf (accessed 1 September 2021).
ECtHR, *Al-Skeini and others v United Kingdom*, App. No. 55721/07, 7 July 2011.
——, *Bankovic and Others v Belgium and Others*, App. No. 52207/99, 10 May 2001.
——, *Big Brother Watch and others v United Kingdom*, App. No. 58170/13 et al., 13 September 2018.
——, *Center for Rättvisa v Sweden*, App. No. 35252/08, 19 June 2018.
——, *Copland v the United Kingdom* App No 62617/00, 3 July 2007.
——, *Tysiąc v Poland*, App no 5410/03, Judgment of 20 March 2007.
——, *Evans v United Kingdom* App no 6339/05, 10 April 2007.
——, *Glukhin v Russia* App No 11519/20, 4 October 2023.
——, *Golder v United Kingdom* App no 4451/70, 21 February 1975.
——, *Grzęda v Poland* App no 43572/18, 15 March 2022.
——, Joined Cases C-402/05 P and C-415/05 P *Yassin Abdullah Kadi and Al Barakaat International Foundation v Council and Commission* ECLI:EU:C:2008:461 (*Kadi Judgment*).
——, *Kopp v Switzerland* App No 13/1997/797/1000, 25 March 1998.
——, *Kruslin v France* App No 11801/85, 24 April 1990.
——, *KU v Finland* App No 2872/02, 2 December 2008.
——, *Muhammad v Spain*, App no 34085/17, 18 October 2022.
——, *Peck v the United Kingdom* App No 44647/98, 28 January 2003.
——, *Pişkin v Turkey* App no 33399/18, 15 December 2020 (not final).

——, *S and Marper v the United Kingdom* App Nos 30562/04 and 30566/04, 4 December 2008.
——, *Tătar v Romania* App no 67021/01, 27 January 2009.
European Patent Office (EPO), Decision no 18 275 163 (27 January 2020).
——, Decision no 18 275 174 (27 January 2020).
Oversight Board, *Case Decision 2020-003-FB-UA* (28 January 2021), available at oversightboard.com/decision/FB-QBJDASCV/ (accessed 13 July 2023).
Rechtbank Den Haag, Case C/09/550982/HA ZA 18-388 (5 February 2020).
The Hague District Court, Case C/09/550982/HA ZA 18-388 (2020).
Tribunal de grande instance de Paris, *LICRA and UEJF v Yahoo! Inc and Yahoo! France* (22 May 2000).
US District Court for the Northern District of California, *Yahoo! Inc v La Ligue Contre le Racisme et l'Antisémitisme* 169 F Supp 2d 1181 (ND Cal 2001).

1

Introduction: Human and Fundamental Rights are at Risk

1.1. General Overview

In recent decades, rapid technological advancements have fundamentally transformed the fabric of contemporary life, exerting a profound and far-reaching influence on social structures, economic systems, and institutional frameworks.[1] These innovations have not only altered how individuals interact, communicate, and work, but have also redefined the organisation of both the private[2] and the public sphere.[3] Digital technologies – ranging from the Internet and artificial intelligence (AI) to big data analytics – have become indispensable tools in daily human activity, permeating all sectors of society. By enabling the efficient processing, analysis, and dissemination of unprecedented volumes of data, these technologies have facilitated new modes of innovation, governance, and decision-making. As a result, data and information have emerged as strategic resources,[4] central to the functioning of what is now referred to as digital[5] or information capitalism.[6] In this context, information is not merely a by-product of technological use but a critical asset that drives economic productivity, shapes social dynamics, and reconfigures power relations.[7]

[1] Across Europe, numerous projects and initiatives are actively examining the societal and economic impacts of emerging technologies. One notable example is the SIENNA Project, which focused on three critical domains: human genomics, human enhancement, and artificial intelligence and robotics. The project produced a series of influential reports that offer valuable insights into the ethical and social implications of these technologies. These publications are available at sienna-project.eu/.

[2] C Véliz, *Privacy is Power: Why and How You Should Take Back Control of Your Data* (Bantam Press, 2020).

[3] J Habermas, *Ein neuer Strukturwandel der Öffentlichkeit und die deliberative Politik* (Suhrkamp, 2022) 54. Habermas argues that new media, especially social platforms, are revolutionary – not merely expanding old media but marking a historic shift. Their novelty lies in their platform nature, as their rise is shaped by commercial exploitation of network communication.

[4] Ö Tene and J Polonetsky, 'Big Data for All: Privacy and User Control in the Age of Analytics' (2013) 11 *Northwestern Journal of Technology and Intellectual Property* 239 ('We live in the age of "Big Data". Data have become the raw material of production, a new source for immense economic and social value … Data creates enormous value for the world economy, driving innovation, productivity, efficiency, and growth.').

[5] D Schiller, Digital Capitalism: Networking the Global Market System (MIT Press, 1999).

[6] JE Cohen, Between Truth and Power: The Legal Construction of Information Capitalism (Oxford University Press, 2020).

[7] M Castells, *The Information Age: Economy, Society and Culture, Volume I: The Rise of the Network Society*, 2nd edn (Wiley-Blackwell, 2010) 21. In a footnote, he distinguishes between 'information

Unlike previous technological transformations, this transformation is advancing not through gradual, time-distributed progress, but with an exponentially accelerating momentum.[8] This rapid and radical shift confronts humanity without adequate preparation. Furthermore, the risks posed by this transformation extend far beyond familiar threats such as mass unemployment.[9] They compel us to confront profound and unsettling questions about the very meaning of human existence – not only at the individual level, but increasingly at the institutional level, as organisations, governments, and global institutions are now being forced to engage with these existential concerns in concrete and systemic ways. In this context, humanity now revisits an age-old philosophical question, echoed by Dolores, the main character of HBO's acclaimed series *Westworld*: 'Have you ever questioned the nature of your reality?'.[10] In addition to questioning our own reality, we are also now compelled to confront the deeper, often obscured reality of a world increasingly governed by algorithms and digital structures.

This digital evolution has produced a dual impact on the exercise of fundamental rights. On the one hand, it has expanded the capacity for individuals to exercise certain rights, notably freedom of expression[11] and the freedom to conduct a business, by creating new platforms for participation and enterprise. On the other hand, the intensification of data collection and processing has generated considerable challenges to other fundamental rights, including the right to privacy, the right to data protection, the principle of non-discrimination, and the broader legal and ethical norm of human dignity.[12] Therefore, while technological innovation

society' as a general descriptor of the social importance of knowledge across history, and 'informational society' as a precise concept tied to contemporary conditions. The latter marks a shift where information is no longer simply embedded in culture or tradition but becomes the very foundation of productivity and power, enabled by new technological conditions.

[8] X Tang, X Li, Y Ding, M Song and Y Bu, 'The Pace of Artificial Intelligence Innovations: Speed, Talent, and Trial-and-Error' (2020) 14(4) *Journal of Informetrics*, article 101094, doi.org/10.1016/j.joi.2020.101094.

[9] J Tasioulas, 'Work and Play in the Shadow of AI' (2024) in D Edmonds (ed), *AI Morality* (Oxford University Press 2024), 118–28.

[10] *Westworld* (HBO, 2016). When I was pursuing my LLM degree at Koç University in Istanbul, the TV series *Westworld* sparked my initial curiosity about the legal dimensions of AI. It was the first time I began to deeply question how society might regulate and respond to the ethical challenges posed by intelligent systems. To this day, I still regard *Westworld* as one of the most compelling and thought-provoking portrayals of AI philosophy in popular media.

[11] Regarding social platforms, see K Klonick, 'The New Governors: The People, Rules, and Processes Governing Online Speech' (2017) 131 *Harvard Law Review* 1599, 1599–1603 (highlighting the increasingly essential role of private social media platforms in regulating free speech and enabling participation in democratic discourse).

[12] On the relationship between human rights and new technologies, see M Klang and A Murray (eds), Human Rights in the Digital Age (Cavendish, 2005); MV De Azevedo Cunha, NNGA De Andrade, L Lixinski and L Tomé Féteira, New Technologies and Human Rights: Challenges to Regulation (Routledge, 2013); O Pollicino and G Romeo (eds), The Internet and Constitutional Law: The Protection of Fundamental Rights and Constitutional Adjudication in Europe (Routledge, 2016); MK Land and JD Aronson, New Technologies for Human Rights Law and Practice (Cambridge University Press, 2018); B Wagner, M Kettemann and K Vieth (eds), Research Handbook on Human Rights and Digital

has facilitated the emergence of novel business models and enhanced access to knowledge and civic engagement, it has simultaneously given rise to complex constitutional and normative dilemmas that demand rigorous legal and policy scrutiny.[13]

Moreover, the COVID-19 pandemic,[14] which emerged as a global crisis in March 2020, significantly accelerated the integration of emerging technologies into daily life and intensified individuals' interactions with these technologies. Simultaneously, it compounded pre-existing regulatory and ethical challenges. As highlighted in a report by the Institute of Electrical and Electronics Engineers (IEEE) on the pandemic's impact on technological adoption and cybersecurity, the crisis notably expedited the deployment of cloud computing, 5G networks, AI, and machine learning (ML).[15] While this rapid technological advancement has facilitated the growth of the digital economy, it has posed substantial difficulties for regulators, policymakers, and judicial actors. These stakeholders are now compelled to respond with both increased urgency and heightened prudence. In particular, the pandemic has magnified the complexities associated with AI systems, many of which remain insufficiently understood, let alone systematically addressed within current legal and policy frameworks.

Therefore, it is imperative to closely examine the digital environment and critically reassess the fundamental and human rights challenges posed by AI systems. Such an analysis necessitates an initial focus on the wider challenges raised by emerging technologies, before turning to legal analysis specific to AI. This is

Technology: Global Politics, Law and International Relations (Edward Elgar, 2019); M Hildebrandt and K O'Hara (eds), Life and the Law in the Era of Data-Driven Agency (Edward Elgar, 2020). In the context of AI systems, at least 12 European documents address values, fundamental rights, and principles: European Parliament, 'Draft Report on Civil Law Rules and Robotics' (2016); European Parliament, 'Report on Civil Law Rules and Robotics' (2017); European Commission, 'Communication – Artificial Intelligence for Europe' (2018); European Commission, 'Statement on Artificial Intelligence, Robotics and Autonomous Systems' (2018); High-Level Expert Group on Artificial Intelligence (HLEGAI), European Commission, 'A Definition of AI' (2018); HLEGAI, European Commission, 'Draft Ethics Guidelines for Trustworthy AI' (2018); HLEGAI, European Commission, 'Ethics Guidelines for Trustworthy AI' (2019); European Commission, 'Communication – Building Trust in Human-Centric Artificial Intelligence' (2019); European Commission, 'White Paper on Artificial Intelligence' (2020); European Commission, 'Shaping Europe's Digital Future' (2020); European Commission, 'Europe's Strategy for Data' (2020); European Commission, 'Report on the Safety and Liability Implications of Artificial Intelligence, the Internet of Things and Robotics' (2020).

[13] O Pollicino and G De Gregorio, 'Constitutional Law in the Algorithmic Society' in HW Micklitz and others (eds), *Constitutional Challenges in the Algorithmic Society* (Cambridge University Press, 2022) 3–24.

[14] World Health Organization, 'WHO Announced COVID-19 Outbreak as a Pandemic on 11 March 2020', available at euro.who.int/en/health-topics/health-emergencies.

[15] IEEE, 'Artificial Intelligence and Machine Learning, 5G and IoT Will Be the Most Important Technologies in 2021, According to New IEEE Study' (19 November 2020), available at https://syncedreview.com/2020/11/23/ieee-ai-ml-5g-and-iot-will-be-the-most-important-technologies-in-2021/#:~:text=Comments%203-,Recent%20IEEE%20study%20released%20the%20results%20of%20a%20survey%20of,say%20AI%20and%20machine%20learning%2C (reporting on the IEEE 2020 Global Survey of CIOs and CTOs, which surveyed 350 technology executives in the US, China, UK, India, and Brazil, and found that 55% had accelerated adoption of cloud computing, 52% of 5G, and 51% of AI and machine learning due to the pandemic).

justified because the most significant developments at the intersection of law and technology have historically arisen in response to earlier waves of advanced technological change. Consequently, this section provides a general overview of the legal and rights-based challenges associated with new technologies rather than limiting the discussion solely to AI-related concerns. To this end, the chapter analyses leading judgments from the European Court of Human Rights (ECtHR) and the Court of Justice of the European Union (CJEU), the two principal judicial bodies actively engaged in the protection of fundamental rights and freedoms in the digital era. The existing jurisprudence primarily focuses on violations of the right to respect for private life, and data protection. Building upon this foundation, the analysis then shifts to AI systems, to assess whether these technologies introduce novel dimensions to the existing legal landscape, particularly in terms of fundamental and human rights. Based on this examination, the chapter identifies and elucidates the distinct and often intensified challenges posed by AI systems, highlighting the ways in which these technologies exacerbate existing rights violations and create new legal complexities.

1.2. Rights Challenges Posed by New Technologies

1.2.1. New Technologies Testing the European Convention on Human Rights

Before examining the specific challenges posed by AI systems, it is essential to first consider the broader issues associated with emerging technologies in general. This step is crucial to determine whether advancements in the AI field have introduced any significant changes in the human rights landscape. In recent years, European courts and institutions have increasingly recognised the growing impact of new technologies on fundamental and human rights, often describing this impact as 'extensive'[16] or 'serious'.[17] These developments have prompted rigorous scrutiny under the European Convention on Human Rights[18] (ECHR), the Charter of Fundamental Rights of the European Union[19] (hereinafter the 'EU Charter'), and

[16] *Rechtbank Den Haag*, Case C/09/550982/HA ZA 18-388 (5 February 2020), para 6.85 (holding that 'collecting and analysing data with the help of those new technologies can interfere extensively with the private lives of those to whom the data pertain').

[17] *Kruslin v France* App No 11801/85 (ECtHR, 24 April 1990), para 33 (holding that 'tapping and other forms of interception of telephone conversations represent a serious interference with private life and correspondence and must accordingly be based on a "law" that is particularly precise. It is essential to have clear, detailed rules on the subject, especially as the technology available for use is continually becoming more sophisticated').

[18] European Convention for the Protection of Human Rights and Fundamental Freedoms (opened for signature 4 November 1950, entered into force 3 September 1953) 213 UNTS 221.

[19] Charter of Fundamental Rights of the European Union [2012] OJ C326/391.

the domestic laws of European Union (EU) Member States, all of which are being tested by this rapidly evolving technological context.[20]

The European Court of Human Rights (ECtHR) has been at the forefront of addressing the regulatory gaps surrounding emerging technologies in Europe, often being the first judicial body to highlight the absence of clear and systematic legal frameworks.[21] In particular, the Court's case law under Article 8 of the ECHR – the right to respect for private and family life[22] – has brought many technology-related challenges to light.[23] While the ECtHR has not provided a definitive legal definition of 'new technologies',[24] it has repeatedly acknowledged their 'rapid development'[25] and 'sophisticated' nature[26] in its judgments. A closer look at selected cases is necessary to illustrate how the Strasbourg Court has responded to these evolving issues.[27]

[20] See the overall fundamental rights framework of the EU in Fundamental Rights Agency of the European Union, Bringing Rights to Life: The Fundamental Rights Landscape of the European Union (Publications Office of the European Union, 2012), available at fra.europa.eu/sites/default/files/fra-2012-bringing-rights-to-life_en.pdf (discussing the major international and Council of Europe human rights instruments, including the 1948 Universal Declaration of Human Rights; the 1965 International Convention on the Elimination of All Forms of Racial Discrimination; the 1966 International Covenant on Civil and Political Rights; the 1966 International Covenant on Economic, Social and Cultural Rights; the 1979 Convention on the Elimination of All Forms of Discrimination against Women; the 1984 Convention against Torture; the 1989 Convention on the Rights of the Child; the 2006 Convention on the Rights of Persons with Disabilities; and the 2006 International Convention for the Protection of All Persons from Enforced Disappearance. It also highlights four Council of Europe conventions addressing technological issues: the Convention for the Protection of Individuals with regard to Automatic Processing of Personal Data (ETS No 108) and its amending protocol (CETS No 223, 'Convention 108+'); the Convention for the Protection of Human Rights and Dignity of the Human Being with regard to the Application of Biology and Medicine (ETS No 164, 'Oviedo Convention'); the Convention on Cybercrime (ETS No 185, 'Budapest Convention'); and the Convention on the Elaboration of a European Pharmacopeia (ETS No 50)).

[21] In this context, the term 'Europe' should be interpreted broadly to encompass not only the Member States of the European Union but also the Contracting Parties to the Council of Europe.

[22] Art 8 ECHR (providing that '1. Everyone has the right to respect for his private and family life, his home and his correspondence. 2. There shall be no interference by a public authority with the exercise of this right except such as is in accordance with the law and is necessary in a democratic society in the interests of national security, public safety or the economic well-being of the country, for the prevention of disorder or crime, for the protection of health or morals, or for the protection of the rights and freedoms of others.').

[23] T Murphy and G Ó Cuinn, 'Work in Progress: New Technologies and the European Court of Human Rights' (2010) 10 *Human Rights Law Review* 601–38.

[24] See Chapter 2 of this book for a detailed analysis of whether and how legal frameworks should engage with the definitional challenges posed by emerging technologies.

[25] *KU v Finland* App No 2872/02 (ECtHR, 2 December 2008), para 22.

[26] *Kopp v Switzerland* App No 13/1997/797/1000 (ECtHR, 25 March 1998) (holding that, 'as interception constituted a serious interference with private life and correspondence, it had to be based on a "law" that was particularly precise, especially as the technology available for use was continually becoming more sophisticated').

[27] The first three leading examples discussed below are drawn from the influential study by Thérèse Murphy and Gearóid Ó Cuinn, which examines the intersection of new technologies and the ECHR. Their analysis systematically reviews the Court's case law through HUDOC, the official database containing both judgments and admissibility decisions. See T Murphy and G Ó Cuinn, 'Work in Progress: New Technologies and the European Court of Human Rights' (2010) 10 *Human Rights Law Review* 601–38.

1.2.1.1. The Right to Respect for Private Life and Correspondence

The first notable tech-related decisions of the ECtHR are related to the protection of privacy. In particular, certain technological advancements challenged the existing boundaries of the 'zone of privacy', prompting the Court to reinterpret and expand those boundaries in response. In *Peck v the United Kingdom*,[28] CCTV (closed-circuit television) footage capturing the applicant carrying a large knife during a suicide attempt was released to the media in order to demonstrate the effectiveness of the surveillance system – without the applicant's consent or any attempt to conceal his identity. The applicant argued that the local authority's disclosure of the CCTV footage violated his right to respect for private life under Article 8 of the Convention. While the government claimed that the events occurred in a public space, the ECtHR dismissed this line of reasoning and affirmed that the notion of private life is not necessarily confined to private settings, and may be implicated even in public contexts:

> Private life is a broad term not susceptible to exhaustive definition. The Court has already held that elements, such as gender identification, name, sexual orientation and sexual life are important elements of the personal sphere protected by Article 8. The Article also protects a right to identity and personal development, and the right to establish and develop relationships with other human beings and the outside world and it may include activities of a professional or business nature. There is, therefore, a zone of interaction of a person with others, even in a public context, which may fall within the scope of 'private life' (P.G. and J.H. v. the United Kingdom, no. 44787/98, § 56, ECHR 2001-IX, with further references).[29]

By assessing the significant impact of CCTV – particularly compared with traditional print media – and noting the absence of an effective remedy for awarding damages, the Court held that 'the disclosure by the Council of the relevant footage constituted a serious interference with the applicant's rights to respect for his private life'.[30] Therefore, the Court found that the applicant's right under Article 8 had been violated.[31] This case remains a key example illustrating how the zone

[28] *Peck v the United Kingdom* App No 44647/98 (ECtHR, 28 January 2003).

[29] In *Peck v the United Kingdom* App No 44647/98 (ECtHR, 28 January 2003), para 57, the Court referenced its earlier reasoning in *P.G. and J.H. v the United Kingdom* App No 44787/98 (ECtHR, 25 September 2001), stating: 'There are a number of elements relevant to a consideration of whether a person's private life is concerned in measures effected outside a person's home or private premises. Since there are occasions when people knowingly or intentionally involve themselves in activities which are or may be recorded or reported in a public manner, a person's reasonable expectations as to privacy may be a significant, though not necessarily conclusive factor. A person who walks down the street will, inevitably, be visible to any member of the public who is also present. Monitoring by technological means of the same public scene (e.g. security guard viewing through closed-circuit television) is of a similar character. Private life considerations may arise, however, once any systematic or permanent record comes into existence of such material from the public domain' (para 56). In this regard, the Court places particular emphasis on 'any systematic or permanent record', in the context of public space.

[30] *Peck v the United Kingdom*, paras 62–63.

[31] *Peck v the United Kingdom*, para 104.

of privacy can extend beyond the personal sphere in response to the novel use of emerging technologies.

Another significant dimension of Article 8 of the ECHR was explored in the case of *Copland v the United Kingdom*.[32] In this case, the focus shifted to the concept of 'correspondence' under Article 8. The Court found that the collection and storage of personal information concerning the applicant's email and Internet usage raised issues on the right to respect for both correspondence and private life.[33] The Court found that the government had violated the applicant's rights through its monitoring of her emails, mobile phone communications, and Internet usage. This interpretation affirmed that the notion of 'correspondence' under the Convention extends to modern forms of communication.

Furthermore, the ECtHR's ruling has illustrated that the new uses of certain technologies give rise to sensitive and critical issues concerning data protection and privacy. In addressing such cases, the Court has reaffirmed its commitment to safeguarding individuals' private life interests, ensuring that the protections enshrined in the Convention are not diminished by the intrusive potential of modern scientific techniques.

A notable example is *S. and Marper v the United Kingdom*, where the government relied on technologies capable of processing fingerprints, cellular samples, and DNA profiles for crime prevention and the identification of potential future offenders.[34] In this case, the central issue concerned the indefinite retention – without consent – of the fingerprints, cellular samples, and DNA profiles of individuals whose criminal proceedings had either ended in acquittal or been discontinued. The applicants claimed that the retention of such biometric data interfered with Article 8 of the Convention, as it was directly related to their individual identities.[35]

According to the Court, all three categories of personal information qualified as personal data under the Data Protection Convention,[36] as they related to 'identified or identifiable individuals'.[37] In its analysis, the Court examined the categories of data separately – considering the retention of cellular samples and DNA profiles, on the one hand, and the retention of fingerprints, on the other.[38] With respect to the first category, the Court emphasised the particularly sensitive nature of this information: cellular samples 'contain a unique genetic code',

[32] Copland v the United Kingdom App No 62617/00 (ECtHR, 3 July 2007).
[33] Copland v the United Kingdom, para 44.
[34] *S and Marper v the United Kingdom* App Nos 30562/04 and 30566/04 (ECtHR, 4 December 2008).
[35] *S and Marper v the United Kingdom*, para 60.
[36] Convention for the Protection of Individuals with regard to Automatic Processing of Personal Data (opened for signature 28 January 1981, ETS No 108) (Council of Europe) (the first binding international instrument on personal data protection, ratified by all Council of Europe Member States and, as of 29 July 2025, by nine non-member states: Argentina, Cabo Verde, Mauritius, Mexico, Morocco, Russian Federation, Senegal, Tunisia, and Uruguay) https://www.coe.int/en/web/conventions/full-list/-/conventions/treaty/108/signatures (Art 2(a) defines 'personal data' as 'any information relating to an identified or identifiable individual ("data subject")').
[37] *S and Marper v the United Kingdom*, para 68.
[38] *S and Marper v the United Kingdom*, paras 70–86.

and DNA profiles 'provide a means of identifying genetic relationships between individuals' and 'stronger potential for future use' – the Court found that the retention of such information constituted an interference with the applicants' right to respect for private life.[39] Regarding the potential future use of cellular material, the Court noted:

> bearing in mind the rapid pace of developments in the field of genetics and information technology, the Court cannot discount the possibility that in the future the private-life interests bound up with genetic information may be adversely affected in novel ways or in a manner which cannot be anticipated with precision today.[40]

Regarding the retention of fingerprints, the Court similarly held that fingerprint records constitute personal data, observing that they 'contain certain external identification features much in the same way as, for example, personal photographs or voice samples'.[41] By drawing attention to the distinctive nature of this technology, which allows the precise identification of individuals, the Court found that the retention of fingerprints likewise constitutes an interference with the right to respect for private life.[42]

Consequently, applying its necessity test, the Court held that, although the degree of interference with the applicants' rights may vary across the three different categories of personal data collected,

> the blanket and indiscriminate nature of the powers of retention of the fingerprints, cellular samples and DNA profiles of persons suspected but not convicted of offences, as applied in the case of the present applicants, fails to strike a fair balance between the competing public and private interests and that the respondent State has overstepped any acceptable margin of appreciation in this regard.[43]

Another significant case was *Basu v Germany*, where the ECtHR addressed racial profiling for the first time, finding that Germany had failed to investigate a discriminatory police check.[44] The applicant, Biplab Basu, a German national of Indian origin, and a lawyer practising in Berlin, was travelling by train from the Czech Republic into Germany in July 2012 with his daughter.[45] He claimed that, during the journey, two German federal police officers entered their train carriage and conducted an identity check exclusively on Basu and his daughter, who were the only visibly dark-skinned passengers present.[46] He subsequently

[39] *S and Marper v the United Kingdom*, paras 72, 75.

[40] *S and Marper v the United Kingdom*, para 71. Indeed, the Court's position is well justified in view of ongoing developments in human genomics. For a detailed analysis, see Sienna Project, 'D2.4: Ethical Analysis of Human Genetics and Genomics' (2019), https://zenodo.org/record/4068016.

[41] *S and Marper v the United Kingdom*, para 81. Such a statement calls for a critical re-evaluation of real-time biometric identification systems, which are capable of continuously capturing and processing facial features on a second-by-second basis. This issue is explored in Chapter 2.

[42] *S and Marper v the United Kingdom*, para 84–86.

[43] *S and Marper v the United Kingdom*, para 125.

[44] *Basu v Germany* App no 215/19 (ECtHR, 18 October 2022).

[45] *Basu v Germany*, paras 2–5.

[46] *Basu v Germany*, para 6.

lodged an administrative complaint in Dresden, Germany, arguing that this stop was discriminatory and the relevant section of the Federal Police Act (Bundespolizeigesetz) could not serve as a legal basis for the interference with his right to self-determination in the sphere of information.[47] However, the domestic courts – the Dresden Administrative Court, the Saxony Administrative Court of Appeal, and the Federal Constitutional Court – dismissed his claim without examining the substance of his allegations or hearing witness testimony.[48] Basu then brought his case before the ECtHR, claiming that Germany had violated his rights under Article 14 (prohibition of discrimination) taken in conjunction with Article 8 of the ECHR.

In its assessment, the ECtHR first underlined that 'Article 8 protects a right to identity and personal development, and the right to establish relationships with other human beings and the outside world. There is therefore an interaction of a person with others, even in a public context, which may fall within the scope of "private life"'.[49] In this regard, the Strasbourg Court found that the identity check constituted an interference with the applicant's right to respect for private life. Furthermore, it emphasised that the public nature of the stop could exacerbate the 'seriousness of the interference', particularly due to the potential for humiliation and embarrassment experienced by the individual concerned.[50] Therefore, the Court noted that it is necessary to assess whether the actions of the police had serious negative effects on the individual's private life. In such cases, according to the Court, the applicant is required to clearly explain and identify the 'concrete repercussions' on their private life, including the nature and extent of their suffering, and to substantiate these allegations in a proper way.[51] Additionally, in cases involving racial discrimination, the Court underlined that, as this form of discrimination constitutes a 'particularly egregious kind of discrimination', it requires from the authorities 'special vigilance and a vigorous reaction'.[52]

Considering all these principles, the Court held that, although not every identity check of a person belonging to an ethnic minority reaches the necessary level of seriousness to fall within the scope of Article 8, the applicant had an 'arguable claim' that he had been subjected to the stop on account of his dark skin colour – an act that 'had serious negative effects' on his private life and caused him to refrain from future train travel.[53] This was sufficient to bring the complaint within the scope of Article 8.

The Court further assessed the case under Article 14 in conjunction with Article 8, focusing on whether the domestic authorities had fulfilled their

[47] *Basu v Germany*, para 6.
[48] *Basu v Germany*, paras 7–9.
[49] *Basu v Germany*, para 21.
[50] *Basu v Germany*, para 22.
[51] *Basu v Germany*, para 23.
[52] *Basu v Germany*, para 24.
[53] *Basu v Germany*, paras 25–27.

procedural obligation to investigate the applicant's claim of racial discrimination. It stated that:

> [O]nce there is an arguable claim that the person concerned may have been targeted on account of facial characteristics, ... the authorities' duty to investigate the existence of a possible link between racist attitudes and a State agent's act is to be considered implicit in their responsibilities under Article 14 of the Convention.[54]

Accordingly, the Court found that the German authorities had failed to conduct an effective and independent investigation into the alleged discriminatory motive behind the identity check.[55] In particular, the internal inquiry carried out by the Federal Police had lacked sufficient independence,[56] and the administrative courts had dismissed the applicant's claim without properly assessing the evidence or hearing witnesses.[57] As a result, the Court concluded that Germany had breached its procedural obligations under Article 14 read in conjunction with Article 8. However, it is important to note that the Court refrained from determining whether the identity check was racially motivated, citing the lack of sufficient fact-finding by the domestic authorities.[58]

1.2.1.2. The Right to Respect for Private Life and the Freedom of Expression

The ECtHR has also examined the deployment of facial recognition technologies in the context of peaceful protests, evaluating their implications for the right to respect for private life and the freedom of expression.[59] Notably, the technology under scrutiny involved a CCTV surveillance system that had been equipped with facial recognition capabilities. In this instance, the applicant, Nikolay Glukhin, had conducted a solo demonstration in the Moscow Metro. He claimed that the public authorities had showed zero tolerance towards his peaceful solo protest. He was subsequently identified and arrested through this technology and fined for failing to notify the public authorities in advance, which is considered an obligation under Russian law when a protest involves a 'quickly de-assembled object'.[60]

The Strasbourg Court found violations of Articles 8 and 10: the right to respect for private life and the freedom of expression. In the context of freedom of expression, the Court found that the legal provision concerning 'quickly de-assembled

[54] *Basu v Germany*, para 35.

[55] *Basu v Germany*, paras 36–38.

[56] *Basu v Germany*, para 36.

[57] *Basu v Germany*, para 37.

[58] *Basu v Germany*, para 38. Despite the judgment's groundbreaking nature, Judge Pavli's partly dissenting opinion highlighted a critical deficiency: its reduction to procedural minimalism. He argued that, by refusing a substantive verdict due to inadequate investigation, the ruling weakens anti-discrimination law and favours state self-protection over accountability (Compare this case with Muhammad v Spain, App no 34085/17, ECtHR 18 October 2022).

[59] *Glukhin v Russia* App No 11519/20 (ECtHR, 4 October 2023).

[60] *Glukhin v Russia*, para 49.

objects' was not foreseeable. It failed to establish any clear criteria 'allowing a person to foresee what kind of objects could be covered by that provision'.[61] This uncertainty had also not been clarified by any Russian higher courts.[62] Furthermore, even in the case of a 'legal' interference which 'pursued the legitimate aims of "prevention of disorder" and "the protection of the rights of others", it was not "necessary in a democratic society"',[63] as Glukhin's protest in the Moscow Metro was peaceful and posed no threat to public order:

> The applicant's solo demonstration was carried out in an indisputably peaceful and non-disruptive manner. The offence of which he was convicted consisted merely of a failure to notify the authorities of his solo demonstration and included no further incriminating element concerning any reprehensible act, such as the obstruction of traffic, damage to property or acts of violence (contrast Kudrevičius and Others, cited above, §§ 164–75). It was not established that the applicant's actions caused any major disruption to ordinary life and other activities to a degree exceeding that which was normal or inevitable in the circumstances. Nor was it claimed that his actions had presented any danger to public order or transport safety. However, the authorities did not show the requisite degree of tolerance towards the applicant's peaceful solo demonstration.[64]

In the context of the right to respect for private life, the Court has reiterated that the concept of 'private life' is a broad term and is

> not limited to [the] 'inner circle' in which the individual may live his or her own personal life without outside interference, but also encompasses the right to lead 'private social life', that is, the possibility of establishing and developing relationships with others and the outside world … There is thus a zone of interaction of a person with others, even in a public context, which may fall within the scope of 'private life'.[65]

In the context of the assessment on the existence of interference, the ECtHR found that 'the processing of the applicant's personal data in the framework of the administrative-offence proceedings against him, including the use of facial recognition technology' amounted to an interference with the applicant's right to respect for his private life.[66] In terms of the assessment on the justification for the interference, it is essential to emphasise that the Strasbourg Court underlined that the need for safeguards under Article 8 increases with technological sophistication, requiring a careful balancing of the advantages offered by modern scientific methods within the criminal justice system against

[61] *Glukhin v Russia*, para 54.
[62] *Glukhin v Russia*, para 54.
[63] *Glukhin v Russia*, para 55.
[64] *Glukhin v Russia*, para 56.
[65] *Glukhin v Russia*, para 64.
[66] *Glukhin v Russia*, para 73. It is important to note that Russian authorities employed several advanced technological methods to identify the applicant, including analysing photographs and videos shared on Telegram, as well as utilising live facial recognition through CCTV cameras. This technology was instrumental in locating and arresting him while he was travelling on the Moscow underground: see paras 68–73.

the private-life interests.[67] Moreover, personal data concerning political opinions, including records of participation in peaceful protests, constitute special categories of sensitive data, thereby warranting a heightened level of protection under the Convention's framework.[68]

In the assessment, the Court examined the legality assessment and the questions regarding the existence of a legitimate aim and whether the interference was 'necessary in a democratic society' together. It stated that the Russian legal framework permitting the processing of any biometric personal data 'in connection with the administrative justice' was 'widely formulated', lacking any limitations 'on the nature of situations which may give rise to the use of facial recognition technology, the intended purposes, the categories of people who may be targeted, or the processing of sensitive personal data'.[69] Within the context of the 'necessity' test, the Court firstly assessed the level of the actual interference and underlined that the use of facial recognition technology is 'particularly intrusive', requiring the 'highest level of justification'.[70] Secondly, the Court considered the 'nature and gravity of the offences' and concluded that the applicant had been prosecuted for an administrative, rather than a criminal, offence under Russian law. Furthermore, it was not alleged that his actions posed any threat to public order.[71] In this case, such a use of facial recognition technology could not be regarded as 'necessary in a democratic society'. Consequently, the Court found a violation of Article 8.[72]

To conclude, new technological developments produce new ways to interfere with fundamental and human rights, particularly the right to respect for private life and correspondence.

In the cases analysed above, technologies such as CCTV, new forms of communication, genetic and information technologies, racial profiling tools, and facial recognition systems have all interfered with the right to respect for private life in distinct and concerning ways. The five judgments delivered by the Strasbourg Court illustrate that existing legal frameworks are often inadequate to address the challenges posed by emerging technologies. These cases underscore the urgent need for both judicial interpretation and legislative action to evolve in response to current technology-related fundamental and human rights issues. Yet the ECtHR is not the only European court to have addressed emerging rights interferences stemming from the use of advanced technologies. The CJEU has also played an increasingly active role in confronting data protection challenges. The following section will, therefore, examine the EU's ongoing efforts to safeguard fundamental rights within the digital environment.

[67] *Glukhin v Russia*, para 75.
[68] *Glukhin v Russia*, para 76.
[69] *Glukhin v Russia*, para 83.
[70] *Glukhin v Russia*, para 86.
[71] *Glukhin v Russia*, para 88.
[72] *Glukhin v Russia*, para 90.

1.2.2. New Technologies Testing the Charter of Fundamental Rights of the EU

In the early phase of sophisticated technological advancement, the EU had not yet engaged in a legal struggle to safeguard the rule of law, fundamental rights, and democratic values in response to the challenges posed by these emerging technologies.[73] During this early period, the EU largely adopted a liberal economic approach, prioritising market development over rights-based regulation.[74]

For instance, the EU's E-Commerce Directive introduced liability exemptions for online intermediaries regarding illegal content shared by users.[75] This special legal regime was based on three key considerations: first, public authorities lacked the technical means to monitor or control user-generated content effectively; second, the EU aimed to promote innovation and stimulate the growth of the digital economy; and third, public institutions at the time had limited insight into the nature and scale of user activity on emerging online platforms, particularly social networks. In other words, the broader implications of digital transformation were not yet fully apparent at the institutional level.[76]

The mechanism of 'notice and takedown' was, therefore, considered an effective solution for addressing illicit content online. Within this framework, platforms were permitted to remove or block such content once they became aware of its presence. This arrangement effectively granted platforms a form of private discretion over matters involving fundamental rights, particularly the right to freedom of expression and the right to respect for private life. The delegation of such public functions to private actors was intended to facilitate the effective implementation of public policy objectives in the online environment.[77] Early policy documents published by European institutions explicitly acknowledged this public role of online platforms, establishing a set of rules, guidelines, and principles aimed at combating illegal and harmful content, and

[73] G De Gregorio, 'The Rise of Digital Constitutionalism in the European Union' (2021) 19 *International Journal of Constitutional Law* 41–70.

[74] G De Gregorio, 'The Rise of Digital Constitutionalism in the European Union' (2021). The US adopted a similar approach through s 230 of the Communications Decency Act, which provides broad immunity to online platforms from liability for user-generated content. S 230(c)(1) of the Act stipulates that 'no provider or user of an interactive computer service shall be treated as the publisher or speaker of any information provided by another information content provider'. See Communications Decency Act 1996, 47 USC § 230(c)(1). For a detailed analysis of this framework in the US context, see Klonick, 'The New Governors' (2017), 1599–1603.

[75] Directive 2000/31/EC of the European Parliament and of the Council of 8 June 2000 on certain legal aspects of information society services, in particular electronic commerce, in the Internal Market (Directive on electronic commerce) [2000] OJ L178/1.

[76] E Biber, 'Digital Constitutionalism in Europe: Exploring a Constellation of Legalities' in G De Gregorio, O Pollicino, & P Valcke (eds), The Oxford Handbook of Digital Constitutionalism, online edn (Oxford University Press, 2025).

[77] G De Gregorio, 'The Rise of Digital Constitutionalism in the European Union' (2021).

thereby reinforcing the platforms' responsibility in upholding these regulatory goals.[78]

The case law of European courts has further illustrated the quasi-public discretion exercised by private actors in the digital sphere. A landmark example is the 2000 decision of the Tribunal de Grande Instance in Paris, which ordered Yahoo! to take all necessary measures to prevent access, within French territory, to an auction website offering Nazi-related objects for sale – conduct prohibited under French criminal law.[79] On one level, the case underscored the limitations of state authorities in effectively monitoring and regulating online criminal activity.[80] At the same time, it revealed the significant role of Internet intermediaries in the enforcement of fundamental rights.[81] Central to the dispute was the tension between Yahoo!'s right to freedom of expression and the claimants' rights under French law, particularly the prohibition of hate-related content.[82] Given the state's limited jurisdiction over the transnational nature of the Internet, the Court held the private platform accountable for the presence of unlawful user-generated content. This decision marked a critical moment in what has been described as the 'privatization of rights enforcement', whereby private companies increasingly assume responsibilities traditionally held by public institutions.[83] This evolving trend – referred to as 'the invisible handshake' – captures the complex and often opaque collaboration between public and private actors.[84] As a result, the exercise of public power in the digital domain has become increasingly hybridised by the influence and operational capacity of private entities.

[78] At least four key policy documents reflect the EU's evolving approach to online platforms: European Commission, 'Online Platforms and the Digital Single Market: Opportunities and Challenges for Europe' COM (2016) 288 final; European Commission, 'Tackling Illegal Content Online: Towards an Enhanced Responsibility of Online Platforms' COM (2017) 555 final; European Commission, 'On Measures to Effectively Tackle Illegal Content Online' C(2018) 1177 final; and Council of the European Union, 'Progress on Combatting Hate Speech Online through the EU Code of Conduct 2016–2019' 12522/19 (2019). These documents collectively encourage self-regulatory initiatives by online platforms and reinforce the special liability regime established under the E-Commerce Directive.

[79] Tribunal de grande instance de Paris, LICRA and UEJF v Yahoo! Inc and Yahoo! France (22 May 2000); US District Court for the Northern District of California, Yahoo! Inc v La Ligue Contre le Racisme et l'Antisémitisme 169 F Supp 2d 1181 (ND Cal 2001).

[80] JR Reidenberg, 'States and Internet Enforcement' (2004) University of Ottawa Law & Technology Journal 213.

[81] M Bassini, 'Fundamental Rights and Private Enforcement in the Digital Age' (2019) 25(2) European Law Journal 188–97. See also the related concepts of 'devolved enforcement' and 'intermediarisation' in European Digital Rights, 'The Slide from "Self-Regulation" to Corporate Censorship' (2011), available at edri.org/files/EDRI_selfreg_final_20110124.pdf; and B Farrand, 'Regulatory Capitalism, Decentered Enforcement, and Its Legal Consequences for Digital Expression: The Use of Copyright Law to Restrict Freedom of Speech Online' (2013) 10(4) Journal of Information Technology and Politics 404–22.

[82] M Bassini, 'Fundamental Rights and Private Enforcement in the Digital Age' (2019).

[83] M Bassini (discussing the enforcement of the right to be forgotten, as recognised by the CJEU in Google Spain SL and Google Inc v Agencia Española de Protección de Datos (AEPD) and Mario Costeja González (Case C-131/12, EU:C:2014:317), within the broader context of the privatisation of fundamental rights enforcement).

[84] M Birnhack and N Elkin-Koren, 'The Invisible Handshake: The Reemergence of the State in the Digital Environment' (2003) 8 *Virginia Journal of Law and Technology* 1–57.

However, the EU has not maintained its initial liberal economic approach in the governance of digital technologies. Since the emergence of advanced technological developments, EU policy has increasingly shifted from a liberal economic perspective to a constitution-oriented approach that aims to protect democratic values and the rights of individuals.[85] This normative reorientation is particularly evident in the judgments of the CJEU, which has taken an increasingly proactive role in addressing the data protection challenges posed by emerging technologies.[86]

A key driver of this judicial activism has been the entry into force of the EU Charter of Fundamental Rights, which acquired binding legal status following the 2009 Lisbon Treaty.[87] The Charter has considerably heightened the Court's authority in adjudicating digital fundamental rights, leading some commentators to characterise the Court as a 'human rights tribunal'.[88] Furthermore, a number of scholars have interpreted the CJEU's technology-related judgments as signalling the emergence of a new phase of European constitutionalism, commonly referred to as 'digital constitutionalism'.[89] This notion seeks to constrain and legitimate the exercise of power in the digital environment.[90] As Suzor aptly puts it, digital constitutionalism involves rethinking 'how the exercise of power ought to be limited (made legitimate) in the digital age'.[91]

A particularly significant illustration of this evolving jurisprudence can be found in the *Google Spain* case, which established the so-called 'right to be forgotten online'.[92] In this landmark decision, the CJEU effectively 'codified' a new right for data subjects, grounded in the rights to privacy and the protection of personal data enshrined in the EU Charter.[93] The Court held that search engine operators may be required to remove links to online content containing

[85] G De Gregorio, 'The Rise of Digital Constitutionalism in the European Union' (2021).

[86] See the 'Fact Sheet' of the CJEU on the 'protection of personal data' published in July 2020, available at https://curia.europa.eu/jcms/upload/docs/application/pdf/2018-10/fiche_thematique_-_donnees_personnelles_-_en.pdf.

[87] Charter of Fundamental Rights of the European Union, [2012] OJ C 326/391.

[88] G de Búrca, 'After the EU Charter of Fundamental Rights: The Court of Justice as a Human Rights Adjudicator?' (2013) 20 *Maastricht Journal of European and Comparative Law* 168–84.

[89] G De Gregorio, 'The Rise of Digital Constitutionalism in the European Union' (2021) (analysing the trajectory and underlying reasons for the shift in the EU from a liberal constitutionalist approach to a digital constitutionalist approach); E Celeste, 'Digital Constitutionalism: A New Systematic Theorization' (2019) 33(1) *International Review of Law, Computers and Technology* 76–99; E Biber and N Hogic, 'Online States and Inter-Legality' in E Chiti and A di Martino (eds), *L'era dell'interlegalità, G Palombella* (Il Mulino, 2021).

[90] C Padovani and M Santaniello, 'Digital Constitutionalism: Fundamental Rights and Power Limitation in the Internet Eco-System' (2018) 80(4) International Communication Gazette 295–301.

[91] N Suzor, 'Digital Constitutionalism: Using the Rule of Law to Evaluate the Legitimacy of Governance by Platforms' (2018) 4(3) Social Media + Society 4. See also the fourth chapter of the book for a critical analysis of the notion of digital constitutionalism.

[92] CJEU, Case C-131/12, *Google Spain SL and Google Inc. v Agencia Española de Protección de Datos (AEPD) and Mario Costeja González*, judgment of 13 May 2014, (Google Spain).

[93] See a comment on the judgment in F Fabbrini and E Celeste, 'The Right to be Forgotten in the Digital Age: The Challenges of Data Protection Beyond Borders' (2020) 21 *German Law Journal* 55–65.

personal information, even if the information was lawfully published by third-party websites, when such content is no longer relevant or adequate in light of the data subject's fundamental rights.[94] In this respect, the right to be forgotten represents a novel *Konkretisierung*[95] – or concretisation – of the right to respect for private life in the digital age.[96] Importantly, the CJEU's intervention in the digital rights landscape did not stop with the right to be forgotten. Its judgments concerning the right to data protection and the right to effective judicial remedy have catalysed a broader struggle for fundamental rights in the digital environment – a development that will be examined in greater depth in the following section.

1.2.2.1. The Right to Data Protection and the Right to Effective Judicial Remedy

On 8 April 2014, the CJEU significantly reinforced its role as a guardian of fundamental rights in the digital realm. In *Digital Rights Ireland Ltd v Minister for Communications, Marine and Natural Resources*, the Court declared invalid the Data Retention Directive,[97] which regulates Internet service providers' (ISPs') storage of telecommunication data in order to prevent serious crimes. The Court held that the Directive violated Articles 7 and 8 of the EU Charter, which respectively guarantee the right to respect for private and family life and the right to the protection of personal data.[98] The ruling was grounded in the Directive's failure to comply with the principle of proportionality – a core element of EU fundamental

[94] The operator of a search engine 'is obliged to remove from the list of results displayed following a search made on the basis of a person's name links to web pages, published by third parties … also in a case where that name or information is not erased beforehand or simultaneously from those web pages, and even, as the case may be, when its publication in itself on those pages is lawful': *Google Spain*, Case C-131/12, para 88.

[95] F Müller and R Christensen, Juristische Methodik: Band I – Grundlegung für die Arbeitsmethoden der Rechtspraxis, 11th edn (Dunker & Humblot, 2013) 263. For the basic premises of the theory on the concretisation of legal norms, see M Klatt, Making the Law Explicit: The Normativity of Legal Argumentation (Hart Publishing, 2008) 54–56 ('the text is only a "guideline, as such it has no claim to normativity … the rule is not the beginning, but the product of the process of the application of the law"').

[96] The right to be forgotten was fully codified under Art 17 of the GDPR after this judgment. See the detailed commentary on Art 17 in C Kuner, LA Bygrave and L Drechsler (eds), *GDPR: A Commentary* (Oxford University Press, 2020) 477.

[97] Directive 2006/24/EC of the European Parliament and of the Council of 15 March 2006 on the retention of data generated or processed in connection with the provision of publicly available electronic communications services or of public communications networks and amending Directive 2002/58/EC [2006] OJ L 105/54.

[98] Art 7 of the Charter states that: 'Everyone has the right to respect for his or her private and family life, home and communications.' Art 8 of the Charter provides that: '1. Everyone has the right to the protection of personal data concerning him or her. 2. Such data must be processed fairly for specified purposes and on the basis of the consent of the person concerned or some other legitimate basis laid down by law. Everyone has the right of access to data which has been collected concerning him or her, and the right to have it rectified. 3. Compliance with these rules shall be subject to control by an independent authority.'

rights jurisprudence.[99] The Court observed that the Directive's interference with fundamental rights was 'wide-ranging', and must be regarded as 'particularly serious'.[100] While it acknowledged that data retention may pursue an objective of general interest – namely the prevention of serious crime – it emphasised that the indiscriminate and blanket retention of data relating to all individuals, all means of electronic communication, and all traffic data, without differentiation, limitation, or exception, constituted a disproportionate intrusion.[101] As such, the Directive exceeded the boundaries established by the principle of proportionality and was deemed incompatible with the Charter.

Furthermore, the CJEU's landmark jurisprudence reveals growing concerns over the misuse of certain technologies in ways that may challenge constitutional values or even threaten the 'essence' of fundamental rights. Such tensions have also contributed to legal and political disagreements between the EU and third countries, particularly in the domains of data protection and national security.[102] A well-known example is the case of *Maximillian Schrems v Data Protection Commissioner* – commonly referred to as *Schrems I* – which is widely regarded as one of the most consequential decisions in international privacy law. In this case, the CJEU invalidated Commission Decision 2000/520/EC of 26 July 2000, which had established the 'Safe Harbor Framework' governing data transfers between the EU and the United States (US). The Court found that the European Commission had failed to ensure that the US provided an 'adequate level of protection for privacy', as required under EU law. In particular, it held that US law did not impose sufficient limitations on the access of national security agencies to the personal data of EU citizens. As a result, the CJEU concluded that such practices compromised the 'essence' of the rights enshrined in Articles 7 and 8 of the EU Charter.[103]

In its reasoning, the Court acknowledged the absence of a precise definition for the concept of an 'adequate level of protection'. However, it clarified that adequacy does not necessitate a third country providing a level of protection identical to that

[99] CJEU, Case C-293/12 *Digital Rights Ireland Ltd v Minister for Communications, Marine and Natural Resources and Others*, judgment of 8 April 2014 *(Digital Rights Ireland).*

[100] *Digital Rights Ireland*, C-293/12, para 37.

[101] *Digital Rights Ireland*, C-293/12, stating that the Directive 'entails an interference with the fundamental rights of practically the entire European population' (para 56). It is worth noting that the judgments of the CJEU on the right to respect for private and family life and the protection of personal data have played an important role in the constitutional shaping of the concept of essence of fundamental rights. See a debate on the issue in M Brkan, 'The Essence of Fundamental Rights to Privacy and Data Protection: Finding the Way through the Maze of the CJEU's Constitutional Reasoning' (Paper presented at the conference 'The Essence of Fundamental Rights in EU Law', Leuven, 17–18 May 2018) 1.

[102] See a discussion on this issue in M Zalnieriute, 'Data Transfers after Schrems II: The EU–US Disagreements over Data Privacy and National Security' (2022) 55(1) *Vanderbilt Journal of Transnational Law*, UNSW Law Research Paper No. 21-35 (discussing that *Schrems II* solidifies the CJEU's principled approach to data protection, refusing data surveillance and data securitisation). See also R Dowd, *The Birth of Digital Human Rights* (Palgrave Macmillan, 2022) 240 (discussing digital human rights abuses outside EU borders).

[103] CJEU, Case C-362/14, *Maximillian Schrems v Data Protection Commissioner (Schrems I)*, judgment of 6 October 2015.

guaranteed under the EU legal order. Rather, the standard requires that the third country provide, 'by reason of its domestic law or its international commitments, a level of protection of fundamental rights and freedoms that is essentially equivalent to that guaranteed in the EU legal order'.[104]

Consequently, the Court held that 'legislation permitting the public authorities to have access on a generalized basis to the content of electronic communications must be regarded as compromising the essence of the fundamental right to respect for private life, as guaranteed by Article 7 of the Charter',[105] adding that

> legislation not providing for an individual to pursue legal remedies in order to have access to personal data relating to him, or to obtain the rectification or erasure of such data does not respect the essence of the fundamental right to effective judicial protection, as enshrined in Article 47 of the Charter.[106]

On this basis, the Court concluded that the Safe Harbor Decision adopted by the European Commission failed to meet the required standard of fundamental rights protection, and therefore declared it invalid.

Following the invalidation of the Safe Harbor Decision, the European Commission adopted the Privacy Shield Decision as its successor, aiming to address the deficiencies identified by the CJEU and to strengthen safeguards for transatlantic data transfers. However, the Privacy Shield framework introduced a new legal landscape that continued to raise concerns, particularly regarding the adequacy of protections against mass surveillance, and the lack of effective legal remedies for EU citizens. These unresolved issues ultimately led to renewed judicial scrutiny, culminating in the CJEU's review of the framework in the case commonly referred to as *Schrems II*.[107]

The central question before the Court, once again, concerned the interpretation of the 'adequate level of protection' required under the General Data Protection Regulation (GDPR)[108] in the context of transferring personal data to a third country. In its assessment, the CJEU outlined a three-step approach to determining whether such an adequate level of protection existed. First, the Court examined the validity of the Privacy Shield Decision adopted by the European Commission. Second, it evaluated the extent to which public authorities in the third country – in this case, the US – had access to the personal data transferred. Third, the Court reviewed the relevant features of the third country's legal system, particularly with

[104] *Schrems I*, C-362/14, para 73.

[105] *Schrems I*, C-362/14, para 94.

[106] *Schrems I*, C-362/14, para 95.

[107] CJEU, Case C-311/18, *Data Protection Commissioner v Facebook Ireland Ltd and Maximillian Schrems (Schrems II)*, judgment of 16 July 2020.

[108] Regulation (EU) 2016/679 of the European Parliament and of the Council of 27 April 2016 on the protection of natural persons with regard to the processing of personal data and on the free movement of such data, and repealing Directive 95/46/EC (General Data Protection Regulation) [2016] OJ L 119/1.

respect to safeguards, oversight mechanisms, and the availability of effective legal remedies for individuals whose data was affected.[109]

In this context, the Court found that the European Commission's Privacy Shield Decision – the legal basis for data transfer from the EU to the US – was invalid due to the invasive nature of US surveillance programmes. According to the Court, both the legal basis for US surveillance programmes, such as PRISM and UPSTREAM,[110] and the ombudsperson mechanism to remedy for breach of rights regarding data processing were inadequate and, therefore, did not comply with the GDPR and the EU Charter.[111]

In this sense, data controllers or operators resorting to transfer of data must ensure that the data subjects are granted a level of protection not identical but 'essentially equivalent' to that guaranteed by the GDPR and the EU Charter, particularly Articles 7 and 8 of the Charter:

> [A]lthough not requiring a third country to ensure a level of protection identical to that guaranteed in the EU legal order, the term 'adequate level of protection' must, as confirmed by recital 104 of that regulation, be understood as requiring the third country in fact to ensure, by reason of its domestic law or its international commitments, a level of protection of fundamental rights and freedoms that is essentially equivalent to that guaranteed within the European Union by virtue of the regulation, read in the light of the Charter.[112]

The Court highlighted that the relevant US law does not indicate any limitations on the power of surveillance programmes that are able to serve as a basis for bulk collection of personal data.[113] Furthermore, the relevant domestic law does not provide data subjects with any actionable rights before the courts against the US authorities.[114] According to the Court, such a lack of any redress mechanism does not respect the 'essence' of the right to effective judicial protection:

> According to settled case-law, the very existence of effective judicial review designed to ensure compliance with provisions of EU law is inherent in the existence of the rule of law. Thus, legislation not providing for any possibility for an individual to pursue legal remedies in order to have access to personal data relating to him or her, or to obtain the rectification or erasure of such data, does not respect the essence of the fundamental right to effective judicial protection, as enshrined in Article 47 of the Charter (judgment

[109] *Schrems II*, Case C-311/18, paras 163–202.

[110] European Parliament, 'The US Surveillance Programmes and Their Impact on EU Citizens' Fundamental Rights' (2013), available at op.europa.eu/en/publication-detail/-/publication/0a3aa9b5-1fe9-4f85-aaae-cc515408cf97.

[111] Schrems II, Case C-311/18. See a discussion of the judgment in O Pollicino, 'Diabolical Persistence: Thoughts on the Schrems II Decision', MediaLaws – Commenti Forum, 24 December 2020, available at medialaws.eu/rivista/diabolical-persistence-thoughts-on-the-schrems-ii-decision (arguing that the parameter of 'adequacy' under the GDPR was transformed by the Court into a requirement of 'essential equivalence').

[112] *Schrems II*, Case C-311/18, para 94.

[113] The relevant domestic laws of the US are s 702 of the Foreign Intelligence Surveillance Act (FISA), Executive Order (EO) 12333, and Presidential Policy Directive (PPD)-28, para 180.

[114] *Schrems II*, Case C-311/18, paras 180–83.

> of 6 October 2015, Schrems, C 362/14, EU:C:2015:650, paragraph 95 and the case-law cited).[115]

In view of these considerations, the Court concluded that the relevant US law fails to provide the minimum safeguards required under EU law. Consequently, the Privacy Shield Decision – intended to affirm an adequate level of protection offered by the US – was declared invalid.[116]

1.2.2.2. The Right to Access Information

Another significant case was decided by the CJEU on 12 January 2023, clarifying the scope of a data subject's right to access information about the recipient of their personal data under Article 15(1) of the GDPR.[117] In this instance, an Austrian citizen, identified as RW, submitted a request to Österreichische Post AG, which is the national postal service of Austria, seeking disclosure of whether his personal data had been shared with any third parties, and if so, the identities of those recipients.[118] The company responded by listing merely broad categories of recipients, such as 'advertisers', 'IT companies', 'charitable organisations' or 'political parties', without naming specific entities.[119] The question of the referring court was:

> Is Article 15(1)(c) of [the GDPR] to be interpreted as meaning that the right of access is limited to information concerning categories of recipient where specific recipients have not yet been determined in the case of planned disclosures, but that right must necessarily also cover recipients of those disclosures in cases where data [have] already been disclosed?[120]

In other words, the referring court asked whether Article 15(1)(c) of the GDPR should be understood to mean that, when a person exercises the right of access to his or her personal data, the data controller must also tell them exactly who has received (or will receive) that data by naming the specific identity of those recipients.[121]

The Luxembourg Court employed multiple methodologies of legal interpretation. By engaging in a literal interpretation of the norm text, examining the Recitals, and applying the principles outlined in Article 5 of the GDPR,

[115] *Schrems II*, Case C-311/18, para 187.

[116] *Schrems II*, Case C-311/18, paras 184–202. The European Data Protection Supervisor issued guidelines entitled 'Strategy for Union institutions, offices, bodies and agencies to comply with the "Schrems II" ruling' on 29 October 2020, available at edps.europa.eu/data-protection/our-work/publications/papers/strategy-union-institutions-offices-bodies-and_en. The purpose of the guidelines was to ensure that future international transfers comply with the EU Charter of Fundamental Rights.

[117] CJEU, Case C-154/21, *RW v Österreichische Post AG*, EU:C:2023:3.

[118] *RW v Österreichische Post*, Case C-154/21, para 17.

[119] *RW v Österreichische Post*, Case C-154/21, paras 18–20.

[120] *RW v Österreichische Post*, Case C-154/21, para 27.

[121] *RW v Österreichische Post*, Case C-154/21, para 28.

particularly the principle of transparency,[122] while also considering the effectiveness of other rights guaranteed under the GDPR, such as the right to rectification, the right to erasure ('right to be forgotten'), and the right to object to the processing of personal data,[123] the Court emphasised that 'the data subject must have, in particular, the right to be informed of the identity of the specific recipients where his or her personal data have been already disclosed'.[124] However, the Court also emphasised that the right to the protection of personal data is not absolute and may be subject to certain limitations. Exceptions may apply in specific circumstances. First, the right of access may be limited to general categories of recipients when it is impossible to identify specific recipients, particularly when such recipients are not yet known.[125] Second, a data controller may lawfully refuse to comply with a data subject's request if it is manifestly unfounded or excessive.[126]

1.2.2.3. The Right not to be Subject to a Decision Based Solely on Automated Processing

Another significant case that illustrates how current technological intrusions into fundamental rights extend beyond the traditional scope of privacy and data protection is the *Schufa* case concerning credit scoring systems.[127] In this case, a German citizen, referred to as OQ, had been denied a loan after her bank received a negative credit score from Schufa, a private credit rating agency. The applicant requested access to her personal data and an explanation of how her score had been calculated. Schufa provided only the score and a general outline of its methodology, citing trade secrets for withholding detailed information. OQ filed a complaint with the Data Protection Authority, which was dismissed. She then appealed to the Administrative Court, which referred questions to the CJEU concerning the interpretation of Article 22 of the GDPR on automated decision-making.

The Advocate General (AG) Pikamäe highlighted three critical issues in interpreting Article 22 of the GDPR: (i) the definition and scope of 'profiling'; (ii) the interpretation of 'automated decision', which hinges on two cumulative criteria,

[122] It is important to highlight that the Court stated that 'the principle of transparency … requires that the data subject have information about how his or her personal data are processed and that that information be easily accessible and easy to understand': see para 35.
[123] *RW v Österreichische Post*, Case C-154/21, paras 30–39.
[124] *RW v Österreichische Post*, Case C-154/21, para 39.
[125] *RW v Österreichische Post*, Case C-154/21, para 48.
[126] *RW v Österreichische Post*, Case C-154/21, para 49.
[127] Advocate General Pikamäe, Opinion in Case C-634/21, *OQ v Land Hesse*, with SCHUFA Holding AG as an intervening party, delivered on 16 March 2023, ECLI:EU:C:2023:220, available at curia.europa.eu/juris/document/document.jsf?docid=271343&doclang=en. See also E Biber, 'Between Humans and Machines: Judicial Interpretation of the Automated Decision-Making Practices in the EU' in CH Hofmann and F Pflücke (eds), *Governance of Automated Decision-Making and EU Law* (Oxford University Press, 2024) 187–212, doi:10.1093/9780198919575.003.0007 (discussing the role of judges in comprehending automation and ensuring meaningful participation in decision-making, with reference to the *Schufa* case).

namely that the decision must produce legal or similarly significant effects and be based solely on automated processing; and (iii) the fundamental requirement of transparency concerning the underlying logic, the significance, and the foreseeable consequences of such processing, as reflected in Article 15(1)(h) of the GDPR. Furthermore, it is important to emphasise that the AG clarified that Article 22(1)[128] sets out a *general prohibition* on decisions based solely on automated processing, rather than conferring a subjective right. He underlined that this interpretation is reinforced by Recital 71[129] and paragraph (2) of Article 22, which delineates the limited circumstances under which such processing may, exceptionally, be permitted.[130]

Regarding the concept of 'profiling', the AG firstly emphasised that the credit scoring by Schufa constituted 'profiling', a legal concept described in Article 4(4),[131] as it involved automated processing of personal data. This processing includes uses of personal data to assess the creditworthiness of the data subject.[132] The AG also stated that, in the present case, the conditions for the decision to produce *legal* and *significant* effects were satisfied:

> [T]he refusal of such an application may have 'legal effects' on the data subject, who can no longer benefit from a contractual relationship in question. Second, it should be noted that such refusal is also likely to have an impact on the financial situation of the data subject. It is therefore logical to conclude that the data subject will in any case be 'similarly' affected within the meaning of that provision.[133]

The AG then turned, secondly, to the crucial question of identifying the relevant 'decision' in the case at hand, specifically whether it was the bank's act of approving or refusing to grant credit to the applicant, or the score generated through Schufa's profiling procedure.[134] He clarified that this question must be assessed on a case-by-case basis, as the process involves multiple distinct procedures:

> In my view, it is impossible to give a categorical answer to this question because the characterisation depends on the circumstances of each particular case. More specifically,

[128] Art 22(1) of the GDPR states that '[t]he data subject shall have the right not to be subject to a decision based solely on automated processing, including profiling, which produces legal effects concerning him or her or similarly significantly affects him or her'.

[129] Recital 71: 'The data subject should have the right not to be subject to a decision, which may include a measure, evaluating personal aspects relating to him or her which is based solely on automated processing and which produces legal effects concerning him or her or similarly significantly affects him or her … However, decision-making based on such processing, including profiling, should be allowed where expressly authorised by Union or Member State law to which the controller is subject.'

[130] Opinion of AG Pikamäe, Case C-634/21, OQ v Land Hesse (Schufa), para 31.

[131] Art 4(4) of the GDPR states that '"profiling" means any form of automated processing of personal data consisting of the use of personal data to evaluate certain personal aspects relating to a natural person, in particular to analyse or predict aspects concerning that natural person's performance at work, economic situation, health, personal preferences, interests, reliability, behaviour, location or movements'.

[132] Opinion of AG Pikamäe, Case C-634/21, OQ v Land Hesse (Schufa), para 33.

[133] Opinion of AG Pikamäe, Case C-634/21, OQ v Land Hesse (Schufa), para 35.

[134] Opinion of AG Pikamäe, Case C-634/21, OQ v Land Hesse (Schufa), para 40.

> the way in which the decision-making process is structured is of crucial importance. That process typically includes several phases, such as profiling, the establishment of the score and the actual decision on the grant of credit.[135]

In light of the referring court's considerations, the AG concluded that:

> [T]he score established by a credit information agency and transmitted to a financial institution *generally tends to predetermine*[136] the financial institution's decision to grant or refuse to grant credit to the data subject, such that this position must be considered only to have purely formal character in the process … the score itself must be regarded as having the status of a 'decision' within the meaning of Article 22(1) of the GDPR.[137]

In other words, the AG focused on the concrete effects that scoring has on the data subject's legal and economic situations.[138] According to him, the most effective way to safeguard the fundamental rights of data subjects under the EU Charter is to hold credit information agencies accountable at the point of score creation:

> Holding the credit information agency responsible based on the establishment of the score – and not by virtue of its further use – would seem to be the most effective way to ensure the protection of the fundamental rights of the data subject, namely the right to protection of personal data … but also the right to respect for private life, as that activity ultimately represents the 'source' of any potential damage.[139]

Thirdly, with respect to the transparency obligations and the scope of the right to information under Article 15(1)(h) of the GDPR, the AG has clarified that the EU legislature seeks to strike a fair balance between the right to the protection of personal data and the right to the protection of intellectual property, as enshrined in the EU Charter.[140] Referring to Recital 63 of the GDPR, the AG has emphasised that considerations related to trade secrets or intellectual property cannot serve as a blanket justification for withholding all information from the data subject. Instead, a minimum threshold of disclosure must be met, to ensure that the core essence of the data subject's right to protection of personal data is not compromised.[141]

In terms of understanding the real objective of Article 15(1)(h), the AG relied on Article 12(1) of the GDPR, and stated that:

> [T]he obligation to provide 'meaningful information about the *logic involved*'[142] must be understood to include sufficiently detailed explanations of the method used to calculate the score and the reasons for a certain result. In general, the controller should provide the data subject with general information, notably on factors taken into account for the decision-making process and on their respective weight on an aggregate level, which is

[135] Opinion of AG Pikamäe, Case C-634/21, OQ v Land Hesse (Schufa), para 40.
[136] Emphasis (italics) is retained from original.
[137] Opinion of AG Pikamäe, Case C-634/21, OQ v Land Hesse (Schufa), para 47.
[138] Opinion of AG Pikamäe, Case C-634/21, OQ v Land Hesse (Schufa), para 49.
[139] Opinion of AG Pikamäe, Case C-634/21, OQ v Land Hesse (Schufa), para 51.
[140] Opinion of AG Pikamäe, Case C-634/21, OQ v Land Hesse (Schufa), para 55. The AG specifically refers to Recitals 58 and 63 to support this balancing approach of the EU legislature.
[141] Opinion of AG Pikamäe, Case C-634/21, OQ v Land Hesse (Schufa), para 56.
[142] Emphasis (italics) is retained from original.

also useful for him or her to challenge any 'decision' within the meaning of Article 22(1) of the GDPR.[143]

1.2.3. Concluding Remarks

The judgments of both the ECtHR and the CJEU have demonstrated that new technologies can test fundamental and human rights – in particular, the rights to data protection, to respect for private life, and to effective judicial protection – in novel ways. In this process, these three rights become prominent in rights struggles.

The experiences observed in the judgments of both the CJEU and the ECtHR require close scrutiny of the impact of AI systems on fundamental and human rights. This scrutiny has two layers. First, it is necessary to see whether AI systems have made a difference in terms of fundamental rights protection, in comparison with the case law analysed above. Second, it is necessary to see how national and supranational actors have reacted to the recent developments of AI systems. The following inquiry will first show how AI systems have exacerbated and enhanced problems and related rights violations. Second, it will signal the variety of current AI governance with diverse legalities surrounding AI-related issues.

1.3. Artificial Intelligence is on the Stage

AI and robotic applications began gaining significant attention on the global legal and regulatory agenda around 2016.[144] In 2017, the European Council stressed the need for the EU to adopt a proactive stance on AI, urging the Union to cultivate a sense of urgency, 'while at the same time ensuring a high level of data protection, digital rights and ethical standards', and invited the EU Commission to 'put forward a European approach to artificial intelligence'.[145] In response, the European Commission issued a Communication in April 2018, aiming to establish 'an appropriate ethical and legal framework based on the Union's values and in line with the Charter of Fundamental Rights of the EU' for the development and use of AI.[146] As outlined in the Communication, the Commission subsequently released, in 2018 and 2019, respectively, the draft and final versions of the Ethics Guidelines

[143] Opinion of AG Pikamäe, Case C-634/21, OQ v Land Hesse (Schufa), para 58.

[144] European Parliament, 'Draft Report on Civil Law Rules and Robotics' (2016), available at europarl.europa.eu/doceo/document/JURI-PR-582443_EN.pdf.

[145] European Council, 'European Council meeting (19 October 2017) – Conclusions', EUCO 14/17 (2017), 8, available at consilium.europa.eu/media/21620/19-euco-final-conclusions-en.pdf.

[146] European Commission, 'Communication on Artificial Intelligence for Europe', COM(2018) 237 final, 25 April 2018.

for Trustworthy AI (hereinafter 'EGTAI'). These guidelines articulate a European human-centric approach to AI governance, placing the respect for human values at the forefront of its objectives.[147]

These developments reflect the sustained and growing engagement of public authorities, policymakers, and private entities within the EU in addressing the implications of AI. A broad array of reports, communications, policy statements, and ethical guidelines has been published with the aim of embedding fundamental European values and principles throughout the entire AI life-cycle – from initial design to final deployment.[148] In this context, Article 2 of the Treaty on European Union (TEU),[149] the EU Charter, and associated provisions of the GDPR are frequently cited as normative references. These documents consistently affirm the importance of core EU values, including human dignity, equality, justice, non-discrimination and non-stigmatisation, autonomy and individual responsibility, informed consent, privacy, and social responsibility.

The EU's legal approach to AI, however, began to take clearer shape in February 2020, when the European Commission published its *White Paper on Artificial Intelligence*. This policy document outlined a proposed regulatory strategy based on a 'risk-based approach', whereby mandatory requirements would, in principle, apply only to AI systems deemed high-risk.[150]

Subsequently, in December 2020, the European Union Agency for Fundamental Rights (FRA) published a report titled *Getting the Future Right – Artificial Intelligence and Fundamental Rights*, which examines the implications of AI for fundamental rights through concrete 'use cases'[151] in selected sectors.[152] The report concentrates on four key areas: social benefits, predictive policing, health services, and targeted advertising. In the section entitled '4.1 Perceived risks', which addresses the impact of current AI applications, the report identifies several significant concerns. These include inaccuracy and potential bias – most frequently observed in relation to public

[147] European Commission, 'Ethics Guidelines for Trustworthy AI', High-Level Expert Group on Artificial Intelligence (HLEG-AI), 8 April 2019, available at op.europa.eu/en/publication-detail/-/publication/d3988569-0434-11ea-8c1f-01aa75ed71a1.

[148] There are at least 12 leading documents dealing with European values, fundamental rights, and principles in the context of AI and robotics. See n 12 above.

[149] Consolidated Version of the Treaty on European Union, [2012] OJ C 326/13. Art 2 TEU provides: 'The Union is founded on the values of respect for human dignity, freedom, democracy, equality, the rule of law and respect for human rights, including the rights of persons belonging to minorities. These values are common to the Member States in a society in which pluralism, non-discrimination, tolerance, justice, solidarity and equality between women and men prevail.'

[150] European Commission, 'White Paper on Artificial Intelligence: A European Approach to Excellence and Trust' COM (2020) 65 final, 19 February 2020, available at ec.europa.eu/info/publications/white-paper-artificial-intelligence-european-approach-excellence-and-trust_en.

[151] FRA, 'Getting the Future Right: Artificial Intelligence and Fundamental Rights' (2020), available at fra.europa.eu/en/publication/2020/artificial-intelligence-and-fundamental-rights (Report I) 17. The report defines the term 'use case' as 'a specific application of a technology for a certain goal used by a specified actor'.

[152] FRA, 'Getting the Future Right' (2020).

administration[153] – alongside risks such as excessive monitoring of people, losing control over automated systems within the context of targeted advertising, and the inability to explain the performance of an algorithm.[154]

The report highlights fundamental rights concerns through concrete, real-world examples that illustrate the risks associated with AI systems. Among these are a human resources algorithm that systematically favoured male over female candidates in recruitment processes; an online chatbot that adopted racist language within a matter of hours; automatic translation tools exhibiting gender bias; facial recognition technologies that demonstrated high accuracy in detecting gender for White men but performed significantly less accurately for Black women; and the use of algorithmic systems by public administrations to categorise unemployed individuals, leading to potentially discriminatory outcomes against those perceived as non-compliant with legal requirements.[155]

One of the most recent and tangible examples highlighting serious fundamental and human rights concerns involves the AI system developed under the 'iBorderCtrl' project (Intelligent Portable Control System), designed to monitor and manage the movement of third-country nationals at the external borders of the EU Schengen Area. The project's most controversial component is an AI-based lie detection system, which analyses facial expressions and behavioural cues to assess the veracity of individuals' statements.[156]

Legal and ethical concerns surrounding the project escalated when the European Commission's Research Executive Agency refused to disclose detailed information regarding the system. This refusal was challenged before the CJEU, with civil society actors requesting the public release of relevant documents, including ethics reports and legal assessments. The CJEU rejected the Commission's motion to dismiss the case, emphasising that the right to freedom of information was central to the matter, and concluded that the public interest in transparency outweighed competing concerns, thereby justifying the disclosure of the requested documentation.[157]

The aforementioned instances of emerging AI practices becoming subjects of CJEU decisions and EU institutional documents underscore that AI represents a

[153] See also European Commission, 'A Union of Equality: EU Anti-Racism Action Plan 2020–2025' COM (2020) 565 final, 18 September 2020 (highlighting that AI-based facial recognition algorithms can exhibit high misclassification rates for women and people from minority racial and ethnic backgrounds).

[154] FRA, 'Getting the Future Right' (2020), 57–58.

[155] FRA, 'Getting the Future Right' (2020), 15.

[156] See the project's website at iborderctrl.eu/The-project, stating that 'the main objective is to enable faster and more thorough border control for third-country nationals crossing the land borders of EU Member States, with technologies that adopt the future development of the Schengen Border Management'.

[157] CJEU, Case T-158/19, *Breyer v REA*, judgment of 15 December 2021, para 200. See also N Lomas, 'Orwellian AI Lie Detector Project Challenged in EU Court', *TechCrunch*, 5 February 2021, available at techcrunch.com/2021/02/05/orwellian-ai-lie-detector-project-challenged-in-eu-court. This judgment is considered in Chapter 2.

breaking point in the present-day protection of fundamental and human rights. Rights-related concerns are no longer confined to the issues of data protection or the right to respect for private life. Rather, new and complex challenges have emerged, implicating a broader array of fundamental rights – including non-discrimination, access to justice, and right to the freedom of information. In other words, AI possesses the capacity to affect individual rights and societal freedoms in ways unparalleled by previous technological developments. This reality necessitates a comprehensive reassessment of the existing legal frameworks. It is essential to adopt a holistic approach that considers the full spectrum of fundamental and human rights in relation to AI,[158] moving beyond the regulatory paradigms established during the Internet era. Tables 1.1. and 1.2. below illustrate this shift, drawing on the judicial cases and the examples discussed above – showing how AI has broadened the scope of rights-related concerns beyond traditional issues of privacy and data protection.[159]

Table 1.1 Fundamental Rights are at Risk I

New Technology (Before AI)	**Problematic Aspects of Technical Capacity or Use**	**Affected Right(s)**
Internet service providers *(Schrems I and II)*	Data transfer outside of the EU	(i) Right to data protection (ii) Right to respect for private life (iii) Right to effective judicial protection
CCTV *(Peck v the United Kingdom)*	Showing the applicant carrying a large knife in the process of attempting suicide	(i) Right to respect for private life
Internet *(Copland v the United Kingdom)*	The collection and storage of personal information related to the applicant's email and Internet usage	(i) Right to respect for private life and correspondence
Genetics and Information Technologies *(S. and Marper v the United Kingdom)*	Processing very sensitive data such as fingerprints, cellular samples, and DNA profiles	(i) Right to respect for private life

(continued)

[158] FRA, 'Getting the Future Right' (2020).
[159] The tables are original contributions of the author of the book, developed in the light of the judicial cases and examples discussed above.

Table 1.1 ***(Continued)***

New Technology (Before AI)	**Problematic Aspects of Technical Capacity or Use**	**Affected Right(s)**
Profiling in the context of identity checks *(Basu v Germany)*	Arbitrary profiling, including forms that may amount to racial profiling	(i) Right to respect for private life (ii) Principle of non-discrimination
CCTV equipped with facial recognition technologies *(Glukhin v Russia)*	A stance of no tolerance toward a solo peaceful protest	(i) Right to respect for private life (ii) Freedom of expression

Table 1.2 Fundamental Rights are at Risk II

AI Systems	**Problematic Aspects of Technical Capacity or Use**	**Affected Right(s)**
Online chatbots *(Report I, FRA 2020)*	(i) Becoming racist; and (ii)deceptive	(i) Principle of non-discrimination (ii) Mental integrity
Biometrics (such as biometric identification or categorisation systems) *(Report I, FRA 2020)*	(i) Excessive monitoring of people (ii) Detecting gender with great accuracy for White men, but not for Black women	(i) Right to data protection (ii) Principle of non-discrimination
AI video lie detector ('iBorderCtrl') *(Breyer v REA)*	(i) Evaluating facial expressions and behaviours to ascertain whether third-country nationals are telling the truth (ii) Not providing information about how it works, or the inability to explain the performance of the algorithm	(i) Right to data protection (ii) Right of access to documents
Credit scoring (Opinion of AG Pikamäe, *Schufa*)	(i) Refusal of a loan application on the basis of a negative score without a clear justification	(i) Right not to be subject to a decision based solely on automated processing (ii) Right to information

The EU has increasingly recognised this shift and the potential risks and challenges posed by AI systems. In response, on 21 April 2021, the European Commission introduced the world's first comprehensive legislative proposal on AI – the Artificial Intelligence Act (hereinafter the 'AI Act').[160] The proposal was broadly welcomed across the EU, as it represents a significant step towards establishing a robust legal framework grounded in high ethical standards and fundamental rights protections.

The disruptive impact of AI systems on the protection of fundamental rights becomes particularly evident when examining the practices explicitly prohibited under the proposed AI Act. These include: (i) manipulation through 'subliminal techniques'; (ii) exploitation of vulnerabilities of specific groups; (iii) general-purpose social scoring; and (iv) mass surveillance via 'real-time' remote biometric identification systems.[161] While it is essential to acknowledge that such practices are fundamentally at odds with the principle of human dignity – the cornerstone of European constitutionalism[162] – it remains uncertain which specific rights are being violated in each case.[163] This ambiguity underscores the need to reassess and potentially reframe existing regulatory approaches. It must be critically examined whether current legal and policy frameworks are adequate to safeguard the full range of fundamental and human rights in the context of increasingly powerful AI technologies.

Recent developments in the EU's approach to AI and digital governance did not stop there. On 26 January 2022, the European Commission published the European Declaration on Digital Rights and Principles for the Digital Decade.[164] The EU's position on the digital transition is articulated in the Declaration's first chapter, which defines the European vision as 'putting people at the centre'. The structural choicc to open with this principle serves to underscore that rights and freedoms must be respected in the digital realm, 'just as they are offline'. Beyond this foundational statement, the Declaration is organised into five additional chapters, each reflecting core European values in the context of

[160] Proposal for a Regulation of the European Parliament and of the Council Laying down Harmonised Rules on Artificial Intelligence (Artificial Intelligence Act) and Amending Certain Union Legislative Acts, COM (2021) 206 final, 2021/0106 (COD), 21 April 2021 (Brussels) ('The AI Act Proposal, COM (2021) 206 final, 21 April 2021').

[161] The AI Act Proposal, COM (2021) 206 final, 21 April 2021.

[162] JQ Whitman, 'On Nazi Honor and New European Dignity' in C Joerges and NS Ghaleigh (eds), *Darker Legacies of Law in Europe: The Shadow of National Socialism and Fascism over Europe and Its Legal Traditions* (Hart Publishing, 2003) 243 ('if we were looking for one phrase to capture the last fifty years of European legal history … we might call it the high era of "dignity"').

[163] These AI practices are closely related to the right to mental integrity. However, the AI Act Proposal does not specifically mention this right. See E Biber and M Capasso, 'The Right to Mental Integrity in the Age of Artificial Intelligence: Cognitive Human Enhancement Technologies' in B Custers and E Fosch-Villaronga (eds), *Law and Artificial Intelligence: Legal, Ethical, and Regulatory Issues of AI, Information Technology and Law Series* (Springer, 2022) 503–20.

[164] See European Commission, 'European Declaration on Digital Rights and Principles for the Digital Decade' COM (2022) 28 final, 26 January 2022 (Brussels).

digital transformation: solidarity and inclusion (Chapter 2);[165] freedom of choice (Chapter 3); participation in the digital public space (Chapter 4); safety, security and empowerment (Chapter 5); and sustainability (Chapter 6). The overarching message is clear: the digital transition must be grounded in European constitutional values. This vision was affirmed by Commission President Ursula von der Leyen, who stated: 'We embrace new technologies. But we stand by our values.'[166] Although the Declaration acknowledges that 'it has a declaratory nature and does not as such affect the content of legal rules or their application', its potential to shape the interpretation and application of rights under the EU Charter should not be underestimated. As an interpretative reference point, it may play an influential role in guiding future legal and policy developments concerning digital and AI governance in the EU.[167]

It is important to restate that the EU has adopted a risk-based approach to the regulation of AI. The proposed AI Act of the European Commission defines this approach as follows:

> [A] balanced and proportionate horizontal regulatory approach to AI that is limited to the minimum necessary requirements to address the risks and problems linked to AI, without unduly constraining or hindering technological development or otherwise disproportionately increasing the cost of placing AI solutions on the market.[168]

However, several legal scholars have criticised the proposed approach for lacking sufficient normative power to effectively safeguard fundamental rights, human rights, and the rule of law.[169] This shortcoming leaves the protection of these rights on an uncertain footing, particularly in the face of increasingly intrusive AI practices.

[165] E Biber, 'Art. 2 The Principle of Solidarity and Inclusion' in R Ducato, A Strowel, and E Marique (eds), The Declaration on European Digital Rights and Principles for the Digital Decade: A Commentary with a Legal Design Perspective (forthcoming).

[166] See President von der Leyen's speech at the high-level opening session of the 2021 Digital Assembly, 'Leading the Digital Decade', 1 June 2021, available at ec.europa.eu/commission/presscorner/detail/en/speech_21_2804.

[167] European Commission, 'European Declaration on Digital Rights and Principles for the Digital Decade' COM (2022) 28 final, 26 January 2022 (Brussels). See also European Commission, 'Communication: Establishing a European Declaration on Digital Rights and Principles for the Digital Decade' COM (2022) 27 final, 26 January 2022 (Brussels).

[168] The AI Act Proposal, COM (2021) 206 final, 21 April 2021, Explanatory Memorandum, 3.

[169] N Smuha, E Ahmed-Rengers, A Harkens, W Li, J MacLaren, R Piselli, and K Yeung, 'How the EU Can Achieve Legally Trustworthy AI: A Response to the European Commission's Proposal for an Artificial Intelligence Act', LEADS Law, University of Birmingham – Legal, Ethical and Accountable Digital Society, 5 August 2021, 9, available at papers.ssrn.com/sol3/papers.cfm?abstract_id=3899991; Ada Lovelace Institute, 'People, Risks, and the Unique Requirements of AI: 18 Recommendations to Strengthen the EU AI Act', Policy Briefing (2022), available at adalovelaceinstitute.org/wp-content/uploads/2022/03/Policy-briefing-People-risk-and-the-unique-requirements-of-AI-18-recommendations-to-strengthen-the-EU-AI-Act.pdf. See also E Biber, 'Machines Learning the Rule of Law: EU Proposes the World's First Artificial Intelligence Act', *Verfassungsblog*, 13 July 2021, available at verfassungsblog.de/ai-rol.

1.3.1. Understanding the Problem

The previous section demonstrated that fundamental and human rights are at significant risk, and it highlighted how these risks diverge from those associated with earlier forms of advanced technology. Building on that analysis, it is essential to situate the problem within its broader context. A thorough examination of the current technological landscape is crucial for effectively addressing the complex legal challenges posed by AI systems.

Understanding the problematic nature of AI systems requires a two-tiered analysis. First, it is crucial to identify who holds power over these technologies.[170] While AI systems may be deployed across both public and private sectors, their development and programming are overwhelmingly driven by private entities – particularly large technology firms.[171] These 'big tech' companies,[172] often among the most powerful globally by market capitalisation, occupy a dominant position on the provider side of the AI ecosystem. As Nemitz has pointed out, such corporations have already had substantial influence in shaping state policies[173] in favour of information or surveillance capitalism.[174] Furthermore, under the European Commission's proposed AI Act, the responsibility for reviewing AI systems lies primarily with the providers themselves. This framework positions private actors not only as key drivers of technological development but also as significant actors in the potential safeguarding – or undermining – of fundamental rights.[175]

Second, it is essential to identify the full range of actors involved in exercising and shaping private digital power over AI (in the use of the private digital power over AI). At a minimum, four distinct categories of actors can be distinguished. First, in the context of public sector applications of AI, public authorities emerge as key actors. These bodies frequently employ AI systems for biometric identification,

[170] See, for instance, K Crawford, who urges researchers to 'focus less on ethics and more on power' because 'AI is invariably designed to amplify and reproduce the forms of power it has been deployed to optimize', in *Atlas of AI: Power, Politics, and the Planetary Costs of Artificial Intelligence* (Yale University Press, 2021) 224.

[171] D Zhang, S Mishra, E Brynjolfsson, J Etchemendy, D Ganguli, B Grosz, T Lyons, J Manyika, JC Niebles, M Sellitto, Y Shoham, J Clark, and R Perrault, 'The AI Index 2021 Annual Report', AI Index Steering Committee, Human-Centered AI Institute, Stanford University (Stanford, CA, March 2021) 93 (showing the dominance of private investment in AI). Furthermore, according to the figures in the report, the US remained the leading destination for private investment, with over USD 23.6 billion in funding in 2020, followed by China (USD 9.9 billion), and the United Kingdom (USD 1.9 billion).

[172] J Surowiecki, 'What Does Breaking Up Big Tech Really Mean?', *MIT Technology Review*, 30 June 2021, available at technologyreview.com/2021/06/30/1026502/big-tech-breakup-monopoly-antitrust.

[173] P Nemitz, 'Constitutional Democracy and Technology in the Age of Artificial Intelligence' (2018) 376(2133) *Philosophical Transactions of the Royal Society A: Mathematical, Physical and Engineering Sciences* 4 (describing four sources of private power: the power of money, the power over infrastructures for democracy and discourse, the power over individuals based on profiling, and dominance in AI innovation).

[174] S Zuboff, *The Age of Surveillance Capitalism: The Fight for a Human Future at the New Frontier of Power* (Profile Books, 2019).

[175] Biber, 'Machines Learning the Rule of Law' (2021).

categorisation, and the administration of social benefits – primarily for purposes related to law enforcement, public order, and the allocation of resources. Second, given the cross-border nature of many AI services, international, transnational, and regional institutions also play a significant role in shaping the regulatory and operational environment surrounding these technologies. Third, at the core of AI systems is the individual, who interacts directly with, and is often the subject of, these technologies. Fourth, society at large represents a collective actor that is profoundly impacted by the widespread deployment of AI. The complexity of this multi-level and interdependent power structure is best illustrated through the analysis of the following two cases.

The Dutch government was the first within the EU to implement AI systems in public administration – and, consequently, the first to be found in violation of individuals' fundamental rights as a result of their use. On 5 February 2020, the District Court of The Hague ruled that the Dutch government's use of the SyRI algorithm ('System Risk Indication') violated Article 8 of the ECHR, which protects the right to respect for private and family life, home, and correspondence.[176] According to the Dutch Legislator, SyRI was a technical infrastructure designed to anonymously link and analyse data, with the capacity to generate risk reports concerning legal or natural persons deemed 'worth investigating in connection with possible fraud, unlawful use of and non-compliance with legislation'.[177] It was implemented by certain government bodies in collaboration with one another, involving the exchange of data to identify the individuals suspected of such abuses.

The claimants, comprising several human rights activists and non-governmental organisations, stated that the national legislation governing SyRI lacked sufficient safeguards for the protection of private life, rendering its binding effect invalid. The District Court of The Hague reviewed both the legislation and the usage of the SyRI algorithm by the Dutch government, primarily in light of Article 8 of the ECHR, the EU Charter, and the key principles of the GDPR – namely the principles of transparency, purpose limitation, and data minimisation. In this context, the court assessed the 'extent and seriousness of the interference' with Article 8 of the ECHR on the basis of the SyRI legislation and the information about the algorithm provided by the state.[178]

To identify the scope of interference, the court focused primarily on the functioning of the SyRI algorithm. It concluded that the SyRI legislation failed to provide sufficient information regarding the functioning of the system, particularly the risk models composed of risk indicators, the methods used for risk

[176] The Hague District Court, Case C/09/550982/HA ZA 18-388 (2020), paras 6.1–6.118.

[177] The Hague District Court, Case C/09/550982/HA ZA 18-388 (2020), paras 6.1–6.118.

[178] It is important to note that the Hague Court highlighted the special responsibility of the state when applying such technologies, and their extensive and increasing interference with the right to respect for private life, in light of the case of *S and Marper v United Kingdom* before the ECtHR. See ECtHR, *S and Marper v United Kingdom*, Apps nos. 30562/04 and 30566/04, judgment of 4 December 2008.

analysis, and the process by which decision trees were generated. As a result of this lack of transparency, the court found that the legislation did not meet the requirements of Article 8 of the ECHR, thus constituting a violation of the right to respect for private life.[179]

The core issue that led to a violation of the Convention was the opacity surrounding the functioning of the SyRI algorithm within the legislative framework.[180] This lack of transparency reflects a broader concern about the concentration of power behind algorithmic systems – power facilitated by the legislation that fails to clearly articulate how the SyRI algorithm operates. In other words, it is the legislative framework, not the algorithmic code, that becomes the real 'black box' for the individual. Furthermore, in today's algorithmic society, individuals often lack the capacity to fully grasp the implications of their digital behaviour or the mechanisms by which technological systems interact with and influence their lives. As Slavin observes, 'we are writing things that we can no longer read'.[181]

This lack of understanding significantly limits individuals' capacity to critically engage with algorithmic systems.[182] As highlighted in a report by the FRA on AI, a Eurobarometer survey found that only 40 per cent of Europeans are aware that they have the right to intervene when decisions about them are made through automated processes.[183] This finding reveals a deeper challenge: AI systems have become so highly complex that even those who use them – and those responsible for regulating them – often cannot fully grasp or explain how these systems function.[184] The Dutch Court recognised this very issue in its judgment and noted that, due to the opacity of the algorithm used, citizens could 'neither anticipate the intrusion into their private life nor … guard themselves against it'.[185]

In this opaque and non-transparent environment – one that effectively blocks individuals from accessing their rights and freedoms – the protection of fundamental rights is situated within an 'irregular square' captured by the interplay of

[179] The Hague District Court, Case C/09/550982/HA ZA 18-388 (2020), paras. 6.1–6.118.

[180] M Turilli and L Floridi, 'The Ethics of Information Transparency' (2015) 11 Ethics and Information Technology 105 (defining transparency as a pro-ethical condition for enabling or impairing other ethical principles or practices); J Burrell, 'How the Machine Thinks: Understanding Opacity in Machine Learning', Big Data & Society (January–June 2016) 1 (arguing that opacity may stem from three forms: state or corporate secrecy, technical illiteracy, and the characteristics of machine learning algorithms and the scale required to apply them usefully). See also M Hildebrandt, 'The Dawn of a Critical Transparency Right for the Profiling Era' in J Bus et al (eds), Digital Enlightenment Yearbook (IOS Press, 2012) 41.

[181] K Slavin, 'How Algorithms Shape Our World', TED Global, 2011, available at ted.com/talks/kevin_slavin_how_algorithms_shape_our_world.

[182] D Neyland, 'Bearing Accountable Witness to the Ethical Algorithmic System' (2016) 41 *Science, Technology & Human Values* 50.

[183] FRA, 'Getting the Future Right' (2020), 12.

[184] FRA, 'Getting the Future Right' (2020), 1.

[185] The Hague District Court, Case C/09/550982/HA ZA 18-388 (2020), paras 6.1–6.118.

the state, the market, extra-state actors, and the individual.[186] It is an irregular square precisely because private power holds a disproportionate influence. In the Dutch case, the SyRI algorithm was developed by private entities, implemented by public authorities to monitor individuals and society, and ultimately assessed by national authorities through an extra-state legality, namely the ECHR. This convergence of private design, public deployment, and supranational review has raised pressing questions for legal scholars concerning institutional inequalities in the governance of algorithmic systems.[187]

The second case is a well-known and widely cited surveillance judgment by the German Constitutional Court – the Bundesverfassungsgericht (BVerfG) – which further illustrates the complex networks of actors operating within the ecosystem of digital power. On 19 May 2020, the German Constitutional Court ruled that the surveillance of telecommunications involving non-German individuals outside German territory violates the German Constitution (Grundgesetz – German Basic Law).[188] The Court conducted a constitutional review *(Rechtssatzverfassungsbeschwerde)* of certain provisions within the German Act on Federal Intelligence Service,[189] which permitted German authorities to collect and process communication data between non-German nationals located outside German territory.[190] The complainants, a group of journalists and non-governmental organisations, argued that these provisions violated their fundamental rights, specifically the right to privacy, and the freedom of the press.[191]

The government argued that it was not bound by the German Basic Law when conducting surveillance activities targeting foreign individuals outside German territory.[192] However, the court rejected this argument and found that the challenged provisions violated Articles 5 and 10 of the German Constitution, which guarantee the freedom of expression and the privacy of telecommunications, respectively. It further stated that legislator must revise the existing provisions to bring them into conformity with the German Basic Law by no later than 31 December 2021.[193]

[186] Klonick, 'The New Governors' (2017), 1599–603 (presenting a triadic model for social platforms situated between the state, speakers, and publishers).

[187] Although the emergence of issues related to institutional inequalities in the context of AI is relatively recent, such challenges have long been present in other domains – particularly in trade, security, and environmental governance.

[188] BVerfG, Case 1 BvR 2835/17, judgment of 19 May 2020.

[189] Gesetz über den Bundesnachrichtendienst (BNDG) of 20 December 1990.

[190] The constitutional complaint mainly challenged §§ 6,7 and §§ 13 to 15 BNDG.

[191] BVerfG, Case 1 BvR 2835/17, judgment of 19 May 2020, para 33. Arts 5(1), second sentence, and 10(1) GG provide: 'Jeder hat das Recht, seine Meinung in Wort, Schrift und Bild frei zu äußern und zu verbreiten und sich aus allgemein zugänglichen Quellen ungehindert zu unterrichten. Die Pressefreiheit und die Freiheit der Berichterstattung durch Rundfunk und Film werden gewährleistet. Eine Zensur findet nicht statt.' (Art 5(1) GG) 'Das Briefgeheimnis sowie das Post- und Fernmeldegeheimnis sind unverletzlich.' (Art 10(1) GG).

[192] BVerfG, Case 1 BvR 2835/17, judgment of 19 May 2020.

[193] BVerfG, Case 1 BvR 2835/17, judgment of 19 May 2020.

The court's reasoning raises several critical questions from both international and European human rights law perspectives. The most significant of these is whether the German Federal Government is bound by the provisions of the German Constitution when it interferes with the rights of non-German individuals outside German territory. The court answered this question with a definitive yes, relying on international human rights law and offering three key arguments to support German accountability on foreign soil, mainly interpreting paragraphs 2 and 3 of Article 1 of the German Constitution.[194] Indeed, pursuant to Article 1(3) of the Basic Law, the court affirmed that all German state authorities are comprehensively bound by the fundamental rights enshrined in the German Constitution, irrespective of territorial boundaries *(Staatsgebiet)* or the individuals concerned *(Staatsvolk)*.[195]

In this context, drawing upon the historical origins of the Basic Law and employing teleological interpretation, the court underscored that the Constitution aims at a comprehensive reading of the fundamental rights rooted in human dignity.[196] Secondly, based on a reading of Article 1, paragraph 2 and the Preamble of the Basic Law, the court found that the Constitution recognises inviolable and inalienable human rights as the basis of every community – of peace and justice in the world.[197] Thus, the fundamental rights enshrined in the Basic Law are situated within a broader framework of international human rights guarantees. This line of reasoning entails that fundamental rights guaranteed by the Basic Law must be interpreted in the light of Germany's obligations under international law.[198] Finally, the court held that emerging technological developments and their usage necessitate a comprehensive reading of Article 1(3) of the Basic Law in order to take into account the threats to fundamental rights and the resulting shifts in power.[199] This interpretation leads to the conclusion that German authorities remain bound by international human rights obligations, regardless of the territorial context of new technologies which offer cross-border services.[200] In other words, the court emphasised that a comprehensive reading of the Constitution is particularly crucial in the context of new technologies that enable state power to extend beyond national borders and affect individuals in third countries.

This case is a perfect example of how AI systems and similar advanced technologies create problems that transcend national borders. This makes legal

[194] Art 1(2), 'Das Deutsche Volk bekennt sich darum zu unverletzlichen und unveräußerlichen Menschenrechten als Grundlage jeder menschlichen Gemeinschaft, des Friedens und der Gerechtigkeit in der Welt.' Art 1(3), 'Die nachfolgenden Grundrechte binden Gesetzgebung, vollziehende Gewalt und Rechtsprechung als unmittelbar geltendes Recht.'

[195] BVerfG, Case 1 BvR 2835/17, judgment of 19 May 2020, paras 87–89.

[196] BVerfG, Case 1 BvR 2835/17, judgment of 19 May 2020, para 89.

[197] BVerfG, Case 1 BvR 2835/17, judgment of 19 May 2020, para 94.

[198] BVerfG, Case 1 BvR 2835/17, judgment of 19 May 2020, paras 94–95.

[199] BVerfG, Case 1 BvR 2835/17, judgment of 19 May 2020.

[200] BVerfG, Case 1 BvR 2835/17, judgment of 19 May 2020.

systems beyond the state – extra-state legalities – highly relevant. Therefore, AI presents an *inter-systemic* issue that connects private entities, the state, and extra-state jurisgenerative entities. Given the increasing influence of private entities in the development and programming of AI systems, it is crucial that legislation and adjudication in this domain do not reinforce the expanding dominance of market forces – either at the local or global level.[201]

The dominance of the free-trade imperative within this field is normatively untenable. This position is grounded in at least three foundational arguments, which can be categorised as follows: (i) the prioritisation of profit over the public interest; (ii) systemic lack of transparency in decision-making processes; and (iii) the hegemonic risks posed by asymmetrical power dynamics.

First, the concentration of power in private entities – whose primary orientation is towards profit maximisation – does not inherently serve the public interest. Second, such entities are not structurally obligated to ensure transparency in the programming and development of AI systems; on the contrary, the disclosure of technical information is often perceived as detrimental to their competitive advantage. Third, the entrenchment of any hegemonic approach – whether market-based or otherwise – poses significant risks not only to the foundational principles of constitutional democracy but also to the proper functioning of the market itself. In light of these concerns, there is a pressing need for a rigorous and legitimacy-seeking legal approach within this 'irregular square' of actors – one capable of rebalancing the asymmetries of power in the AI governance landscape. Such a framework must be committed to the robust protection of fundamental and human rights, and must actively counter the risk of institutionalising rights violations through automated systems. Figure 1.1. below illustrates the complex and problematic interdependencies between AI systems and their socio-technical and legal environments.[202]

[201] While I was editing my PhD dissertation, Russia invaded Ukraine, on 24 February 2022. The EU immediately took restrictive measures in response to the crisis. See Council of the European Union, 'EU restrictive measures in response to the crisis in Ukraine', available at consilium.europa.eu/en/policies/sanctions/restrictive-measures-ukraine-crisis. I also observed the reactions of the big tech companies to this crisis. They took major decisions that demonstrated their global impact. For instance, on 1 March 2022, Google blocked mobile apps connected to RT (Russian state-controlled international television) and Sputnik from its Play Store. This was a clear sign that private digital power challenges conventional power relationships between states and private actors. As big tech companies are at the heart of the war, they can play a powerful role. This situation also challenges several concepts, including global justice and digital sovereignty. It also requires considering whether the company, in this example, should autonomously decide on the scope of its responsibility regarding the crisis, and what kind of technological sanctions it should apply. See P Dave, 'Exclusive: Google Blocks RT, Sputnik from Play App Store in Europe', Reuters, 2 March 2022, available at reuters.com/technology/exclusive-google-blocks-rt-sputnik-play-app-store-europe-2022-03-02. See also M Schaake, 'Big Tech Faces Moral Reckoning in Ukraine', Financial Times, 7 March 2022, available at ft.com/content/d35c5e95-e0cb-4350-9dbd-e971e7070b63 (arguing that these companies should follow some moral lines globally).

[202] The figure has been developed with inspiration from Nemitz's article. See Nemitz, 'Constitutional Democracy and Technology in the Age of Artificial Intelligence' (2018).

Figure 1.1 AI Ecosystem

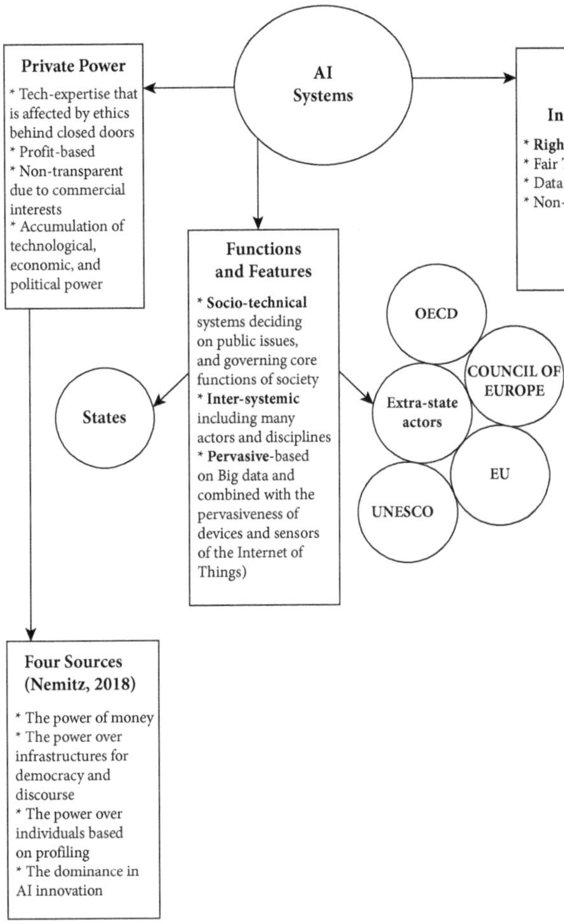

1.3.2. Existing Approaches

The field of AI regulation is characterised by five principal legal approaches: the black letter law, and emergent, ethical, risk regulation, and rights-based models.[203] While the limitations of these models have been critiqued in the existing literature,[204] it is significant to underscore key issues. Beyond the specific

[203] N Petit and J De Cooman, 'Models of Law and Regulation for AI', EUI Working Paper RSCAS 2020/63, Robert Schuman Centre for Advanced Studies (2020) 1–21. These models are analysed in Chapter 3 of this book.
[204] Petit and De Cooman, 'Models of Law and Regulation for AI' (2020), 15.

'risks' associated with the risk-based model – discussed in detail in chapter three of this book – other legal approaches also raise critical concerns. These models, along with their respective shortcomings, are further examined in chapter three; however, a number of these issues will also be briefly addressed in this section, for conceptual clarity.

The black letter law model, at its core, may involve blind spots and pose the risk of becoming irrelevant to the rapidly evolving technologies it aims to regulate.[205] Laws, after all, are designed based on a specific representation, and often a static state of the world, and could seem highly abstract in a new context. Therefore, reasoning based on existing rules without a thorough comprehension of the technology can lead to wrong normative results.[206]

The emergent model that captures the intellectual attitude known as the 'law of the horse' is also subject to significant critique. This approach, which ridicules the adoption of a new law whenever a new technology emerges – in the nineteenth century, the horse,[207] – presents a primary problem of redundancy.[208] Given that AI is designed to replicate certain aspects of human capacities, legal frameworks governing AI may closely resemble those regulating human actions, potentially leading to overlaps and redundancies in legislation.[209]

The ethical model, meanwhile, faces substantial critique due to its vulnerability to manipulation and ambiguity. The key fallacies of this approach are aptly captured by a trio of terms. First, the term 'ethics washing', also referred to as 'ethics lobbying', describes a deceptive practice whereby an organisation presents a superficial or performative commitment to ethical principles to create the illusion of moral responsibility, while avoiding meaningful legal regulation.[210] Second, 'ethical relativism' highlights the lack of universal, objective ethical standards, as these criteria can be seen as dependent on non-moral variables such as culture, time, and location, which makes it difficult to establish a consistent framework.[211] Third, 'ethics shopping', as defined by Luciano Floridi, describes the strategic and self-serving misuse of ethics. It is the 'malpractice of choosing, adapting, or revising … ethical principles … in order to retrofit some pre-existing behaviours … and hence justify

[205] Petit and De Cooman, 'Models of Law and Regulation for AI' (2020), 8–9.

[206] Petit and De Cooman, 'Models of Law and Regulation for AI' (2020), 8.

[207] FH Easterbrook, 'Cyberspace and the Law of the Horse', *University of Chicago Legal Forum* (1996), 207–16.

[208] Petit and De Cooman, 'Models of Law and Regulation for AI' (2020), 9.

[209] Petit and De Cooman, 'Models of Law and Regulation for AI' (2020), 9.

[210] B Wagner, 'Ethics as an Escape from Regulation: From Ethics-Washing to Ethics-Shopping?' in E Bayamlioglu, I Baraliuc, LAW Janssens, and M Hildebrandt (eds), Being Profiled: Cogitas ergo sum – 10 Years of Profiling the European Citizen (Amsterdam University Press, 2019) 84–89, doi:10.1515/9789048550180-016 ('Ethical frameworks that provide a way to go beyond existing legal frameworks can also provide an opportunity to ignore them.').

[211] Ethical relativism is a thesis of meta-ethics according to which moral criteria depend on non-moral variable factors such as culture, time, and location. See 'Moral Relativism' in EN Zalta (ed), *Stanford Encyclopedia of Philosophy* (first published 2004, substantive revision 2019, Stanford University), available at plato.stanford.edu/entries/moral-relativism/.

them a posteriori'.[212] These practices collectively expose the ethical model's fundamental weaknesses, demonstrating how it can be co-opted to serve commercial interests rather than protect the public interest.[213]

Among these regulatory approaches, the rights-based approach is particularly crucial. Its core focus is on establishing legal obligations rooted in the 'trinitarian formula'[214] of Western constitutionalist faith: democracy, human rights, and the rule of law.[215] The relationship between human rights and new technologies has been a long-standing subject of legal scholarship. Scholars have long been aware of the fact that scientific and technological developments bring both risks and benefits to fundamental and human rights.[216] This dynamic has led scholars and practitioners to rigorously examine how these technologies can be abused in ways that violate human rights, while simultaneously exploring creative ways to use them to improve the human condition. This tension – between risk and opportunity – is what makes the field of human rights and new technologies both dynamic and ever-evolving. However, it is important to note that a crucial challenge lies in the fragmented nature of the existing scholarship. Studies on the risks and opportunities of new technologies for human rights often suffer from a lack of a systemic, concrete, and analytical framework. This is evident in a tendency to overgeneralise technological applications and overlook the specific characteristics of present-day technological systems. Furthermore, the legal literature on advanced technologies

[212] Floridi defines it as follows: 'the malpractice of choosing, adapting, or revising ("mixing and matching") ethical principles, guidelines, codes, frameworks, or other similar standards (especially but not only in the ethics of AI), from a variety of available offers, in order to retrofit some pre-existing behaviours (choices, processes, strategies, etc.), and hence justify them a posteriori, instead of implementing or improving new behaviours by benchmarking them against public, ethical standards'. See L Floridi, 'Translating Principles into Practices of Digital Ethics: Five Risks of Being Unethical' (2019) 32 Philosophy & Technology 186.

[213] Petit and De Cooman, 'Models of Law and Regulation for AI' (2020), 10–11. See Chapter 3 of this book for a detailed analysis.

[214] The term was coined by M Kumm: see M Kumm, 'The Cosmopolitan Turn in Constitutionalism: An Integrated Conception of Public Law' (2013) 20 *Indiana Journal of Global Legal Studies* 609.

[215] Nemitz, 'Constitutional Democracy and Technology in the Age of Artificial Intelligence' (2018); FA Raso, H Hilligoss, V Krishnamurthy, C Bavitz, and L Kim, 'Artificial Intelligence & Human Rights: Opportunities & Risks', Berkman Klein Center for Internet & Society at Harvard University, 25 September 2018, available at cyber.harvard.edu/sites/default/files/2018-09/2018-09_AIHumanRightsSmall.pdf?subscribe=Download+the+Report; KM Manheim and L Kaplan, 'Artificial Intelligence: Risks to Privacy and Democracy' (2019) 21 Yale Journal of Law and Technology 106; J Fjeld et al, 'Principled Artificial Intelligence: Mapping Consensus in Ethical and Rights-Based Approaches to Principles for AI', Berkman Klein Center for Internet & Society at Harvard University, 15 January 2020, available at dash.harvard.edu/server/api/core/bitstreams/c8d686a8-49e8-4128-969c-cb4a5f2ee145/content; M Hildebrandt, 'The Artificial Intelligence of European Union Law' (2020) 21 (1) *German Law Journal* 74; A Mantelero, *Beyond Data: Human Rights, Ethical and Social Impact Assessment in AI, Information Technology and Law Series, vol 36* (Asser Press Springer, 2022).

[216] It is not possible to cite all relevant legal literature here. However, see some crucial studies on the relationship between human rights law and new technologies: MK Land and JD Aronson, New Technologies for Human Rights Law and Practice (Cambridge University Press, 2018); MV de Azevedo Cunha, NN Gomes, L Lixinski, and LT Féteira, New Technologies and Human Rights: Challenges to Regulation (Routledge, 2013).

is overwhelmed by definitional inconsistencies.[217] Different studies often employ different or conflicting definitions for the same or similar systems, leading to considerable confusion. While a detailed discussion on the origins of this issue is beyond the scope of this analysis, these developments may stem from a broader lack of a foundational theoretical framework in the field of law and technology.[218]

This line of thinking has led some legal scholars to wrongly analogise emerging technologies with earlier technological developments.[219] However, such analogical reasoning often proves inadequate, as it fails to account for the distinct ontological and functional characteristics of specific technologies. Consequently, these mischaracterisations can obscure essential features and lead to wrong normative conclusions within legal discourse. This issue was explicitly acknowledged by the District Court of The Hague, which argued that, when our understanding of technologies is based on properties and terms such as 'self-learning', and when wrong analogies are drawn between human beings and new technologies, we become unable 'to properly justify actions and to properly substantiate decisions' within institutional or administrative systems.[220]

Research on the impact of AI systems on fundamental rights has often followed a similar pattern. In the absence of a solid conceptual foundation, many studies have examined these impacts without adequately identifying the distinctive characteristics of AI – such as its high degree of automation, inherent complexity, and socio-technical dimensions. This approach not only complicates an already intricate issue but also fails to interrogate the broader need for new social values and normative frameworks in response to AI's growing influence.[221] Moreover, there is a notable lack of critical scholarship examining the EU's risk-based approach to AI regulation. Current analyses of this framework, especially in relation to the European Commission's proposed AI Act, are still emerging, and remain limited in both theoretical and practical scope.

[217] M Hildebrandt, 'Smart Technologies' (2020) 9(4) *Internet Policy Review* 2 ('A wide range of products and services is currently discussed under the heading of "smart", loosely overlapping with the technologies of (cloud) robotics, the Internet of Things (IoT), and more generally with hardwired applications of AI.').

[218] Although it is crucial to have a theoretical background in the field of law and technology, the legal literature remains relatively weak on this issue. One early contribution was AJ Cockfield, 'Towards a Law and Technology Theory' (2004) 30(3) *Manitoba Law Journal* 383.

[219] Klonick illustrates this pattern by analysing analogies between states and social platforms in 'The New Governors' (2017), 1599–1603.

[220] The Hague District Court, Case C/09/550982/HA ZA 18-388 (2020), para 6.46, citing the opinion of the Advisory Division: 'The term "self-learning" is confusing and misleading: an algorithm does not know and understand reality. There are predictive algorithms which are fairly accurate in predicting the outcome of a court case. However, they do not do so on the basis of the substantive merits of the case. They can therefore not substantiate their predictions in a legally sound manner, while that is required for all legal proceedings for each individual case. … The reverse also applies: the human user of such a self-learning system does not understand why the system concludes that there is a link. An administrative organ that partially bases its actions on such a system is unable to properly justify its actions and to properly substantiate its decisions.'

[221] See S Ranchordás, 'Empathy in the Digital Administrative State' (2022) 71 *Duke Law Journal* 1341–89, available at ssrn.com/abstract=3946487 (proposing the concept of 'administrative empathy').

Moreover, current legal scholarship on AI systems often fails to adequately recognise the *inter-systemic* nature of AI-related issues. Rather than critically engaging with the autonomous dimensions of distinct legal frameworks and the contextual factors that shape them, much of the literature remains focused on identifying surface-level 'common points' across jurisdictions – an approach exemplified by initiatives such as GlobalPolicy.AI, which will be discussed below. However, as Virginia Dignum highlights, 'AI means different things to different people'.[222] This fundamental lack of a unified understanding has a direct consequence: AI legislation is likewise interpreted and applied differently across various individuals, institutions, and jurisdictions.[223]

This observation proves that there is no such phenomenon as 'global AI', but, rather, inter-systemic AI systems that concern national, regional, international, and transnational authorities. The *inter-systemic* nature of AI can be seen in reports from the Center for AI and Digital Policy. For example, their 2022 report reviewed AI policies and practices in 50 countries and provided a global network analysis of AI.[224] This review included recent policy developments from the G7, G20, Council of Europe, EU, and UNESCO, demonstrating the breadth of stakeholders involved. Moreover, a 'datavisualisation' from the Council of Europe reinforces this point, revealing over 450 AI policy initiatives from a diverse array of sources.[225] Notably, international organisations are just as productive as their national counterparts in this domain.[226] As of 9 November 2021, international bodies had published 166 documents, compared with 156 from national authorities. The most prolific international organisations in this field are the Council of Europe, the EU, the OECD, and UNESCO.[227]

[222] V Dignum, 'Relational Artificial Intelligence', arXiv:2202.07446 (2022), available at arxiv.org/abs/2202.07446.

[223] M Hildebrandt, 'Global Competition and Convergence of AI Law' in JM Smith, J Husa, C Valcke, M Barreto, and T de Mendonca (eds), *Elgar Encyclopaedia of Comparative Law* (Edward Elgar, 2022).

[224] Center for AI and Digital Policy, 'Artificial Intelligence and Democratic Values Index' (Washington, DC, 2022), available at caidp.org/reports/aidv-2021. The report has four goals: (i) documenting AI policies and practices of countries; (ii) establishing a methodology based on global norms; (iii) providing a basis for comparative evaluation; and (iv) encouraging countries to ensure that AI is trustworthy and human-centric. It identifies seven key findings: (i) the OECD/G20 AI Principles have framed the global debate over AI policy; (ii) governments have both national ambitions and collaborative goals; (iii) AI safeguards build on data protection law; (iv) facial surveillance is identified as an AI "red line"; (v) concerns about autonomous weapons remain; (vi) NGOs are powerful advocates for the public; and (vii) AI policy is still in its early days, but the pace is accelerating. The Center has also published two other reports relevant to AI issues, namely 'Privacy and Human Rights' and 'Cryptography and Liberty'. See also M Rotenberg, 'Time to Assess National AI Policies', Communications of the ACM (2020), available at cacm.acm.org/blogs/blog-cacm/248921-time-to-assess-national-ai-policies/fulltext (noting that there are more than 300 AI policy initiatives worldwide).

[225] See the Council of Europe's datavisualisation of AI initiatives, which compiles over 450 documents from national authorities, the private sector, international organisations, and multi-stakeholder initiatives, available at coe.int/en/web/artificial-intelligence/national-initiatives.

[226] Council of Europe, 'Datavisualisation of AI National Initiatives'.

[227] Council of Europe, 'Datavisualisation of AI National Initiatives'. According to the datavisualisation, the golden year for international organisations was 2020: they produced 47 frameworks on AI, the highest number recorded between 2015 and 2021. It is also important to note that, on 4 April 2022,

The principles and recommendations set forth by international institutions constitute a form of soft law that is highly relevant to the regulation of AI. As a result, the frameworks developed by these bodies may concurrently emerge in a single legal case, alongside national legislative approaches. However, a significant gap exists in the current legal scholarship, which largely fails to critically examine the autonomous quality of each published document. Instead, the literature often focuses on the quantitative analysis of recurring concepts – such as human rights, privacy, responsibility, and accountability – that are emphasised within these documents.[228]

At the policy level, a dominant trend in the discourse on global AI governance has been the proliferation of AI ethics principles.[229] This has led to what can be described as an 'ethics congestion',[230] a condition characterised by a vast number of non-binding guidelines and recommendations. A notable aspect of this trend is the increasing emphasis on ethical frameworks over established fundamental and human rights.[231]

The debate over the future architecture of AI governance – specifically, whether it should be fragmented or centralised – is another key area of discussion.[232] Proponents of centralisation face known risks, such as the potential for creating a brittle institution and the difficulty of ensuring adequate participation while implementing deep-seated rules.[233] Consequently, some scholars advocate

the Council of Europe and the Italian Chairmanship of the Committee of Ministers co-organised the 'High-Level Segment – Inaugural Meeting of the Committee on Artificial Intelligence (CAI)' in Rome, to elaborate an appropriate legal framework on AI, based on the Council of Europe's standards on human rights, democracy, and the rule of law, available at coe.int/en/web/artificial-intelligence/-/inaugural-meeting-of-the-committee-on-artificial-intelligence-cai-.

[228] Raso et al, 'Artificial Intelligence & Human Rights: Opportunities & Risks' (2018).

[229] EV Garcia, 'Multilateralism and Artificial Intelligence: What Role for the United Nations?' in M Tinnirello (ed), *The Global Politics of Artificial Intelligence* (Chapman & Hall, 2006) 1–20.

[230] I am inspired by the term 'treaty congestion', developed in international environmental law. See DK Anton, 'Treaty Congestion in Contemporary International Environmental Law' in S Alam, JH Bhuiyan, TMR Chowdhury, and EJ Techera (eds), *Routledge Handbook of International Environmental Law* (Routledge, 2012).

[231] A Berthet, 'Why Do Emerging AI Guidelines Emphasize "Ethics" over Human Rights?', *Open Global Rights* (2019), available at openglobalrights.org/why-do-emerging-ai-guidelines-emphasize-ethics-over-human-rights. However, such a tendency is not acceptable. As Palombella argues in his well-known article 'The Rule of Law and Its Core', justice in law is fundamentally different from ethics because of its conceptual claim of the 'hindering of a hindrance to freedom' (citing Kant), meaning that the condition of co-existence through liberty must be ensured before pursuing any ethical objective. It is this transcendental ideal of law that makes it possible to pursue ethical objectives. See G Palombella, 'The Rule of Law and Its Core', in G Palombella and N Walker (eds), *Relocating the Rule of Law* (Hart Publishing, 2009).

[232] P Cihon, MM Maas and L Kemp, 'Fragmentation and the Future: Investigating Architectures for International AI Governance' (2020) 11(5) *Global Policy*. In fact, the question of regime centralisation is not new. It has been discussed in the environmental context for at least 50 years. In 1970, the US diplomat George Kennan proposed the establishment of an 'International Environmental Agency' outside the United Nations. See 'Kennan Now Backs an Agency in UN on World Pollution' (*New York Times*, 3 March 1972), available at nytimes.com/1972/03/03/archives/kennan-now-backs-an-agency-in-un-on-world-pollution.html.

[233] Cihon, Maas and Kemp, 'Fragmentation and the Future: Investigating Architectures for International AI Governance' (2020).

for a decentralised approach, grounded in global standards, soft law, or existing international legal instruments.[234] However, a crucial dimension remains under-recognised in this debate: the *inter-systemic* aspect of AI. Given that AI issues transcend individual systems and jurisdictions, a truly effective governance model must be collaborative. Such a model would facilitate the engagement of all interested and relevant parties in addressing international issues, moving beyond the current focus on fragmented or centralised paradigms.

1.4. Focus of the Book

The focus of the research lies on the most significant AI practices affecting the protection of fundamental and human rights. Given the core purpose of the EU's legislative proposals – namely, to secure fundamental values and principles throughout the production process of AI, from the design phase to its deployment – and considering the challenges outlined above, this book poses the following central research question: How can European human rights and fundamental rights be effectively protected from the risks posed by AI systems, particularly those employed in the domains of biometric and social welfare distribution, within the context of an 'irregular square' captured by the state, the market, extra-state actors, and the individual?

To answer this question, it is first necessary to develop a foundational understanding of the nature of AI systems and to classify their key features. At this stage, the book draws on illustrative cases that exemplify the most significant AI practices impacting the protection of fundamental and human rights. Accordingly, the research addresses the following sub-questions: what are the fundamental characteristics of AI systems used by public authorities in the fields of social benefits and biometrics? In exploring this, the inquiry begins by asking, what is AI? How is AI defined across different disciplines – such as computer science, philosophy, and law? Can law, as a normative system, adequately define AI? Moreover, should legal scholars focus primarily on defining AI, or should they examine its practical applications? The analysis then turns to the specific uses of AI systems in the domains of social benefits and biometrics, identifying the key features of these systems.

The second set of sub-questions focuses on the current legal approaches to AI systems used by public authorities. It asks, do these approaches adequately serve the protection of European values and fundamental rights? What is the European legal approach to AI systems in the public domain? Does the current regulatory framework take into account the key characteristics of AI systems, and

[234] P Cihon, 'Standards for AI Governance: International Standards to Enable Global Coordination in AI Research & Development', Technical Report, Centre for the Governance of AI, Future of Humanity Institute, University of Oxford (2019), available at fhi.ox.ac.uk/wp-content/uploads/Standards_-FHI-Technical-Report.pdf.

is it adequate to safeguard fundamental and human rights? Finally, the research examines the nature of the legal framework within which this approach operates, considering whether it is capable of responding to the unique challenges posed by AI technologies deployed in the public sector.

The third dimension of the inquiry considers whether the theory of inter-legality can provide a useful perspective and methodology for addressing the *inter-systemic* nature of AI-related legal challenges in the context of fundamental and human rights protection. It asks, can the theory of inter-legality offer a viable framework for understanding and regulating the misuse of AI systems across different normative orders? If so, why is this approach particularly relevant to the legal and ethical issues raised by AI? In pursuing these questions, the research further explores the relationship between inter-legality and other relevant doctrinal approaches, including the theory of the horizontal effect of fundamental rights, and the emerging notion of digital constitutionalism. Finally, it considers how an inter-legality approach might be concretely applied to specific cases involving the use of AI or advanced technologies by public authorities.

1.5. Methodology

This book develops a rights-based inter-legal approach; a theoretical framework and methodology aimed to address the challenges that artificial intelligence poses to fundamental and human rights. This approach enables a comprehensive consideration of the full spectrum of rights within the AI context. By addressing the power imbalances between the state, the market, extra-state legalities, and the individual, it overcomes the disequilibrium often present in these interactions. The framework also integrates the theory of inter-legality with other relevant doctrinal perspectives, including the horizontal effect of fundamental rights and the notion of digital constitutionalism.

The rights-based component of this approach is defined by two elements: (i) it relies on the corpus of European fundamental and human rights law to establish its normative commitments; and (ii) it focuses on accountability strategies that are derived from established fundamental and human rights practices. In this sense, the book adopts a 'rights-based approach' in a specific sense – referring not to a general proxy for 'social good', but to a concrete framework of recognised legal norms and established practices. Framing this approach within the context of European fundamental and human rights law is particularly significant, as it enhances the external impact and influence of such a framework on the protections of rights. This framing critiques the self-referential and isolated legal reasoning, such as that sometimes found in the jurisprudence of the CJEU,[235]

[235] G de Búrca, 'After the EU Charter of Fundamental Rights: The Court of Justice as a Human Rights Adjudicator?' ('the three years since the Charter came into force reveals that the CJEU is referring even

which is seen as an unsustainable position in a technology-driven world where rights require outward-looking protection.

A thorough understanding of how EU fundamental rights law and broader human rights law and practice intersect with AI is critical. This approach not only establishes a global baseline for addressing the cross-border implications of AI systems, but also provides essential guidance for human rights advocates who are developing new techniques or responding to the impacts of AI. The justification for this framework involves a comparative analysis of current digital legal strategies, including an examination of key features of AI systems in areas of social benefits and biometrics. It also specifically scrutinises the EU's risk-based approach to AI regulation, assessing its effectiveness in protecting rights in these contexts.

With respect to the inter-legal dimension of the approach, the fundamental features of AI systems necessitate its development and application at five distinct levels.

First, AI systems deployed in the public sector are both interdisciplinary and institutionally *inter-systemic*. This is because their development and use involve a variety of academic disciplines and a wide range of different institutions. From an institutional standpoint, the 'GlobalPolicy.AI'[236] initiative provides a compelling justification for the inter-systemic nature of AI governance and the necessity of an inter-legal approach. It is an online platform designed to facilitate international co-operation among policymakers and intergovernmental organisations. It serves as a one-stop shop for AI policy experts and the public, helping users to navigate the complex landscape of international AI governance. The platform provides access to essential tools and best practices. As of September 2021, the platform's eight partners include the Council of Europe, the European Commission, the European Agency for Fundamental Rights, the Inter-American Development Bank, the OECD and its AI Policy Observatory (OECD.AI), the United Nations, UNESCO, and The World Bank Group (WBG).

The platform has two primary objectives. First, it aims 'to provide information about each organization's work on AI, thereby helping policy makers and the wider public navigate the international AI governance landscape and access relevant resources'. Second, it seeks 'to strengthen co-operation between the different organizations, leveraging each other's work and making progress together towards

less now to the ECHR than it did before, and even more rarely to the case law of the Court of Human Rights'). It is important to note that European legality does not represent a complex legal universe. As stated by the CJEU, European legality achieved legal integration through an 'autonomous legal order'. See CJEU, Case 26/62, Van Gend en Loos, ECLI:EU:C:1963:1; and Case 6/64, Costa v ENEL, ECLI:EU:C:1964:66 ('By contrast with ordinary international treaties, the EEC Treaty has created its own legal system which, on the entry into force of the Treaty, became an integral part of the legal systems of the Member States and which their courts are bound to apply.'). See also G Palombella, '"Formats" of Law and Their Intertwining', in J Klabbers and G Palombella (eds), *The Challenge of Inter-Legality* (Cambridge University Press, 2019) 30–31.

[236] See the GlobalPolicy.AI platform website, available at globalpolicy.ai/en.

common goals'.[237] Aligning AI with human rights and democracy is identified as a key objective of the platform.[238]

At first glance, the GlobalPolicy.AI platform serves as a powerful example of how different legal and institutional regimes can be interwoven. It brings together eight diverse international organisations to focus on the common issue of AI governance. The platform highlights that AI is a transboundary concern, similar to security or climate change. By calling for international co-operation and the establishment of common goals that affect all of humanity, the initiative effectively characterises AI as a 'global' issue.

Striving to develop common goals for AI through this platform naturally fosters a fertile ecosystem for inter-legality, as at the descriptive level 'inter-legality captures the crossing threads of originally separate regulators as well as legalities'.[239] All the intergovernmental organisations involved have published statements, reports, communications, and guidelines examining the societal, ethical, legal, and economic impacts of AI. By recognising AI as a common concern, they collectively demonstrate that it is a global phenomenon, not merely a 'national' issue. This proliferation of extra-state regimes and international organisations focused on AI creates an ecosystem where, as Merry notes, 'two or more legal systems coexist in the same social field'.[240]

Second, the use of AI to address other major challenges creates a material interconnection between AI and a host of global concerns. This framing directly addresses the interdisciplinary inter-systemic aspect of AI systems. For instance, regulating AI-driven surveillance technologies like biometric identification would be naive without considering the broader implications for global security. This connection can be understood as an 'issue-linkage', a concept described by Axelrod and Kehohane, where 'most issues are linked to other issues. This means that games being played on different issues – different "chessboards," in Stanley Hoffmann's wording – they affect one another. Connections between games become important when issues are linked'.[241] The United Nations also recognises this potential. On 15 September 2021, UN High Commissioner for Human Rights, Michelle Bachelet, underscored AI's potential role in solving global issues, highlighting how technology can be a force for both progress and peril:

> Artificial intelligence can be a force for good, helping societies overcome some of the great challenges of our times. But AI technologies can have negative, even catastrophic,

[237] GlobalPolicy.AI platform website.

[238] There are three key areas of the platform. The other two are 'responsible development and use of trustworthy AI' and 'AI to advance the sustainable development goals'. See the key areas at globalpolicy.ai/en/key-focus-areas.

[239] G Palombella, 'Exploring the Rationale of Inter-Legality' (on file with author) 9.

[240] SE Merry, 'Legal Pluralism' (1988) 22 *Law & Society Review* 869, 870 (defining legal pluralism as 'a situation in which two or more legal systems coexist in the same social field').

[241] R Axelrod and RO Keohane, 'Achieving Cooperation under Anarchy: Strategies and Institutions' (1985) 38(1) World Politics 239.

effects if they are used without sufficient regard to how they affect people's human rights.[242]

Third, AI systems used in the public sector are *dynamic* in both their development and adoption. Since static, closed legal systems cannot effectively capture such a rapidly changing field and its societal impacts,[243] an inter-legal approach is essential. This dynamism demands up-to-date and flexible approaches. An inter-legal approach is particularly promising, as its core idea excludes the monopoly or hegemony of a single legal order. In fact, this dynamic quality of the approach ensures both stability within the legal system – a feat that a closed legal system cannot achieve – and a genuine compatibility with the constant evolution of technology.

Fourth, as discussed in chapters two and three, AI systems used in the public sector are marked by *complexity*. This complexity arises from three interrelated dimensions: (a) their reliance on black-box mechanisms that obscure internal decision-making processes; (b) the use of heterogeneous terminology that complicates identification and classification; and (c) the integration of diverse techniques and applications. Moreover, such systems are inherently *social*, in that (a) they mediate and facilitate key aspects of the functioning of social institutions and structures; (b) they recognise and respond to the social components of their environment; (c) they structure interactions between individuals and the system through processes of identification, categorisation, and detection; and (d) they weave broader social contexts by aggregating and interpreting individual data within collective frameworks.

Legal scholars argue that the challenges posed by AI systems have not been adequately addressed, rendering current legal regimes insufficient. This inadequacy also proves the necessity for an inter-legal approach, as a closed legal system is ill-equipped to handle these problems. Moreover, the regulatory landscape is further complicated by the emergence of new technologies and their own private regulations, often supported by an 'invisible handshake' between the state and private actors.[244] These extra-state normative sources, however, face a significant problem: they lack democratic legitimacy. This deficit in both democratic and substantive legitimacy can disrupt their function, potentially making them dysfunctional when interacting with the systems they aim to regulate.[245]

Given these factors, AI issues become increasingly complex, demanding a reconsideration of the dynamics within this regulatory context. It is foreseeable that such a broad and interconnected issue will test the limits of existing legal

[242] United Nations, UN News, 'Urgent Action Needed over Artificial Intelligence Risks to Human Rights', 15 September 2021, available at news.un.org/en/story/2021/09/1099972.

[243] Palombella, 'Exploring the Rationale of Inter-Legality' (on file with author) 4.

[244] MD Birnhack and N Elkin-Koren, 'The Invisible Handshake: The Reemergence of the State in the Digital Environment' (2003) *Virginia Journal of Law and Technology* 1–57.

[245] G Palombella, 'Inter-Legality: On Interconnectedness and "External Sources"' (2021) 7(2) *Italian Law Journal*.

regimes. Inter-legality requires us to question the *law of the case* by looking within this interwoven legal texture rather than a single legal system.[246] While this composite legal practice may be more demanding than applying law from a single source, an inter-legal approach is necessary to effectively address the complex issues surrounding AI systems.

Fifth, the perceived inadequacy of existing law when confronted with AI systems may create a regulatory vacuum – or even a 'rightless' zone. Unlike other approaches, inter-legality is uniquely suited to address such a lacuna by offering a bridge between legal systems and revealing the connections between them. From an inter-legal perspective, the diversity of jurisgenerative entities, regimes, and orders collectively contributes to filling this gap, thereby producing a composite law governing the issue at stake.[247]

The book is structured into theoretical and methodological parts. Chapters three and four provide the theoretical foundation, presenting the backdrop for the subsequent methodological discussion. These chapters explore the theory of inter-legality within the context of relevant legal methodologies and perspectives, while also interrogating the specific demands of a rights-based approach. This analysis of the rights-based approach also clarifies how the proposed EU AI Act fits within the broader EU digital regulatory framework, particularly by examining its interactions with the GDPR.

Chapter two presents multidisciplinary research on the definition of AI systems, drawing insights from the philosophy of technology, and from computer science, and law. This research is conducted with the aim of neither overstating nor underestimating the complex capacities of AI, thus avoiding both over- and under-inclusive definitions. Consequently, it adopts a fact-based, legal realist approach, to ensure that the analysis remains concrete.[248] This approach focuses on the digital and social experiences of AI systems, to ground its conclusions.

The rights-based inter-legal approach is designed for use in both the regulation of AI systems and the judicial interpretation of incidents they cause. Given the reality of legislative inertia in technology regulation,[249] however, this book's current focus is on the judiciary. While the burden of addressing the negative impacts of AI systems is not theirs alone, judges are nonetheless positioned to play a critical role in shaping the legal approach through their interpretations and decisions. In the absence of meaningful legislation, judicial interpretation will inevitably establish key standards that influence how AI systems are governed.[250]

[246] Palombella, 'Inter-Legality: On Interconnectedness and "External Sources"' (2021).

[247] Palombella, 'Exploring the Rationale of Inter-Legality' (on file with author) 4.

[248] G Gilmore, 'Legal Realism: Its Cause and Its Cure' (1961) 70 Yale Law Journal 1038 ('The life of the law … has not been logic: it has been experience … Law is not static but dynamic. It changes as society changes, both forever in an equilibrium precarious and unstable.').

[249] Pollicino and De Gregorio, 'Constitutional Law in the Algorithmic Society' (2022).

[250] Biber, 'Between Humans and Machines: Judicial Interpretation of the Automated Decision-Making Practices in the EU' (2024).

Following the theoretical chapters, a methodological section at the end of chapter four outlines a three-step process for applying this approach to concrete judgments. This method involves: (i) adopting the vantage point of the affair – the case at hand – under scrutiny; (ii) identifying the relevant normativities governing the case; and (iii) considering the demands of justice stemming from the case.

1.6. Contribution

In 2021, 115 civil society organisations raised concerns and offered recommendations to strengthen fundamental rights protections within the proposed AI Act.[251] However, a significant gap exists. Current analyses of this legislative approach, including the European Commission's proposal, often lack a robust theoretical and practical underpinning. This book aims to bridge that gap. By providing a deeply theoretical framework grounded in the current ecosystem of ongoing work, this book seeks to empower these recommendations and transform them from mere suggestions into a coherent and defensible strategy for effective AI regulation.

The main contribution of this book is a meaningful shift in perspective. Its central contribution moves beyond the prevailing market-driven perspectives on AI. It instead advocates for a legitimate approach by demanding a serious consideration of the *publicness* of AI systems, and of 'the reasons stemming from the diverse perspectives involved'.[252]

Indeed, it invites the reader to consider AI-related issues from a fresh and more nuanced perspective. While the public dimension of AI systems supports the adoption of a rights-based approach, their *inter-systemic* nature gives rise to a complex landscape where inter-legal issues are likely to emerge. It is unlikely that a singular legal regime will arise from the present case. Rather, disputes involving AI systems inherently span multiple domains – engaging state actors, transnational or non-state entities, and frameworks driven by market logic or technological innovation.

As Pollicino and De Gregorio put it, 'There is thus no definitive "recipe" for protecting democratic values, but there are different means to achieve this result, among which there is also technology.'[253]

As their reasoning makes clear, technological or market-oriented perspectives are not merely relevant to the discourse surrounding AI – they are profoundly influential. As such, non-state actors possessing technical expertise – such as universities and multinational corporations – wield significant power in identifying, assessing, managing and mitigating the risks posed by AI systems.

[251] Access Now, 'An EU Artificial Intelligence Act for Fundamental Rights: A Civil Society Statement' (2021), available at accessnow.org/cms/assets/uploads/2021/11/joint-statement-EU-AIA.pdf.

[252] Palombella, 'Inter-Legality: On Interconnectedness and "External Sources"' (2021).

[253] Pollicino and De Gregorio, 'Constitutional Law in the Algorithmic Society' (2022).

This dynamic highlights a crucial point: computational code carries normative power.[254] It diffuses into the normative space by actively shaping social relations, thus becoming a potent component of an inter-legal ecosystem. In this context, code emerges as a 'dangerous competitor' to the rule of law itself.[255] Within this framework, an inter-legal perspective becomes essential. It enables the identification of relevant perspectives from various frameworks and allows for a critical examination of their correlations, grounded in the specificities of a given case rather than pre-emptively excluding actors. By seeking a digital equilibrium,[256] this approach rejects both the dominance of market-oriented perspectives and the legal hegemony of any single order. It thus provides a more nuanced and inclusive model for addressing the complex challenges of AI governance.

1.7. Structure of Research

The book is structured into four substantive chapters, culminating in a concluding chapter. Building upon the foundational themes of this introduction, the first chapter provides an in-depth examination of the fundamental and human rights challenges posed by AI systems and a comprehensive overview of the legal approaches already developed within the EU. This chapter, therefore, establishes the essential background and contextual framework for the four subsequent chapters.

Chapter two, titled 'Artificial Intelligence Systems', provides a conceptual framework for understanding the defining features and capabilities of these systems. This chapter outlines two primary criteria guiding the selection of AI systems for analysis. The first is the *relevance condition*, which requires that the AI system be actively deployed by the public sector in the delivery of public services. The second is the *sensitivity condition*, which pertains to systems that raise significant concerns regarding the protection of fundamental and human rights. This focused selection is justified by the significant potential for these systems to produce profound

[254] L Lessig, *Code and Other Laws of Cyberspace* (Basic Books, 1999). However, it is crucial to see that ethical aspects might also shape the computational code.

[255] M Hildebrandt, 'Closure: On Ethics, Code and Law' in M Hildebrandt, Law for Computer Scientists *and Other Folk* (Oxford University Press, 2020) 284–318.

[256] The concept of 'digital equilibrium' has been discussed in workshops at the Department of Law of the European University Institute that I attended in Florence. It has been defined as follows: when it comes to the digital public sphere, the regulatory spectrum has two sides – the public, consisting of state and supranational institutions, and the private, consisting of corporate forces. In this spectrum, digital equilibrium describes how public and private forces maintain the digital public sphere in a healthy regulatory balance, and how it shields the sphere from regulatory extremism. See a short explanation in European University Institute, 'The Digital Services Act (DSA): Views of the Cathedral' (2022), available at eui.eu/events?id=547317; see also F de Abreu Duarte, 'The Internet Is for Porn! (but is it?) – The Digital Equilibrium Hypothesis', *The Digital Constitutionalist* (2022), available at digi-con.org/the-internet-is-for-porn-but-is-it-the-digital-equilibrium-hypothesis.

consequences for individuals, marginalised groups, and society at large, thereby necessitating a concentrated examination.

Before analysing the systems that are selected according to these two criteria, chapter two first begins with a multidisciplinary inquiry into the definition of AI systems. Drawing on perspectives from computer science, the philosophy of technology, and legal scholarship, this initial section provides a comprehensive overview that lays the conceptual understanding for the analysis that follows. Crucially, this section does not aim to furnish a single comprehensive definition of AI; such an exercise would likely prove fruitless, as the term, in many respects, resembles a comet – broadening and evolving with the particles of its usage. Following this conceptual groundwork, the chapter proceeds to a focused analysis of specific applications in the fields of social benefits and biometrics. This empirical research is grounded in a fact-based approach, utilising three official reports from EU institutions to investigate the 'where, how, and for what purpose' of these systems' deployment. Based on this analysis of real-world digital and social experiences, the chapter identifies six fundamental characteristics of the examined AI systems: (i) the *inter-systemic* aspect; (ii) the *dynamic* aspect; (iii) the *complexity* aspect; (iv) the *social* aspect; (v) the *privateness*; and (vi) the *publicness*. Moving beyond a generic treatment, the chapter examines the scope, dimensions, and dynamics of these features at a granular level within the context of the selected AI systems. The chapter concludes with a summary of its key findings.

Chapter three, titled 'Steering the Pendulum[257] towards the Rule of Technology: Analysing the Artificial Intelligence Act', evaluates the normative power of the EU's risk-based approach to AI. It asks whether this approach is strong enough to protect the rule of law which requires considering diverse needs and goals, and whether it can prevent the law 'from turning into a sheer tool of domination'.[258] From an inter-legal perspective, this analysis undertakes a critical examination of the normative ecosystem governing AI systems, using selected use cases to evaluate its resilience to various forms of dominance. It further explores whether this ecosystem constitutes a 'legal-friendly functional normative ground' that facilitates interaction among diverse legalities and normative actors. The chapter's initial section is dedicated to mapping and critically analysing existing regulatory models and approaches to AI systems. Subsequently, it narrows its focus to the EU's risk-based approach. This approach is given particular attention as it represents the world's first concrete and comprehensive legal proposal for AI regulation.[259] Following a critical analysis of the AI Act from the perspective of the rule of law and fundamental rights, this analysis concludes that the model's normative power is insufficient. Its primary weakness is an over-reliance on a market-oriented,

[257] I use the term 'pendulum' deliberately, drawing inspiration from Umberto Eco, as a metaphor to illustrate the oscillation between the rule of technology and the rule of law. See U Eco, *Il pendolo di Foucault* (Bompiani, 2014).

[258] G Palombella, 'The Rule of Law at Home and Abroad' 2016(8) *Hague Journal on the Rule of Law* 1.

[259] The AI Act Proposal, COM (2021) 206 final, 21 April 2021.

technocratic approach that overlooks the six fundamental characteristics of AI systems discussed in the previous chapter.[260] This deficiency renders the current legal framework vulnerable to the dominance of this technocratic approach, ultimately leading to a 'rule of technology' where market interests prevail over legal principles.[261]

The concrete reasoning for this conclusion is fourfold. First, the intrinsic value of fundamental and human rights is undermined by overlooking the *publicness* of AI systems. Second, the risk profiles are inadequately assessed, due to a limited engagement with the *complexity* and *dynamic* nature of these technologies. Third, private power gains disproportionate influence as a result of underemphasising both the *inter-systemic* dynamics and the *publicness* of AI. Finally, the precautionary bans are formulated in opaque ways, often without due consideration of the broader *social* context in which AI operates. This comprehensive analysis leads to the chapter's final conclusion: the imperative for a rights-based approach that places the *publicness* of AI systems at its core.

Chapter four, titled 'Steering the Pendulum Towards the Rule of Law: A Rights-Based Inter-Legal Approach', contends that, in light of the additional fundamental characteristics of AI systems discussed in Chapter two, a rights-based approach – while essential – is insufficient on its own to address the challenges posed by the public deployment of AI. The *inter-systemic*, *social*, *complex*, and *dynamic* dimensions of these systems necessitate the adoption of an inter-legal approach to ensure a more comprehensive and context-sensitive response. The justification for this approach is constructed upon a five-tiered framework, progressing from a macro-level overview to a micro-level application. The chapter begins by situating the theory of inter-legality within its broader theoretical context, explicating its relationship to competing and complementary conceptual frameworks such as monism, dualism, pluralism, regime complex, polycentrism, and global law, as articulated within the literatures of international law and political administration theory. Subsequently, the analysis delineates the theory's three fundamental characteristics: (i) the simultaneous emergence of diverse legalities; (ii) a shift in focus from contestations to functions; and (iii) the emergence of a 'law of the case' derived from composite interweaving norms. Building upon a rigorous analysis of these three fundamental features, the chapter proceeds to examine the doctrinal mechanisms proposed by legal scholars to protect the rights and freedoms of individuals in the digital environment. This section specifically addresses

[260] See Chapter 2, on this issue.

[261] For the term 'rule of technology', see R Brownsword and K Yeung, *Regulating Technologies: Legal Futures, Regulatory Frames and Technological Fixes* (Hart Publishing, 2008). Moreover, as analysed below, the AI Act provides legal mechanisms for AI providers to claim legitimacy through self-assessed checks. It is worth considering that these legal mechanisms might create new ways for the 'masters of the code of capital' – the lawyers – to circumvent the legal rules defined in the AI Act. Therefore, the problem could be not only the 'rule of technology' but also the 'rule of lawyers'. See K Pistor, *The Code of Capital: How the Law Creates Wealth and Inequality* (Princeton University Press, 2019). Pistor explains how the law has been placed in the service of capital, and thus increases inequality in society.

(i) the theories of the horizontal application of fundamental rights; (ii) the notion of digital constitutionalism; (iii) rights; and (iv) the rule of law. The fourth level of analysis, at a highly specific and concrete level, explains how the theory of inter-legality is profoundly relevant to AI systems used by public authorities. It defends the position that these systems are 'inter-legal by default'. Finally, the fifth level demonstrates the application of a rights-based inter-legal approach in a concrete case. This is achieved through a three-step process: first, taking the vantage point of the affair under close scrutiny; second, understanding the relevant normativities that control the case; and third, considering the demands of justice stemming from it.

Overall, the book as a whole takes a comprehensive inter-legal path. It analyses the core features of AI systems in chapter two, and subsequently examines the legalities governing these systems in chapter three. Chapter four advances the discussion by proposing a rights-based inter-legal approach aimed at reinforcing the rule of law in the context of AI governance. The concluding chapter, titled 'Inter-Legalizing the Pendulum', synthesises the overarching arguments of the book and articulates its central contribution: a principled defence of a rights-based inter-legal approach as a normative foundation for governing AI systems.

2

Artificial Intelligence Systems

2.1. General Overview

When Esra, the leading character of the series *Midnight at the Pera Palace*,[1] uses the 'magical' key that she found at the Pera Palace – a legendary hotel in Istanbul – she has no idea how it works and what the social consequences might be. She accidentally discovers the key's true power – its ability to transport her through time – when it unexpectedly sends her back to the year 1919. As she navigates this unfamiliar past, she soon finds herself entangled in a web of political conspiracy. Her presence in 1919 begins to alter the social and political fabric of the era, triggering a series of unforeseen consequences – including a shocking murder. Even more interestingly, the story reaches a point where Esra begins to lose her sense of identity and can no longer discern exactly which time she truly belongs to.

The series leaves its audience with a single, resonant truth: you do not belong in a time or place where you cannot be yourself. Yet, this seemingly simple tale also reveals another deeper reality – one that reminds us how difficult it is to predict the consequences of a power that is not fully understood. Such power, especially when rooted in shifting social dynamics, can profoundly reshape the structures of society and politics. Preparing for the transformations brought about by a new power requires first understanding its potential. In this light, AI systems – much like the magical key in Esra's story – are not just tools, but social systems. They monitor individuals, influence decisions, and shape societal outcomes. But unlike Esra's key, they are not magical.[2] AI is created by people, and as such, it can – and must – be understood in meaningful ways.

[1] The series is based on the book by C King, *Midnight at the Pera Palace: The Birth of Modern Istanbul* (WW Norton & Company, 2015). It is available at netflix.com/title/81212136.

[2] It is important to recognise that so-called 'magical' narratives surrounding AI systems significantly affect developments in science, policy, and society. In science fiction, see *Westworld*, created by Jonathan Nolan and Lisa Joy, HBO, US, 2016 (engaging with the philosophy of cognition); *Interstellar*, directed by Christopher Nolan, US, 2014 (engaging with robots Tars, Case, and Kipp that assist researchers working at NASA); *Ex Machina*, directed by Alex Garland, US, 2014 (engaging with the deceptive capabilities of AI); *HUM∀NS*, created by Sam Vincent and Jonathan Brackley, UK/US, 2015; *Her*, directed by Spike Jonze, US, 2013; *I, Robot*, directed by Alex Proyas, US/Germany, 2004; *Blade Runner*, directed by Ridley Scott, US/Hong Kong, 1982; *A Space Odyssey*, directed by Stanley Kubrick, UK/US, 1968. In literature, see K Čapek, *R.U.R. (Rossum's Universal Robots)* (1921); C Stross, *Saturn's Children* (2008); I Tregillis, *The Mechanical* (2015); M Shelley, *Frankenstein* (1818). Interestingly, Shelley and Čapek are cited by the European Parliament: 'whereas from Mary Shelley's Frankenstein's Monster to the classical

In this regard, this chapter provides a conceptual framework for understanding the defining features and capabilities of these systems. It outlines two primary criteria guiding the selection of AI systems for analysis. The first is the *relevance condition*, which requires that the AI system be actively deployed by the public sector in the delivery of public services. The second is the *sensitivity condition*, which pertains to systems that raise significant concerns regarding the protection of fundamental and human rights. This focused selection is justified by the significant potential for these systems to produce profound consequences for individuals, marginalised groups, and society at large, thereby necessitating a concentrated examination.

Before analysing the systems that are selected according to these two criteria, chapter two begins, in section 2.2., with a multidisciplinary inquiry into the definition of AI systems. Drawing on perspectives from computer science, the philosophy of technology, and legal scholarship, this initial section provides a comprehensive overview that lays the conceptual understanding for the analysis that follows. Crucially, this section does not aim to furnish a single, comprehensive definition of AI; such an exercise would likely prove fruitless, as the term, in many respects, resembles a comet – broadening and evolving with the particles of its usage. Following this conceptual groundwork, the chapter proceeds to a focused analysis of specific applications in the fields of social benefits and biometrics. This empirical research is grounded in a fact-based approach, utilising three official reports from EU institutions to investigate the 'where, how, and for what purpose' of these systems' deployment. Based on this analysis of real-world digital and social experiences, the chapter identifies six fundamental characteristics of the examined AI systems: (i) the *inter-systemic* aspect; (ii) the *dynamic* aspect; (iii) the *complexity* aspect; (iv) the *social* aspect; (v) the *privateness*; and (vi) the *publicness*. Moving beyond a generic treatment, the chapter examines the scope, dimensions, and dynamics of these features at a granular level within the context of the selected AI systems. The chapter concludes with a summary of its key findings.

2.2. Artificial Intelligence: An Eternal Quest?

Artificial intelligence (AI), as an academic discipline, has emerged from a profound question: 'Can machines think?'. This inquiry was first rigorously explored by Alan Turing, English mathematician and computer scientist, in his groundbreaking 1950

myth of Pygmalion, through the story of Prague's Golem to the robot of Karel Čapek, who coined the word, people have fantasised about the possibility of building intelligent machines, more often than not androids with human features', in European Parliament, Civil Law Rules on Robotics, Resolution of 16 February 2017 with recommendations to the Commission on Civil Law Rules on Robotics (2015/2103(INL)), available at europarl.europa.eu/doceo/document/TA-8-2017-0051_EN.pdf. See also S Cave, K Dihal, and S Dillon, *AI Narratives: A History of Imaginative Thinking about Intelligent Machines* (Oxford University Press, 2020) (discussing the impacts of narratives of AI on science, policy, and society). Such narratives also show different cultural approaches to robotics and AI technologies: see M Funk and B Irrgang, *Robotics in Germany and Japan: Philosophical and Technical Perspectives, Dresdner Studien zur Philosophie der Technologie, vol 5* (Peter Lang, 2014).

paper, 'Computing Machinery and Intelligence', which challenged conventional notions of cognition and laid the philosophical groundwork for the field.[3] However, the conceptual roots and imaginative underpinnings of AI can be traced back to ancient myths and philosophies; echoes of the creative genius and craftmanship mastery embodied by the Greek pantheon, particularly Hephaestus. Renowned as the divine artisan and master blacksmith, Hephaestus is famed for crafting Talos, a remarkable bronze automaton entrusted with safeguarding Crete.[4]

The essence of such a craftmanship lies in humanity's natural desire to imitate the divine by crafting tools that mirror human qualities, a pattern evident in inventions spanning centuries of innovation. For instance, the Greek Antikythera mechanism, an ancient marvel recovered from a shipwreck off the Greek coast, stands as the oldest analogue computer, meticulously designed to predict celestial events and reveal the sophisticated astronomical knowledge of its era.[5] Centuries later, al-Jazari, often addressed as 'the father of robotics', an Arab polymath from Mesopotamia, revolutionised mechanical engineering with his seminal work, *The Book of Knowledge of Ingenious Mechanical Devices ('Kitab fi Ma'rifat al-Hiyal al-Handasiyya')*.[6] His groundbreaking inventions included a diverse array of humanoid automata, such as a highly complex elephant water-clock with automated servants,[7] a musical boat with a flautist,[8] and a servant designed to pour water over the king's hands and entertain the king.[9] Nearly three centuries later, al-Jazari's ambition on automation inspired the imagination of Leonardo da Vinci,[10] the visionary master of the Italian Renaissance.[11] Da Vinci invented a

[3] AM Turing, 'Computing Machinery and Intelligence' (1950) 59(236) *Mind* 433–60.

[4] The earliest known reference to an automaton appears in *The Argonautica* by Apollonius Rhodius, where Talos, the bronze guardian of Crete, is depicted as a self-moving mechanical being. See A Rhodius, *The Argonautica*, with an English translation by RC Seaton, MA (William Heineman/GP Putnam's Sons, 1912) Book IV, 407 ('And Talos, the man of bronze, as he broke off rocks from the hard cliff, stayed them from fastening hawsers to the shore, when they came to the road-stead of Dicte's haven. He was of the stock of bronze, of the men sprung from ash-trees, the last left among the sons of the gods; and the son of Cronos gave him to Europa.'). See also the history of automaton, in AG Drachmann, *The Mechanical Technology of Greek and Roman Antiquity* (University of Wisconsin Press, 1963); JG Landels, *Engineering in the Ancient World* (Chatto & Windus, 1978); G Cambiano, 'Automaton' (1994) 25 *Studi Storici* 613–33; S Bär, *Artificial Intelligence in Greek and Roman Epic* (Bloomsbury, 2024). It is worth emphasising the profound connection between art and innovation when reflecting on the commitment to protecting the Phoenician princess Europa, a theme masterfully depicted in Tiziano Vecellio's iconic Renaissance masterpiece, Il Ratto di Europa (The Abduction of Europa), painted between 1559 and 1562. This remarkable work holds historical significance as the first of Tiziano's paintings to arrive in the United States and is currently on display at the Isabella Stewart Gardner Museum in Boston.

[5] T Freeth et al, 'A Model of the Cosmos in the ancient Greek Antikythera Mechanism' (2021) 11 *Scientific Reports* 5821, available at doi.org/10.1038/s41598-021-84310-w.

[6] I al-Razzaz al-Jazari, *The Book of Knowledge of Ingenious Mechanical Devices (Kitab fi Ma'rifat al-Hiyal al-Handasiyya)*, trans and annotated by DR Hill (D Reidel Publishing Company, 1974). The translator has noted that al-Jazari completed this book in 1204 or 1206, 3.

[7] al-Jazari, *Book of Knowledge of Ingenious Mechanical Devices* (1974), 58–82.

[8] al-Jazari, *Book of Knowledge of Ingenious Mechanical Devices* (1974), 107–09.

[9] al-Jazari, *Book of Knowledge of Ingenious Mechanical Devices* (1974), 133–35.

[10] 'al-Jazari', *Encyclopaedia Britannica*, available at britannica.com/biography/al-Jazari.

[11] D Kiecol, *Leonardo* (Koenemann, 2023).

mechanical knight (*'automa del cavaliere'* or *'robot di Leonardo'*, in Italian) that captured the Renaissance spirit of blending art, science, and the ambition to create lifelike machines.[12] Reflecting his deep appreciation for mechanics, he once remarked, 'Mechanics are the Paradise of mathematical science, because here we come to the fruits of mathematics.'[13]

Finally, the Mechanical Turk, a chess-playing automaton that captivated audiences with its apparent intelligence, exemplified the tantalising yet elusive pursuit of replicating human thought, even as its true nature was eventually exposed as a cleverly orchestrated illusion.[14] Together, these inventions underscore an enduring human fascination with replicating our own form and intellect, driving forward the evolution of technology and imagination. This relentless pursuit naturally raises a profound question: *can machines truly think, or are they simply sophisticated extensions of our natural desire to mirror the human mind?*

The question of whether machines can truly think, as first scientifically posed by Turing, is indeed deeply intertwined with a timeless philosophical challenge – *what it truly means to be human* – a question that ancient philosophers such as Plato[15] and Aristotle pondered.[16] Although they did not conceptualise 'artificial intelligence' in the modern sense, their explorations of what constitutes thinking and knowing laid the groundwork for later debates on whether machines could replicate or even surpass human intellect.[17]

Indeed, the journey initiated by Alan Turing was carried forward by a cohort of scientists, notably John McCarthy and Marvin Minsky, who formally established the

[12] Biblioteca Ambrosiana, Codex Atlanticus: The Largest Existing Collection of Writings and Drawings by Leonardo da Vinci (Milan), available at codex-atlanticus.ambrosiana.it/#/. In 1957, Carlo Pedretti was the first to identify the mechanical knight in the Codex Atlanticus. See C Pedretti (ed), Leonardo da Vinci: Fragments at Windsor Castle from the Codex Atlanticus (Phaidon, 1957), 39–40, no 12705.

[13] JP Richter, Scritti Letterari di Leonardo da Vinci (The Literary Works of Leonardo da Vinci) (S Low, Marston, Searle & Rivington, 1883), available at archive.org/details/literaryworksofl02leon/page/n3/mode/2up, 289. Even in the twenty-first century, the collaborative spirit and cross-disciplinary exchange that characterised Renaissance Florence provide a compelling model for innovation, potentially offering a more sustainable and holistic approach than Silicon Valley's often singular focus on market dominance. See E Weiner, 'Renaissance Florence Was a Better Model for Innovation than Silicon Valley Is', Harvard Business Review, 25 January 2016, available at hbr.org/2016/01/renaissance-florence-was-a-better-model-for-innovation-than-silicon-valley-is.

[14] E Stephens, 'The Mechanical Turk: A Short History of "Artificial Artificial Intelligence"' (2023) 31(1) Cultural Studies 65–87.

[15] Pinpointing a definitive *Platonic* view on human nature is a complex undertaking, far exceeding the scope of this book. However, I would like to leave the reader with a questioning from Plato's Republic to reflect on: 'Is there one element in us for learning, another for feeling spirited, and yet a third for our desire for the pleasures of food, sex, and things like that? Or do we do each of these things, when we embark upon them, with our entire soul? Those are questions to which it will be hard to give a convincing answer', in Plato, *The Republic*, Book 4 435a–436c, ed by GRF Ferrari, trans by T Griffith (Cambridge University Press, 2000) 131.

[16] See an excellent project on how Aristotelian ethics provide a compelling framework for addressing the challenges and opportunities of AI systems, in The Lyceum Project, J Ober and J Tasioulas, 'AI Ethics with Aristotle White Paper' (17 June 2024), available at oxford-aiethics.ox.ac.uk/lyceum-project-ai-ethics-aristotle-white-paper.

[17] See an excellent discussion on this issue in 'Lyceum Project Philosophers' Panel – White Paper on Aristotelian AI Ethics', available at youtube.com/watch?v=trVqxqToknQ&t=1965s.

field of AI by coining the term 'artificial intelligence' in their seminal 1955 summer research project proposal at Dartmouth College.[18] The proposal challenged researchers with a question of how to make machines to solve problems *'reserved for humans'*:

> The study is to proceed on the basis of the conjecture that every aspect of learning or any other feature of intelligence can in principle be so precisely described that a machine can be made to *simulate* it. An attempt will be made to find how to make machines use language, form abstractions and concepts, *solve kinds of problems now reserved for humans* and improve themselves. We think that a significant advance can be made in or more of these problems if a carefully selected group of scientists work on it together for a summer.[19]

The question of 'could machines be designed to tackle problems once thought to be exclusively within the realm of human cognition?' set the stage for decades of interdisciplinary research that would ultimately transform how we think about intelligence, both artificial and human. Perhaps due to the inherent complexity and breadth of this inquiry, a clear and universally accepted definition of AI remains elusive within the scientific community.[20] Frequently described as an 'umbrella term' ('it isn't any one thing'),[21] AI does not refer to any single technology or concept, but rather encompasses a broad array of systems and applications. This definitional ambiguity has also been empirically observed by the European Union Agency for Fundamental Rights (FRA), which conducted interviews with public and private sector representatives across five EU Member States – Estonia, France, Finland, Spain, and the Netherlands. The interviews revealed divergent understandings of what AI entails, with several participants explicitly acknowledging the absence of a clear or consistent definition.[22]

Given its inherent generality and abstraction, this section does not attempt to provide a singular, comprehensive definition of AI. Such an endeavour would likely be unproductive, as the term 'AI' functions much like a comet – its meaning continually expanding and evolving, shaped by the trajectories and contexts of its usage.[23] Rather, this section concentrates on prevailing approaches to AI, in order to develop

[18] See the original document in J McCarthy, M Minsky, N Rochester, and CE Shannon, 'Proposal for the Dartmouth Summer Research Project on Artificial Intelligence', 31 August 1955, reprinted in (2006) 27(4) *AI Magazine*. The author intentionally uses italics to emphasise key points.

[19] McCarthy et al, 'Proposal for the Dartmouth Summer Research Project on AI' (1955).

[20] Council of Europe, Ad Hoc Committee on Artificial Intelligence (CAHAI), 'Feasibility Study', 17 December 2020, available at rm.coe.int/cahai-2020-23-final-eng-feasibility-study-/1680a0c6da, 3.

[21] P Stone, R Brooks, E Brynjolfsson, R Calo, O Etzioni, G Hager, J Hirschberg, S Kalyanakrishnan, E Kamar, S Kraus, K Leyton-Brown, D Parkes, W Press, A Lee, J Shah, M Tambe, and A Teller, 'Artificial Intelligence and Life in 2030: One Hundred Year Study on Artificial Intelligence' (Stanford University, September 2016), available at ai10020201023.sites.stanford.edu/sites/g/files/sbiybj18871/files/media/file/ai100report10032016fnl_singles.pdf.

[22] European Union Agency for Fundamental Rights (FRA), 'Getting the Future Right: Artificial Intelligence and Fundamental Rights' (2020), available at fra.europa.eu/en/publication/2020/artificial-intelligence-and-fundamental-rights ('Report I').

[23] It is worth noting that calling AI a 'term' is intentional here because it is questionable to call AI a 'concept', as it is not bordered. See the difference between concepts and terms in M Uschold, 'The Importance of Distinguishing between Terms and Concepts', Semantic Arts (2013), available at semanticarts.com/the-importance-of-distinguishing-between-terms-and-concepts. See also M Uschold and M Gruninger, 'Ontologies: Principles, Methods and Applications' (1996) 11 Knowledge Engineering Review 93–136.

a clearer understanding of its current dynamics. Instead of offering an exhaustive evaluation, it aims to present a broad overview of the state of the discipline across three key domains: computer science, philosophy, and law.

2.2.1. Artificial Intelligence in Computer Science: An Interdisciplinary Area?

As mentioned earlier, the term 'artificial intelligence' was introduced by John McCarthy, who defined it as 'the science and engineering of making intelligent machines'.[24] This foundational idea was echoed by Nils J. Nilsson, who described AI as an 'activity devoted to making machines intelligent'.[25] Building upon these definitions, Stuart Russell and Peter Norvig offered a more comprehensive framework by categorising eight definitions of AI in computer science into four distinct approaches: 'thinking humanly', 'thinking rationally', 'acting humanly', and 'acting rationally'.[26] These categories are illustrated by the authors, in Table 2.1. below, using quotations from different sources.[27]

Table 2.1 Defining Artificial Intelligence in Computer Science

Thinking Humanly 'The exciting new effort to make computers think … machines with minds, in the full and literal sense.' (Haugeland, 1985) '[The automation of] activities that we associate with human thinking, activities such as decision-making, problem solving, learning.' (Bellman, 1978)	**Thinking Rationally** 'The study of mental faculties through the use of computational models.' (Charniak and McDermott, 1985) 'The study of the computations that make it possible to perceive, reason, and act.' (Winston, 1992)
Acting Humanly 'The art of creating machines that perform functions that require intelligence when performed by people.' (Kurzweil, 1990) 'The study of how to make computers do things at which, at the moment, people are better.' (Rich and Knight, 1991)	**Acting Rationally** 'Computational Intelligence is the study of the design of intelligent agents.' (Poole et al, 1998) 'AI … is concerned with intelligent behavior in artifacts.' (Nilsson, 1998)

[24] P Hamet and J Tremblay, 'Artificial Intelligence in Medicine' (2017) 69 Metabolism – Clinical and Experimental 36–40. However, this definition has been challenged by philosophers, as mechanical intelligence was discussed prior to the emergence of AI. See S Bringsjord and NS Govindarajulu, 'Artificial Intelligence' in EN Zalta and U Nodelman (eds), The Stanford Encyclopedia of Philosophy (Fall 2024 Edition), available at plato.stanford.edu/archives/fall2024/entries/artificial-intelligence/.

[25] NJ Nilsson, *The Quest for Artificial Intelligence: A History of Ideas and Achievements* (Cambridge University Press, 2010) 13, available at ai.stanford.edu/~nilsson/QAI/qai.pdf.

[26] SJ Russell and P Norvig, *Artificial Intelligence: A Modern Approach*, 3rd edn (Pearson, 2010) 1.

[27] Russell and Norvig, Artificial Intelligence: A Modern Approach (2010), 1. The table was prepared by the authors of the cited book.

These definitions reveal that, in its initial stages, AI was conceptualised by computer scientists through the lens of distinctly human traits – namely, the mind, intelligence, and mental faculties such as decision-making, perception, reasoning, and action. From the outset, this trajectory reflects a core ambition of AI: to engineer machines that *replicate* the mental capacities of the human mind. This defining characteristic sets AI apart from other technological inventions. Unlike a secondary tool that assists a human in achieving a purpose – functioning in a supportive or subordinate role – AI systems have the potential to occupy a *primary* position by making their own decisions, thereby functioning as 'machines with minds'[28] in social environments. This foundational link to human cognitive attributes is a key reason why AI has become a major topic of discussion across diverse disciplines, including philosophy,[29] economics,[30] mathematics,[31] psychology,[32] and neuroscience.[33] As a result, the field of AI emerges as a highly dynamic, inter-systemic, and inherently interdisciplinary area.[34]

2.2.2. Artificial Intelligence in Philosophy: Anthropocentric or Non-Anthropocentric Arguments?

The field of AI philosophy often distinguishes between two types of AI, based on their ultimate goals: 'strong' AI and 'weak' AI.[35] 'Strong' AI seeks to achieve all the mental faculties of a human, including phenomenal consciousness, with the aim of creating a truly artificial person.[36] 'Weak' AI, however, has a more limited goal;

[28] Russell and Norvig, Artificial Intelligence: A Modern Approach (2010), 1.

[29] This is especially evident when it comes to humanoid AI robots. See MS Archer and AM Maccarini (eds), What Is Essential to Being Human? Can AI Robots Not Share It? (Routledge, 2021). See also an interview with a computer scientist at the Technical University of Munich, available at tum.de/en/about-tum/news/press-releases/details/33313 ('Robots help us understand humans.'). See also D Deutsch, 'Philosophy That Will Be the Key That Unlocks Artificial Intelligence' (The Guardian, 3 October 2012), available at theguardian.com/science/2012/oct/03/philosophy-artificial-intelligence. See also 'Artificial Intelligence' in *Stanford Encyclopedia of Philosophy* (n 24), noting that many philosophical approaches and techniques are used in AI, including first-order logic, intensional logics, deontic reasoning, inductive logic, probability theory, probabilistic reasoning, practical reasoning, and planning.

[30] CF Camerer, 'Behavioral Economics and Artificial Intelligence', paper presented at the NBER Conference (2017), available at governance40.com/wp-content/uploads/2018/12/Camerer.pdf (discussing the use of AI on two behavioural variables: bargaining and risky choice).

[31] A Garrido, 'Mathematics and Artificial Intelligence, Two Branches of the Same Tree' (2010) 2 *Procedia – Social and Behavioral Sciences* 1133–36.

[32] Russell and Norvig, Artificial Intelligence: A Modern Approach (2010).

[33] Russell and Norvig, Artificial Intelligence: A Modern Approach (2010).

[34] Notably, within this process, engineers often perceive the human being as a technical challenge to be modelled, while social scientists frequently interpret AI as a societal threat.

[35] D Cole, 'The Chinese Room Argument', *The Stanford Encyclopedia of Philosophy* (Winter 2024 Edition), Edward N Zalta & Uri Nodelman (eds), available at plato.stanford.edu/archives/win2024/entries/chinese-room (14 January 2025). See also J Preston and M Bishop (eds), *Views into the Chinese Room: New Essays on Searle and Artificial Intelligence* (Oxford University Press, 2002).

[36] 'Artificial Intelligence' in *Stanford Encyclopedia of Philosophy* (n 24).

it does not aim for real consciousness, but instead focuses on *simulating* the full repertoire of mental functions of the human person.[37]

The most renowned critique of the concept of 'strong' AI is the 'Chinese Room Argument', introduced by Searle in his 1980 paper 'Mind, Brains and Programs'.[38] In this work, Searle presents a thought experiment *(Gedankenexperiment)* designed to challenge the argument that syntactic manipulation of symbols is sufficient for semantic understanding. He imagines himself locked inside a room, equipped with a set of Chinese characters and a rule book written in English. Outside the room, a native Chinese speaker – unaware of who and what is inside – slides questions written in Chinese through a slot. Searle, who understands no Chinese, uses the English-language rule book to correlate one set of formal symbols with another, based purely on their shapes. By following this rule book, Searle is able to produce seemingly coherent responses in Chinese, which he passes back through the slot. Notably, while his outputs are indistinguishable from those of a native speaker, Searle himself possesses no semantic understanding of the symbols he is processing.[39]

Searle uses the outcome of this thought experiment to argue against the plausibility of strong AI. The logical structure of his argument is designed as follows:

(i) If the notion of strong AI is true, then in the case of a program for Chinese-language operating, any system running that program thereby *understands* Chinese.
(ii) Searle could run the program without actually *understanding* Chinese.
(iii) Therefore, the assumption of strong AI is false.

These premises highlight that the capacity for genuine *understanding* lies at the core of the distinction between 'strong' and 'weak' AI:

> If I do not understand Chinese solely on the basis of running a computer program for understanding Chinese, neither does any other digital computer solely on that basis. Digital computers merely manipulate formal symbols according to rules in the program. … Just manipulating the symbols is not by itself enough to guarantee cognition, perception, understanding, and thinking.[40]

In philosophy of technology, methodological approaches are also applied to the analysis of AI systems. Guttman and Decker propose a structured framework for evaluating emerging technologies, in their well-known book *Robo- and Informationethics.*[41] According to their approach, it is first necessary to

[37] 'Artificial Intelligence' in *Stanford Encyclopedia of Philosophy* (n 24). See also JR Searle, *The Mystery of Consciousness* (New York Review Books, 1997) 61. It is necessary to note that Searle emphasises that simulation is not the same as duplication.

[38] JR Searle, 'Minds, Brains, and Programs' (1980) 3 *Behavioral and Brain Sciences* 417–57.

[39] Searle, 'Minds, Brains, and Programs' (1980) 418.

[40] JR Searle, 'Is the Brain's Mind a Computer Program?', *Scientific American*, January 1990, 26. In this paper, Searle presents three axioms while explaining his thought experiment, namely: (i) computer programs are formal (syntactic); (ii) human minds have mental contents (semantics); and (iii) syntax by itself is neither constitutive of, nor sufficient for, semantics.

[41] M Decker and M Gutmann, 'Robo- and Informationethics: Some Introducing Remarks' in A M Esser, A Grunwald, and M Gutmann (eds), *Robo- and Informationethics: Some Fundamentals, Hermeneutics and Anthropology, vol 3* (Lit Verlag, 2012) 3.

identify whether a new technology possesses features that differentiate it from traditional technologies. Second, one must observe 'anthropological problems' related to how the technology might impact the human body and mental integrity. The final step is to focus on the specific ethical concerns that emerge from these observations.[42]

Despite the lack of a clear answer as to which field of ethics should be the focus for regulating AI systems,[43] the *Ethics Guidelines* issued by the High-Level Expert Group on Artificial Intelligence[44] (HLEGAI) outline three key functions of ethics in addressing AI-related challenges: (i) understanding how technologies may give rise to different considerations; (ii) providing finer-grained guidance on what we *ought to* do with technology rather than what we can do; and (iii) grounding and complementing fundamental rights. In this context, fundamental rights are described as the 'bedrock for the formulation of ethical principles', serving both as a foundation for identifying abstract ethical principles and as a framework for specifying how concrete ethical values can be operationalised in the development and deployment of AI.[45]

When examining the key ethical debates in AI and robotics, philosophers have identified at least 10 essential areas of discussion:[46] privacy and surveillance; manipulation of behaviour; opacity of AI systems; bias in decision systems; human–robot interaction; automation and employment; autonomous systems; machine ethics; artificial moral agents; and singularity.

In particular, privacy and surveillance, behavioural manipulation, opacity of AI systems, and bias in decision-making deserve special attention, as they are closely tied to AI systems in the domains of biometrics and social welfare systems – the primary focus of this book. Addressing the critical dimensions of these four ethical concerns is, therefore, both essential and urgent.[47]

Firstly, in the context of privacy and surveillance, two critical dimensions deserve attention: the evolving scope of privacy studies, and the depth of contemporary privacy concerns. The rise of AI systems has marked a critical turning point in how privacy is understood and studied. Earlier scholarship largely focused on state surveillance, particularly the activities of secret services. With the advent and widespread deployment of AI, however, the focus has shifted beyond state

[42] Decker and Gutmann, 'Robo- and Informationethics' (2012), 3.

[43] Five prominent fields of ethics have emerged in relation to technological development: roboethics, computer ethics, machine ethics, bioethics, and humanistic ethics. Key works in these areas include: P Lin, K Abney, and GA Bekey, Robot Ethics: The Ethical and Social Implications of Robotics (MIT Press, 2014); L Floridi (ed), The Cambridge Handbook of Information and Computer Ethics (Cambridge University Press, 2010); and M Anderson and S L Anderson, Machine Ethics (Cambridge University Press, 2011). For a recent discussion of humanistic ethics in the context of AI, see J Tasioulas, 'Artificial Intelligence, Humanistic Ethics' (2022) 151(2) Dædalus: The Journal of the American Academy of Arts & Sciences 232–43.

[44] European Commission, HLEG-AI, 'Ethics Guidelines for Trustworthy AI' (2019), available at aepd.es/sites/default/files/2019-12/ai-ethics-guidelines.pdf.

[45] European Commission, HLEG-AI, 'Ethics Guidelines for Trustworthy AI' (2019).

[46] For a comprehensive framework on ethical issues, see VC Müller, 'Ethics of Artificial Intelligence and Robotics' in *Stanford Encyclopedia of Philosophy* (2018), available at plato.stanford.edu/entries/ethics-ai.

[47] It should be noted that Chapters 1 and 3 of this book discuss privacy and surveillance, manipulation of behaviour, opacity of AI systems, and bias in decision-making systems in detail from a legal perspective.

actors, encompassing businesses, public institutions, and even individuals, who now wield surveillance capabilities.[48]

As emphasised in chapter three of this book, private power holds a dominant position in the development of AI systems. In terms of the magnitude of the privacy concerns, Smolan captures the challenge concisely: 'In this vast ocean of data, there is a frighteningly complete picture of us.'[49]

This suggests that AI systems possess the capacity to generate insights about individuals that surpass even their own self-knowledge. In other words, they may come to know us more intimately than we know ourselves.[50] As Harari notes in *Homo Deus*, this raises a critical question for contemporary scholarship and public debate: 'what will happen to society, politics and daily life when non-conscious but highly intelligent algorithms know us better than we know ourselves?'.[51]

Secondly, private companies developing AI and other related advanced technologies such as large language models (LLMs) – including the so-called 'Big Five' (Amazon, Google/Alphabet, Microsoft, Apple, and Facebook) – have increasingly embraced manipulation as a central element of their business model. These firms have demonstrated not only an unprecedented capacity to accumulate vast amounts of data, but also to deploy that data in ways that actively shape and influence both online and offline behaviour.[52] As the digital sphere expands to encompass smart systems, urban infrastructures, and new models of governance – alongside the intensifying engagement of individuals with such technologies – it becomes evident that users are critically vulnerable to manipulation, deception, and behavioural nudges.[53] Such practices pose a profound threat to rational, autonomous decision-making and, ultimately, to individual autonomy itself.[54]

Thirdly, AI systems often lack transparency – not only for end users, but, in many cases, even for the experts who design or operate them.[55] This opacity is particularly pronounced in systems that rely on machine-learning techniques,

[48] 'Ethics of Artificial Intelligence and Robotics' in *Stanford Encyclopedia of Philosophy* (n 46).

[49] S Smolan, *The Human Face of Big Data* (PBS Documentary, 24 February 2016).

[50] N Thompson, 'When Tech Knows You Better Than You Know Yourself' (*Wired*, 4 October 2018), available at wired.com/story/artificial-intelligence-yuval-noah-harari-tristan-harris.

[51] YN Harari, *Homo Deus: A Brief History of Tomorrow* (Harper, 2016).

[52] See a comprehensive study in F Jongepier and M Klenk, *The Philosophy of Online Manipulation* (Routledge, 2022).

[53] E Costa and D Halpern, 'The Behavioural Science of Online Harm and Manipulation, and What to Do About It – An Exploratory Paper to Spark Ideas and Debate' (*The Behavioural Insight Team*, 2019), available at bi.team/publications/the-behavioural-science-of-online-harm-and-manipulation-and-what-to-do-about-it. See also A Mathur, G Acar, MJ Friedman, E Lucherini, J Mayer, M Chetty and A Narayanan, 'Dark Patterns at Scale: Findings from a Crawl of 11K Shopping Websites', Proceedings of the ACM on Human-Computer Interaction 3(CSCW), art 81 (2019), available at arxiv.org/abs/1907.07032 (analysing shopping websites to show how they use dark patterns to influence users).

[54] D Susser, B Roessler, and H Nissenbaum, 'Technology, Autonomy, and Manipulation' (2019) 8(2) Internet Policy Review, available at policyreview.info/articles/analysis/technology-autonomy-and-manipulation (explaining that online manipulation targets and exploits decision-making vulnerabilities of individuals).

[55] M Whittaker et al, 'AI Now Report 2018' (AI Now Institute, December 2018), available at ainowinstitute.org/AI_Now_2018_Report.pdf.

where the internal logic by which patterns are recognised or classifications are made becomes increasingly difficult to interpret.[56] The most pressing concern here lies in the limited capacity of such systems to be explained or held accountable, a challenge that is especially critical in contexts such as public administration.[57] It has been provocatively argued that AI systems must be democratised to avoid a Kafkaesque future, relying on Kafka's book *The Trial*,[58] which portrays an opaque and unaccountable order.[59]

Finally, the presence of bias in AI-based decision-making systems raises profound ethical concerns. These concerns are particularly noticeable in the context of predictive systems employed in policing. A prominent example is COMPAS (Correctional Offender Management Profiling for Alternative Sanctions), a tool designed to predict the likelihood of a defendant reoffending.[60] Research has revealed that COMPAS exhibits systematic bias against Black defendants, thereby undermining the fairness and legitimacy of its use.[61] This case highlights a broader and more disturbing implication: AI systems deployed in predictive policing risk reinforcing existing social inequalities and disproportionately disadvantaging marginalised or minority groups.

In terms of methodology for analysing and examining new technologies, analogical thinking[62] – defined as the 'ability to think about relational patterns'[63] – becomes especially significant. Within the context of AI systems, this approach entails examining both the similarities and the differences between human beings and the technologies under consideration.[64] However, focusing

[56] 'Ethics of Artificial Intelligence and Robotics' in *Stanford Encyclopedia of Philosophy* (n 46).

[57] HA Kissinger, 'How the Enlightenment Ends: Philosophically, Intellectually – in Every Way – Human Society Is Unprepared for the Rise of Artificial Intelligence' (The Atlantic, June 2018), available at theatlantic.com/magazine/archive/2018/06/henry-kissinger-ai-could-mean-the-end-of-human-history/559124.

[58] F Kafka, The Trial, trans M Mitchell (Oxford World's Classics, 2009) ('Someone must have been telling tales about Josef K., for one morning, without having done anything wrong, he was arrested.'). See also C Kamper, 'Kafkaesque AI? Legal Decision-Making in the Area of Machine Learning' (2020) 24(2) University of San Francisco Intellectual Property and Technology Law Journal 251.

[59] S Cave, 'To Save Us from a Kafkaesque Future, We Must Democratise AI' (*The Guardian*, 4 January 2019), available at theguardian.com/commentisfree/2019/jan/04/future-democratise-ai-artificial-intelligence-power.

[60] COMPAS was designed by a professor of statistics, Tim Brennan, and is used by criminal justice agencies in the US. See T Brennan, W Dieterich, and B Ehret, 'Evaluating the Predictive Validity of the COMPAS Risk and Needs Assessment System' (2009) 36(1) Criminal Justice and Behavior 21–40. In this article, it is explained that COMPAS is 'an automated decision-support software package that integrates risk and needs assessment with several other domains, including sentencing decisions, treatment and case management, and recidivism outcomes'.

[61] E Yong, 'A Popular Algorithm Is No Better at Predicting Crimes Than Random People' (The Atlantic, 17 January 2018), available at theatlantic.com/technology/archive/2018/01/equivant-compas-algorithm/550646. See also J Angwin, J Larson, S Mattu, and L Kirchner, 'Machine Bias' (ProPublica, 23 May 2016), available at propublica.org/article/machine-bias-risk-assessments-in-criminal-sentencing.

[62] D Gentner, KJ Holyoak, and BN Kokinov (eds), *The Analogical Mind: Perspectives from Cognitive Science* (Bradford, 2001).

[63] D Hofstadter, 'Epilogue: Analogy as the Core of Human Cognition' in Gentner, Holyoak, and Kokinov (eds), *The Analogical Mind* (2001), 499–538.

[64] Indeed, there are philosophical discussions on whether AI systems can be trusted, loved, and capable of learning in literature. Regarding the concept of 'trust', see F Fossa, '"I Don't Trust You, You Faker!" On Trust, Reliance, and Artificial Agency" (2019) 39 Teoria 63–80. Regarding the concept of 'love', see

first on the differences, rather than the more immediately apparent similarities, provides a more effective approach to minimising conceptual confusion.[65] Among the key distinctions, the notion of autonomy emerges as central.[66] Human beings are 'self-determined' and 'purpose-setting agents',[67] whereas technologies designed to replicate human-specific functions, such as AI systems and robots, remain fundamentally 'purpose-built artifacts'.[68]

However, relatively little attention has been given to the question of why discussions in this field so often begin with the concept of autonomy,[69] despite the existence of numerous definitions of what constitutes a 'human being'. For example, Cassirer defines the human person as follows:

> He [the human person] has so enveloped himself in linguistic forms, in artistic images, in mythical symbols or in religious rites that he cannot see or know anything except by the interposition of this artificial medium. Man does not live in a world of hard facts, or according to his immediate needs and desires … He lives rather in the midst of imaginary emotions, in hopes and fears, in illusions and disillusions, in his fantasies and dreams. 'What disturbs and alarms man', said Epictetus, 'are not things but his opinions and fancies about things'[70] … 'Man's outstanding characteristic, his distinguishing mark, is not his

S Nyholm, J Danaher, and BD Earp, 'The Technological Future of Love' in N McKeever, A Grahle, and J Saunders (eds), Love: Past, Present, and Future (Routledge, 2022). Regarding the concept of 'self-learning', see S Vallor, 'Artificial Intelligence and the Ethics of Self-Learning Robots' in P Lin, K Abney, and R Jenkins (eds), Robot Ethics 2.0: From Autonomous Cars to Artificial Intelligence (Oxford University Press, 2017).

[65] In 2020, I had the opportunity to discuss this issue with Fabio Fossa, research fellow at the Polytechnic University of Milan, during a workshop in Pisa, where the idea first emerged. I sincerely thank him for this insightful exchange.

[66] A considerable body of research has been conducted by M Gutmann, B Rathgeber, and T Syed on the concept of autonomy. See M Gutmann, B Rathgeber, and T Syed, 'Action and Autonomy: A Hidden Dilemma in Artificial Autonomous Systems' in M Decker and M Gutmann (eds), *Robo- and Informationethics: Some Fundamentals, Hermeneutics and Anthropology*, vol 3 (Lit Verlag, 2012) 231–54. First, the distinction between behaviour and action should be highlighted for a clear definition of the concept of autonomy. According to the authors, behaviour is governed by natural laws. The reason for a specific behaviour is explained in terms of causes: it is not arbitrary or deliberate, but causal. By contrast, an action is a voluntary activity which is governed by reasons. When an actor acts, she wills to act voluntarily, since there is a reason for this specific action. In other words, 'the logical grammar of action is that of results generated under the guidance of explicit and explicable purposes' (235). Therefore, an action addresses a 'richer game' than behaviour, due to its origin in an argumentative ability to justify. Autonomy can be attributed to both concepts, meaning that an actor may behave or act autonomously. However, the difference between these two divides autonomy into two levels, namely weak and strong autonomy. An actor with strong autonomy is free to set ends that can be realised by applying means. There are no existing robotic (or AI) applications with this ability yet, meaning that such technologies are not autonomous in the strong sense. By contrast, an actor with weak autonomy is autonomous in choosing between ends, but not free to set a new end, being limited to predetermined ones.

[67] Fossa, '"I Don't Trust You, You Faker!"' (2019), 10.

[68] JJ Bryson and PP Kime, 'Just an Artifact: Why Machines Are Perceived as Moral Agents' in Proceedings of the 22nd International Joint Conference on Artificial Intelligence (IJCAI 2011) (Barcelona, 16–22 July 2011). See also JM Balkin, 'The Path of Robotics Law' (2015) 6 California Law Review 45–60 (arguing that people treat robots and AI agents as 'special-purpose animals' or 'special-purpose human beings').

[69] This may be because many philosophical debates on this issue have focused on the Kantian tradition, which links autonomy to fully rational persons.

[70] E Cassirer, An Essay on Man: An Introduction to a Philosophy of Human Culture (Doubleday Anchor Books, 1944) 43. See also E Cassirer, 'A Clue to the Nature of Man: The Symbol' (Yale University Blog, 16 June 2021), available at blog.yalebooks.com/2021/06/16/a-clue-to-the-nature-of-man-the-symbol.

> metaphysical of physical nature– but his work. It is his work, it is the system of human activities, which defines and determines the circle of 'humanity'. Language, myth, religion, art, science, history are the constituents, the various sectors of his circle. A 'philosophy of man' would therefore be a philosophy, which would give us insight into the fundamental structure of each of these human activities, and which at the same time would enable us to understand them as an organic whole.[71]

He ultimately advances the notion of *animal symbolicum*, arguing that while the concept of *animale rationale* is not incorrect per se, it is nonetheless insufficient.[72] Reasoning, therefore, should not be regarded as the sole capacity that defines the human person. Cassirer's observation is particularly significant because his emphasis on human creativity suggests that defining the human person is a dynamic rather than a static endeavour. Human creativity not only shapes her nature but also transforms it, rendering her subject to continual change through her own work. As Gutmann and Decker note: 'Humans literally are what they are transforming themselves into.'[73]

This perspective helps to explain why Floridi and Coeckelbergh introduce concepts such as 'technological beings' and 'inforg' when reflecting on the contemporary human condition within the philosophy of technology. Coeckelbergh underscores the inherently transformative role of technology in human existence, observing that

> technological transformation is natural. This is also true for the transformation of human being. We changed ourselves because we are the kind of beings that change ourselves and the world by using technology; … this is part of our nature. It does not happen in spite of being natural. We are … artificial by nature.[74]

Similarly, Floridi emphasises the informational dimension of the human person, writing: 'we are all becoming connected informational organisms ("inforgs"). This is happening not through some fanciful transformation in our body, but, more seriously and realistically, through the re-ontologization of our environment and of ourselves.'[75]

Extending these perspectives, several discussions seek to move beyond anthropocentric arguments in examining the nature of AI systems. Floridi and Sanders, in their well-known and controversial article 'On the Morality of Artificial Agents', argue that scholars have constrained themselves within anthropocentric conceptions and, in doing so, have missed the opportunity to engage with alternative types of agenthood:

> *Limiting the ethical discourse to individual agents* hinders the development of a satisfactory investigation of *distributed morality* … insisting on the necessarily *human-based*

[71] Cassirer, *An Essay on Man* (1944), 93.
[72] Cassirer, *An Essay on Man* (1944).
[73] M Decker and M Gutmann, 'Robo- and Informationethics: Some Introducing Remarks' (2012), 4.
[74] M Coeckelbergh, Human Being @ Risk: Enhancement, Technology, and the Evaluation of Vulnerability Transformations (Springer, 2013) 27.
[75] L Floridi, 'A Look into the Future Impact of ICT on Our Lives' (2007) 9–10, available at ssrn.com/abstract=3844463.

> *nature* of the agent means undermining the possibility of understanding another major transformation in the ethical field.[76]

They further underscore the widening gap between moral patients – the receivers of actions, who can be affected for good or ill – and moral agents – the sources of actions, capable of performing deeds that are morally good or evil:

> Secularism has contracted A [moral agents], while environmentalism has justifiably expanded P [moral patients], so the gap between A and P has been widening; this has been accompanied by an enormous increase in the moral responsibility of the individual.[77]

In this way, they seek to articulate a new form of agenthood – one that is liberated from anthropocentric arguments.[78] To this end, they draw upon the framework of 'computer ethics' to defend a conception of the moral agent that does not necessarily presuppose free will, mental states, or traditional notions of responsibility. This perspective of 'mind-less morality' enables them to avoid many of the debates and concerns surrounding the definitional factors of AI.[79]

These perspectives demonstrate that both anthropocentric and non-anthropocentric arguments concerning AI systems adopt overly narrow approaches to defining them. Anthropocentric accounts tend to reduce the human person primarily to the notion of autonomy,[80] whereas non-anthropocentric accounts often centre on concepts derived from computer ethics – concepts that are, in fact, even narrower than anthropocentric ones. For this reason, such non-anthropocentric perspectives are frequently described as 'deflationary accounts' of autonomy.[81]

[76] L Floridi and JW Sanders, 'On the Morality of Artificial Agents' (2004) 14 *Minds and Machines* 351 (italic emphasis in original).

[77] Floridi and Sanders, 'On the Morality of Artificial Intelligence' (2004), 350 (emphasis added).

[78] Floridi and Sanders, 'On the Morality of Artificial Intelligence' (2004). He also notes that some efforts have been made to redress this gap by extending the concept of agenthood to include legal persons.

[79] However, Floridi does not offer a new definition of agenthood. He argues that there is no unified definition of the concept: 'People disagree on what can and cannot count as an "agent", even in principle, e.g. Franklin and Graesser (1996)', and notes that 'One cannot define with sufficient accuracy things like life, intelligence, agenthood and mind because they all admit of subtle degrees and continuous changes.' In his words, instead of seeking sufficient and necessary conditions to establish a definiens, he suggests considering the protean definiendum – not a procrustean definiens – since 'attempts follow one another without a final identikit ever being nailed to the definiendum in question'. He therefore proposes a solution: 'to give up altogether or at best be resigned to be vague, and rely on indicative examples'. See Floridi and Sanders, 'On the Morality of Artificial Intelligence' (2004).

[80] Indeed, there are international instruments that focus on human dignity rather than autonomy, as the latter is a narrower concept. For instance, the Universal Declaration on Bioethics and Human Rights (UDBHR) was the first international instrument to broaden the scope of bioethics from personal autonomy to human dignity. See A Bagheri, JD Moreno, and S Semplici, Global Bioethics: The Impact of the UNESCO International Bioethics Committee (Springer, 2016). See also M-H Parizeau, 'The Tension between Autonomy and Dignity' in P Kemp, J Rentorff, and NM Johansen (eds), Bioethics and Biolaw, vol. II: Four Ethical Principles (Rhodos International Science and Art Publishers and Centre for Ethics and Law, 2000) 47–59 (arguing that the concept of autonomy is qualified by an 'over-correction in favour of individual choice'). See also R Brownsword and D Beyleveld, Human Dignity in Bioethics and Biolaw (Oxford University Press, 2001) (explaining the non-autonomous aspect of human beings in the context of care).

[81] C Allen, 'Artificial Life, Artificial Agents, Virtual Realities: Technologies and Autonomous Agency' in L Floridi (ed), The Cambridge Handbook of Information and Computer Ethics (Cambridge University Press, 2010) 218–33. It is important to note that Allen defines the concept of an agent as 'any system that can use information adaptively to achieve some goals'.

Instead of engaging with conscious reflection on the reasons for actions and beliefs – what is commonly referred to as the 'Kantian conception'[82] – these approaches emphasise a more limited understanding, namely the *reasonable* selection among different behavioural options.[83] Within this 'deflationary account', what becomes crucial is that the technological system possesses a mechanism enabling it to function with a degree of flexibility in the absence of direct human supervision.[84] In this sense, the AI systems examined in this book qualify as 'autonomous agents', insofar as they are capable of deciding, identifying, categorising, and detecting within designed environments without direct human supervision.

Although the question of AI autonomy remains highly controversial, philosophers of technology have examined specific ethical challenges arising from the potential for autonomous agency afforded by computational agents and their environments.[85] From the non-anthropocentric perspective, or the so-called 'deflationary account', it is emphasised that the ethics of the designed environment must also be taken into account, since it is within this environment that the 'autonomous agent' makes its reasonable selections. Put differently, on the 'deflationary account', questions of autonomy cannot be disentangled from the ethical considerations embedded in the design of the environment itself. In this context, the most pressing ethical concern is that such systems may either be ethically challenged or altogether 'ethically blind'.[86] The notion of 'ethical blindness' is defined as 'the temporary inability of a decision maker to see the ethical dimension of a decision at stake'.[87] As Allen explains, in the case of artificial agents, 'ethically blind' AI systems 'lack specific information that would be relevant to ethical decision making, they have no means of assessing the ethically relevant effects of their decisions, and they lack other capacities such as empathy that are important to human morality'.[88]

2.2.3. Artificial Intelligence in Law: Technical Approaches or Social Practices?

To begin with, legal definitions for AI systems must remain compatible with the principle of the rule of law, which is defined as 'one of the features of the common spiritual heritage of the member States of the Council of Europe'[89] and 'a fundamental component of European public order for the protection of human rights

[82] See the Kantian tradition on the concept of autonomy in M Gutmann, B Rathgeber, and T Syed, 'Action and Autonomy: A Hidden Dilemma in Artificial Autonomous Systems' in M Decker and M Gutmann (eds), Robo- and Informationethics (2012), 231–54.

[83] Allen, 'Artificial Life, Artificial Agents, Virtual Realities' (2010), 221–22.

[84] Allen, 'Artificial Life, Artificial Agents, Virtual Realities' (2010), 222.

[85] Allen, 'Artificial Life, Artificial Agents, Virtual Realities' (2010), 218–33.

[86] W Wallach and C Allen, Moral Machines: Teaching Robots Right from Wrong (Oxford University Press, 2008) 42.

[87] G Palazzo, F Krings, and U Hoffrage, 'Ethical Blindness' (2012) 109 *Journal of Business Ethics* 325.

[88] Allen, 'Artificial Life, Artificial Agents, Virtual Realities' (2010), 230.

[89] The concept of the rule of law first appeared in the case of Golder v United Kingdom (ECtHR, App no 4451/70, 21 February 1975), para 34.

and fundamental freedoms',[90] by the ECtHR. From an operational perspective, the 2011 *Venice Commission Report* identified several core elements of the rule of law, rather than limiting itself to a purely theoretical definition,[91] namely (1) legality; including a transparent, accountable, and democratic process for enacting law; (2) legal certainty; (3) prohibition of arbitrariness; (4) access to justice before independent and impartial courts, including judicial review of administrative acts; (5) respect for human rights; and (6) non-discrimination and equality before the law.[92] In this regard, the report emphasised that the principle of legal certainty requires legal rules to be *foreseeable*, *accessible*, *precise*, and *clear*.[93] The principle thus exert normative impact, serving as a 'lodestar',[94] 'inherent in all the articles of the Convention',[95] and going well beyond mere 'rhetorical references'.[96]

Therefore, any legal definition of AI systems must satisfy these normative requirements in order to remain consistent with the principle of the rule of law.[97] The final AI Act[98] defines 'AI systems' in Article 3(1) as:

> 'AI system' means a machine-based system that is designed to operate with varying levels of autonomy and that may exhibit adaptiveness after deployment, and that, for explicit or implicit objectives, infers, from the input it receives, how to generate outputs such as predictions, content, recommendations, or decisions that can influence physical or virtual environments.

In total, Article 3 sets out an encyclopaedic catalogue of 68 distinct definitions pertaining to AI systems and practices.[99]

Compared with the European Commission's original proposal for the AI Act, the definition of AI provided in the final Act is considerably more

[90] See a recent judgment in *Grzęda v Poland* (ECtHR, App no 43572/18, 15 March 2022), para 253.

[91] For theoretical discussions, see G Palombella and N Walker (eds), Relocating the Rule of Law (Hart Publishing, 2009). For a comprehensive discussion, see also BZ Tamanaha, On the Rule of Law: History, Politics, Theory (Cambridge University Press, 2012).

[92] European Commission for Democracy through Law (Venice Commission), 'Report on the Rule of Law' (adopted at the 86th plenary session, Venice, 25–26 March 2011, rapporteurs: P van Dijk, G Haller, J Jowell, and K Tuori), available at venice.coe.int/WebForms/pages/?p=02_Rule_of_law&lang=EN.

[93] Venice Commission, 'Report on the Rule of Law' (2011), paras 44–51.

[94] R Spano, 'The Rule of Law as the Lodestar of the European Convention on Human Rights: The Strasbourg Court and the Independence of the Judiciary' (2021) 27 *European Law Journal* 211–27. The term 'lodestar' is defined as 'a star that is used to guide the course of a ship, especially the pole star; a person or thing that serves as an inspiration or guide' (211).

[95] See Pişkin v Turkey (ECtHR, App no 33399/18, 15 December 2020) (not final), para 153.

[96] See Golder v United Kingdom (n 89), where the Court stated that 'it would be a mistake to see in this reference a merely "more or less rhetorical reference", devoid of relevance for those interpreting the Convention. One reason why the signatory Governments decided to "take the first steps for the collective enforcement of certain of the Rights stated in the Universal Declaration" was their profound belief in the rule of law' (para 34).

[97] See also J Schuett, 'A Legal Definition of AI' (2019) arXiv:1909.01095, available at arxiv.org/abs/1909.01095 (listing five requirements for legal definitions, namely (i) inclusiveness, (ii) precision, (iii) comprehensiveness, (iv) practicability, and (v) permanence).

[98] Regulation (EU) 2024/1689 of the European Parliament and of the Council of 13 June 2024 laying down harmonised rules on artificial intelligence and amending Regulations (EC) No 300/2008, (EU) No 167/2013, (EU) No 168/2013, (EU) 2018/858, (EU) 2018/1139 and (EU) 2019/2144 and Directives 2014/90/EU, (EU) 2016/797 and (EU) 2020/1828 (Artificial Intelligence Act), OJ L 1689, 12 July 2024.

[99] AI Act (n 98).

accessible. In the Proposal, AI systems were defined in a distinctly technical manner as:

> software that is developed with one or more of the techniques and approaches listed in Annex I and can, for a given set of human-defined objectives, generate outputs such as content, predictions, recommendations, or decisions influencing the environments they interact with.[100]

Annex I, in turn, enumerated predominantly technical approaches, including machine learning, logic- and knowledge-based methods, and statistical techniques.

As I have argued elsewhere,[101] such definitional attempts risk encountering the so-called odd paradox[102] – namely the absence of a widely accepted definition of AI – precisely because of AI's dynamic and continuously evolving nature. For instance, viewed from the perspective of the Proposal, one might ask whether, if software were to operate without a *human-defined* objective, but instead with a *computer-defined* objective, the AI Act would still apply. Furthermore, can the techniques enumerated in Annex I truly be defined, understood, and exhaustively followed in practice? The European Commission indirectly acknowledged these difficulties in 2021 when it described AI as a 'fast-evolving family of technologies'.[103] This recognition highlights the need for the AI Act to account for both the technical complexities and the legal dimensions of AI and its ongoing development.[104] An approach that does not maintain balance among these elements may diminish legal certainty and enable providers to evade obligations under the AI Act, with potential consequences for fundamental rights and the rule of law.

In 2020, the challenges posed by 'connectionist AI' illustrated this issue with particular clarity.[105] Such systems, capable of defining their own technical purpose, tested the boundaries of European patent law – raising profound questions, such as whether a machine itself could be considered an inventor. This example exposed the limits of rigidly technical definitions. The issue has become even more notable with the emergence of LLMs in late 2022, which presented a definitional challenge for the AI Act, as their general-purpose character resists straightforward incorporation into the Act's original categorical framework. It is, therefore, essential to sustain a balance

[100] Proposal for a Regulation of the European Parliament and of the Council laying down harmonised rules on artificial intelligence (Artificial Intelligence Act) and amending certain Union legislative acts, COM (2021) 206 final, 2021/0106 (COD), 21 April 2021 (Brussels) ('The AI Act Proposal, COM (2021) 206 final, 21 April 2021').

[101] E Biber, 'Machines Learning the Rule of Law: EU Proposes the World's First Artificial Intelligence Act' (*Verfassungsblog*, 13 July 2021), available at verfassungsblog.de/ai-rol.

[102] P McCorduck, Machines Who Think: A Personal Inquiry into the History and Prospects of Artificial Intelligence (AK Peters, 2004).

[103] The AI Act Proposal, COM (2021) 206 final, 21 April 2021 (n 100).

[104] While this book was being edited, the European Commission published guidelines on the definition of AI: Communication from the Commission, 'Commission Guidelines on the definition of an artificial intelligence system established by Regulation (EU) 2024/1689 (AI Act)', C(2025) 5053 final, 29 July 2025.

[105] European Patent Office (EPO), Decision no 18 275 163 (27 January 2020); Decision no 18 275 174 (27 January 2020). See also EPO, 'EPO Refuses DABUS Patent Applications Designating a Machine Inventor' (20 December 2019), available at epo.org/news-events/news/2019/20191220.html.

between the technical complexities of AI, its legal dimensions, and its continuous evolution, in order to safeguard the rule of law.[106]

2.3. AI in Europe: Illustrative Case Studies

This section examines the deployment of AI systems in Europe with a focus on two domains that are particularly sensitive from both a social and legal perspective: social benefits and biometrics. It begins by setting out the definitional frameworks proposed by the European Commission and the Council of Europe, which provide the conceptual foundation for understanding how such systems are identified and classified. Building on this, it turns to two detailed case studies that explore the practical use of AI in these areas, highlighting not only their technical operation but also their broader implications for governance and accountability.

In 2019, the European Commission's HLEGAI defined AI as follows:

> Artificial intelligence (AI) refers to systems that display intelligent behaviour by analysing their environment and taking actions – with some degree of autonomy – to achieve specific goals. AI-based systems can be purely software-based, acting in the virtual world (e.g. voice assistants, image analysis software, search engines, speech and face recognition systems) or AI can be embedded in hardware devices (e.g. advanced robots, autonomous cars, drones or Internet of Things applications).[107]

The Council of Europe, on the other hand, offers the following definition in its *Feasibility Study*:

> AI systems act in the physical or digital dimension by recording their environment through data acquisition, analyzing certain structured or unstructured data, reasoning on the knowledge or processing information derived from the data, and on that basis decide on the best course of action to reach a certain goal.[108]

[106] See the material scope of a regulation, in J Schuett, 'A Legal Definition of AI' (2019), 1 (stating that a typical regulation has four dimensions: the material scope, the personal scope, the territorial scope, and the temporal scope. The material scope of a regulation, which is usually defined at the beginning, can refer to an object or an activity.).

[107] 'A Definition of AI: Main Capabilities and Disciplines', developed for the purpose of the AI HLEG's Deliverables (8 April 2019), available at ec.europa.eu/digital-single-market/en/news/definition-artificial-intelligence-main-capabilities-and-scientific-disciplines, 1. See also European Parliament, Resolution of 20 January 2021 on artificial intelligence: questions of interpretation and application of international law in so far as the EU is affected in the areas of civil and military uses and of state authority outside the scope of criminal justice (2020/2013(INI)), stating that '"AI system" means a system that is either software-based or embedded in hardware devices, and that displays behaviour simulating intelligence by, inter alia, collecting and processing data, analysing and interpreting its environment, and by taking action, with some degree of autonomy, to achieve specific goals'.

[108] Council of Europe, Ad Hoc Committee on Artificial Intelligence (CAHAI), 'Feasibility Study' (17 December 2020) 4, available at rm.coe.int/cahai-2020-23-final-eng-feasibility-study-/1680a0c6da. However, it is worth noting that the Council of Europe also highlighted that 'a future Council of Europe legal framework on AI should adopt a simplified and technology-neutral definition of its purpose, covering those practices or application cases where the development and use of AI systems, or automated decision-making systems more generally, can impact on human rights, democracy and the rule of law, and taking into account all of the systems' socio-technical implications'.

A comparison of the two definitions reveals that the latter is more accessible and operational. The material scope of the Council of Europe's definition places emphasis on processes such as analysing, recording, reasoning, processing, and deciding, rather than on the technical approaches underlying such processes.[109] Moreover, the Council of Europe explicitly identifies three distinct characteristics of AI systems that differentiate them from other technologies: their 'scale, connectedness and reach', their 'complexity and opacity', and their 'ability to recalibrate through feedback and reinforcement learning'. The *Feasibility Study* goes further by linking these characteristics to specific risks, including the amplification of unjust bias,[110] the difficulty of attributing responsibility for adverse outcomes, and the possibility of systems functioning maliciously.[111]

When considering specific applications of AI, however, an important gap becomes evident in the existing literature: there is a lack of systematic analysis of concrete use cases in the public sector. Three major reports provide rare but significant contributions in this respect: the Fundamental Rights Agency's *Getting the Future Right: Artificial Intelligence and Fundamental Rights* ('Report I'),[112] the European Commission's *AI Watch: Artificial Intelligence in Public Services* ('Report II'),[113] and the updated second edition of Report II, published in 2022 ('2022 Report').[114]

It is important to note that an earlier version of this analysis was developed in a chapter published in 2024,[115] where the focus was limited to Report I and Report II. The present analysis offers a more comprehensive examination and integrates revisions based on the updated version of Report II, which will be referred to here as the 2022 Report.[116] Drawing on a detailed analysis of 24 national AI strategies, an overview of 686 AI use cases collected from 30 different European countries,[117] and eight in-depth case studies, the 2022 Report highlights a growing trend of AI deployment to improve the quality of public services, administrative efficiency, and public engagement. Key applications include chatbots, fraud detection, predictive maintenance, and traffic management, with most projects focused on enhancing service quality rather than automating decision-making. The report also underscores

[109] Therefore, this definition appears to be consistent with the rule of law.

[110] Council of Europe (CAHAI), 'Feasibility Study' (n 108), 5.

[111] Council of Europe, (CAHAI), 'Feasibility Study' (n 108), 5–6.

[112] FRA, 'Getting the Future Right' (2020) ('Report I').

[113] See the full name of the report in European Commission, 'AI Watch: Artificial Intelligence in Public Services. Overview of the Use and Impact of AI in Public Services in the EU', Science for Policy Report (2020), available at publications.jrc.ec.europa.eu/repository/handle/JRC120399. At the civil society level, see also European Digital Rights (EDRi), 'Use Cases: Impermissible AI and Fundamental Rights Breaches' (2020), available at edri.org/wp-content/uploads/2021/06/Case-studies-Impermissible-AI-biometrics-September-2020.pdf.

[114] L Tangi et al, 'AI Watch: European Landscape on the Use of Artificial Intelligence by the Public Sector' (Publications Office of the European Union, 2022), EUR 31088 EN, doi.org/10.2760/39336.

[115] E Biber, 'Between Humans and Machines: Judicial Interpretation of the Automated Decision-Making Practices in the EU' in CH Hofmann and F Pflücke (eds), *Governance of Automated Decision-Making and EU Law* (Oxford University Press, 2024) 187–212, doi:10.1093/9780198919575.003.0007.

[116] Tangi et al, 'AI Watch: European Landscape' (2022).

[117] The 2022 Report (at 36) highlights that the Netherlands, with 125 use cases, has the highest number of detected cases – largely due to its national case-tracking repository – followed by Italy, with 75 use cases, and Portugal, with 60.

challenges such as limited internal AI capacity, ethical risks, and uneven implementation across regions. It concludes with clear policy recommendations, including building internal expertise, promoting widespread employee awareness, carefully selecting partners, implementing structured risk management to prevent discriminatory use, and adapting organisational structures – potentially requiring new task allocations – to ensure responsible and human-centric implementation.[118]

However, it is important to note that in the 2022 Report, no systems were identified as being directly related to the fields of social benefits and biometrics. Nevertheless, several systems were found to be closely associated with these areas, highlighting their relevance and potential connections. Ultimately, these three reports offer empirical insights into how AI is currently being deployed in public services, and they constitute the analytical anchor for this section's examination of AI use in the fields of social benefits and biometrics.

2.3.1. Use Case I: AI systems in the Area of Social Benefits

The OECD defines social benefits as 'current transfers received by households intended to provide for the needs that arise from certain events or circumstances, for example, sickness, unemployment, retirement, housing, education or family circumstances'.[119] This definition highlights the fundamental purpose of social benefits: to serve as a safety net. They extend beyond mere financial assistance, functioning as essential instruments of income redistribution and social protection. By design, they safeguard individuals and families against life's uncertainties, such as sudden illness, unemployment, or the challenges associated with old age.

Report I highlights that AI systems in public administration are increasingly being deployed in areas such as benefit calculations, fraud prevention and detection, eligibility assessments, and risk scoring.[120] Governments pursue these technologies with the stated aim of making such decisions more efficient and more consistent with principles of fairness.

In the domain of social benefits, Report I draws particular attention to two critical areas where AI-based decision-making is already in use: housing benefits and unemployment benefits.[121] In these contexts, the systems rely primarily on rule-based decision-making, structured around 'if-then rules'.[122] For example, a person will be eligible for a certain benefit if her income falls below a specified threshold.[123]

Table 2.2. outlines three distinct practices of AI within the field of social benefits.

[118] Tangi et al, 'AI Watch: European Landscape' (2022), 4–6.

[119] OECD, 'Glossary of Statistical Terms: Social Benefits Definitions', available at stats.oecd.org/glossary/detail.asp?ID=2480.

[120] FRA, 'Getting the Future Right' (2020).

[121] FRA, 'Getting the Future Right' (2020). It is worth noting that, according to the report, the organisation employing this AI system has initially relied on image processing to process applications, in order to decide on such social benefit applications.

[122] FRA, 'Getting the Future Right' (2020), 27.

[123] FRA, 'Getting the Future Right' (2020), 27.

Table 2.2 AI Systems in the Area of Social Benefits

AI Systems in the Area of Social Benefits[124]			
System/Report	**Primary Purpose**	**Data Source of the System**	**Techniques and Decision Logic**
Housing Benefits (Report I)	Increase efficiency by accelerating benefit determination.	Internal database of benefit applications (pseudonymised).	- Processing applications - Rule-based decision-making - Decision-tree model following the rules - Simple statistical model (linear regression): it is used 'where the input is the income and the cost limits, and the outcome is the amount of benefit'.[125]
Unemployment Benefits (Report I)	Improve efficiency of benefit allocation.	Various databases: population registers, tax authority databases (salaries and work history).	- Processing applications - Rule-based decision-making: when eligibility criteria are met, the system calculates benefit duration and amount based on payment period and average daily salary.[126]
Multiple Social Assistance Programmes (Report II)[127] Processing applications on home care, sickness benefits, unemployment benefits, and taxes.	Efficiency Streamline processing across diverse benefits (home care, sickness, unemployment, taxation).	Personal data submitted via the self-service portal.	- Robotic Process Automation (RPA)[128] - Rule-based decision-making

(continued)

[124] The table constitutes an original contribution by the author of this book. An earlier version was first published in E Biber, 'Between Humans and Machines' (2024), 187–212, doi:10.1093/9780198919575.003.0007. The present version has been substantially expanded and refined, incorporating additional insights and developments, including those set out in the 2022 Report.

[125] FRA, 'Getting the Future Right' (2020).

[126] FRA, 'Getting the Future Right' (2020).

[127] Report II notes that this system was introduced in Trelleborg, Sweden, in 2015. By 2020, 75% of citizens were using the online platform to access welfare payments (43–44). See European Commission, AI Watch (2022).

[128] Report II does not provide sufficient information about this system. It only considers the system as an 'automated decision-making system'. Therefore, this part of the research is conducted on the basis of the report of AlgorithmWatch, which reported on this issue in 2020. See K Lind, 'Central Authorities Slow to React as Sweden's Cities Embrace Automation of Welfare Management' (2020), available at algorithmwatch.org/en/trelleborg-sweden-algorithm/.

Table 2.2 ***(Continued)***

AI Systems in the Area of Social Benefits			
System/Report	**Primary Purpose**	**Data Source of the System**	**Techniques and Decision Logic**
Estimation of Income (2022 Report, Links beyond Direct Social Benefits)[129]	Efficiency Estimating the income of SMEs and self-employed individuals who choose to pay taxes using a simplified 'module'.	Using data from similar taxpayers, based on activity, location, and other factors.	– Automated reasoning, optimisation – 'Phyton with learning libraries in a specialised multiprocessor system for resource-intensive calculations.'[130]

In this sector, AI systems typically operate in two stages: first, by processing applications, and subsequently by making determinations on them. Given the inherent complexity of these systems, the techniques underlying decision-making should be understood as constituting the 'black-box' dimension of AI practice. This aspect is particularly significant, as underscored by the Hague Court, which noted that citizens could 'neither anticipate the intrusion into their private life nor can they guard themselves against it'.[131] The 'black-box' domain thus represents the locus where both the dynamism and the opacity of AI systems become most apparent.

The first three practices are designed as forms of rule-based decision-making. One such case is the use of Robotic Process Automation (RPA) in the municipality of Trelleborg, Sweden, where it has been implemented since 2016, as documented in Report II.[132] Despite extensive public debate, including coverage in major media outlets, neither public officials nor the company responsible for developing the system have provided satisfactory explanations of how the system functions or how its decisions are reached.[133] Moreover, such systems necessarily base their determinations on the data sources provided. It is, therefore, crucial to recognise that these data sources may be insufficient, incomplete,

[129] This practice is provided in Annex II, 'Case Studies Description' in L Tangi et al, 'AI Watch: European Landscape' (2022).
[130] Annex II of the 2022 Report in L Tangi et al, 'AI Watch: European Landscape' (2022).
[131] The Hague District Court, Case no C/09/550982/HA ZA 18-388 (2020), paras 6.1–6.118.
[132] L Tangi et al, 'AI Watch: European Landscape' (2022).
[133] K Lind, 'Central Authorities Slow to React as Sweden's Cities Embrace Automation of Welfare Management' (n 128). It is worth noting that a journalist, Freddi Ramel, lodged an appeal to the administrative court of appeal to obtain access to the system's code under Sweden's Freedom of Information Act. Trelleborg argued that the code was a trade secret. However, the Court decided that the code of the system is a public document and, therefore, 'the source code has to be made accessible to the public and is fully included in the principle of public access'. See also A Kaun, 'Suing the Algorithm: The Mundanization of Automated Decision-Making in Public Services through Litigation' (2021) Information, Communication & Society 1–17.

or even inaccurate. This critical observation underscores the continuing importance of human oversight and intervention in these domains.

The last practice is a practice of automated reasoning and optimisation, applied to the domain of taxation. The Spanish Tax Agency has developed an AI-based system to estimate the income of SMEs and self-employed individuals who opt for the simplified 'module' scheme rather than declaring exact income figures. The model applies optimisation techniques to learn from patterns across similar taxpayers – based on activity, location, and other factors – thus improving the accuracy of income forecasting and enabling scenario analysis of alternative taxation options.[134]

2.3.2. Use Case II: AI Systems in the Area of Biometrics

The final AI Act defines 'biometric data' in Article 3(34) as:

> personal data resulting from specific technical processing relating to the physical, physiological or behavioural characteristics of a natural person, such as facial images or dactyloscopic data.[135]

Biometric data can be used in different kinds of AI systems, including emotion recognition systems,[136] biometric categorisation systems,[137] and biometric identification systems.[138] In the case of such biometrical systems, two fields are prominent in public use: predictive policing, and migration and border control management. Table 2.3. sketches the three use cases in this area, based on Report I,[139] Report II,[140] and the 2022 Report.[141]

[134] This practice is provided within Annex II of the 2022 Report: L Tangi et al, 'AI Watch: European Landscape' (2022).

[135] Regulation (EU) 2024/1689 of the European Parliament and of the Council of 13 June 2024 laying down harmonised rules on artificial intelligence and amending Regulations (EC) No 300/2008, (EU) No 167/2013, (EU) No 168/2013, (EU) 2018/858, (EU) 2018/1139 and (EU) 2019/2144 and Directives 2014/90/EU, (EU) 2016/797 and (EU) 2020/1828 (Artificial Intelligence Act), OJ L 1689, 12 July 2024.

[136] The AI Act defines, in Art 3(39), that an '"emotion recognition system" means an AI system for the purpose of identifying or inferring emotions or intentions of natural persons on the basis of their biometric data'.

[137] The AI Act defines this, in Art 3(40), as an 'AI system for the purpose of assigning natural persons to specific categories on the basis of their biometric data, unless it is ancillary to another commercial service and strictly necessary for objective technical reasons'.

[138] Art 3 of the AI Act identifies three categories of biometric identification systems: (i) remote; (ii) real-time; and (iii) post-remote. These are defined as follows in AI Act 3(41): '"remote biometric identification system" means an AI system for the purpose of identifying natural persons, without their active involvement, typically at a distance through the comparison of a person's biometric data with the biometric data contained in a reference database'; 3(42): '"real-time remote biometric identification system" means a remote biometric identification system, whereby the capturing of biometric data, the comparison and the identification all occur without a significant delay, comprising not only instant identification, but also limited short delays in order to avoid circumvention'; 3(43) '"post-remote biometric identification system" means a remote biometric identification system other than a real-time remote biometric identification system'.

[139] FRA, 'Getting the Future Right' (2020).

[140] European Commission, 'AI Watch: Artificial Intelligence in Public Services' (2020).

[141] L Tangi et al, 'AI Watch: European Landscape' (2022).

Table 2.3 AI Systems in the Area of Biometrics – Law Enforcement

AI Systems in the Area of Biometrics – Law Enforcement[142]			
System/ Report	**Primary Purpose**	**Data Source of the System**	**Techniques and Decision Logic**
Predictive Policing (eg mapping crime patterns, detecting online hate speech,[143] preparing risk assessments on gender-based violence) (Report I)	Increase efficiency by automating tasks). Enhance public security.	Historical police and crime data (including crime reports, witness statements, suspect declarations). Environmental and contextual data (population density, the locations of public services and gathering places, and large events or holidays). Personal data (both real-time and historical), including criminal records, addresses, phone numbers, location data.	– Application of data mining, machine learning, and predictive analytics – Simulation techniques and data visualisation – Construction of predictive models for identifying potential crimes, perpetrators, and victims – Generation of 'heat maps' to highlight geographical concentrations of certain crimes – In gender-based violence cases, the system produces a 'risk score' based on the likelihood of recurrence, which is subsequently evaluated by law enforcement in light of severity and nature of threats.
Migration and Border Control Management	Improve efficiency in border management. Strengthen security.	Biometric data (facial images, body movement, micro-expressions, behavioral cues). Other personal data relevant to migration and identity verification processes.	– Biometric identification and categorisation techniques – Emotion recognition systems.

(continued)

[142] The table constitutes an original contribution by the author of this book. An earlier version was first published in E Biber, 'Between Humans and Machines' (2024), 187–212, doi:10.1093/9780198919575.003.0007. The present version has been substantially expanded and refined, incorporating additional insights and developments, including those set out in the 2022 Report.

[143] According to the FRA report, a public agency uses an AI system to detect online hate speech (FRA, 'Getting the Future Right' (2020)), 36.

Table 2.3 ***(Continued)***

AI Systems in the Area of Biometrics – Law Enforcement			
System/ Report	**Primary Purpose**	**Data Source of the System**	**Techniques and Decision Logic**
Intelligent Control Platform (ICP) Danish Business Authority (2022 Report)	Provide an automated assessment of the risk of a company being fraudulent. Strengthen trust and security in business environment.	Data from 800,000+ companies, and a variety of other data from administrative databases, merged in the Graph database. Company registration data (including identity papers, assets, audits).	– Predictive ML models (≈30 models) combined with Graph database analysis – Automated risk-scoring system (fraud likelihood) integrated into case-handling – Controls identity papers, verifies assets, flags negligence/ unstructured data – Risk monitoring with 'Record Keeper' framework ensuring transparency, explainability, and traceability.

An example of predictive policing, provided in Report I, illustrates how AI is applied to enhance public security by predicting potential criminal activity. These systems draw on historical police and crime data, including reports, witness statements, and suspect records, as well as contextual information such as population density, public spaces, and major events.

With respect to migration and border control management, the three reports do not offer concrete examples illustrating how AI systems are being deployed in this domain. However, newer AI techniques are being developed to control borders, and to provide a decision support system for border authorities.[144] Moreover, this area is particularly significant as all the three systems of biometrics mentioned above can be used in this area.[145] Indeed, due to the rich variety of AI systems, this field is called a 'human laboratory',[146] where people are used as 'test subjects' for such systems.

[144] See, for instance, the project of iBorderCtrl, available at perma.cc/L7KM-TPFK.

[145] New technologies serving in this area are categorised as 'smart borders' technologies. See J Sánchez-Monedero and L Dencik, 'The Politics of Deceptive Borders: "Biomarkers of Deceit" and the Case of iBorderCtrl' (2022) 25(3) Information, Communication & Society 414. See also a research briefing on the UK's smart border technology to detect deception, available at post.parliament.uk/research-briefings/post-pn-375/. See further the US version, called 'AVATAR', an automated lie detector and deception detection technology based on eye tracking, available at discernscience.com/avatar/.

[146] European Digital Rights (EDRi), 'Technological Testing Ground: Migration Management Experiments and Reflections from the Ground Up' (2020) 16, available at edri.org/our-work/european-court-supports-transparency-in-risky-eu-border-tech-experiments/. See also T Cardoso, 'Ottawa's Use of AI for Immigration a "High-Risk Laboratory": Report' (The Globe and Mail, 25 September 2018), available at theglobeandmail.com/politics/article-ottawas-use-of-ai-for-immigration-a-high-risk-laboratory-report/.

As a use case, the project of iBorderCtrl is to be considered in this regard. The main objective of the project is 'to enable faster and thorough border control for third country nationals crossing the land borders of EU Member States (MS), with technologies that adopt the future development of the Schengen Border Management'.[147] The project brings together many technologies, including biometric verification, automated deception detection, document authentication, and risk assessments.[148] However, the 'black-box' aspect of the project has not been unlocked. The project was filed before the CJEU to disclose detailed information about how the AI systems used in it work, and the ethics reports and legal assessments regarding these systems.[149] The CJEU argued that the public interest justifies the disclosure of the relevant documents:

> the public is interested in participating in an informed, open, and democratic debate regarding the question, whether control technologies, as the one mentioned, are desirable, if they should be funded via public money, and that this public interest must be duly respected.[150]

Despite this judgment, the project's website is currently not accessible.[151]

Another critical example that can be considered within this domain is the Intelligent Control Platform (ICP) developed by the Danish Business Authority to provide an automated assessment of the risk of a company being fraudulent, as mentioned in the 2022 Report.[152] The platform draws on data from more than 800,000 companies, and a variety of other data coming from administrative databases, combining them in a Graph database that supports around 30 machine learning models. These models calculate fraud risk scores with about 75 per cent accuracy, which are then integrated into case-handling processes to automatically verify identity papers, asset declarations, and audit records. To ensure accountability and explainability, the ICP includes a 'Record Keeper' framework that traces all data-handling and decision-making. Its development was supported by managerial commitment, internal data science expertise, and close collaboration between technical staff and domain experts.

[147] See the project's website at iborderctrl.eu/The-project.

[148] iBorderCtrl project website (n 147).

[149] CJEU, Case T-158/19 *Breyer v REA*, 15 December 2021.

[150] CJEU, *Breyer v REA*, para 200 (unofficial translation): '[es besteht] ein Interesse der Öffentlichkeit daran … an einer informierten öffentlichen und demokratischen Diskussion über die Frage teilzunehmen, ob Kontrolltechnologien wie die in Rede stehenden wünschenswert sind und ob sie durch öffentliche Gelder finanziert werden sollen, und dass dieses Interesse gebührend gewahrt werden muss'.

[151] There is only a warning, stating that 'the resource is not available via this channel', as of 21 March 2022, available at iborderctrl.eu/restricted.html.

[152] Annex II of the 2022 Report: Tangi et al, 'AI Watch: European Landscape' (2022). It is worth highlighting that the 2022 Report explicitly stated that the platform's status was classified as 'in production'.

2.4. The Fundamental Characteristics of AI Systems in the Areas of Social Benefits and Biometrics

In order to establish an effective framework for regulating AI systems, a necessary preliminary step is to engage in a closer examination of their defining features. This section, therefore, presents the most prominent characteristics of AI systems, with particular reference to their deployment in the domains of social benefits administration and biometrics. Six distinctive aspects call for systematic scrutiny within the legal discourse on AI regulation: (i) the inter-systemic aspect; (ii) the dynamic aspect; (iii) the complexity aspect; (iv) the social aspect; (v) the privateness aspect; and (vi) the publicness aspect. It is imperative to transcend generic references to these features and instead meticulously analyse their scope, dimensions, and dynamics at a more granular level within the specific context of the aforementioned AI systems.

2.4.1. The Inter-Systemic Aspect of AI systems

The inter-systemic dimension of AI systems manifests across three distinct levels, which can be organised into two overarching categories. The first two levels (Levels 1 and 2) fall within (i) the interdisciplinary inter-systemic category, reflecting the ways in which AI systems intersect with and draw upon multiple fields of knowledge and methodologies. The third level (Level 3), by contrast, belongs to (ii) the institutionally inter-systemic category, which captures the interaction of AI systems with existing organisational, legal, and administrative structures.

First, within the interdisciplinary inter-systemic category (i), the field of AI is inherently interdisciplinary at its foundational level (Level 1). This implies that the design and development of AI systems are informed by a convergence of diverse theories, methods, and techniques drawn from multiple disciplines. As observed by Russell and Norvig, mentioned earlier in this chapter, the conceptual and methodological underpinnings of AI derive from philosophy, mathematics, economics, neuroscience, and psychology, among others. In light of the use cases discussed above, one illustrative example is rule-based decision-making, which is constructed on the basis of formal logical principles.

Second, at the relational level (Level 2) within the interdisciplinary inter-systemic category, AI systems exhibit extensive interconnections with a wide range of societal domains, thereby generating significant cross-sectoral 'spillover potential'.[153] As previously discussed, the large-scale deployment of AI in the

[153] It is important to note that the 'spillover effect' is defined as a type of 'networked effect' in economics, referring to the impact of seemingly unrelated events in one nation on the economies of other nations. See a basic definition in *Investopedia*, available at investopedia.com/terms/s/spillover-effect.asp.

public sector may produce unintended externalities, for example the considerable environmental impact associated with the energy-intensive training of AI models. A further illustration can be found in the case of Trelleborg, discussed in this chapter, where the system has been employed across multiple domains, including home care services, sickness benefits, and unemployment management. This integration produces what may be described as an 'inter-systemic spiral', whereby diverse policy areas become increasingly interwoven within a single technological framework.[154]

Third, AI systems can be characterised as (ii) institutionally inter-systemic, insofar as they implicate the activities of private entities, state authorities, and extra-state actors (Level 3). This dimension is a direct outgrowth of the broader processes of globalisation, of which AI systems are both a product and a driver. By their very design and application, AI systems can operate across borders: they may be employed by governments for security and surveillance purposes, or by private corporations to monitor consumers on both local and global scales.[155] A noticeable example arises in the field of biometrics, particularly in the context of migration management and border control, where AI technologies function within inherently transnational frameworks. This globalised character is further reinforced by the extraterritorial and ubiquitous nature of data flows. As a result, risks to fundamental and human rights that originate in one jurisdiction may have direct implications for individuals located outside that jurisdiction who nonetheless become subject to the operation of such systems. Accordingly, these risks acquire a persistent and pervasive quality, extending beyond the remit of national institutions to encompass global and transnational actors.[156]

Taken together, these three levels situate AI systems within both an interdisciplinary and an institutionally inter-systemic category. They are institutionally inter-systemic insofar as they involve interventions across multiple layers of governance and practice, including those originating in the private sector. At the same time, they are interdisciplinarily inter-systemic because their deployment raises a range of cross-cutting issues, most notably those relating to environmental

[154] This situation excludes a legal approach that takes one single rationale.

[155] Heyvaert suggests that some global issues pose 'intersystemic risks' that 'possess the potential to cascade across different systems and hence, entail a liability to exponential growth across numbers of linked systems'. Moreover, she notes that such risks are globalised, ubiquitous, and entrenched. Her article makes this argument with respect to climate change and zoonotic disease risks, yet she adds that the case could also be considered for challenges such as cybersecurity and biodiversity depletion. See V Heyvaert, 'Governing Intersystemic Systemic Risks: Lessons from Covid and Climate Change' (2022) Modern Law Review 1. It is also crucial to note that the interoperability activities of governments on AI systems institutionalise the inter-systemic dimension of such systems. See European Commission, 'New European Interoperability Framework: Promoting Seamless Services and Data Flows for European Public Administrations' (2017), available at ec.europa.eu/isa2/sites/default/files/eif_brochure_final.pdf.

[156] This situation requires consideration of the 'poverty of the legislative state' in such cases. See G Palombella, 'The Rule of Law as an Institutional Ideal' (2010) 9(1) Comparative Sociology 10 (arguing that 'the poverty of the legislative state is generated by the hierarchical model of law, and mainly by the lack of a plurality of equally relevant protagonists and actors on the (institutional) scene).

protection.[157] Moreover, the inter-systemic character of AI systems is inseparable from their dual nature: while they create novel opportunities for innovation, development, and systemic transformation, they simultaneously pose significant risks to hard-won achievements at the global, regional, and national levels. Put differently, the dual nature of AI use necessitates the engagement of diverse perspectives and disciplinary approaches within even a single case.[158] As a result, AI systems have the potential to generate cascading risks across interconnected social and legal systems.

It is important to underscore that the inter-systemic dimension of AI systems highlights a fundamental distinction between AI and the Internet. In the case of the Internet, the institutionally inter-systemic aspect has been the most prominent, owing to its inherently borderless and transnational character. By contrast, AI systems demand a more multifaceted approach: they are not only institutionally inter-systemic, but also interdisciplinarily inter-systemic, given the wide range of disciplinary intersections involved in their design, deployment, and governance.

2.4.2. The Dynamic Aspect of AI systems

AI systems are characterised by an exceptionally dynamic nature. According to the 2019 *Stanford AI Index Report* – produced in partnership with McKinsey & Company, Google, PwC, OpenAI, Genpact, and AI21 Labs – the pace of AI development is outstripping Moore's Law.[159] Moore's Law, an empirical observation, holds that the number of transistors in a dense integrated circuit doubles approximately every two years, thereby enabling application developers to expect a corresponding doubling in performance for the same hardware cost within that time frame.[160] The *Stanford Report* observed that, 'prior to 2012, AI results closely tracked Moore's Law, with compute doubling every two years. Post-2012, compute has been doubling every 3.4 months.'[161] This accelerated trajectory not only underscores the unprecedented speed of AI advancement but also reflects the shifting conceptual boundaries of the field – rightly captured in the observation that, 'as soon as [AI] works, no one calls it AI anymore'.[162]

The dynamic quality of AI systems is further reinforced by their rapid diffusion across both the public and private sectors. According to the *European Enterprise*

[157] M Coeckelbergh, Green Leviathan or the Poetics of Political Liberty: Navigating Freedom in the Age of Climate Change and Artificial Intelligence (Routledge, 2021).

[158] This feature becomes particularly evident when an AI system under examination threatens several rights at both domestic and transnational levels. See Chapter 3 of the book on this issue.

[159] R Perrault et al, 'Stanford Human-Centered Artificial Intelligence, Artificial Intelligence Index 2019 Annual Report' (2019), available at hai.stanford.edu/sites/default/files/ai_index_2019_report.pdf.

[160] Stanford HAI, 'AI Index 2019 Annual Report' (n 159).

[161] Stanford HAI, 'AI Index 2019 Annual Report' (n 159), 'Chapter 3 Technical Performance – Computational Capacity' 66.

[162] B Meyer, 'John McCarthy' (2011), available at cacm.acm.org/blogs/blog-cacm/138907-john-mccarthy/fulltext (quoting McCarthy).

Survey, at the beginning of 2020, 42 per cent of companies in the EU reported using at least one AI technology.[163] The combination of this exponential technological development and its swift cross-sectoral adoption underscores the need for constantly updated regulatory and policy approaches, capable of keeping pace with both the evolving capabilities of AI and its expanding social, economic, and institutional footprint.

2.4.3. The Complexity Aspect of AI systems

The case studies discussed above demonstrate that AI systems are marked by a high degree of complexity. They often operate through so-called 'black-box'[164] mechanisms, generating outputs without providing transparent or easily comprehensible explanations. Even comparatively 'simple' AI systems, such as rule-based decision-making systems in the administration of social benefits, pose significant challenges to explanation and accountability, as illustrated by the Trelleborg example.

Furthermore, public officials employing AI systems in the fields of social benefits and biometrics frequently rely on heterogeneous terminology to describe and classify these technologies. This terminological inconsistency contributes to the absence of a common nomenclature, which in turn hampers the clear identification and categorisation of such systems. For instance, in the Swedish context, officials refer to their system as 'Robotic Process Automation' rather than identifying it more accurately as a rule-based decision-making system. This divergence in terminology illustrates a broader pattern: the adoption and use of AI systems across European countries is highly heterogeneous, with states deploying different functionalities, techniques, and practices even when pursuing comparable objectives. Such heterogeneity underscores the difficulty – if not impossibility – of establishing a standardised conceptual language for these systems.

Moreover, the case studies have shown that certain AI systems – particularly those deployed in the contexts of migration management and border control – integrate multiple techniques to surveil, identify, categorise, and detect individuals, as well as their expressions. This multilayered design significantly compounds the complexity of such systems, rendering their underlying decision-making processes highly opaque and exceedingly difficult to articulate in plain, accessible language.

[163] FRA, 'European Enterprise Survey on the Use of Technologies Based on Artificial Intelligence' (2020), available at op.europa.eu/en/publication-detail/-/publication/f089bbae-f0b0-11ea-991b-01aa75ed71a1#:~:text=The%20survey%20reached%20a%20total,have%20adopted%20at%20least%20two (noting that larger companies have the potential to benefit most from AI systems compared with small and micro-sized enterprises, due to their larger economies of scale).

[164] F Pasquale, The Black Box Society: The Secret Algorithms That Control Money and Information (Harvard University Press, 2015).

2.4.4. The Social Aspect of AI systems

The use cases have demonstrated that AI systems function as social systems, actively mediating and reshaping social institutions and structures.[165] Their applications extend across diverse domains of social, public, and human services. Within the social sciences, three principal areas of application have been identified: (i) enhancing the effectiveness of diagnosis and prediction of various conditions; (ii) advancing understanding of human development and functioning; and (iii) improving the management and organisation of data in social and human services.[166] As the use cases above illustrate, AI systems employed in contexts such as the allocation of social benefits, the assessment of risk, the generation of individual risk scores, and the identification, categorisation, and detection of human behaviours and emotions[167] exert a direct influence on the configuration of social structures and the operation of social institutions.

Within the philosophy of technology, the social dimension of AI systems is often conceptualised through the lens of relational ethics.[168] From this perspective, AI is understood not merely as a technical tool but as a system embedded within, and responsive to, the interplay between individuals, technologies, and broader social infrastructures. Relational understandings of AI emphasise how such systems both shape and are shaped by human behaviour and societal dynamics. Put differently, AI systems exert influence on individuals, interpersonal interactions, and collective structures, precisely because they are capable of recognising and engaging with the social components of their environment. Consequently, the framework of relational ethics posits that AI should be approached as a *socio-technical* system, rather than being reduced to a mere automation technique. In this regard, it calls for situating ethical evaluation within the concrete dynamics of decision-making contexts, thereby assessing what may be considered 'right' in relation to the specific circumstances in which an AI system operates.[169]

As I have examined elsewhere, the relational understanding of AI provides a useful framework for distinguishing between the technical and social dimensions of

[165] N Smuha, E Ahmed-Rengers, A Harkens, W Li, J MacLaren, R Piselli, and K Yeung, 'How the EU Can Achieve Legally Trustworthy AI: A Response to the European Commission's Proposal for an Artificial Intelligence Act', LEADS Law, University of Birmingham – Legal, Ethical and Accountable Digital Society, 5 August 2021, available at papers.ssrn.com/sol3/papers.cfm?abstract_id=3899991, 12 (stating that such systems cannot be considered solely as consumer or technical products).

[166] M Robila and SA Robila, 'Applications of Artificial Intelligence Methodologies to Behavioral and Social Sciences' (2020) 29 Journal of Child and Family Studies 2957.

[167] See an interesting discussion stating that emotion AI systems detect physical signals or muscle movements rather than emotions, in LF Barrett, 'Darwin Was Wrong: Your Expressions Do Not Reveal Your Emotions' (Scientific American, 27 April 2022), available at scientificamerican.com/article/darwin-was-wrong-your-facial-expressions-do-not-reveal-your-emotions.

[168] For some leading studies see V Dignum, 'Relational Artificial Intelligence' (2022) arXiv:2202.07446, available at arxiv.org/abs/2202.07446.

[169] However, this is not an easy task, as it requires both multidisciplinary and multi-stakeholder participation.

AI systems, even though the two remain deeply intertwined.[170] The technical dimension is primarily associated with the black-box mechanisms or decision trees that structure an AI system's operations, thereby giving rise to significant epistemic challenges. By contrast, the social dimension concerns the nature of the data on which AI systems rely. Such data is inherently social, as it is drawn from human societies and reflects collective behaviours, practices, and expressions. The AI systems examined above, for instance, capture and process social data in the form of expressions, behaviours, events, emotional responses, and recurrent patterns or errors.

This observation highlights a critical feature of AI systems: individuals are not only subjected to the data generated by their own actions and choices but are also influenced by aggregated data derived from similarly situated individuals, which together construct broader social contexts. In the specific case of AI systems deployed in migration management and border control, these social contexts are transnational in scope, encompassing diverse populations across multiple countries.

In other words, the evaluative framework underpinning AI systems is constructed on the basis of actions and behaviours that cannot be attributed to a single individual. This means that the decisions generated by the AI systems examined above are never purely personal; rather, they are fundamentally social decisions, encompassing not only individual communities but also a plurality of diverse social groups. Consequently, the protection of rights and interests in this context must extend beyond the individual to encompass collective interests as well. This conclusion underscores the need to critically reassess prevailing formulations of the rule of law, many of which remain primarily oriented towards safeguarding individual interests, while insufficiently accounting for the collective dimensions of AI-driven decision-making.[171]

2.4.5. The *Privateness* of AI Systems

The *privateness* of AI systems derives from the fact that their technical expertise is largely developed and directed by private initiatives. These private actors employ specialists with the most advanced knowledge of the 'black-box' mechanisms underlying AI systems. However, as the use cases above have demonstrated, when such systems are deployed within the public sphere, considerations of public interest may justify the disclosure of relevant documents, even when these are protected as trade secrets. This tension highlights the need for a critical examination of the *publicness* of AI systems and the balance between proprietary rights and the demands of transparency and accountability in contexts that directly affect individuals and communities.

[170] E Biber, 'Between Humans and Machines' (2024).

[171] See a discussion on this issue in A Puri, 'Rule of Law, AI, and the "Individual"' (Verfassungsblog, 2022), available at verfassungsblog.de/roa-individual/. See also Chapter 4 of this book for a discussion on the rule of law.

2.4.6. The *Publicness* of AI Systems

The AI systems examined above process data and information concerning public(s)[172] and generate decisions on matters of public relevance. In other words, they translate information about public(s) from the analogue world into the digital domain. The publicness of AI systems arises from their deployment within the public sphere[173] – the 'space of appearance'[174] – where individuals come together, are bound by the same legal frameworks ('legal publics'), are shaped by shared infrastructures ('infrastructural publics'), and are subject to common power relations that may condition or constrain their autonomy ('normative publics').[175]

This aspect of AI systems, as examined in this chapter, can be further concretised by reference to the infrastructures within which such systems operate. At the outset, it is important to recognise that AI systems themselves constitute a distinctive form of digital infrastructure,[176] shaping and mediating social, legal, and institutional practices. In this context, Appel offers a useful definition of the concept of *infrastructure*, as follows: 'Critical locations [infrastructures] through which sociality, governance and politics, accumulation and dispossession, and institutions and aspirations are formed, reformed, and performed.'[177]

As identified in the discussion of the *social* aspect of AI systems, these technologies mediate social institutions and structures through their relational nature,[178] as they are used to determine access to social benefits and to identify, categorise, and detect individuals and their expressions. In this sense, AI systems constitute

[172] According to a Kantian understanding, the public refers to 'unavoidable-living-side-by-side': 'When you cannot avoid living side by side with all others, you ought to leave the state of nature and proceed with them into a rightful condition'. See I Kant, The Metaphysics of Morals (Cambridge University Press, 2005).

[173] See the concept of 'public sphere' in J Habermas, S Lennox, and F Lennox, 'The Public Sphere: An Encyclopedia Article (1964)' (1974) 3 New German Critique 49–55; J Habermas, The Structural Transformation of the Public Sphere: An Inquiry into a Category of Bourgeois Society (trans by T Burger with the assistance of F Lawrence, MIT Press, 1989); S Benhabib, 'The Embattled Public Sphere: Hannah Arendt, Jürgen Habermas and Beyond' (1997) 90 *Theoria: A Journal of Social and Political Theory* 1–24.

[174] H Arendt, The Human Condition (University of Chicago Press, 1998) ('everything that appears in public can be seen and heard by everybody and has the widest possible publicity').

[175] B Kingsbury and N Maisley, 'Infrastructures and Laws: Publics and Publicness' (Institute for International Law and Justice, NYU School of Law, Working Paper 2021/3).

[176] P Edwards, 'We Have Been Assimilated: Some Principles for Thinking About Algorithmic Systems', Working Conference on Information Systems and Organizations (IS&O) (San Francisco, CA, 2018) 19–27. See also OECD, 'Global Information Infrastructure and Global Information Society (GII-GIS): Statement of Policy Recommendations Made by the ICCP Committee' (1996) OECD Digital Economy Papers No 18, OECD Publishing, Paris, doi:10.1787/237382063227.

[177] H Appel, N Anand, and A Gupta, 'Introduction: Temporality, Politics and the Promise of Infrastructure' in H Appel, N Anand, and A Gupta (eds), The Promise of Infrastructure (Duke University Press, 2018) 3.

[178] GC Bowker, K Baker, F Millerand, and D Ribes, 'Toward Information Infrastructure Studies: Ways of Knowing in a Networked Environment' in J Hunsinger et al (eds), International Handbook of Internet Research (Springer, 2010) 97–117 (stating that infrastructure refers to 'pervasive enabling resources in network form').

critical systems for individuals, with the potential to produce life-changing social consequences. In light of the definition above, they are dynamic – continually being formed, reformed, and performed. Moreover, the effects of AI-driven infrastructures on social relations have not emerged in an unplanned or incidental manner, but have been deliberately engineered according to specific designs and objectives – particularly evident in the context of law enforcement.[179]

In this way, the AI systems examined above have generated a new form of *publicness*: one grounded in algorithmic practices and decision-making processes that are shaped by private dynamics and embedded within broader power relations.[180] Individuals thus become subject to a novel configuration of power – one that is largely opaque and difficult, if not impossible, for them to fully comprehend. More importantly, this particular 'vague' configuration of power relations can have profound implications for individual and collective autonomy. Put differently, the autonomy of publics is increasingly conditioned by an infrastructure that is not governed solely by a 'single mind'[181] such as the state, but also by AI systems developed by private entities, even when these systems are deployed by public authorities. This dynamic illustrates the normative impact of AI systems, revealing how they reshape the foundations of autonomy, authority, and governance.

From an observational standpoint, AI systems embody highly significant social elements in a formal sense, given their deployment by state authorities. This is particularly evident in the context of migration and border control management, where their operation can generate far-reaching global impacts. As emphasised in the discussion of the inter-systemic aspect of AI systems, such technologies engage with diverse publics in a transnational manner, thereby extending their influence well beyond the confines of any single jurisdiction.[182]

Therefore, the *publics* surrounding this particular digital infrastructure have the right to demand that it be 'structured, governed, and operated in a manner according to their claims and interests'.[183] This aligns with Kingsbury's normative claim that infrastructures ought to be designed, oriented, and operated in accordance with the requirements of *publicness*. As Kingsbury explains, legal ideas and mechanisms play a crucial role in operationalising *publicness* for infrastructural *publics*, thereby enabling them to act and to be heard.[184] In this regard,

[179] See engineered and non-engineered infrastructures, in Kingsbury and Maisley, 'Infrastructures and Laws' (2021), 7.

[180] Kingsbury and Maisley, 'Infrastructures and Laws' (2021), 2 (stating that 'infrastructures are socio-technical assemblages infused in politics and power relations').

[181] For the expression 'single directing mind', see B Kingsbury, 'International Law and Inter-Public Law' (2009) 49 Nomos: Moral Universalism and Pluralism 167–204.

[182] This requires understanding the public sphere in a transnational or a pluralist sense, as Habermas calls the public sphere 'an open and inclusive network of overlapping, subcultural publics having fluid, temporal, social, and substantive boundaries': see J Habermas, Between Facts and Norms: Contributions to a Discourse Theory of Law and Democracy (MIT Press, 1996) 307.

[183] Kingsbury and Maisley, 'Infrastructures and Laws' (2021).

[184] Kingsbury and Maisley, 'Infrastructures and Laws' (2021).

publicness entails adherence to three core principles: *accessibility*, *exposure*, and *consideration*. The AI systems examined above must, therefore, be analysed within this framework.

First, *accessibility* requires that relations be open and available to all members of the public.[185] In the context of the AI systems examined above, this principle applies not only to access to the systems themselves but also to the decision-making processes underpinning them. It further entails that the legal rules governing these systems must be accessible and open to everybody.

Second, *exposure* recognises that the public sphere is constituted by individuals with diverse values, priorities, experiences, and interests, and therefore insists that events and expressions in this space be subject to the 'widest possible publicity'.[186] Applied to the AI systems discussed above, this principle requires that such technologies actively prevent and eliminate discriminatory practices based on race, gender, class, disability, religion, or other grounds, thereby ensuring that all individuals can be equally visible and audible within these spaces.

Third, *consideration* refers to the reciprocal expectations inherent in public life, whereby individuals are called upon to view issues not solely from their own standpoint but also from the perspective of society as a whole.[187] In this regard, questions concerning the AI systems analysed above must be assessed not only through the lens of individual perspectives but also from a broader public standpoint that reflects collective values and societal wellbeing.

2.5. Concluding Remarks

The characteristics identified above collectively provide a normative framework for developing a legal approach to AI systems deployed in the public sector. Put differently, these six features constitute the key dynamics and sources that must be taken into account when designing regulatory frameworks and adjudicating disputes involving AI. The six features may be summarised as follows:

(i) AI systems deployed in the public sector are simultaneously institutionally and interdisciplinarily *inter-systemic*, insofar as they operate across multiple institutional settings while drawing upon insights, methods, and techniques from a wide range of disciplines.
(ii) AI systems used in the public sector are inherently *dynamic*, both in terms of their rapid technological development and in their patterns of adoption across different institutional and societal contexts.

[185] Kingsbury and Maisley, 'Infrastructures and Laws' (2021).
[186] Kingsbury and Maisley, 'Infrastructures and Laws' (2021), 21. See also Arendt, The Human Condition (1998) (stating that 'everything that appears in public can be seen and heard by everybody and has the widest possible publicity').
[187] Kingsbury and Maisley, 'Infrastructures and Laws' (2021), 21.

(iii) AI systems employed in the public sector are characterised by significant *complexity*. This complexity arises from three interrelated dimensions: (a) their reliance on black-box mechanisms that obscure internal decision-making processes; (b) the use of heterogeneous terminology that complicates identification and classification; and (c) the integration of diverse techniques and applications.

(iv) AI systems used in the public sector are fundamentally *social* in nature. This social dimension is manifested in several ways: (a) they mediate and facilitate key aspects of the functioning of social institutions and structures; (b) they recognise and respond to the social components of their environment; (c) they structure interactions between individuals and the system through processes of identification, categorisation, and detection; and (d) they weave[188] broader social contexts by aggregating and interpreting individual data within collective frameworks.

(v) AI systems used in the public sector possess a *private* dimension, insofar as their development depends heavily on specialised technical expertise that is primarily concentrated within private entities and initiatives.

(vi) AI systems used in the public sector embody the quality of *publicness*. By operating within the public sphere – the 'space of appearance'[189] – they become embedded in existing power relations and exert a normative impact on the autonomy of individuals. The quality of *publicness*, in this sense, requires adherence to three fundamental principles: *accessibility*, *exposure*, and *consideration*.[190]

The following chapter will, therefore, examine the current regulatory approach of the EU – the world's first comprehensive framework for AI regulation – in order to assess whether, and to what extent, it takes into account these crucial characteristics.

[188] The term 'weaving' is employed intentionally, rather than 'coding', in order to underscore the social dimension of AI systems, and to distinguish it from their purely technical dimension.

[189] Arendt, The Human Condition (1998).

[190] Kingsbury and Maisley, 'Infrastructures and Laws' (2021).

3

Steering the Pendulum Towards the 'Rule of Technology'

Analysing the Artificial Intelligence Act

3.1. General Overview

This chapter evaluates the normative power of the European Union (EU)'s risk-based approach to AI systems, specifically examining whether it possesses sufficient power to safeguard the rule of law while simultaneously accommodating diverse needs and objectives, as required. Central to this inquiry is the question of whether such an approach can achieve these aims while 'preventing the law from turning into a sheer tool of domination'.[1] From an inter-legal perspective, this analysis involves interrogating and clarifying the normative ecosystem of AI systems in light of specific use cases, in order to assess whether that ecosystem is sufficiently resilient against forms of dominance. It further examines whether it provides a 'legal-friendly functional normative ground' within which diverse normative actors and legalities are able to interact with one another. This chapter begins by mapping the current regulatory models, and approaches governing AI systems. Following a critical examination of these frameworks, it then turns to the EU's risk-based approach, which receives particular attention as the first concrete legal framework worldwide for the regulation of AI.[2] After critically assessing the AI Act,[3] approved in June 2024, in light of the rule of law and the protection of fundamental rights, the chapter concludes that the normative power of the model remains inadequate to ensure the rule of law. This inadequacy stems primarily from the model's heavy reliance on a market-oriented technocratic approach, a stance that fails to account of the six fundamental characteristics of AI systems identified

[1] G Palombella, 'The Rule of Law at Home and Abroad' (2016) 8 *Hague Journal on the Rule of Law* 1.

[2] Regulation (EU) 2024/1689 of the European Parliament and of the Council of 13 June 2024 laying down harmonised rules on artificial intelligence and amending Regulations (EC) No 300/2008, (EU) No 167/2013, (EU) No 168/2013, (EU) 2018/858, (EU) 2018/1139 and (EU) 2019/2144 and Directives 2014/90/EU, (EU) 2016/797 and (EU) 2020/1828 (Artificial Intelligence Act), OJ L 1689, 12 July 2024.

[3] Throughout this chapter, the European Commission's Proposal is referred to as the 'AI Act Proposal', while the adopted legislation is referred to as the 'AI Act'.

in the previous chapter of this book.[4] As a result, the current legal framework cannot be considered resilient against the dominance of a market-oriented technocratic approach, thereby raising the risk of a shift towards a 'rule of technology'.[5]

The line of reasoning proceeds as follows: (i) the intrinsic value of fundamental and human rights is undermined by the failure to account for the *publicness* of AI systems; (ii) the misidentification of risk profiles arises from neglecting the *complexity* and *dynamic* dimensions of such systems; (iii) the dominance of private power results from overlooking both the *inter-systemic* and *publicness* aspects; and (iv) the imposition of opaque precautionary bans stems from disregarding the *social* dimension of AI systems. On the basis of this analysis, the chapter concludes by underscoring the necessity of adopting a *rights-based inter-legal* approach.

3.2. What is Regulation?

Karen Yeung defines regulation as 'the sustained and focused attempt by the state to alter behaviour thought to be of value to the community'.[6] On the basis of this definition, Yeung identifies two critical features of regulation: its 'instrumental nature' and its 'public aspect'.[7] With respect to the first, the instrumental nature of regulation implies that its collective value must be assessed primarily in terms of effectiveness – namely, the extent to which a regulatory programme successfully achieves its stated objectives. The public aspect, by contrast, highlights that regulatory goals are pursued through the authority, means, and resources of the state – particularly its unique power of compulsion.[8] Put more clearly, the regulated community is required to conform to prescribed forms of conduct under the threat of sanctions. This coercive capacity, exercised through the issuance of sanctions, is framed as a form of 'public law' that cannot be superseded by private agreements.[9]

[4] See Chapter 2 of this book on this issue.

[5] For the term the 'rule of technology', see R Brownsword and K Yeung, *Regulating Technologies: Legal Futures, Regulatory Frames and Technological Fixes* (Hart Publishing, 2008). As analysed below, the AI Act provides legal mechanisms for AI providers to claim legitimacy through self-assessed checks. It is worth considering that these mechanisms may create new and innovative ways for the 'masters of the code of capital' – namely, lawyers – to circumvent the legal rules defined in the AI Act. Thus, the problem may not be limited to the 'rule of technology' but also extend to the 'rule of lawyers'. See K Pistor, *The Code of Capital: How the Law Creates Wealth and Inequality* (Princeton University Press, 2019). Pistor explains how law has been placed in the service of capital and thereby exacerbates inequality in society.

[6] K Yeung, *Securing Compliance: A Principled Framework* (Hart Publishing, 2004) 5. P Drahos (ed), *Regulatory Theory: Foundations and Applications* (Australian National University Press, 2017); T Wischmeyer and T Rademacher (eds), *Regulating Artificial Intelligence* (Springer, 2020).

[7] Yeung, *Securing Compliance* (2004), 29.

[8] Yeung, *Securing Compliance* (2004), 29–30.

[9] Yeung, *Securing Compliance* (2004), 29–30.

In this regard, regulatory programmes can be analysed and evaluated through the lens of these two defining characteristics of regulation. On the one hand, their instrumental nature can be concretised by specifying particular regulatory goals that serve to advance the overarching purposes of regulation. On the other hand, their public aspect can be framed in relation to a variety of factors that shape and constrain regulatory decision-making, particularly those derived from constitutional values grounded in liberal democratic theory.[10] Within this framework, regulatory goals and constitutional values may be classified separately, as follows in Table 3.1 below.[11]

Table 3.1 Regulatory Goals and Constitutional Values

Regulatory Goals	Constitutional Values
Efficiency	Authorised by Law
Clarity and Predictability	Certainty and Stability
Flexibility, Responsiveness, and Timeliness	Accountability and Transparency
	Procedural Fairness and Due Process
	Proportionality, Consistency, and Rationality

Because of the public aspect of regulation, constitutional values and principles inevitably shape and constrain the design and implementation of regulatory programmes for AI systems. Accordingly, such regulations must be assessed not only in terms of their efficiency and timeliness in achieving policy objectives, but also in light of their consistency with underlying constitutional values and principles. With this fundamental dimension of regulation in view, this chapter proceeds to analyse the current legal models discussed in the literature on AI governance, before turning to an examination of the EU's risk-based approach.

3.3. Existing Approaches Surrounding Artificial Intelligence Systems

There are five primary legal approaches to the regulation of AI: the black-letter law model, the emergent model, the ethical model, the risk regulation model, and the rights-based model.[12] This section sets out to define each of these approaches,

[10] Yeung, *Securing Compliance* (2004), 29–30.

[11] Yeung, *Securing Compliance* (2004), 29–55. The table was constructed by the author of this book, drawing on content from the cited literature.

[12] A clear overview of legal and regulatory initiatives concerning AI can be found in N Petit and J De Cooman, 'Models of Law and Regulation for AI' (2020) EUI Working Papers, Robert Schuman Centre for Advanced Studies 2020/63, 1–21. The authors identify four regulatory models in this article: the black-letter law model, the emergent model, the ethical model, and the risk regulation model. Within this framework, they subsume the rights-based model under the category of black letter law. However,

and to assess their respective advantages and disadvantages. The latter two models – the risk regulation model and the rights-based model – are given more detailed consideration in the following sections.

The black-letter law[13] model focuses on the application of existing legal frameworks to emerging AI systems. Its starting point is the identification of relevant legal provisions that may govern or intersect with the operation of such technologies.[14] Within the law and AI scholarship, the most frequently discussed areas include intellectual property, product safety and liability, legal personhood, consumer protection, labour law, privacy, civil liability, criminal liability, insurance, and tax law.[15]

The emergent model, by contrast, focuses on specific classes of AI applications and asks whether such applications necessitate the creation of an entirely 'new branch of law'.[16] Given that AI systems raise novel and often highly specific legal challenges, this model seeks a *sui generis* legal framework, typically naming it after the application in question – for example, 'the law of drones',[17] 'the law of driverless cars',[18] or 'the law of robots'.[19] In the literature, this approach is often linked to the notion of 'the law of the horse', an intellectual stance that characterises the need to establish a new body of law each time a transformative technology emerges.[20]

it is important to distinguish between the black-letter law model and the rights-based model. Whereas the former refers to a narrower, more formal approach, the rights-based approach embodies a more dynamic and expansive perspective, owing to the abstract normative forms of fundamental and human rights. Accordingly, the rights-based approach merits separate analysis. For a comparison between ordinary legal norms and fundamental rights, see D Grimm, 'Fundamental Rights in the Interpretation of German Constitutional Court' in D Grimm, *Constitutionalism: Past, Present, and Future* (Oxford University Press, 2016) 167–69 (discussing that the classic legal norm has an 'if-then' structure containing a condition and a consequence, while fundamental rights declare a certain conduct or a certain state or social institutions to be free). See also R Alexy, *A Theory of Constitutional Rights* (Oxford University Press, 2010) 44 (rather than focusing on the vagueness of the respective legal norm, he explains fundamental rights as 'principles' ('optimization commands') that depend on other norms and factual circumstances to be fulfilled. Rules, on the other hand, depend on the respective case where it is applicable or not. In other words, while the fulfilment of a fundamental right is relative, and is subjected to balancing, the fulfilment of a rule must be realised as long as it is applicable).

[13] See a definition published by the Legal Information Institute of Cornell Law School, 'Black Letter Law', available at law.cornell.edu/wex/black_letter_law ('Basic standard rules that are generally known and free from doubt. The black letter law on any subject consists of rules that can be applied in a very mechanical way without moral qualms or other considerations.').

[14] Petit and De Cooman (2020), 2.

[15] W Barfield (ed), *The Cambridge Handbook of the Law of Algorithms* (Cambridge University Press, 2021). See also E Palmerini and E Stradella (eds), *Law and Technology: The Challenge of Regulating Technological Development* (Pisa University Press, 2013).

[16] Petit and De Cooman (2020), 3–4.

[17] European Parliament, 'Civil and Military Drones: Navigating a Disruptive and Dynamic Technological Ecosystem' (2019), available at europarl.europa.eu/RegData/etudes/BRIE/2019/642230/EPRS_BRI(2019)642230_EN.pdf.

[18] M Channon, L McCormick, and K Noussia, *The Law and Autonomous Vehicles* (Informa Law from Routledge, 2019).

[19] U Pagallo, *The Laws of Robots: Crimes, Contracts, and Torts* (Law, Governance and Technology Series, vol 10, Springer, 2013).

[20] FH Easterbrook, 'Cyberspace and the Law of the Horse' (1996) *University of Chicago Legal Forum* 207–16.

The expression 'law of the horse' gained prominence in a 1996 cyberlaw conference presentation by Justice Frank H. Easterbrook.[21] In that presentation, Easterbrook argued that, rather than adopting a *sui generis* and fragmented approach that tailors distinct legal regimes to each new technological development, legal analysis should focus on the study of general rules and principles, and on how these can be applied to 'new' circumstances:

> Lots of cases deal with sales of horses; others deal with people kicked by horses; still more deal with the licensing and racing of horses, or with the care veterinarians give to horses, or with prizes at horse shows. Any effort to collect these strands into a course on 'The Law of the Horse' is doomed to be shallow and to miss unifying principles. … Only by putting the law of the horse in the context of broader rules about commercial endeavours could one really understand the law about horses.[22]

Easterbrook further argued that 'the law of the horse' risks becoming both outdated and weak, as it stands isolated from the broader legal system. He therefore concluded that it is preferable to 'develop a sound law of intellectual property, then apply it to computer networks' rather than crafting entirely new and fragmented legal domains.[23] From this non-law-of-the-horse perspective, the regulation of AI should not centre on creating a distinct 'law of AI'. Instead, the emphasis should be placed on examining how existing branches of law – and the general rules and principles underpinning them – can be applied, interpreted, and adapted to the regulation of contemporary AI systems.

The third approach is the ethical model. As Tasioulas explains, two interlocking questions lie at the heart of ethics: '*what is it to live a good or flourishing life*?' and '*what is it that we owe to others, notably fellow human beings, but also nonhuman animals or even inanimate nature*?'[24] Building on these foundational inquiries, the ethical model emphasises the role of ethical reasoning in shaping the law and regulation of AI systems. As discussed in chapter two, although there is no consensus regarding which particular field of ethics should serve as the foundation for AI regulation[25] – a divergence that may, in fact, represent one of ethics' key strengths – the Ethics Guidelines produced by the High-Level Expert Group

[21] FH Easterbrook, 'Cyberspace and the Law of the Horse' (1996).

[22] FH Easterbrook, 'Cyberspace and the Law of the Horse' (1996), 206–07.

[23] FH Easterbrook, 'Cyberspace and the Law of the Horse' (1996), 207.

[24] J Tasioulas, 'Artificial Intelligence, Humanistic Ethics' (2022) 151(2) *Dædalus: Journal of the American Academy of Arts & Sciences* 232.

[25] There are four prominent fields of ethics in this context: roboethics, computer ethics, machine ethics, and bioethics. These fields are explored in several leading works: P Lin, K Abney, and GA Bekey, *Robot Ethics: The Ethical and Social Implications of Robotics* (MIT Press, 2014); L Floridi (ed), *The Cambridge Handbook of Information and Computer Ethics* (Cambridge University Press, 2010); and M Anderson and SL Anderson, *Machine Ethics* (Cambridge University Press, 2011). With respect to bioethics, see PE Ekmekci and B Arda, *Artificial Intelligence and Bioethics* (Springer, 2020); and B Feuillet-Liger and K Orfali, *The Reality of Human Dignity in Law and Bioethics: Comparative Perspectives* (Springer, 2018). See also J Tasioulas, 'Artificial Intelligence, Humanistic Ethics' (2022), 232–43.

on Artificial Intelligence (HLEGAI)[26] propose three key functions of ethics in addressing AI-related challenges: (i) identifying how technologies may give rise to distinct moral considerations; (ii) offering more fine-grained guidance on what we ought to do with technology, as opposed to what we can do; and (iii) grounding and complementing the protection of fundamental rights.

The shortcomings of these models have been extensively examined in the literature.[27] The black-letter law model, for example, risks generating significant blind spots, and, over time, may lose relevance in relation to the evolving technological landscape.[28] This is because laws are typically designed with reference to specific representations of the world at a given moment, and may therefore appear overly abstract or ill-suited when applied to new contexts. Although the black-letter law model initially appears economical and efficient, given its reliance on existing legal frameworks, it nonetheless carries the potential to generate unforeseen social and economic costs. Therefore, reasoning that relies exclusively on existing rules while resting on an imperfect understanding of the underlying technology risks producing incorrect normative outcomes.[29]

Moreover, the relationship between legal and practical discourse is particularly salient when considered through the lens of Alexy's 'special case thesis' *(Sonderfallthese)*.[30] According to this thesis, legal discourse represents a special case of practical discourse.[31] This can be clarified in two steps. First, legal discourse is an instance of general practical discourse insofar as it addresses questions of what is obligatory, prohibited, and/or permitted – questions that are practical in nature.[32] Second, legal discourse is a special case because it resolves these questions within the framework of a particular legal system which constrains practical reasoning through binding norms, statutes, precedents, and doctrines. These constraints endow legal discourse with its authoritative and institutional character, thereby distinguishing it from general practical

[26] European Commission, HLEGAI, 'Ethics Guidelines for Trustworthy AI' (2019), available at aepd.es/sites/default/files/2019-12/ai-ethics-guidelines.pdf.

[27] Petit and De Cooman (2020), 1–21. See also R Brownsword and M Goodwin, *Law and the Technologies of the Twenty-First Century* (Cambridge University Press, 2012) 46–71 (addressing four failures of lawmakers: (i) failing to take sensible precautionary measures relative to the risks posed by emerging technologies; (ii) pursuing illegitimate objectives; (iii) introducing ineffective interventions not fully fit for purpose; and (iv) failing to establish sustainable regulatory connections, or to make appropriate reconnections where regulation has become disconnected).

[28] Petit and De Cooman (2020), 8–9.

[29] Petit and De Cooman (2020), 8.

[30] Alexy first introduced the 'special case thesis' *(Sonderfallthese)* in his doctoral dissertation 'A Theory of Legal Argumentation', originally published in 1978. See R Alexy, *Theorie der juristischen Argumentation: Die Theorie des rationalen Diskurses als Theorie der juristischen Begründung* (Suhrkamp, 1991) 263. See also R Alexy, *A Theory of Legal Argumentation*, trans R Adler and N MacCormick (Clarendon Press, 1989).

[31] R Alexy, 'The Special Case Thesis' (1999) 12(4) *Ratio Juris* 374 (examining the objections against the 'special case thesis' raised by J Habermas in 1996). See also J Habermas, *Between Facts and Norms: Contributions to a Discourse Theory of Law and Democracy* (MIT Press, 1996) 204, 206.

[32] For a clear explanation, see also M Klatt, 'Robert Alexy's Philosophy of Law as System' in M Klatt (ed), *Institutionalized Reason: The Jurisprudence of Robert Alexy* (Oxford University Press, 2012) 4–5.

discourse.[33] In this sense, the claim to correctness in legal discourse arises from its grounding in a legal order that is valid, institutionalised, and authoritative.[34] Nevertheless, the relationship between legal and practical discourse endures, owing to the open texture of law. As Klatt clearly observes in his analysis of Alexy's jurisprudence: 'The intentions of the lawmaker may be unclear, the language of the law may be vague, norms may stand in conflict, and precedents may be overruled.'[35]

When applied to advanced technologies, the practical discourse surrounding AI has the potential to influence legal discourse, particularly where the latter has not yet adequately addressed the novel features of such systems. In this context, it becomes important to consider what may constitute the elements of practical discourse when legal discourse remains underdeveloped. Extra-legal factors, such as ethical frameworks or guidelines formulated by technology providers, may begin to fill this gap. As a result, judicial reasoning may be shaped, at least in part, by these external norms as they diffuse across the broader normative space.[36]

The emergent model, which reflects the so-called 'law of the horse' intellectual attitude – namely, the creation of a new legal branch whenever a new technology arises – is not without controversy. Its primary shortcoming lies in the risk of redundancy.[37] Since AI systems are designed to mimic human behaviours, the legal issues they generate may often overlap with those already addressed by existing legal frameworks governing human conduct, thereby raising the problem of duplicative or unnecessary legal regimes.[38] Furthermore, the emergent model differs fundamentally from the black-letter law model. While the emergent model is concerned with questions of *ex ante* legal design, seeking to establish new legal frameworks in anticipation of technological developments, the black-letter law model focuses on *ex post* legal design, relying on the application of existing laws to new technological contexts.

However, the *ex ante* orientation of the emergent model may prove ineffective in practice. On the one hand, the model has the advantage of capturing the specific transformations introduced by AI systems, since its focus lies on the unique features of the technology at issue. As argued in chapter one of this book, AI systems represent a breaking point in the protection of fundamental and human rights. On the other hand, as Easterbrook cautioned in his critique of the 'law of the horse', the rapidly evolving nature of AI – belonging to a 'fast-evolving

[33] Klatt, 'Robert Alexy's Philosophy of Law as System' (2012), 4–5.
[34] Alexy, 'The Special Case Thesis' (1999), 375.
[35] Klatt, 'Robert Alexy's Philosophy of Law as System' (2012), 5.
[36] M Hildebrandt, 'Closure: On Ethics, Code and Law' in M Hildebrandt, *Law for Computer Scientists* (Oxford University Press, 2020) 284–318 (arguing that, although ethics does not have the force of law, it may acquire the force of technology, as it can be developed by technology developers; in this way, ethics can diffuse into the normative space).
[37] Petit and De Cooman (2020), 9.
[38] Petit and De Cooman (2020), 9.

family of technologies'[39] – renders arguments grounded in this model particularly vulnerable to becoming outdated, weak, and isolated from broader legal discourse.

The challenges of 'ethics washing' (or 'ethics lobbying'),[40] 'ethical relativism', and 'ethics shopping'[41] have been highlighted in the literature, to illustrate the fallacies of the ethical model.[42] In this context, 'ethics washing' refers to the practice of ethical 'window-dressing'. Here, ethics becomes an industry-driven tool of self-regulation, strategically employed to prioritise corporate interests and circumvent legal accountability.[43] Put differently, ethics initiatives – particularly those sponsored by industry actors – may be deployed to delay, weaken, or even replace binding legislation, thereby undermining their normative value.[44]

Ethical relativism is a thesis in meta-ethics which holds that moral criteria depend on non-moral variables, such as culture, time, and location.[45] Accordingly, as Tasioulas explains,

> judgments that are true or justified according to one set of standards may not be true or justified according to a different set, and … between the two sets of standards no assessment of rational superiority can be made or could in principle be made that is not simply question-begging.[46]

Applied to AI systems, ethical relativism raises a critical question: which culture's moral standards or customs should be adopted? As Bostrom underscores, this question becomes particularly important in light of AI's global reach and transnational deployment.[47]

[39] Proposal for a Regulation of the European Parliament and of the Council Laying down Harmonised Rules on Artificial Intelligence (Artificial Intelligence Act) and Amending Certain Union Legislative Acts, COM (2021) 206 final, 2021/0106 (COD), 21 April 2021 (Brussels), Explanatory Memorandum, 1.

[40] B Wagner, 'Ethics as an Escape from Regulation: From Ethics-Washing to Ethics-Shopping?' in M Hildebrandt and S Gutwirth (eds), *Being Profiled: Cogitas ergo sum* (Amsterdam University Press, 2018) 84 ('Ethical frameworks that provide a way to go beyond existing legal frameworks can also provide an opportunity to ignore them.').

[41] L Floridi, 'Translating Principles into Practices of Digital Ethics: Five Risks of Being Unethical' (2019) 32 *Philosophy & Technology* 185–93.

[42] Petit and De Cooman (2020) 10–11.

[43] In this regard, Wagner gives a clear example of the Google DeepMind Ethics Team, which avoided any legal responsibility regarding data protection despite repeated emphasis on how ethically Google DeepMind was acting. See Wagner, 'Ethics as an Escape from Regulation: From Ethics-Washing to Ethics-Shopping?' (2018) 84.

[44] B Mittelstadt, 'Principles Alone Cannot Guarantee Ethical AI' (2019) 1(11) *Nature Machine Intelligence* 501.

[45] I kindly thank Prof Damiano Canale, professor of philosophy of law and critical thinking at Bocconi University, Milan, for his valuable feedback, which helped to clarify the discussion of this issue.

[46] J Tasioulas, 'Consequences of Ethical Relativism' (1998) 6(2) *European Journal of Philosophy* 156–71.

[47] N Bostrom, *Superintelligence: Paths, Dangers, Strategies* (Oxford University Press, 2014). 'The trolley problem' can also be considered to illustrate ethical relativism: 'suppose you are the driver of a trolley. The trolley rounds a bend, and there come into view ahead five track workmen, who have been repairing the track. The track goes through a bit of a valley at that point, and the sides are steep, so you must stop the trolley if you are to avoid running the five men down. You step on the brakes, but alas they don't work. Now you suddenly see a spur of track leading off to the right. You can turn the

The practice of 'ethics shopping' further illustrates the problematic dimensions of the ethical model. This phenomenon is closely connected to the 'ethics congestion' produced by the proliferation of hundreds of guidelines and recommendations on AI ethics. Such congestion generates confusion and inconsistency as to which ethical framework should be regarded as authoritative or appropriate. Consequently, both private and public actors engaged in the development or deployment of AI systems tend to 'shop' for the ethical approach that best aligns with and legitimates their existing behaviours or agendas. In the literature, Floridi has offered a compact definition of this practice:

> [T]he malpractice of choosing, adapting, or revising ('mixing and matching') ethical principles, guidelines, codes, frameworks, or other similar standards (especially but not only in the ethics of AI), from a variety of available offers, in order to retrofit some pre-existing behaviours (choices, processes, strategies, etc.), and hence justify them a posteriori, instead of implementing or improving new behaviours by benchmarking them against public, ethical standards.[48]

In this regard, one may observe that companies often conduct AI research in ethically weak jurisdictions or export ethically weak AI systems to such contexts. The broader risk is the creation of a 'market of principles and values'[49] in which actors select not the most socially accepted or normatively robust ethical framework, but rather the one that best serves their own interests. Taken together, these three fallacies of the ethical model demonstrate that, while ethics remains inescapable in the governance of AI, the ethical model on its own can neither serve as a concrete policy alternative nor as an easy alternative for governmental regulation.[50]

Within these models, the rights-based approach has emerged as a central focus of legal scholarship from the very outset of discussions on AI law and regulation. While this model will be explored in greater detail in the following sections, it should already be noted that the 'rights-based approach' is fundamentally grounded in the frameworks of human rights, democracy, and the rule of law.[51]

trolley on to it, and thus save the five men on the straight track ahead. Unfortunately, ... there is one track workman on that spur of track. He can no more get off the track in time than the five can, so you will kill him if you turn the trolley onto him. Is it morally permissible for you to turn the trolley?'. See JJ Thomson, 'The Trolley Problem' (1995) 94(6) *Yale Law Journal* 1395–415. See also Massachusetts Institute of Technology (MIT), 'Moral Machine Experiment', available at moralmachine.net/; and J-F Bonnefon, *The Car That Knew Too Much: Can a Machine Be Moral?* (MIT Press, 2021).

[48] Floridi, 'Translating Principles into Practices of Digital Ethics: Five Risks of Being Unethical' (2019), 186.

[49] Floridi, 'Translating Principles into Practices of Digital Ethics' (2019), 185–93.

[50] See Wagner, 'Ethics as an Escape from Regulation: From Ethics-Washing to Ethics-Shopping?' (2018), 84.

[51] There are at least 12 leading documents dealing with European values, fundamental rights, and principles in the context of AI and robotics. See European Parliament, 'Draft Report on Civil Law Rules and Robotics' (2016); European Parliament, 'Report on Civil Law Rules and Robotics' (2017); European Commission, 'Communication: Artificial Intelligence for Europe' (2018); European Commission, 'Statement on Artificial Intelligence, Robotics and Autonomous Systems' (2018); European Commission, HLEG-AI, 'A Definition of AI' (2018); European Commission, HLEG-AI, 'Draft Ethics

The fifth model is the risk regulation model. This approach is concerned with developing strategies to mitigate the potential harms associated with AI systems. Its primary focus lies in the monitoring and management of risks that may have serious consequences for individuals and communities. The European Commission has explicitly endorsed this model, emphasising that 'a regulatory framework should concentrate on how to minimise the various risks of potential harm'.[52] This orientation has subsequently been formalised in the AI Act Proposal, introduced by the European Commission in April 2021.[53] Given that the EU has clearly committed itself to a risk-based approach to AI regulation,[54] it becomes crucial to critically reflect on the notion of risk regulation in order to determine whether it is capable of ensuring the protection of the rule of law, and of fundamental rights and freedoms in the digital sphere.

3.4. The Analysis of the European Union's Legal Approach

3.4.1. The Notion of Risk Regulation

The notion of risk regulation has held significant influence across legal systems worldwide, attracting considerable attention from legal scholars in diverse fields.[55] It has been described as 'governmental interference with market or social processes to control potential adverse consequences to health'.[56] Despite the apparent simplicity of this definition, the practice of risk regulation has given rise to a wide range of approaches to both risk assessment and risk management. This may be due to the fact that, as Beck observes, the essence of risk lies not in the present

Guidelines for Trustworthy AI' (2018); European Commission, HLEG-AI, 'Ethics Guidelines for Trustworthy AI' (2019); European Commission, 'Communication: Building Trust in Human-Centric Artificial Intelligence' (2019); European Commission, 'White Paper on Artificial Intelligence' (2020); European Commission, 'Shaping Europe's Digital Future' (2020); European Commission, 'Europe's Strategy for Data' (2020); European Commission, 'Report on the Safety and Liability Implications of Artificial Intelligence, the Internet of Things and Robotics' (2020).

[52] European Commission, 'White Paper on Artificial Intelligence: A European Approach to Excellence and Trust' (Brussels, 19 February 2020) COM(2020) 65 final, 10.

[53] AI Act Proposal (n 39).

[54] It is important to note that the risk-based approach is not only applied in the context of AI systems but also in other domains of advanced technologies. Indeed, risk has become a central feature of EU regulation of digital technologies. See G De Gregorio and P Dunn, 'The European Risk-Based Approaches: Connecting Constitutional Dots in the Digital Age' (2022) 59(2) *Common Market Law Review* 473–500.

[55] C Hood, H Rothstein, and R Baldwin, *The Government of Risk: Understanding Risk Regulation Regimes* (Oxford University Press, 2001). According to Hood, there are three key factors that establish the regime context of risk regulation: the type of risk, public preferences and attitudes, and organised interests.

[56] Hood, Rothstein and Baldwin, *The Government of Risk* (2001), 3.

but in the uncertainty of the future, compelling us to act today in anticipation of the crises of tomorrow:

> The center of risk consciousness lies not in the present, but in the future. In the risk society, the past loses the power to determine the present. Its place is taken by the future, thus, something non-existent, invented, fictive as the 'cause' of current experience and action. We become active today in order to prevent, alleviate or take precautions against the problems and crises of tomorrow and the day after tomorrow – or not to do so.[57]

This future-oriented standpoint closely aligns with the precautionary principle, which seeks to prevent or minimise actions that may generate risks of harm.[58] As Harramoes notes, this orientation may arise from the inherent tension between two dimensions of scientific practice: 'Society's growing commitment to the precautionary principle is essentially a response to a growing tension between two aspects of science: its growing innovative powers were increasingly outrunning its capacity to anticipate the consequences.'[59]

As long as the tension between these two aspects of science endures, scholarly and practical engagement with the precautionary principle will remain persistent. For this reason, the principle constitutes the primary focus of the following section.

3.4.1.1. The Precautionary Principle

The precautionary principle calls for *ex ante* measures aimed at preventing potential harms before they materialise.[60] Its origins lie in philosophy, specifically the *Vorsorgeprinzip*,[61] which subsequently evolved into a recognised legal standard.[62] The principle was first acknowledged at the international level in 1982, when the United Nations World Charter for Nature declared that,

[57] U Beck, *Risk Society: Towards a New Modernity* (Sage Publications, 1992) 34.

[58] CR Sunstein, 'Beyond the Precautionary Principle' (2002) University of Chicago, John M Olin Law & Economics Working Paper No 149, 2.

[59] P Harremoes et al (eds), *The Precautionary Principle in the 20th Century: Late Lessons from Early Warnings* (European Environment Agency Earthscan, 2002) 209.

[60] CR Sunstein, *Laws of Fear Beyond the Precautionary Principle* (Cambridge University Press, 2005).

[61] S Boehmer-Christiansen, 'The Precautionary Principle in Germany: Enabling Government' in T O'Riordan and J Cameron (eds), *Interpreting the Precautionary Principle* (Earthscan, 1994) 31–66; H Jonas, *Das Prinzip Verantwortung: Versuch einer Ethik für die Technologische Zivilisation*, 5th edn (Suhrkamp, 2003); H Jonas, The Imperative of Responsibility: In Search of Ethics for the Technological Age, trans H Jonas with the collaboration of D Herr (University of Chicago Press, 1984) x (suggesting an epistemic interpretation of the precautionary principle on the basis of a 'heuristic of fear' *(Heuristik der Furcht)*, meaning to give more weight to pessimistic forecasts than to optimistic ones, given the insufficiency of our predictive knowledge). See also N Dinneen, 'Precautionary Discourse: Thinking Through the Distinction Between the Precautionary Principle and the Precautionary Approach in Theory and Practice' (2013) 32(1) *Politics and the Life Sciences* 2–21 (discussing the theoretical foundation of the precautionary principle in the philosophy of Hans Jonas).

[62] The ECtHR clearly emphasised this point in *Tătar v Romania* App no 67021/01 (ECtHR, 27 January 2009), para 65: 'l'évolution du principe d'une conception philosophique vers une norme juridique'.

whenever 'potential adverse effects are fully understood, the activities should not proceed'.[63] Since then, the principle has gained broad international acceptance and support.[64]

In 1992, the principle was explicitly articulated in Principle 15 of the Rio Declaration, which affirms that:

> in order to protect the environment, the precautionary approach shall be widely applied by States according to their capabilities. Where there are threats of serious or irreversible damage, lack of full scientific certainty shall not be used as a reason for postponing cost-effective measures to prevent environmental degradation.[65]

Put differently, the Rio Declaration underscores that the absence of conclusive evidence of harm or full scientific certainty should not serve as a justification for regulatory inaction.[66] More recently, in 2001, the principle was recognised beyond the legal and environmental sphere, being listed by the *New York Times Magazine* as one of the most important ideas of the year.[67]

Within the EU, the precautionary principle has become a fundamental governing policy tool, particularly in the fields of health and environmental protection. Article 191 of the Treaty on the Functioning of the European Union (TFEU) explicitly provides that Union policy on the environment 'shall be based on the precautionary principle'.[68] One of the earliest judicial interpretations of this principle emerged in the decision of the Court of First Instance (CFI) in *Pfizer*,[69] where the Court observed that:

> the Community institutions may, by reason of the precautionary principle, take protective measures without having to wait until the reality and seriousness of those risks

[63] IM Goklany, *The Precautionary Principle: A Critical Appraisal of Environmental Risk Assessment* (Cato Institute, 2001) 4. See also United Nations, *World Charter for Nature* (28 October 1982), available at refworld.org/docid/3b00f22a10.html.

[64] A Trouwborst, *Evolution and Status of the Precautionary Principle in International Law* (Springer, 2002).

[65] United Nations, 'Rio Declaration on Environment and Development', in 'Report of the United Nations Conference on Environment and Development' (12 August 1992), available at un.org/en/development/desa/population/migration/generalassembly/docs/globalcompact/A_CONF.151_26_Vol.I_Declaration.pdf.

[66] In this regard, see Art 3(3) of the United Nations Framework Convention on Climate Change (opened for signature 9 May 1992, entered into force 21 March 1994) 1771 UNTS 107, which provides: 'where there are threats of serious or irreversible damage, lack of full scientific certainty should not be used as a reason for postponing measures, taking into account that policies and measures to deal with climate change should be cost-effective so as to ensure global benefits at the lowest possible cost', available at unfccc.int/files/essential_background/background_publications_htmlpdf/application/pdf/conveng.pdf.

[67] 'The Year in Ideas: A to Z' (*New York Times*, 9 December 2001), available at nytimes.com/2001/12/09/magazine/the-year-in-ideas-a-to-z-precautionary-principle.html.

[68] Consolidated Version of the Treaty on the Functioning of the European Union (2012) OJ C 326/47. Art 191. See also K Purnhagen, *The Politics of Systematization in EU Product Safety Regulation: Market, State, Collectivity, and Integration* (Springer, 2013). It has been argued that the 'European risk regulation regime' has been systematised by the CJEU. The Court did not create another brick for the 'right to safety'; instead, it cited previous judgments and tested whether they had been applied properly in the case at hand. Accordingly, one can predict that the European risk regulation regime for AI is also likely to be shaped through the case law of the CJEU.

[69] Case T-13/99 *Pfizer Animal Health SA v Council of the European Union* [2002] ECR II-3305.

> become fully apparent[70] … If the Community institutions were unable to take any preventive protective measures until such research was completed, the precautionary principle, the aim of which is to prevent the occurrence of any such adverse effects, would be rendered devoid of purpose.[71]

In the legal scholarship, a particularly clear definition of the precautionary principle has been advanced by Stewart, who identifies four specific subcategories of the principle, which Sunstein paraphrased accurately, namely:

(i) the 'nonpreclusion precautionary principle', meaning that regulation should not be precluded by the lack of scientific uncertainty about activities that pose a potential significant risk of harm;
(ii) the 'margin of safety precautionary principle', meaning that regulation should cover a margin of safety – that is to say, limiting activities below the level at which adverse effects have not been observed or predicted;
(iii) the 'best available technology precautionary principle', meaning that best technology requirements should be provided for activities that present an uncertain potential for substantial harm, unless 'the proponent of the activity shows that they present no appreciable risk of harm'; and
(iv) the 'prohibitory precautionary principle', meaning that prohibitions should be applied to activities that present an uncertain potential for substantial harm unless 'the proponent of the activity shows that it presents no appreciable risk of harm'.[72]

A significant debate within the legal literature concerns whether the precautionary principle should be applied in stronger or weaker forms. In these discussions, the principle is often conceptualised as a 'scale', assessing how approaches to these activities may raise threats of harm.[73] This scale ranges from weaker to stronger expressions, applications, or levels of the principle. It is also important to recognise, as Fisher emphasises, that 'how the precautionary principle will be formulated, interpreted and implemented will be largely a product of legal culture'.[74]

Although the precautionary principle was initially developed within the field of environmental law,[75] it has more recently been applied across a broader range

[70] Case T-13/99 *Pfizer*, para 139.

[71] Case T-13/99 *Pfizer*, paras 139, 386. E Vos, 'Antibiotics, the Precautionary Principle and the Court of First Instance: Cases T-13/99 *Pfizer Animal Health SA v Council of the European Union* and T-70/99 *Alpharma Inc v Council of the European Union*' (2004) 11(2) Maastricht Journal of European and Comparative Law 187–200.

[72] CR Sunstein, 'Beyond the Precautionary Principle' (2002) University of Chicago, John M Olin Law & Economics Working Paper No 149, 10–11. RB Stewart, 'Environmental Regulatory Decision Making Under Uncertainty' (2001) *University College London Symposium on the Law & Economics of Environmental Policy* 20, available at ucl.ac.uk/cserge/Stewart.pdf.

[73] See nn 58 and 60.

[74] E Fisher, 'Precaution, Precaution Everywhere: Developing a "Common Understanding" of the Precautionary Principle in the European Community' (2002) 9(1) *Maastricht Journal of European and Comparative Law* 18.

[75] A Trouwborst, *Evolution and Status of the Precautionary Principle in International Law* (Springer, 2002).

of contexts, including the regulation of emerging technologies.[76] A cursory overview of its application reveals the growing appeal of the principle as a form of 'regulatory insurance' – a mechanism designed to anticipate and prevent potential disasters before they materialise.[77]

One of the major criticisms of the precautionary principle is that it lacks the capacity to adequately address all dimensions of complex social situations.[78] In 1980, David Collingridge crystallised this challenge in the context of emerging technologies, a problem that has since become known in philosophical discourse as the 'Collingridge dilemma':

> Attempting to control a technology is difficult and not rarely impossible, because during its early stages, when it can be controlled, not enough can be known about its harmful social consequences to warrant controlling its development; but by the time these consequences are apparent, control has become costly and slow.[79]

Given that AI systems function as *social* systems, as outlined in chapter two of this book, the Collingridge dilemma carries profound implications. Most notably, it highlights the difficulty of applying the precautionary principle to AI, since the inherently *social* character of these systems brings with it a multiplicity of social factors and values that may ultimately hinder the sustained application of precautionary measures. A vivid illustration of this can be found in the rapid emergence of large language models (LLMs) in late 2022. These systems exemplify how technological capabilities can diffuse quickly into social and professional domains, generating new opportunities while simultaneously creating risks of over-reliance. As LLMs become increasingly integrated into decision-making, education, and communication, their social embedding amplifies both their utility and their potential for harm, making early intervention difficult and raising the very dilemma Collingridge described: the tendency for risks to become most visible only after widespread adoption, when corrective action is most difficult to pursue.

This situation also suggests that the common assumption that technology simply develops too quickly for the law to keep pace may be somewhat misguided. The gap does not arise solely from the speed of technological change, but also from the fact that the law lacks sufficiently informed and qualified observations about technological practices – an issue that should not be regarded as the law's concern alone. The law's first step, therefore, should be to render such experiences more visible; that is, to ensure greater transparency. Providers, who enjoy direct access

[76] R Andorno, 'The Precautionary Principle: A New Legal Standard for a Technological Age' (2004) 1(1) *Journal of International Biotechnology Law* 11–19, available at doi.org/10.1515/jibl.2004.1.1.11.

[77] CR Sunstein, 'The Paralyzing Principle' (Winter 2002–03) 25(4) *Regulation* 32–37.

[78] CR Sunstein, 'Beyond the Precautionary Principle' (2002), 5. In this paper, Sunstein draws on insights from behavioural economics to explain the inadequacy of the precautionary principle. He identifies five main reasons: loss aversion, the myth of a benevolent nature, the availability heuristic, probability neglect, and system neglect (see discussion at 5–7).

[79] D Collingridge, *The Social Control of Technology* (St Martin's Press, 1980) 19.

to and partly observe these experiences, hold a position of advantage – and, as is sometimes evident, this advantage may be used in ways that are far from beneficial. Such asymmetries of access and knowledge can create a sense of unfairness in the regulatory landscape.

Moreover, the highly pervasive reach of AI, spanning virtually every domain of human activity, propels us into boundless uncertainty, as each recognised social impact inevitably gives rise to further, unforeseen, consequences. In this sense, one is situated within a vast sea of social uncertainty, wherein hidden currents operate beyond immediate perception or control.[80] At the same time, it is crucial to recognise that debates and conflicts surrounding AI are grounded less in economic interests than in ethical and social values. Accordingly, questions of fundamental rights and the rule of law in the context of AI demand regulatory decision-making processes that incorporate a broader range of considerations than those typically encompassed by market mechanisms. As Feintuck observes with regard to the purpose of a regulatory system:

> Underlying the regulatory system as a whole are the immanent, fundamental values of rationality and accountability on which the polity is premised, and an acceptance, albeit often an implicit one, that the system should acknowledge moral values beyond economic and instrumental values.[81]

The scepticism directed at the precautionary principle and the broader framework of risk regulation necessitates a closer examination of the defining characteristics of risk analysis itself.

3.4.1.2. *The Characteristics of Risk Analysis*

The Society for Risk Analysis (SRA) defines risk analysis as 'a distinct science covering risk assessment, perception, communication, management, governance and policy in the context of risks of concern to individuals, public- and private-sector organizations, and society at a local, regional, national, or global level'.[82] Building on this understanding, Apostolakis identifies three central questions that any risk analysis must address: '(1) What can go wrong? (2) How likely is it? and (3) What are the consequences?'[83]

Before turning to the characteristics of risk analysis, it is essential to distinguish between the notions of risk and uncertainty. A significant distinction was

[80] This situation reminds us of the vital role that methodological and interdisciplinary research plays in this field.

[81] M Feintuck, 'Precautionary Maybe, but What's the Principle? The Precautionary Principle, the Regulation of Risk, and the Public Domain' (2005) 32(3) *Journal of Law and Society* 392 (arguing that, although the principle is largely applied as a procedural tool rather than a substantive one, its utility can be realised if substantive content and value orientation are established).

[82] Society for Risk Analysis, 'Risk Analysis Introduction', available at sra.org/risk-analysis-introduction/.

[83] GE Apostolakis, 'How Useful Is Quantitative Risk Assessment?' (2004) 24(3) *Risk Analysis* 516.

articulated by Knight in 1921.[84] According to Knight, risk pertains to situations in which the decision-maker knows the probabilities of possible outcomes and can, therefore, calculate the odds with reasonable accuracy. Uncertainty, by contrast, arises in situations where the decision-maker lacks sufficient information to determine probabilities or establish accurate odds.[85]

In the case of AI systems, as outlined in chapter two, their *complex*, *dynamic*, and *social* characteristics render their impacts uncertain and not yet fully understood.[86] As Wallach and Marchant observe, AI systems and robotics 'present exceptionally broad and intractable uncertainties about their benefits, risks, and future trajectories'.[87] Such uncertainty poses a significant obstacle to effective decision-making, and if it is overlooked or misinterpreted, decisions made under conditions of profound uncertainty risk generating serious social costs and policy failures.[88] Within the current landscape of AI systems deployed by the public sector in support of public policy decisions, three dynamics can be identified as central sources of uncertainty: (i) the vagueness in the definition of AI; (ii) the unpredictable outcomes of AI applications; and (iii) the pacing problem – the persistent gap between rapid technological innovation and the slower processes of law and governance.[89]

Setting aside, for the moment, the fundamental question of whether uncertainty can, in fact, be overcome through risk analysis methods, it is clear that the EU has embraced a risk-based approach to the regulation of AI systems. Accordingly, before turning to an analysis of the Union's specific approach, it is necessary to outline the defining characteristics of the risk regulation model and to consider its potential advantages and disadvantages.

The risk regulation model is generally understood to rest on three interrelated pillars: risk assessment, risk management, and risk communication. These components are not isolated but, rather, mutually reinforcing, functioning as an integrated framework. Nonetheless, it is important to emphasise that one way to strengthen the input legitimacy of this model is to maintain a clear and stringent distinction

[84] FH Knight, *Risk, Uncertainty and Profit* (Houghton Mifflin Company 1921), 516.

[85] P Dizikes, 'Explained: Knightian Uncertainty – The Economic Crisis Has Revived an Old Philosophical Idea About Risk and Uncertainty. But What Is It, Exactly?' (*MIT News Office*, 2 June 2010), available at news.mit.edu/2010/explained-knightian-0602#:~:text=Therefore%2C%20according%20to%20Knight%2C%20risk,odds%20in%20the%20first%20place.

[86] N Smuha, 'From a "Race to AI" to a "Race to AI Regulation": Regulatory Competition for Artificial Intelligence' (2021) 13(1) *Law, Innovation and Technology* 57–84.

[87] W Wallach and GE Marchant, 'Toward the Agile and Comprehensive International Governance of AI and Robotics' (2019) 107(3) *Proceedings of the IEEE* 505.

[88] Uncertainty is also presented as a 'wicked problem', a concept referring to complex and unpredictable challenges. See BW Head and J Alford, 'Wicked Problems: Implications for Public Policy and Management' (2015) 47(6) *Administration & Society* 711–39.

[89] M Nordström, 'AI under Great Uncertainty: Implications and Decision Strategies for Public Policy' (2021) *AI & Society*, available at doi.org/10.1007/s00146-021-01263-4. Nordström proposes incorporating elements of an argumentative approach framing and temporal strategies to address the uncertainty associated with AI systems in the public sector. By reading the notion of 'framing' as 'a decision problem being formulated in different but logically equivalent ways', Nordström argues that the AI governance community needs to reflect on how issues surrounding AI systems are framed and whether the tech industry is setting the agenda for AI regulation.

between risk assessment and risk management.[90] The purpose of this separation is to safeguard the objectivity of the risk assessment process, and to prevent it from being distorted or manipulated by predetermined policy objectives.[91]

The first pillar, risk assessment, is a process that relies primarily on statistical evidence to evaluate the nature and magnitude of a given risk.[92] Put simply, it constitutes a scientific undertaking. The process begins with the identification of the risk at issue and the factors contributing to it. It then seeks to reach scientifically grounded judgements through the analysis of statistical evidence. In this way, risk assessment provides essential support for decision-making regarding the measures to be adopted.[93] However, under conditions of scientific uncertainty, risk assessment loses much of its effectiveness and efficiency. As a result, the overall effectiveness of a risk regulation model is heavily dependent on the accuracy of the measurements and calculations carried out during the risk assessment process.

In the context of AI systems deployed in criminal justice – for example, a risk assessment tool[94] designed 'to measure the future behavioural risk posed by a defendant and to inform a variety of decisions at different steps of the criminal justice process'[95] – it becomes crucial to conduct an objective evaluation of the risks such systems pose. These risks may concern accuracy, transparency, accountability, privacy, freedom of expression, and fairness, and the key question is whether they can be considered acceptable within a legal system grounded in the rule of law.[96] It is also important to note that, while system designers determine the features and classifications of such tools, they do not directly design the

[90] C Joerges and J Neyer, 'Politics, Risk Management, World Trade Organization Governance and the Limits of Legalization' (2003) 30(3) *Science and Public Policy* 220.

[91] N Doorn and SO Hansson, 'Factors and Margins of Safety' in N Möller et al (eds), *Handbook of Safety Principles* (Wiley, 2018) 100.

[92] D Wright and J Copas, 'Prediction Scores for Risk Assessment' in R Baldwin (ed), *Law and Uncertainty: Risks and Legal Processes* (Kluwer Law International, 1997) 21–38.

[93] T Aven and BS Krohn, 'A New Perspective on How to Understand, Assess and Manage Risk and the Unforeseen' (2014) 121 *Reliability Engineering & System Safety* 1–10.

[94] A well-known example is COMPAS, one of the most widely used risk-assessment tools in the United States. Designed by statistician Tim Brennan, COMPAS is used by criminal justice agencies across the country. See T Brennan, W Dieterich, and B Ehret, 'Evaluating the Predictive Validity of the COMPAS Risk and Needs Assessment System' (2009) 36(1) *Criminal Justice and Behavior* 21–40. In this article, COMPAS is described as 'an automated decision-support software package that integrates risk and needs assessment with several other domains, including sentencing decisions, treatment and case management, and recidivism outcomes'. For a detailed analysis of risk-assessment tools used in the United States, see Electronic Privacy Information Center, 'AI in the Criminal Justice System', available at epic.org/issues/ai/ai-in-the-criminal-justice-system/.

[95] T Scantamburlo, A Charlesworth, and N Cristianini, 'Machine Decisions and Human Consequences' in K Yeung and M Lodge (eds), *Algorithmic Regulation* (Oxford University Press, 2019) 58. See also K Crawford, *Atlas of AI: Power, Politics and the Planetary Cost of Artificial Intelligence* (Yale University Press, 2021) 116–19.

[96] The risk-assessment process of the risk-regulation model should not be confused with that of an AI system designed to evaluate defendants. Whereas the risk-regulation model concerns the assessment of risks posed by the subject matter of regulation, a risk-assessment AI system is concerned with estimating the future behavioural risks posed by an individual defendant. For the sake of clarity, such systems are referred to in this book as 'risk-assessment tools'.

actual decision function.[97] Instead, the decision function is generated by the learning process of the AI system itself, which draws on extensive training data and produces predictions based on statistical correlations.[98]

Risk management, by contrast, is not a scientific undertaking; it has been defined as the 'task of transforming assessments into policies by taking due account of non-scientific concerns'.[99] Its starting point lies in the outcomes of the risk assessment process.[100] The overarching objective of risk management is, as one formulation describes, 'to achieve an appropriate balance between realizing opportunities to achieve benefits on the one hand, and minimizing losses on the other'.[101] To this end, the process involves determining what measures should be adopted in order to mitigate or minimise identified risks.

The final pillar of the risk regulation model, and an integral component of the risk management process, is risk communication; it is defined as 'the exchange of information among interested parties about the nature, magnitude, significance, or control of a risk'.[102] Importantly, the purpose of risk communication is 'not to diffuse public concern or avoid action, but rather to produce an informed public that is involved, interested, reasonable, thoughtful, solution-oriented, and collaborative'.[103] In this regard, Covello and Allen, in 1988, set out seven foundational rules for effective risk communication:

(1) Accept and involve the public as a legitimate partner.
(2) Plan carefully and evaluate performance.

[97] See Scantamburlo, Charlesworth, and Cristianini, 'Machine Decisions and Human Consequences' (2019), 55. According to the authors, in the language of AI, 'features' describe the 'items', and items are assigned to 'classes' referred to as 'labels'. The purpose of an algorithm is to build a 'classifier' that assigns a class label – 'spam' in the case of emails, for instance – to any item that has not previously been classified or labelled.

[98] Scantamburlo, Charlesworth and Cristianini, 'Machine Decisions and Human Consequences' (2019), 55–56.

[99] See Joerges and Neyer, 'Politics, Risk Management, WTO Governance and the Limits of Legalization' (2003), 220.

[100] See Doorn and Hansson, 'Factors and Margins of Safety' (2018), 100.

[101] R Flage, 'Maintenance Optimization and Its Relation to Safety' in N Möller et al (eds), *Handbook of Safety Principles* (2018), 543. See also T Aven and J-E Vinnem, *Risk Management: With Applications from the Offshore Petroleum Industry* (Springer, 2007).

[102] VT Covello, 'Risk Communication: An Emerging Area of Health Communication Research' (1992) 15(1) *Communication Yearbook* 359. See also VT Covello, D von Winterfeldt, and P Slovic, 'Communicating Risk Information to the Public' in JC Davies, VT Covello, and FW Allen (eds), *Risk Communication* (Conservation Foundation, 1987) 109–34. Furthermore, the WHO defines risk communication as 'the real-time exchange of information, advice and opinions between experts or officials and people who face a threat (from a hazard) to their survival, health or economic or social wellbeing': WHO, 'Communication and Community Engagement', available at who.int/emergencies/risk-communications. See also MJ Palenchar and RL Heath, 'Strategic Risk Communication: Adding Value to Society' (2007) 33(2) *Public Relations Review* 120–29.

[103] Covello, 'Risk Communication' (1992), 364. The WHO emphasises that the purpose of risk communication is 'to enable people at risk to make informed decisions to mitigate the effects of a threat (hazard) – such as a disease outbreak – and take protective and preventive measures': WHO, 'Communication and Community Engagement', available at who.int/emergencies/risk-communications.

(3) Listen to your audience.
(4) Be honest, frank, and open.
(5) Coordinate and collaborate with other credible sources.
(6) Meet the needs of the media.
(7) Speak clearly and with compassion.[104]

Four major problems have been identified in the effective communication of risk-related information: (i) the characteristics and limitations of scientific data concerning risks; (ii) the characteristics and limitations of government officials, industry representatives, and other spokespersons responsible for communicating such information; (iii) the characteristics and limitations of the media in reporting on risks; and (iv) the characteristics and limitations of the public in evaluating and interpreting risk information.[105] Taken together, these difficulties reveal four inherent limitations of the risk regulation model itself, namely those arising from science, interested parties, media, and the public:

Figure 3.1 Risk Communication

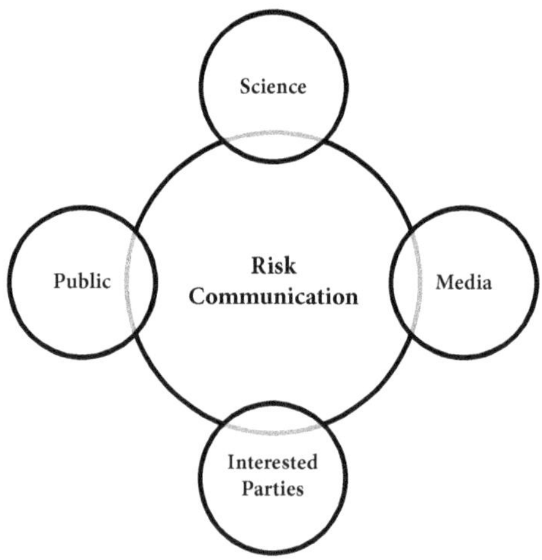

The 'Science' circle of the Venn diagram[106] concerns the uncertainties inherent in scientific data, models, and methods. It has been emphasised that, even when risk assessments are conducted with rigour, they seldom provide sufficient answers.[107] In other words, the outcomes of most risk assessments are, at best,

[104] V Covello and FW Allen, *Seven Cardinal Rules of Risk Communication* (US Environmental Protection Agency, Office of Policy Analysis, 1988), available at archive.epa.gov/publicinvolvement/web/pdf/risk.pdf. These seven rules were designed to guide the risk-communication policy of the US Environmental Protection Agency in 1988.
[105] Covello, 'Risk Communication' (1992), 360–67.
[106] The Venn diagram is an original contribution of the author of the book.
[107] Covello, 'Risk Communication' (1992), 360.

approximations. These scientific uncertainties inevitably undermine effective communication with the public, as they generate incomplete representations of risk-related issues.

The 'Media' circle addresses the role of mass media in transmitting risk-related information.[108] Media coverage may prove deficient when risks are oversimplified, distorted, or misreported.[109] As has been noted, such deficiencies arise 'not only in what is contained in stories, but in what is left out'.[110] In the context of AI, for example, deficiencies occur when reporting emphasises speculative or futuristic portrayals – often shaped by popular culture and science fiction – rather than offering accurate accounts of existing AI systems and their actual applications. Such coverage risks misleading the public and obscuring pressing regulatory challenges. Furthermore, the media ecosystem may reflect the market-oriented rhetoric. 'AI snake oil', a term promoted by Arvind Narayanan and Sayash Kapoor in their book *AI Snake Oil: What Artificial Intelligence Can Do, What It Can't, and How to Tell the Difference*, refers to the marketing strategy whereby companies exaggerate the capabilities of AI to promote products or services that fail to deliver substantive value.[111] Furthermore, it is important to underline that, while the market exploits such language for profit, this kind of hype is far from new in the field. As Weizenbaum observed as early as 1976, even highly educated individuals are prone to exaggerating the capabilities of these machines.[112] Evidently, these dynamics significantly undermine the possibility of accessing accurate and reliable information about risk.

The 'Interested Parties' circle concerns the public and private actors responsible for communicating information about risks. Although these actors are often regarded as the most knowledgeable sources, they are simultaneously perceived as the least trustworthy. For instance, the 2022 Edelman Trust Barometer, based on surveys in 28 countries, found that distrust has become society's 'default emotion', with 60 per cent of respondents indicating that they 'distrust until they see evidence [that] something is trustworthy'.[113] Furthermore, two-thirds of those surveyed expressed the belief that they are routinely misled by government and business leaders, as well as by journalists and reporters.[114]

[108] Covello, 'Risk Communication' (1992), 364.

[109] Covello, 'Risk Communication' (1992), 365.

[110] Covello, 'Risk Communication' (1992), 365.

[111] A Narayanan and S Kapoor, *AI Snake Oil: What Artificial Intelligence Can Do, What It Can't, and How to Tell the Difference* (Princeton University Press 2024).

[112] 'The reaction to ELIZA showed me more vividly than anything I had seen hitherto the enormously exaggerated attributions an even well-educated audience is capable of making, even strives to make, to a technology it does not understand.' In J Weizenbaum, *Computer Power and Human Reason: From Judgment to Calculation* (The MIT, WH Freeman and Co 1976) 7.

[113] Edelman Trust Barometer 2022, available at edelman.com/trust/2022-trust-barometer. See also World Economic Forum, 'Edelman Trust Barometer: Cycle of Distrust Threatens Action on Global Challenges' (2022), available at weforum.org/agenda/2022/01/edelman-trust-barometer-2022-report/.

[114] Edelman Trust Barometer 2022 (n 113), 15.

Finally, the 'Public' circle reflects the attitudes and beliefs that shape how individuals interpret and evaluate risk information.[115] A number of characteristics and limitations influence public risk perception. These include 'inaccurate perceptions of levels of risk', 'exaggerated expectations about the effectiveness of regulatory actions', and 'difficulties in understanding probabilistic information related to unfamiliar activities or technologies', among others.[116] In addition, the acceptability of risk for the public is closely tied to the values held within that community. As Covello properly explains:

> They [the public] weigh the various factors according to their own values, senses of risk, and stakes in the outcome. Because acceptability is a matter of values and opinions, and because values and opinions differ, debates about risk are often debates about values, accountability, and control.[117]

These aspects of risk communication demonstrate that cultural, political, and psychological factors significantly shape the operation of the risk regulation model. Furthermore, the value-oriented and future-oriented *ex ante* perspective of this model marks a critical distinction between the risk regulation model and the rights-based model. A risk-oriented approach may, however, suffer from an inherent inadequacy with respect to accountability. Experience has shown that the European risk regulation regime has been largely systematised through the case law of the CJEU, which tends to build upon past experiences.[118] This reliance on judicial development implies that the accountability framework within a risk-oriented approach does not fully emerge in its initial stages, but only emerges during its more mature and settled phases. In the meantime, individuals and society are left in a position of delicate uncertainty.

Furthermore, the risk profiles of AI systems are in constant flux due to their inherently dynamic character, as discussed in chapter two of this book. Attempts to regulate these shifting risk profiles and their magnitude through the application of the precautionary principle may, therefore, prove unnecessary once a risk has already materialised.[119] In such cases, the risk-oriented approach risks becoming ineffective, as it is unable to keep pace with the evolving nature of AI systems. Table 3.2 below[120] provides a schematic overview of the models discussed in this section. The risk regulation model and the rights-based model are examined in greater depth in the subsequent sections of this book, particularly in relation to the use of AI systems by public authorities.

[115] Covello, 'Risk Communication' (1992), 366.
[116] Covello, 'Risk Communication' (1992), 366.
[117] Covello, 'Risk Communication' (1992), 367.
[118] Purnhagen, *The Politics of Systematization in EU Product Safety Regulation* (2013).
[119] Petit and J De Cooman (2020), 12.
[120] This table is a developed version created and inspired by the study in Petit and De Cooman (2020), 1.

Table 3.2 Main Legal Approaches to AI Regulation and Their Respective Pros and Cons

Main Legal Approaches to AI Regulation and Their Respective Pros and Cons					
	Black Letter Law Model	**Emergent Model ('Law of the horse')**	**Ethical Model**	**Risk Regulation Model**	**Rights-based Model**
Focus	Application of existing laws to AI	Creation of a new branch of law for each new technology	Reliance on ethics frameworks to guide AI regulation	Prevention and mitigation of potential harms through the precautionary principle	Grounding regulation in human rights, democracy, and the rule of law
Examples	Intellectual property; product safety and liability; privacy	'The law of drones'; 'the law of driverless cars'; 'the law of AI'	Industry self-regulation	EU Artificial Intelligence Act	European Declaration on Digital Rights and Principles for the Digital Decade
Timing	*Ex post* (after risks or harms occur)	*Ex ante* (before risks materialise)	*Ex ante*	*Ex ante*	*Dynamic*
Advantages	Economical; time-saving; builds on established legal structures	Technology-specific; captures the novelty of the system; provides tailored legal attention	Provides normative guidance; highlights moral questions about what we *ought to* do; complements fundamental rights	Balances potential benefits with minimisation of harms	Strong accountability regime; triggers duty of justification; limits arbitrary power; ensures robust protection of individual autonomy (See section 3.5)

(continued)

Table 3.2 ***(Continued)***

Main Legal Approaches to AI Regulation and Their Respective Pros and Cons					
	Black Letter Law Model	**Emergent Model ('Law of the horse')**	**Ethical Model**	**Risk Regulation Model**	**Rights-based Model**
Disadvantages	Risks of incorrect analogies; production of blind spots; and potential irrelevance as technology evolves	Redundancy; fragmentation; easily outdated; weak and isolated from broader legal system	Risks of ethics washing, ethics relativism, ethics shopping; lacks binding force; easily co-opted by industry interests	Ineffective under conditions of scientific uncertainty; weak accountability in early stages; highly dependent on quality of risk assessment; shaped by limitations of science, officials, media, and the public (Covello, 1992)	May be criticised as abstract; requires careful operationalisation in practice

3.4.2. The Risk-Based Approach of the AI Act

The EU has long recognised both the opportunities and the potential dangers posed by advanced AI systems. On 21 April 2021, the European Commission introduced the world's first comprehensive regulatory proposal for artificial intelligence – the Artificial Intelligence Act (AI Act).[121] The Proposal was broadly welcomed across the Union, particularly because it introduced substantial legal provisions reflecting ethical standards.[122] Central to the

[121] AI Act Proposal (n 39).

[122] It is important to note that there are two distinct Western approaches to AI governance. See H Roberts and L Floridi, 'The EU and the US: Two Different Approaches to AI Governance' (Oxford Internet Institute, 2021), available at oii.ox.ac.uk/news-events/news/the-eu-and-the-us-two-different-approaches-to-ai-governance/ (discussing the greater hesitancy in the US to introduce legal obligations, compared with the EU).

Proposal is its adoption of a risk-based approach, which the Commission defines as follows:

> a balanced and proportionate horizontal regulatory approach to AI that is limited to the minimum necessary requirements to address the risks and problems linked to AI, without unduly constraining or hindering technological development or otherwise disproportionately increasing the cost of placing AI solutions on the market.[123]

It is important to emphasise that the approach outlined above is not confined to the EU; rather, the Proposal carries global significance. This is most evident in the case of Brussels, which in recent years has evolved not only into the centre of EU policy-making, but also into a leading hub for global regulatory initiatives in high-technology sectors. The Proposal exemplifies what has been termed the 'Brussels Effect' – the phenomenon whereby EU legislation, such as the AI Act, transcends its 'local' scope and effectively sets global standards, owing to the Union's extensive regulatory influence and power.[124] The consequence, however, is that an ineffective regulatory model adopted by the EU risks generating harmful consequences on a global scale. Moreover, as highlighted in chapter two, the AI Act extends beyond merely addressing the functioning of the internal market; it also engages directly with socio-technical challenges, carrying profound implications for both individual rights and societal structures.

Within the risk-based framework, the AI Act Proposal establishes a hierarchy of AI practices, categorising them into unacceptable risk, high-risk, limited risk, and minimal risk.[125] The European Commission places particular emphasis on high-risk AI systems, a category that encompasses the safety components of products already regulated under existing product safety legislation, including machinery, medical devices, and toys. In addition, Annex III identifies a range of stand-alone systems, such as those employed in recruitment processes and in law enforcement, that pose direct threats to fundamental rights. Figure 3.2 below illustrates the risk hierarchy set out in the AI Act Proposal.[126]

[123] See the AI Act Proposal (n 39), Explanatory Memorandum, 3.

[124] A Bradford, *The Brussels Effect: How the European Union Rules the World* (Oxford University Press, 2020).

[125] See the AI Act Proposal (n 39).

[126] It is important to note that a similar risk hierarchy approach has been adopted in the final AI Act (n 2). It classifies AI systems into four categories: 'unacceptable risk', prohibited under Art 5; 'high-risk', subject to strict, mandatory *ex ante* requirements; 'transparency risk', subject to disclosure obligations under Art 50; and 'minimal or no risk', largely left to voluntary codes of conduct.

Figure 3.2 The Risk Hierarchy in the AI Act

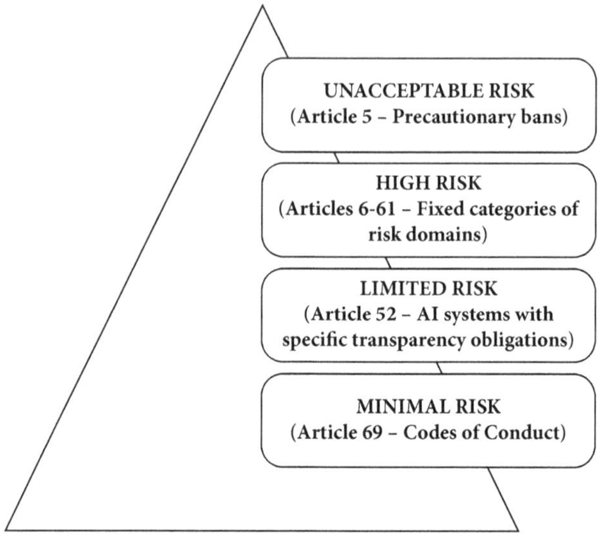

As recognised in the Explanatory Memorandum,[127] high-risk AI systems pose 'significant risks' to security, health, and fundamental rights. To address these concerns, the AI Act sets out a series of special requirements designed to safeguard fundamental rights and ensure non-discrimination. These obligations include the establishment of appropriate data governance and management practices; the preparation of technical documentation demonstrating compliance with regulatory standards; mechanisms to ensure traceability of system functioning; sufficient operational transparency; effective human oversight; and the maintenance of an appropriate level of accuracy, robustness, and cybersecurity.[128]

Although the AI Act aspires to align AI with EU values and the protection of fundamental rights, questions remain as to whether it will fully achieve this objective. A critical approach can, however, serve to strengthen a rights-based approach, understood as compromising two core elements: (i) reliance on the corpus of European fundamental and human rights law as the basis for its normative commitments; and (ii) an emphasis on accountability strategies rooted in established fundamental and human rights practices. In this regard, this chapter identifies four critical challenges that may weaken the AI Act's objectives: (i) the undermining of the intrinsic value of fundamental and human rights by overlooking the *publicness* of AI systems; (ii) the misidentification of risk profiles resulting from neglecting the *complexity* and *dynamic* dimensions of AI; (iii) the

[127] See the AI Act Proposal (n 39).
[128] See the AI Act Proposal (n 39).

entrenchment of private power due to disregarding both the *inter-systemic* and *publicness* aspects of AI; and (iv) the imposition of opaque precautionary bans stemming from the neglect of AI's *social* aspect. It is important to note that the analysis is based on the final AI Act, published in July 2024 and in force since August 2024.

3.4.2.1. Undermining the Intrinsic Value of Fundamental and Human Rights

The core aim of the AI Act, as articulated in its recitals, is the protection of fundamental rights.[129] The final text refers to 'fundamental rights' more than 90 times, underscoring its stated priority. However, questions arise as to whether the provisions introduced are sufficient to realise this objective,[130] particularly in light of the Act's limited engagement with the *publicness* of AI systems deployed in the public sector. This shortcoming becomes particularly evident in the Act's tendency to conflate fundamental rights with safety standards,[131] thereby reducing rights protections to questions of technical compliance. Such an orientation has been characterised as 'excessively technocratic', a description that underscores how such an approach risks undermining the distinctive normative character of fundamental and human rights.[132]

Put simply, by equating fundamental rights with safety standards, the AI Act effectively reduces rights to the status of mere interests.[133] Yet, fundamental and human rights cannot be regarded simply as 'interests';[134] they possess an intrinsic value,[135] as well as distinct moral strength and importance.[136] Failure to recognise

[129] See the AI Act (n 2). See also E Biber, 'Machines Learning the Rule of Law: EU Proposes the World's First Artificial Intelligence Act' (*Verfassungsblog*, 13 July 2021), available at verfassungsblog.de/ai-rol/.

[130] See N Smuha et al, 'How the EU Can Achieve Legally Trustworthy AI: A Response to the European Commission's Proposal for an Artificial Intelligence Act' (LEADS Law, University of Birmingham, 5 August 2021) 9, available at papers.ssrn.com/sol3/papers.cfm?abstract_id=3899991 ('while the Proposal's text is infused with fundamental-rights language, it seems to take an overly technocratic approach to the protection of fundamental rights').

[131] Smuha et al, 'How the EU Can Achieve Legally Trustworthy AI' (2021), 9. See also theories of fundamental rights in E-W Böckenförde, 'Grundrechtstheorie und Grundrechtsinterpretation' (1974) 27 *Neue Juristische Wochenschrift (NJW)* 1529–38 (presenting five fundamental rights theories, namely the liberal, the institutional, the democratic-functional, the welfare-state, and the value theory of fundamental rights).

[132] Smuha et al, 'How the EU Can Achieve Legally Trustworthy AI' (2021), 9–10.

[133] Smuha et al, 'How the EU Can Achieve Legally Trustworthy AI' (2021).

[134] Smuha et al, 'How the EU Can Achieve Legally Trustworthy AI' (2021).

[135] However, it is a demanding intellectual task to understand what makes something valuable. For instance, one might ask what separates our first salary from the next one. Is it only our subjective judgement, shaped by human perception, or is there an independent 'quality'? As Dworkin observes, 'value is something independent of what people happen to enjoy or want or need or what is good for them'. In this sense, value refers to something external and independent. Following this reasoning, Palombella explains that the intrinsic value of fundamental rights 'could be achieved by ascribing to them a raison d'être external to the state and certainly autonomous, even of the deliberations of democratic majorities'. See R Dworkin, *Life's Dominion* (HarperCollins, 1993) 71; G Palombella, 'Fundamental Rights: From Limits to Common Goals' (2021, on file with author) 3.

[136] J Raz, 'On the Nature of Rights' (1984) XCIII *Mind* 194–214.

this particular status risks obscuring the EU Institutions' obligations to respect and promote, and refrain from actions or policies that could adversely affect, the rights enshrined in the EU Charter of Fundamental Rights.[137] Even more concerningly, such a reductionist approach may erode the foundational values of the Union, namely human dignity, freedom, democracy, equality, and the rule of law. To protect these values, fundamental rights have been granted a particular status within the broader architecture of rights protection in European fundamental and human rights law. This special legal status entails a requirement of robust and well-founded justification for any interference with such rights.[138]

This mechanism is elaborated in German legal discourse through the so-called 'two-tiered approach'.[139] According to this framework, the first step is to determine whether a particular state action falling within the scope of a fundamental right constitutes an infringement. The second step is to evaluate whether such an infringement can be justified under the applicable limitation regime and the specific clauses governing the respective fundamental right. In addition, certain provisions apply to all fundamental rights, most notably the prohibition on infringing the essence of a fundamental right *(Wesensgehalt)*.[140] Within this structure, an interference with any fundamental right may only be justified where it pursues (i) a legitimate purpose prescribed by law, and (ii) is subject to review by a legitimately established and independent body.[141] Because the distinctive features of fundamental and human rights are not adequately recognised in the AI Act, these essential elements are left unconcretised therein.[142] This limitation appears

[137] See, in this regard, Arts 51(1) and 54 of the EU Charter, which provide that 'The provisions of this Charter are addressed to the institutions, bodies, offices and agencies of the Union with due regard for the principle of subsidiarity and to the Member States only when they are implementing Union law. They shall therefore respect the rights, observe the principles and promote the application thereof in accordance with their respective powers and respecting the limits of the powers of the Union as conferred on it in the Treaties'; 'Nothing in this Charter shall be interpreted as implying any right to engage in any activity or to perform any act aimed at the destruction of any of the rights and freedoms recognised in this Charter or at their limitation to a greater extent than is provided for herein'. See also T Tridimas, 'The General Principles of EU Law and the Europeanisation of National Laws' (2020) 13(2) Review of European Administrative Law 5–31.

[138] See, in this regard, Art 52 of the EU Charter, which provides that 'Any limitation on the exercise of the rights and freedoms recognised by this Charter must be provided for by law and respect the essence of those rights and freedoms. Subject to the principle of proportionality, limitations may be made only if they are necessary and genuinely meet objectives of general interest recognised by the Union or the need to protect the rights and freedoms of others.'

[139] See D Grimm, 'Fundamental Rights in the Interpretation of the German Constitutional Court' in D Grimm, *Constitutionalism: Past, Present, and Future* (Oxford University Press, 2016) 169–70. This mechanism has been adopted in many domestic, regional, and international courts.

[140] Furthermore, in Germany, the Federal Constitutional Court (BVerfGE) established limits to the limitations of fundamental rights, known as 'Schranken-Schranken', in its early judgments. See D Grimm, 'Fundamental Rights in the Interpretation of the German Constitutional Court' (2016), 171.

[141] In this process, the proportionality test has particular significance for the protection of rights. See A Barak, *Proportionality: Constitutional Rights and Their Limitations* (Cambridge University Press, 2012).

[142] For a discussion on the concretisation of legal norms, see F Müller, 'Arbeitsmethoden des Verfassungsrechts', in *Enzyklopädie der Geisteswissenschaftlichen Arbeitsmethoden* (R Oldenburg Verlag, 1971) 123–90 (arguing that the concretisation of legal norms occurs through engagement with legal materials, doctrines, commentaries, case law, and comparative legal documents, and thus with a large body of texts that are not identical to the respective legal norm).

to be connected to the 'risk-based approach' that lies at the very core of the AI Act's regulatory architecture.[143]

Therefore, rather than engaging with the *publicness* of AI systems and adopting a fundamental and human rights-based approach, the proposed AI Act transforms fundamental rights into a set of technical and bureaucratic requirements.[144] In doing so, it reduces the protection of rights to a largely 'technocratic and bureaucratic process'. Such an approach, however, fails to establish a meaningful mechanism of accountability or to ensure effective protection of fundamental rights. The principal concern appears instead to be the safeguarding of the functioning of the internal market. Yet, considerations of market efficiency cannot be regarded as more important than the protection of fundamental rights. In other words, the market cannot be permitted to reign over fundamental and human rights – particularly in circumstances where AI systems automate the decision-making powers of public authorities and thereby pose life-changing risks to individuals.

Moreover, because the AI Act places its emphasis on risks rather than rights, it engages only to a partial extent with the limits of European and international human rights law in safeguarding fundamental rights within the digital sphere. For example, although AI systems deployed in the public sector raise profound concerns about the manipulation of the human mind, neither international human rights law nor European fundamental rights law currently afford explicit legal status to the human mind as such.[145] The case law of the ECtHR nonetheless makes clear that the notion of private life is not confined to bodily integrity or physical places, but also extends to the mental sphere:

> The Court … reiterates that 'private life' is a broad term, encompassing, inter alia, aspects of an individual's physical and social identity, including the right to personal autonomy, personal development and to establish and develop relationships with other human beings and the outside world. The Court has … held that private life includes a person's physical and psychological integrity and that the State is also under a positive obligation to secure to its citizens their right to effective respect for this integrity.[146]

[143] This point is examined in greater detail below.

[144] Smuha et al, 'How the EU Can Achieve Legally Trustworthy AI' (2021).

[145] E Biber and M Capasso, 'The Right to Mental Integrity in the Age of Artificial Intelligence: Cognitive Human Enhancement Technologies' in B Custers and E Fosch-Villaronga (eds), *Law and Artificial Intelligence: Legal, Ethical, and Regulatory Issues of AI* (Springer, Information Technology and Law Series, 2022). Similar concerns are also highlighted in the context of the prohibition of discrimination. It has been argued that the formulation of the prohibition of discrimination in international and European human and fundamental rights law does not sufficiently protect individuals against the risks posed by AI systems. See T Krupiy, 'Why the Proposed Artificial Intelligence Regulation Does Not Deliver on the Promise to Protect Individuals from Harm' (*European Law Blog*, 23 July 2021), available at europeanlawblog.eu/2021/07/23/why-the-proposed-artificial-intelligence-regulation-does-not-deliver-on-the-promise-to-protect-individuals-from-harm/ (highlighting the shortcomings of the definitions of direct and indirect discrimination in the context of AI systems, and underlining that expressing genders as mathematical equations is not compatible with recognising that individuals have plural gender identities).

[146] ECtHR, *Tysiąc v Poland*, App no 5410/03, Judgment of 20 March 2007, para 107.

In this context, privacy serves to protect 'against unwanted intrusions into people's private lives in a traditional sense of guarding a person's private space – be that in their head or in their home'.[147] However, the precise meaning and scope of 'mental integrity' remain underdeveloped and imprecise. As a result, several human rights scholars have argued that existing legal frameworks are ill-equipped to confront the novel challenges posed by emerging technologies. To address this gap, they have proposed the recognition of a new free-standing human right: the 'right to mental self-determination'.[148] In this sense, reform is necessary to develop mind-protecting legal norms. Advances in cognitive sciences, which increasingly provide novel technical means to alter and influence the human mind, constitute one of the central justifications for recognising and regulating such a new right.[149] However, notwithstanding these calls for reform, the AI Act remains ambiguous as to whether its provisions on prohibited or high-risk AI systems in themselves establish rights not to be subjected to prohibited AI practices, or rights not to be manipulated, and not to be exposed to non-compliant high-risk AI systems.[150]

This stance does little to advance the project of 'rights constitutionalism'[151] in the digital sphere. Given that AI systems have emerged in an era where new rights have been progressively recognised since 1946,[152] this lacuna in the Act is particularly problematic. Once again, the burden of developing 'rights constitutionalism' is placed on the courts, notwithstanding the extensive advancements and accumulated experience in European data protection and fundamental rights law.[153] This approach neglects the considerable potential of fundamental and human rights to

[147] J Marshall, *Personal Freedom through Human Rights Law? Autonomy, Identity and Integrity under the European Convention on Human Rights* (Martinus Nijhoff, 2009).

[148] J-C Bublitz, 'The Nascent Right to Psychological Integrity and Mental Self-Determination' in A von Arnauld et al (eds), *The Cambridge Handbook of New Human Rights Recognition* (Cambridge University Press, 2020) 387–408. In the US, the 'NeuroRights Initiative', established at Columbia University, works to incorporate five specific neuro-rights into international human rights law: the right to personal identity, the right to free will, the right to mental privacy, the right to equal access to mental augmentation, and the right to protection from algorithmic bias. See NeuroRights Foundation, 'Mission', available at neurorightsfoundation.org/mission. Globally, Chile was the first country to take legislative steps on neuro-rights to prevent the misuse of AI and neurotechnology. See JM Munoz, 'Chile: Right to Free Will Needs Definition' (*Nature*, 29 October 2019), available at nature.com/articles/d41586-019-03295-9.

[149] C-J Bublitz, 'The Nascent Right to Psychological Integrity and Mental Self-Determination' (2020), 387. (arguing that, although legal systems address bodily integrity in detail – even in exceptional situations such as pregnancy or organ transplantation – they largely disregard interventions affecting the human mind).

[150] G Malgieri and M Ienca, 'The EU Regulates AI but Forgets to Protect Our Mind' (*European Law Blog*, 7 July 2021), available at europeanlawblog.eu/2021/07/07/the-eu-regulates-ai-but-forgets-to-protect-our-mind/ (arguing that the nexus between AI systems and the human mind is absent from the AI Act Proposal).

[151] See M Versteeg and A Chilton, *How Constitutional Rights Matter* (Oxford University Press, 2020) 79 (capturing the rights found in 194 countries).

[152] See a graph illustrating the proliferation of constitutional rights from 1946 to 2016, in M Versteeg and A Chilton, How Constitutional Rights Matter (2020), 83.

[153] Indeed, the CJEU has played a significant role in the development and concretisation of the fundamental right to data protection, as examined in Chapter 1.

serve as a powerful 'normative anchor' in addressing the challenges posed by new technologies.[154] In this context, courts may seek to interpret novel interferences arising from AI systems and practices through the lens of the principle of human dignity. From this perspective, one could argue that the framework of fundamental and human rights protection leaves no gaps, even in the digital sphere. However, given the complexity of AI systems and the limited substantive understanding of what the principle of human dignity requires *(hermeneutische Unsicherheit)*,[155] combined with the limitations of European fundamental and human rights law in addressing digital challenges, this task may ultimately prove too demanding for judges.

3.4.2.2. *Entrenchment of Private Power*

The entrenchment of private power within the AI Act can be observed on two distinct levels: first, in the technocratic processes through which the special requirements are concretised; and second, in the technocratic reviews designed to verify compliance with those requirements. By 'technocratic', this chapter refers to highly technical and bureaucratic management techniques, developed largely within private law structures and primarily concerning private actors.[156] This regulatory pattern suggests that the AI Act has overlooked both the *inter-systemic* and the *publicness* dimensions of AI systems deployed in the public sphere.

3.4.2.2.1. Technocratic Processes

The technocratic orientation of the AI Act, which entrenches the dominance of private power, is most clearly reflected in its regulatory regime establishing mandatory requirements for high-risk AI systems. Notably, the AI Act does not provide a substantive definition of the concept of 'high risk'; rather, it enumerates specific

[154] Indeed, it has been highlighted that, in the context of new technologies, an anchor point for addressing regulatory dilemmas can 'be found in the common heritage of human rights and values'. See R Leenes et al, 'Regulatory Challenges of Robotics: Some Guidelines for Addressing Legal and Ethical Issues' (2017) 9(1) *Law, Innovation and Technology* 1–44. See also an example of using human rights as 'normative anchor points of governance' in the context of human enhancement technologies, in D Ruggiu, 'Implementing a Responsible Research and Innovation Framework for Human Enhancement According to Human Rights: The Right to Bodily Integrity and the Rise of "Enhanced Societies"' (2018) 10(1) *Law, Innovation and Technology* 1–40.

[155] C McCrudden, 'Human Dignity and Judicial Interpretation of Human Rights' (2008) 19(4) *European Journal of International Law* 654–724. See also the notions of 'practical certainty' and 'hermeneutic uncertainty' of the principle, in D Marten and H-J Papier, *Handbuch der Grundrechte in Deutschland und Europa*, vol IV: *Grundrechte in Deutschland – Einzelgrundrechte I*, 1st edn (CF Müller, 2011) 5 ('der Satz von der Menschenwürde ist beides zugleich: einleuchtend und dunkel; einleuchtend beim ersten Hinsehen, dunkel, je mehr man ihn rational zu fassen versucht') (discussing that the principle of human dignity is both self-evident and opaque, and that attempts at rationalisation only deepen its opacity).

[156] There is an ongoing European Research Council (ERC) project in the EU that examines 'extractive' private law structures. See N-EXTLAW, coordinated by M Bartl, available at nonextractivefuture.eu/the-project/.

categories of AI systems that fall within this designation.[157] There are two groups of high-risk AI systems. The first group comprises AI systems intended for use as safety components of products already governed by existing product safety legislation and subject to third-party *ex ante* conformity assessments. This category is set out in Article 6 and Annex I of the AI Act,[158] and includes, inter alia, machinery, medical devices, and toys.[159] The second group, listed in Annex III, encompasses a wider range of stand-alone AI systems deployed in sensitive domains, such as law enforcement, education, recruitment, and the enjoyment of public services and social benefits.

The new regime on mandatory requirements set out in the AI Act closely follows the 2019 HLEG Ethics Guidelines, which identified seven requirements to be met before an AI system may be placed on the market or put into service.[160] However, while the AI Act draws significantly on these Guidelines, several of the requirements articulated therein have not been explicitly or precisely transposed into the legislative text. Table 3.3 below sets out, in parallel, the key similarities and divergences between the two instruments:

Table 3.3 AI Act and Ethics Guidelines

AI Act	Ethics Guidelines
Human oversight	Human agency and oversight
Accuracy, robustness, and cybersecurity	Technical robustness and safety
Appropriate data governance and management practices	Privacy and data governance
Technical documentation Ensuring traceability of functioning Transparency and provision of information to deployers	Transparency
Risk management system	Diversity, non-discrimination, and fairness
	Societal and environmental wellbeing
	Accountability

Although the mandatory requirements introduced in the AI Act appear promising in addressing the dangers posed by AI systems, the wide discretion conferred upon AI providers in implementing these requirements is deeply problematic,[161] particularly given its potential to reinforce the hegemony of

[157] Annex III of the AI Act (n 2).
[158] See the AI Act (n 2).
[159] It is important to note that these high-risk AI systems are covered by the Machinery Directive (2006/42/EC), the Toy Safety Directive (2009/48/EC), and the Medical Devices Regulation (2017/745). See Annex I of the AI Act (n 2).
[160] European Commission, HLEGAI, 'Ethics Guidelines for Trustworthy AI' (2019).
[161] Smuha et al, 'How the EU Can Achieve Legally Trustworthy AI' (2021).

private power within the public digital sphere. This issue becomes evident from the very outset, in the first obligation set out under Article 9, which mandates the establishment, implementation, documentation, and maintenance of a 'risk management system'.[162]

The obligation to establish a risk management system is structured around four steps: (i) the 'identification and analysis of the known and foreseeable risks'; (ii) the 'estimation and evaluation of the risks that may emerge when the high-risk AI system is used in accordance with its intended purpose, and under conditions of reasonably foreseeable misuse'; (iii) the 'evaluation of other risks possibly arising, based on the analysis of data gathered from the post-market monitoring system'; and (iv) the 'adoption of suitable risk management measures'.[163] In addition, Article 9(4) specifies that these risk management measures 'shall give due consideration to the effects and possible interactions resulting from the combined application of the requirements', and should be embraced 'with a view to minimising risks more effectively while achieving an appropriate balance in implementing measures'.[164] This provision demonstrates that the risk management system constitutes the foundational requirement upon which the development, coherence, and effectiveness of the entire set of mandatory obligations ultimately depend.[165] In other words, the effectiveness of the entire set of mandatory requirements ultimately depends on the quality of the risk management system.[166] A weak or insufficiently designed risk management framework has the potential to undermine the fulfilment of all other obligations.

What is particularly striking in this process is that the AI provider – the very actor seeking to place the system on the market or put it into service[167] – is entrusted with primary responsibility for executing this critical process. Furthermore, Article 9(3) establishes a sort of discretion for the provider. The provision applies only to risks that can be 'reasonably mitigated or eliminated' through development or design or the provision of technical information. Importantly, what is considered 'reasonable' depends on context and must be assessed in light of available technology, industry standards, and the circumstances of use.

Moreover, pursuant to Article 9(5), it is the provider who determines whether a risk to health, security, or fundamental rights may be considered 'acceptable'. The provider is authorised to adopt measures ensuring that 'the relevant residual risk associated with each hazard as well as the overall residual risk of the high-risk AI system is judged acceptable'.[168] However, Article 9 does not impose any obligation to consult individuals directly subjected to the system when deciding what level

[162] Art 9 of the AI Act (n 2).
[163] Art 9(2) of the AI Act (n 2).
[164] Art 9(4) of the AI Act (n 2).
[165] Art 8 of the AI Act (n 2) states that the risk management system referred to in Art 9 shall be taken into account when ensuring compliance with the requirements.
[166] See also the discussion in Smuha et al, 'How the EU Can Achieve Legally Trustworthy AI' (2021).
[167] Art 3(3) of the AI Act (n 2).
[168] Art 9(5) of the AI Act (n 2).

of risk may be deemed acceptable. Given that such individuals hold a legitimate stake in the process, this provider-centred framework, which places hegemonic authority in the hands of private actors, raises serious normative and democratic concerns.[169]

Furthermore, the testing procedure for determining the most appropriate risk management measures remains elusive. Although paragraphs (6) and (7) of Article 9 state that testing procedures may include testing in real-world conditions, to identify the most appropriate risk management measures in accordance with Article 60,[170] it is the AI provider who bears the ultimate responsibility for ensuring the sufficiency of the testing procedures:

> Testing shall ensure that high-risk AI systems perform consistently for their intended purpose and that they are in compliance with the requirements set out in this Section.[171]

It is crucial to recognise that such systems may pose risks not only to the health and security of individuals, but also to their fundamental rights. In practice, this means that in situations where fundamental rights are implicated, it is the AI provider who determines whether a given risk is deemed 'acceptable', what measures should be adopted in response, and how the system should be tested. Considering that AI systems deployed in the public sector function as *social* systems and embody a quality of *publicness*, thereby impacting rights-sensitive domains involving highly vulnerable groups such as children and refugees, such an extensive margin of discretion entrusted to private providers cannot be regarded as legitimate.

However, it is significant to note that one notable element of Article 9 is found in paragraph 9, which requires providers of high-risk AI systems to consider potential adverse impacts on children and other vulnerable groups as part of their risk management system. This provision has the potential to strengthen the risk management framework by embedding a precautionary principle, ensuring that harms are anticipated rather than merely remedied after they occur. At the same time, it reflects a rights-sensitive approach to AI governance, acknowledging that vulnerable populations face disproportionate risks and, therefore, require heightened protection.

The critical role of private power is equally evident in the Proposal's provisions on data governance and management.[172] Here again, it is the AI provider

[169] Smuha et al, 'How the EU Can Achieve Legally Trustworthy AI' (2021). In the AI Act Proposal (n 39), Art 9 required the provider to communicate at least with the user, in Art 9(4). Furthermore, under the GDPR, the affected data subjects may have a say in the process of data impact assessment, according to Article 35(9): 'Where appropriate, the controller shall seek the views of data subjects or their representatives on the intended processing, without prejudice to the protection of commercial or public interests or the security of processing operations.'

[170] Art 60 states that the Commission shall specify the detailed elements of the real-world testing plan. For the term 'real-world testing plan', see Art 3(53) of AI Act (n 2).

[171] Art 9(6) of the AI Act (n 2).

[172] Art 10 of the AI Act (n 2).

who manages the quality of data governance and management. As stipulated in Article 10(2):

> training, validation and testing data sets shall be subject to data governance and management practices *appropriate* for the intended purpose.[173]

Furthermore, in light of the extensive reliance of AI systems on personal data, it has been argued for a stronger dialogue between the AI Act and the GDPR, particularly with regard to data protection rights.[174] Such dialogue is essential in order to capture the *inter-systemic* character of AI systems. Absent this dialogue, the regulatory landscape risks devolving into an archipelago of isolated normative spheres rather than forming a weave of normative spheres constituting an interconnected fabric of norms capable of meaningful legal interaction. If this isolation persists, the AI Act may ultimately fall short of providing a 'legal-friendly functional normative ground' in which diverse regulatory actors and legal frameworks can effectively engage. In other words, the regulation of AI risks being reduced to a single-cell phenomenon despite the fact that the GDPR already imposes obligations concerning the collection and processing of data.[175]

The transparency requirements likewise reveal an unbalanced constellation, privileging both the user – as distinct from the individual subjected to the system – and the AI provider. First, the Proposal grants the provider a wide margin of discretion in determining the adequacy of transparency, employing indeterminate terms, such as 'sufficiently' transparent and an 'appropriate type and degree of transparency'.[176] Second, although European policy documents consistently underscore that the core transparency challenge in AI concerns the protection of fundamental and human rights,[177] it is important to note that the AI Act's transparency provisions do not specifically address the position of individuals directly subjected to AI systems. Instead, the focus is placed on the users of such systems, and on the accompanying instructions for their operation.[178] This orientation prevents affected individuals from effectively engaging with a high-risk AI system

[173] The italic emphasis on the term '*appropriate*' is intentional.

[174] Furthermore, beyond data governance requirements, there are additional issues that relate to both the GDPR and the AI Act Proposal, such as the treatment of biometric data, the 'special data category', and the use of AI regulatory sandboxes. Similar criticism has been raised in the context of law enforcement, where the Proposal's relationship with the Law Enforcement Directive remains unclear. See Smuha et al, 'How the EU Can Achieve Legally Trustworthy AI' (2021), 42–43.

[175] However, it is important to note that the AI Act considers such a dialogue in relation to 'special categories or personal data'. Specifically, Art 10(5) establishes an exception, which is referred to in Art 9 of the GDPR. While the GDPR generally prohibits the processing of such sensitive categories of data, the AI Act permits their processing for the limited purpose of bias detection and correction, provided that adequate safeguards are implemented to protect fundamental rights.

[176] Art 13(1); see n 2.

[177] O Pollicino and G De Gregorio, 'Constitutional Law in the Algorithmic Society' in H-W Micklitz et al (eds), *Constitutional Challenges in the Algorithmic Society* (Cambridge University Press, 2022) 3–24.

[178] Paras (2) and (3) of Art 13 of the AI Act (n 2).

in a critical and informed manner, thereby undermining their capacity to exercise rights of contestation and accountability.

It is worth noting that certain technical innovations may contribute to fostering a more critical interaction between individuals and AI systems. For example, researchers at the University of Palermo have developed a robot capable of explaining its decision-making processes by 'thinking out loud'. This is achieved by enabling the robot to vocalise its internal reasoning through the simulation of inner speech,[179] thereby offering individuals greater insight into the system's functioning.[180] In a series of experiments, the researchers examined how inner speech influences the behaviour of a robot. In one illustrative case, they programmed the AI robot 'Pepper'[181] to assist a human in setting a lunch table in accordance with the requirements of etiquette. When the human instructed the robot to place the cutlery incorrectly, the machine faced a dilemma whether to follow the human's instructions or to comply with the established rules of etiquette. According to the researchers, enabling inner speech allowed the robot to resolve such dilemmas more effectively.[182] Given that AI systems are often notoriously difficult to interpret or explain, this mechanism has significant potential to enhance both transparency and reliability, as it enables humans to understand the motivations underpinning the robot's decisions and behaviour.[183] In this way, such research makes an important contribution to the broader debate on 'explainable AI'.[184]

A further area of concern arises in relation to the requirement of human oversight, as set out in Article 14 of the AI Act. This provision mandates the establishment of 'human oversight' mechanisms with the stated aim of ensuring the protection of individuals' fundamental rights:[185]

> Human oversight shall aim to prevent or minimise the risks to health, safety or fundamental rights that may emerge when a high-risk AI system is used in accordance with

[179] For more on the qualities of 'inner speech', see A Morin, 'Characteristics of an Effective Internal Dialogue in the Acquisition of Self-Information' (1995) 15 *Imagination, Cognition and Personality* 45–58.

[180] N Grover, 'Study Explores Inner Life of AI with Robot That Thinks Out Loud' (*The Guardian*, 21 April 2021), available at amp.theguardian.com/technology/2021/apr/21/study-inner-life-ai-robot-thinks-out-loud?__twitter_impression=true.

[181] Pepper AI is a humanoid, programmable robot created in 2014 that is able to recognise faces and basic human emotions. For more information, see SoftBank Robotics, 'Pepper', available at softbankrobotics.com/emea/en/pepper.

[182] Morin, 'Characteristics of an Effective Internal Dialogue' (1995); Grover, 'Study Explores Inner Life of AI with Robot That Thinks Out Loud' (2021).

[183] A Pipitone and A Chella, 'What Robots Want? Hearing the Inner Voice of a Robot' (2021) 24 *iScience* 102371, 1.

[184] A Rai, 'Explainable AI: From Black Box to Glass Box' (2020) 48 *Journal of the Academy of Marketing Science* 137–41.

[185] The human oversight requirement is applied differently in Germany. The German approach excludes the use of automated systems for administrative acts requiring the exercise of discretion. This means that only a human can exercise discretion. See P Nemitz and E Gräf, 'Artificial Intelligence Must Be Used According to the Law, or Not at All' (*Verfassungsblog*, 2022), available at verfassungsblog.de/roa-artificial-intelligence-must-be-used-according-to-the-law/.

> its intended purpose or under conditions of reasonably foreseeable misuse, in particular when such risks persist despite the application of other requirements set out in this Section.[186]

Moreover, Article 14(4)(d) expressly acknowledges the importance of individual autonomy by authorising the person responsible for human oversight to 'decide, in any particular situation, not to use the high-risk AI system or otherwise disregard, override or reverse the output'.[187] However, the normative power of Article 14 may remain insufficient to achieve its stated purpose, as it does not take into account the fundamental differences between AI systems and human beings with respect to 'cognition'.[188] It is evident that human overseers cannot realistically examine the entirety of the data mining process, nor can they meaningfully validate the often opaque outputs produced by complex AI systems.[189] In practice, the human overseer may only be able to detect obvious failures, making it particularly difficult to identify more subtle problems, such as the replication of gender bias within an AI system.[190] This limitation effectively neutralises the protective potential of Article 14, which might otherwise have operated in favour of the individual subject to the system, and instead reinforces the existing power imbalance within the AI Act to the benefit of the AI provider and the user. Consequently, the provisions on human oversight cannot be regarded as an adequate response to the fundamental rights challenges posed by AI systems. On their own, such measures can legitimise neither the deployment of AI systems nor the decisions they generate. Indeed, no AI system can be considered a legitimate device in a democratic society unless its use can be demonstrated to be lawful, necessary, and proportionate.[191] That said, the requirement of human oversight still remains crucial and may be advanced as one of the key mechanisms for humanising digital government. Indeed, the AI Act explicitly cautions the individual responsible for oversight to remain 'aware of the possible tendency of automatically relying or over-relying on the output produced by a high-risk AI system'.[192] This concern refers to the well-documented phenomenon of 'automation bias'; that is, the 'undue deference to automated systems by human actors that disregard contradictory information from other sources or do

[186] Art 14(2) of the AI Act (n 2).

[187] Art 14(4)(d) of the AI Act (n 2).

[188] See a debate on this issue in M Alfonseca et al, 'Superintelligence Cannot Be Contained: Lessons from Computability Theory' (2021) 70 *Journal of Artificial Intelligence Research*, available at jair.org/index.php/jair/article/view/12202.

[189] See an empirical study on the inadequacy of human oversight, in B Green, 'The Flaws of Policies Requiring Human Oversight of Government Algorithms' (2022) 45 *Computer Law & Security Review* 1–22 (demonstrating that people are unable to perform the desired oversight function, and proposing institutional oversight). See also B Green and A Kak, 'The False Comfort of Human Oversight as an Antidote to AI Harm' (*Future Tense*, 2021), available at slate.com/technology/2021/06/human-oversight-artificial-intelligence-laws.html.

[190] See World Wide Web Foundation, 'Policy Brief W20 Argentina: Artificial Intelligence – Open Questions about Gender Inclusion' (2018), available at webfoundation.org/docs/2018/06/AI-Gender.pdf.

[191] See the discussion in this chapter on the intrinsic value of fundamental and human rights.

[192] Art 14(4)(b) of the AI Act (n 2).

not (thoroughly) search for additional information'.[193] It is promising that the AI Act acknowledges this risk.[194] Nevertheless, additional dimensions require careful consideration if human oversight is to function as a meaningful safeguard.

In future iterations, the AI Act should also take into account that the excessive digitalisation of government services and the automation of decision-making may eliminate the uniquely human capacity to forgive trivial mistakes, for example the misspelling of names or errors in dates in applications for social benefits or tax returns.[195] More broadly, a rigorous regulatory approach must recognise that bias may emerge at multiple levels: within the system itself; within the human overseer who is vulnerable to 'automation bias'; and within the individual subject to the system, who may make minor errors due, for instance, to digital illiteracy or lack of familiarity with bureaucratic processes. The AI Act falls short of this standard, as it does not adequately address either the systemic biases inherent in AI or the vulnerabilities of those subject to it. Consequently, the normative space surrounding the Act's essential requirements appears disproportionately shaped by private digital power, with insufficient acknowledgement of the role that critical interactions among other relevant actors should play within this framework.

Furthermore, alongside the essential requirements, it is important to recognise that technical standards for AI providers will be developed through the process of European standardisation.[196] These standards are closely tied to the practical application of AI systems and, therefore, directly affect the experiences of individuals subjected to them. Yet, it remains unclear whether individuals – or the public more broadly – will have any meaningful opportunity to participate in the

[193] S Alon-Barkat and M Busuioc, 'Human–AI Interactions in Public Sector Decision-Making: "Automation Bias" and "Selective Adherence" to Algorithmic Advice' (2022) *Journal of Public Administration Research and Theory* 7–8, available at papers.ssrn.com/sol3/papers.cfm?abstract_id=3794660 (discussing two reasons for this bias: 'the perceived inherent superiority of automated systems by humans', and 'cognitive laziness', referring to 'human reluctance to engage in cognitively demanding mental process') It is important to emphasise that the 'cognitive laziness' of a human reviewing an AI system cannot serve as an excuse for an unfair situation produced by that system. Ultimately, any such system must satisfy the necessity test and cannot be justified if it exacerbates injustice in society.

[194] Over-reliance on the outputs of high-risk AI systems poses significant dangers. A striking example is the Spanish government's use of the 'VioGén' system, designed to estimate the risk of recidivism in cases of gender-based violence. As reported by AlgorithmWatch, the system produced deeply flawed assessments: of 15 women killed in domestic violence incidents in 2014 – despite having previously reported their aggressors – 14 had been classified by VioGén as facing either low or non-specific risk. See AlgorithmWatch, 'Automating Society Report 2020' (2020) 227, available at automatingsociety.algorithmwatch.org/wp-content/uploads/2020/12/Automating-Society-Report-2020.pdf. Similar concerns were highlighted in the Spanish press. See 'Las asesinadas que denunciaron se valoraron como "riesgo bajo o nulo"' (*El Mundo*, 9 December 2014), available at elmundo.es/espana/2014/12/09/54861553ca4741734b8b457e.html. For a more detailed account of the system's design and operation, see JL González et al, 'Integral Monitoring System in Cases of Gender Violence: VioGén System' (2018) 4(1) *Behavior & Law Journal* 29–40.

[195] S Ranchordás, 'Empathy in the Digital Administrative State' (2022) 71 *Duke Law Journal* 1341–89 (examining the role of empathy as a key value in administrative law).

[196] M Veale and F Zuiderveen Borgesius, 'Demystifying the Draft EU Artificial Intelligence Act' (2021), available at arxiv.org/abs/2107.03721v1.

creation of such standards. As has already been emphasised, standardisation bodies such as CEN-CENELEC[197] suffer from a well-documented democratic deficit in standard-setting, with individuals and civil society organisations frequently underrepresented due to limited resources.[198] These concerns render the process of standardisation in this context highly controversial.

3.4.2.2.2. Technocratic Reviews

The AI Act establishes a number of significant oversight institutions, including the 'notifying authority', 'market surveillance authority', 'conformity assessment body', 'post-marketing monitoring system', 'AI Office', and 'European Artificial Intelligence Board'. Under Article 3(48), the first two of these are categorised as 'national competent authorities'. Without entering into a detailed discussion of the specific roles and responsibilities of these institutions – or, more fundamentally, questioning the necessity of creating multiple oversight bodies – their presence in the AI Act at least appears promising in scope.

However, the robustness of the regulatory system is significantly undermined by Article 43(2) and Annex VI of the AI Act, which set out the framework for reviewing compliance with the mandatory requirements. According to these provisions, most reviews are carried out through internal 'conformity assessment procedures' undertaken by the providers themselves, a mechanism adapted from EU product safety law.[199] In practice, this means that providers are entrusted with the task of self-assessing whether high-risk AI systems comply with the essential requirements.[200]

[197] See the website of the standardisation body CEN-CENELEC, available at https://www.cencenelec.eu/.

[198] Smuha et al, 'How the EU Can Achieve Legally Trustworthy AI' (2021) (a similar argument is highlighted in the context of the conformity assessment mechanism, since the technical rules governing the performance of this mechanism will be defined by notified bodies, which are private bodies).

[199] The conformity assessment procedure is defined in Art 2(12) of Regulation (EC) No 765/2008 as 'the process demonstrating whether specified requirements relating to a product, process, service, system, person or body have been fulfilled'. See Regulation (EC) No 765/2008 of the European Parliament and of the Council of 9 July 2008, available at eur-lex.europa.eu/legal-content/EN/TXT/PDF/?uri=CELEX:32008R0765&from=EN. See also European Commission, The 'Blue Guide' on the Implementation of EU Product Rules 2016 (2016), available at eur-lex.europa.eu/legal-content/EN/TXT/PDF/?uri=CELEX:52016XC0726(02)&from=EN, clarifying the conformity assessment procedure and the CE marking. The AI Act similarly defines the procedure, in Art 3(20), as 'the process of demonstrating whether the requirements set out in Chapter III, Section 2 relating to a high-risk AI system have been fulfilled'. The conformity assessment procedure is linked to the CE marking, defined in Art 3(24) of the AI Act as 'a marking by which a provider indicates that an AI system is in conformity with the requirements'.

[200] Considering the specificities of AI systems, regarding the conformity assessment procedure, two main concerns have been highlighted. First, the term 'conformity' may acquire a substantially new meaning. Second, this new understanding of conformity could conflict with other parallel assessments and requirements imposed on technology providers, particularly the obligations of data controllers under the GDPR, and conformity assessment procedures previously implemented for other products. See N Ioannidis and O Gkotsopoulou, 'The Palimpsest of Conformity Assessment in the Proposed Artificial Intelligence Act: A Critical Exploration of Related Terminology' (*European Law Blog*, 2 July 2021), available at europeanlawblog.eu/2021/07/02/

The only exception concerns high-risk AI systems deployed in the field of biometrics, which are subject to a conformity assessment conducted by an independent 'notified body'.[201] Within this framework, private power is assigned a notably significant role in the oversight process. On the one hand, this situation raises the challenge of the legitimacy of entrusting such authority to private actors; on the other, it highlights the challenge of their capacity to conduct adequate assessments of AI systems. In particular, private actors on their own may face challenges in sufficiently evaluating these systems with respect to fundamental and human rights.[202]

This problem can be illustrated through a notable case in the United Kingdom, where a technological system analysing voices was deployed to detect cheating in English language tests.[203] While its initial purpose was narrowly defined as identifying irregularities, the system's outputs went on to shape government decisions concerning visa applications. When the system accused foreign students of cheating, the government consequently decided to deport them. However, subsequent review revealed that the system produced false accusations in approximately 20 per cent of cases,[204] resulting in the wrongful deportation of more than 7,000 students. According to the *Financial Times*,

> some were detained by immigration officials, lost their jobs, and were left homeless as a result. Most of the students were not allowed to appeal the Home Office decision; nor were they able to obtain evidence against them, or given the opportunity to prove their proficiency in English.[205]

To fully understand this example and to assess it in a practical way, it is first necessary to identify the system in question. Broadly, such systems may fall under the category of 'online proctoring technologies' designed to monitor and prevent

the-palimpsest-of-conformity-assessment-in-the-proposed-artificial-intelligence-act-a-critical-exploration-of-related-terminology/. These authors also clarify the distinctions between the terms 'compliance', 'conformity', 'impact', and 'accountability'. Three of these terms – 'conformity', 'impact', and 'accountability' – share the element of compliance, but with significant nuances. The scope of 'compliance' is broader, encompassing 'overall abidance', whereas 'conformity' refers specifically to 'compliance with specific requirements'. The comparison between conformity and impact derives from the 'data protection impact assessment' in Art 35 GDPR: conformity is essentially a formal, pre-deployment commercial control, while impact assessment is broader, addressing not only legal but also societal implications of data processing. The difference is that accountability regulates responsibility, while conformity regulates the procedure for identifying who is responsible. The authors conclude that conformity is narrower in scope than compliance, impact, and accountability. It must also be noted that such terminological and procedural complexity risks hindering the concretisation of the rule of law.

[201] Recital 125 of the AI Act (n 2).

[202] It should be added that they might also make categorical errors regarding the identification of the right(s) affected.

[203] C Baynes, 'Government "Deported 7,000 Foreign Students after Falsely Accusing Them of Cheating in English Language Tests"' (*The Independent*, 14 June 2019), available at independent.co.uk/news/uk/politics/home-office-mistakenly-deported-thousands-foreign-students-cheating-language-tests-theresa-may-windrush-a8331906.html.

[204] 'Home Office Told Thousands of Foreign Students to Leave UK in Error' (*Financial Times*, 6 May 2018), available at ft.com/content/2ae9b7d2-4d0c-11e8-8a8e-22951a2d8493.

[205] *Financial Times* (n 204).

cheating in examinations.[206] While we do not have sufficient information regarding the functioning of the system in question, let us suppose that the system used in the United Kingdom relied on an 'AI system intended to be used for monitoring and detecting prohibited behaviour of students during the test', which is one of the high-risk categories listed in Annex III of the AI Act. Furthermore, since passing the English language test constitutes a visa requirement, the system functioned as part of the examination of visa applications, thereby situating it within another category of Annex III, 'migration, asylum and border control management'.

At first glance, the system implicates at least two groups of rights under the framework of the ECHR: the right to privacy, including the right to family life; and the right to a fair trial, encompassing both the right of access to a court and the right to be heard. This example demonstrates that even 'minor' technical errors can produce life-changing consequences for individuals, while simultaneously raising pressing concerns regarding a wide spectrum of potential risks, scenarios, and adverse effects on fundamental and human rights. Indeed, such systems may not only give rise to a single instance of 'high risk' but may also create cumulative risks – double or even triple risks – thereby exacerbating threats to health, security, and rights. This example illustrates that AI systems possess a significant potential to surpass the risk contexts and categories envisaged in the AI Act.[207] In such a complex landscape, it is evident that an AI provider cannot reasonably claim the expertise necessary to anticipate the full range of ways in which their systems may affect security, health, and fundamental and human rights.

Moreover, it remains unclear whether it is the AI provider who ultimately determines what qualifies as 'necessary' and 'proportionate'. Should this be the case, it is difficult to imagine that a provider could meaningfully engage with the complex necessity and proportionality tests elaborated in constitutional jurisprudence. Two additional factors render this process particularly challenging. First, as noted above, even European and international human rights law, including the EU Charter of Fundamental Rights, display certain limitations in addressing the protection of rights within the digital sphere. Second, AI systems are inherently multipurpose technologies, capable of being deployed in diverse contexts. Thus, if the provider is tasked with making determinations of necessity and proportionality, she would be required to adapt to a constantly evolving landscape of AI practices – an expectation that appears both unreasonable and legally problematic.

Furthermore, it has already been demonstrated that conformity assessment procedures involving notified bodies create circumstances for the abuse of power in the context of major pharmaceutical companies ('Big Pharma') and medical

[206] K Lee and M Fanguy, 'Online Exam Proctoring Technologies: Educational Innovation and Deterioration?' (2022) *British Journal of Educational Technology* 1–16.

[207] In the context of COVID-19 and climate change, see V Heyvaert, 'Governing Intersystemic Systemic Risks: Lessons from Covid and Climate Change' (2022) *Modern Law Review* 1–30 (arguing that climate change and zoonotic disease risks present distinctive profiles due to their potential to trigger cascading risks beyond the original risk context).

devices.[208] Considering the substantial risks that high-risk AI systems present to fundamental rights, such a laissez-faire legal system is simply inadequate. Ultimately, delegating important tasks to private companies without proper regulation and oversight is not acceptable.

Another significant concern that reinforces the existing asymmetry of power is the lack of a clearly defined path to redress for individuals subjected to AI systems. Although the AI Act explicitly seeks to safeguard European values and fundamental rights in response to emerging challenges, there remains a risk that affected individuals could find themselves without effective remedies in cases involving the misuse of prohibited or high-risk AI systems.

Under the AI Act, individuals and legal persons are granted a right to lodge a complaint with a market surveillance authority:[209]

> any natural or legal person having grounds to consider that there has been an infringement of the provisions of this Regulation may submit complaints to the relevant market surveillance authority.

Given that the main focus of the AI Act is on the provider and the deployer, and that it is built on the language and structure of product safety regulation, such a right appears promising. However, given the Act's highly technical nature, it may be difficult in practice for individuals to identify and assess what constitute an 'infringement' of its provisions.[210] In this regard, Recital 58 is particularly significant, as it underlines the importance of accountability and effective redress:

> the exercise of important procedural fundamental rights, such as the right to an effective remedy and to a fair trial as well as the right of defence and the presumption of innocence, could be hampered, in particular, where such AI systems are not sufficiently

[208] S Kierkegaard and P Kierkegaard, 'Danger to Public Health: Medical Devices, Toxicity, Virus and Fraud' (2013) 29(1) *Computer Law & Security Review* 14 (arguing that the EU has prioritised the health of the single market over the health of the community). See also H van Kolfschooten, 'EU Regulation of Artificial Intelligence: Challenges for Patients' Rights' (2022) 59 *Common Market Law Review* 106 (arguing that the Proposal focuses on companies rather than patients).

[209] Art 85 of the AI Act (n 2). Within the AI Act, there are only two titles which explicitly mention a 'right': right to lodge a complaint with a market surveillance authority under Art 85, and 'right to explanation of individual decision making' under Art 86.

[210] This provision should be compared with the GDPR. Art 57 GDPR provides that each supervisory authority has the task 'to handle complaints lodged by a data subject, or by a body, organisation or association in accordance with Article 80, and investigate, to the extent appropriate, the subject matter of the complaint and inform the complainant of the progress and the outcome of the investigation within a reasonable period, in particular if further investigation or coordination with another supervisory authority is necessary'. In addition, the GDPR enshrines both the 'right to lodge a complaint with a supervisory authority' and the 'right to an effective remedy against a supervisory authority', in Arts 77 and 78. Art 77 states that, 'without prejudice to any other administrative or judicial remedy, every data subject shall have the right to lodge a complaint with a supervisory authority, in particular in the Member State of his or her habitual residence, place of work or place of the alleged infringement if the data subject considers that the processing of personal data relating to him or her infringes this Regulation'. Art 78 further establishes that, 'without prejudice to any other administrative or non-judicial remedy, each natural or legal person shall have the right to an effective judicial remedy against a legally binding decision of a supervisory authority concerning them'.

> transparent, explainable and documented. It is therefore appropriate to classify as high-risk, insofar as their use is permitted under relevant Union and national law, a number of AI systems intended to be used in the law enforcement context where accuracy, reliability and transparency is particularly important to avoid adverse impacts, retain public trust and ensure accountability and effective redress.

Given the foundational character of the right of access to justice,[211] this aspect of the AI Act requires particularly close examination. A regulatory framework that is excessively bureaucratic or technical may obstruct the effective concretisation of the rule of law and the meaningful protection of fundamental rights. In such circumstances, the law itself, by virtue of its overly *technocratic* design, may inadvertently produce a legal regime within which individuals are unable to exercise their rights and freedoms in practice. This, in turn, undermines the possibility of securing genuine accountability for AI providers and both private and public users.

Furthermore, the efforts of non-governmental organisations (NGOs) to raise concerns regarding AI are of particular importance in the context of the review processes for AI systems deployed in the public sphere. According to the 2022 Report of the Center for AI and Digital Policy, NGOs serve as powerful advocates for the public interest.[212] They have produced substantive reports on AI policy and regulation, and have documented various forms of abuse arising from the deployment of AI technologies.[213] Their meaningful participation in both the legislative and the review processes is, therefore, crucial. The European Parliament has recognised this democratic function by granting NGOs standing to challenge environmental issues, thereby 'strengthen[ing] the role which civil society can play as watchdog in the democratic space'.[214] Given the demonstrated capacity of NGOs to act on behalf of individuals and the public in AI-related matters, a comparable mechanism should be introduced in the field of AI governance, to ensure algorithmic justice.

As highlighted by the Fundamental Rights Agency ('Report I'), it is essential to establish robust mechanisms for the protection of fundamental rights rather

[211] See the discussion on the 'right to law' or the 'right of access to justice' proposed by G Palombella, 'Some Reflections upon Access to Justice in the Transnational Setting, as a "Right to Law"' in JE David et al (eds), *Strengthening Human Rights Protection* (Cambridge University Press, 2021) 61–81; and G Palombella, 'Access to Justice: Dynamic, Foundational, and Generative' (2021) 34(2) *Ratio Juris* 121–38 (arguing that access to justice refers to the protection of law itself, resembling the significance of a right to have rights. Palombella further parses the right of access to justice by identifying its 'dual nature', namely its structural and foundational character and its status as a fundamental right).

[212] Center for AI and Digital Policy, 'Artificial Intelligence and Democratic Values Index' (2022), available at caidp.org/reports/aidv-2021/.

[213] Center for AI and Digital Policy (n 212).

[214] See Regulation (EU) 2021/1767 of the European Parliament and of the Council amending Regulation (EC) No 1367/2006 on the application of the provisions of the Aarhus Convention on Access to Information, Public Participation in Decision-Making and Access to Justice in Environmental Matters to Community Institutions and Bodies, PE-CONS 63/21, 5 October 2021, available at data.consilium.europa.eu/doc/document/PE-63-2021-INIT/en/pdf.

than relying predominantly on self-assessment checks conducted by providers.[215] The AI Act itself, in both its provisions and its recitals, expressly references several fundamental rights enshrined in the EU Charter,[216] including the right to human dignity, respect for private life, the protection of personal data, and the principle of non-discrimination. However, despite this evident awareness, the Act's risk-based approach may, in practice, place these fundamental and human rights at significant risk within the digital sphere.

3.4.2.3. *Opaque Precautionary Bans*

Article 5 of the AI Act establishes the legal boundaries of permissible AI use within the EU by enumerating a set of practices that are prohibited. In the European Commission's 2021 Proposal, the area of prohibition was limited to four domains: manipulative techniques beyond an individual's consciousness; the exploitation of vulnerabilities; social scoring by public authorities; and real-time remote biometric identification in public spaces, subject to narrow exceptions.[217] The final text of the AI Act, however, significantly broadens the scope of proscribed practices. It now explicitly encompasses manipulative or deceptive techniques likely to cause harm, the exploitation of vulnerabilities, social scoring in general (not restricted to public authorities), predictive systems assessing or forecasting an individual's risk of committing criminal offences, the untargeted scraping of facial images for the creation of recognition databases, the use of emotion recognition technologies in employment and educational settings, biometric categorisation inferring protected characteristics, and, with reinforced safeguards, real-time remote biometric identification in publicly accessible spaces. It is significant to note that the European Commission released its draft Guidelines on Prohibited AI Practices on 4 February 2025.[218] Although the Guidelines do not carry binding legal force, they function as an important interpretive instrument within the Union's emerging regulatory architecture for AI.

Article 5 of the AI Act prohibits AI practices deemed to pose an *unacceptable risk*

> because they contradict Union values of respect for human dignity, freedom, equality, democracy and the rule of law and fundamental rights enshrined in the Charter, including the right to non-discrimination, to data protection and to privacy and the rights of the child.[219]

[215] European Union Agency for Fundamental Rights, 'Getting the Future Right: Artificial Intelligence and Fundamental Rights' (2020), available at fra.europa.eu/sites/default/files/fra_uploads/fra-2020-artificial-intelligence_en.pdf.
[216] Charter of Fundamental Rights of the European Union [2012] OJ C 326/391.
[217] Art 5 of the AI Act Proposal (n 39).
[218] European Commission, 'Annex to the Communication to the Commission Approval of the Content of the Draft Communication from the Commission' – Commission Guidelines on Prohibited Artificial Intelligence Practices established by Regulation (EU) 2024/1689 AI Act (4 February 2025) ('Guidelines on Prohibited AI Practices').
[219] AI Act (n 2), Recital 28.

In addition, the Guidelines underline that the prohibitions in Article 5 of the AI Act are also designed to protect a wider set of rights protected under the Charter of Fundamental Rights, including

> the right to freedom of expression and information (Article 11), freedom of assembly and of association (Article 12), freedom of thought, conscience and religion (Article 10), the right to an effective remedy and to a fair trial (Article 47), and the presumption of innocence and the right of defence (Article 48).[220]

Such a close dialogue with fundamental rights suggests that Article 5 may be regarded as the provision of the EU AI Act that most explicitly and directly engages with fundamental rights protection. In so doing, it offers perhaps the most powerful articulation of the European legal perspective on the regulation of AI, anchoring the Union's approach within the constitutional framework of rights and values enshrined in the Charter.[221]

For instance, the prohibition on social scoring in the AI Act clearly reflects concern regarding the recent practices in China, where reports have documented a rapid proliferation[222] of dystopian AI systems.[223] The Guidelines clarify the rationale behind this prohibition and state that:

> The prohibition of 'social scoring' aims to protect, in particular, the right to human dignity and other fundamental rights, including the right to non-discrimination and equality, to data protection, and to private and family life, as well as relevant social and economic rights, as applicable. It also aims to safeguard and promote the Union values of democracy, equality (including equal access to public and private services), and justice.[224]

Among the prohibitions, particular attention should be given to the ban on harmful manipulation and deception, which is intended to safeguard the principle of individual autonomy. The European Commission's Guidelines make clear that

> the underlying rationale of these prohibitions is to protect individual autonomy and well-being from manipulative, deceptive, and exploitative AI practices that can subvert and impair an individual's autonomy, decision-making, and free choices. The prohibitions aim to protect the right to human dignity (Article 1 of the Charter), which also constitutes the basis of all fundamental rights and includes individual autonomy as an essential aspect.[225]

[220] 'Guidelines on Prohibited AI Practices' (n 218), para 8.

[221] E Biber, 'A Close Reading of the European Commission's Guidelines on Prohibited Artificial Intelligence Practices: A Powerful Reflection of the European Approach to AI' (2025) (2)3 *Journal of AI Law and Regulation* 266–73.

[222] R Anderson, 'The Panopticon is Already Here' (*The Atlantic*, September 2020), available at theatlantic.com/magazine/archive/2020/09/china-ai-surveillance/614197/.

[223] See a recent debate on this issue in 'Debate: China's Social Credit System', *Verfassungsblog*, available at verfassungsblog.de/category/debates/chinas-social-credit-system/.

[224] 'Guidelines on Prohibited AI Practices' (n 218), para 148. See also Recital 31 AI Act (n 2).

[225] 'Guidelines on Prohibited AI Practices' (n 218), para 59.

In line with this rationale, the Guidelines identify three distinct categories of prohibited manipulative techniques: (a) subliminal techniques beyond a person's consciousness; (b) purposefully manipulative techniques; and (c) deceptive techniques.[226] However, it is highly significant that this prohibition applies only where the harm resulting from these three categories of manipulative techniques is deemed 'significant'.[227] The Guidelines emphasise that the determination of such harm is inherently fact-specific, requiring a careful evaluation of the particular circumstances of each individual case.[228]

However, the threshold of 'significant harm' presents certain challenges, as it introduces a degree of ambiguity and indeterminacy into the scope of the prohibition. Determining what qualifies as 'significant' will often prove challenging, given the fact-sensitive nature of the assessment and the diversity of contexts in which manipulative techniques may be deployed. Moreover, the consequences of such applications may not be immediately observable; rather, their full impact on autonomy, decision-making, and social structures may only become apparent in the longer term, once cumulative effects and broader societal implications have materialised.

Indeed, the Guidelines acknowledge this challenge through an example involving children: a game powered by AI that monitors their behaviour and preferences, generating personalised reward loops designed to exploit their vulnerability to instant gratification and limited self-control. Such design choices deliberately foster compulsive play and addictive tendencies, which in turn can lead to physical health issues, diminished concentration, declining academic performance, and social difficulties.[229] The Guidelines note that such a practice 'can significantly impact a child's development and well-being, *with potential longer-term consequences that may also extend to adulthood*'.[230] Considering this issue, therefore, the conceptual uncertainty on the notion of 'significant harm' tends to overlook the *social* dimensions of AI systems and risks narrowing the protective reach of the prohibition and limiting its effectiveness as a safeguard of human dignity and individual autonomy.

Furthermore, in relation to the qualification of the 'significant harm', it is essential to remember the critical role of NGOs in scrutinising AI systems. As noted above, NGOs operate as powerful advocates for the public interest.[231] They have produced detailed and critical analyses of AI policy and regulation, systematically drawing attention to documented cases of misuse and abuse.

[226] 'Guidelines on Prohibited AI Practices' (n 218), para 63. It is worth emphasising that this rationale equally informs the prohibition set forth in Art 5(1)(b), wherein the notion of 'exploitation' is addressed.

[227] The AI Act leaves the concept of 'significant harm' undefined. However, as the Guidelines note (para 91), reference to Recital 29 suggests that it should be understood as 'implying significant adverse impacts on physical or psychological health, as well as on financial and economic interests'.

[228] 'Guidelines on Prohibited AI Practices' (n 218), para 91.

[229] 'Guidelines on Prohibited AI Practices' (n 218), para 105.

[230] 'Guidelines on Prohibited AI Practices' (n 218), para 105. The italic emphasis is intentional.

[231] Center for AI and Digital Policy, 'Artificial Intelligence and Democratic Values Index' (2022).

The importance of this point is also demonstrated by the 'Reclaim Your Face' movement,[232] a Europe-wide civil society initiative advocating for a ban on indiscriminate biometric surveillance. Equally, the landmark *SyRI* judgment – widely recognised as one of the most significant technology-related cases worldwide – was brought about through the efforts of human rights activists and NGOs.[233] These examples underscore the crucial role of civil society in advancing rights-based oversight of emerging technologies. In other words, they highlight the need to ensure the meaningful participation of NGOs in both the legislative design and the review processes governing AI systems. Such an approach would also ensure that both the *social* and *publicness* dimensions of AI systems are properly taken into account, thereby reducing the risk that the threshold of 'significant harm' is construed in a way that privileges technocratic or market-oriented perspectives at the expense of broader commitments to fundamental rights and social justice.[234]

It should be noted, however, that the AI Act does not provide a clear participation right for NGOs. Although the Commission notes in its Guidelines on Prohibited AI Practices that their drafting was informed by input from a variety of stakeholders, including civil society organisations,[235] the AI Act itself does not establish a clear mechanism for such actors to participate in deliberations on whether specific AI practices should fall within the scope of the prohibition regime. There are, nevertheless, certain avenues that can be discussed at two levels. First, as Recital 96 of the AI Act indicates, civil society organisations may be involved in the process of conducting fundamental rights impact assessments, which certain deployers of high-risk AI systems are required to carry out:[236]

> Where appropriate, to collect relevant information necessary to perform the impact assessment, deployers of [a] high-risk AI system, in particular when AI systems are used in the public sector, could involve relevant stakeholders, including the representatives of groups of persons likely to be affected by the AI system, independent experts, and *civil society organisations* in conducting such impact assessments and designing measures to be taken in the case of materialisation of the risks. The European Artificial Intelligence Office (AI Office) should develop a template for a questionnaire in order to facilitate compliance and reduce the administrative burden for deployers.[237]

[232] As of March 2022, 68,758 had signed the petition of the movement. The movement classifies biometric mass surveillance into five categories, namely general monitoring, predictive policing, government databases, border and migrant control, and social media and online scraping. It asks the European Commission to 'prohibit indiscriminate or arbitrarily-targeted uses of biometrics'. See 'Reclaim You Face', available at reclaimyourface.eu/ (access 13 July 2023).

[233] The Hague District Court, Case C/09/550982/HA ZA 18-388 (2020), paras 6.1–6.118.

[234] See Chapter 2 of this book for the explanations of the *social* and *publicness* aspects of AI systems.

[235] 'Guidelines on Prohibited AI Practices' (n 218), para 6.

[236] Art 27 of the AI Act (n 2).

[237] Recital 96 of the AI Act (n 2) (emphasis added).

The second avenue, reflected in Article 67(2) of the AI Act, lies at the enforcement level and provides for the participation of civil society as members of the advisory forum,[238] a forum that provides technical expertise and advises the European Artificial Intelligence Board and the Commission.[239] However, according to Article 67(3),

> the Commission shall appoint the members of the advisory forum … among stakeholders with recognised expertise in the field of AI.

This preference raises the question of whether civil society will, in practice, obtain a seat on the advisory forum – an issue that commentators have noted depends on how lived experience is framed, and the extent to which it is prioritised in decision-making.[240]

Therefore, in order to preserve the role of civil society organisations as active participants in the review processes of AI systems, the existing avenues for their involvement require further clarification. This need was already underscored in 2019 by the HLEG, which highlighted the need for inclusive and participatory governance mechanisms in the regulation of AI:

> Questions about the kinds of risks deemed unacceptable must be deliberated and decided upon by the community at large through open, transparent and accountable deliberation, taking into account the EU's legal framework and obligations under the Charter of Fundamental Rights.[241]

Moreover, the regulation of prohibited AI practices is deeply related to European legal culture, particularly through its close relationship with the protection of human dignity.[242] As such, it is essential that this legal culture, together with the broader values of the European community, be fairly represented in the regulatory and review processes. This objective can only be meaningfully achieved through a clear establishment of participation rights, ensuring that diverse societal voices contribute to shaping the boundaries of what is deemed unacceptable in the governance of AI.[243]

[238] See also Recital 150 of the AI Act (n 2).

[239] Art 67(1) of the AI Act (n 2).

[240] ME Kaminski and G Malgieri, 'Impacted Stakeholder Participation in AI and Data Governance' (2025) 27(1) *Yale Journal of Law & Technology* 265.

[241] European Commission, HLEGAI, 'Policy and Investment Recommendations for Trustworthy AI' (2019), available at europarl.europa.eu/italy/resource/static/files/import/intelligenza_artificiale_30_aprile/ai-hleg_policy-and-investment-recommendations.pdf.

[242] P Häberle, *Europäische Rechtskultur: Versuch einer Annäherung in zwölf Schritten* (Nomos Verlagsgesellschaft, 1994) 72 ('Diese Menschenwürde ist ein Element der sich im Gang der europäischen Geschichte entwickelnden Gerechtigkeitsprinzipien: von Aristoteles' Klassikertexten (Nikomachische Ethik) bis zum angloamerikanischen due process-Gedanken bzw. zur 'Gerechtigkeit als Fairness' (J Rawls)').

[243] This point has also been emphasised by the European Commission in its 'Communication on Establishing a European Declaration on Digital Rights and Principles for the Digital Decade', COM(2022) 27 final, 26 January 2022, 1 ('The digital transformation should be shaped according to our European values and laws.').

In this regard, it is also significant to recall that the European Declaration on Digital Rights, presented by the European Commission on 26 January 2022, places the individual at the centre of the digital transformation.[244] While this emphasis highlights the importance of freedom of choice and individual agency, it also raises the question of how to respond to the societal risks posed by AI systems. These technologies affect not only individuals but also the wider social fabric, reshaping institutions and collective practices. For this reason, reliance on individual agency alone is insufficient; what is required is a structural framework of legal protection that addresses both individual and societal dimensions.[245]

Moreover, such protection is also necessary at the individual level. Many AI systems rely on techniques, developed in behavioural economics, that can subtly undermine individual choice. Indeed, such techniques can manipulate the individual on the basis of dark patterns.[246] Without clear safeguards to prevent or restrict these practices, an individual may find herself no longer acting as the 'subject' of decision-making, but rather as the 'object' of decisions effectively determined by the system. In this context, it becomes difficult to safeguard individual agency or freedom of choice within a coded ecosystem that may, in some cases, know more about the individual than she knows about herself,[247] and which therefore carries a powerful capacity for persuasion and influence.[248] This underlines the need, at the individual level, for structural legal mechanisms that can help ensure respect for, and protection of, human agency.

3.4.2.4. *Misidentifications of Risk Profiles*

Another challenge with the AI Act, when viewed from the perspective of fundamental rights, lies in its limited attention to the nature of the risks posed by AI systems. For regulation to function effectively, it is essential first to obtain a good grip on the nature of the risks under examination.[249] This step is particularly important because different types of risk inevitably demand different regulatory

[244] J-H Hoepman, 'The European Declaration on Digital Rights Puts People in the Firing Line of the Digital Transformation' (2022), available at blog.xot.nl/2022/03/06/the-european-declaration-on-digital-rights-puts-people-in-the-firing-line-of-the-digital-transformation/index.html (arguing that the Declaration ignores the systemic risks of AI systems and fails to provide more structural legal protection).

[245] J-H Hoepman, 'The European Declaration on Digital Rights' (2022).

[246] It should be noted that no concrete example could be identified of biometrics being employed by public authorities as a form of 'persuasive technology'. Nevertheless, such a scenario is not implausible, given the *dynamic* aspect of AI systems discussed in Chapter 2.

[247] J Carmichael, 'Google Knows You Better than Yourself' (*The Atlantic*, 19 August 2014), available at theatlantic.com/technology/archive/2014/08/google-knows-you-better-than-you-know-yourself/378608/.

[248] P Tokamani, 'Persuasive Technology and Human Rights' (LLM thesis, Tilburg University, 2016), available at arno.uvt.nl/show.cgi?fid=142041.

[249] V Heyvaert, 'Governing Intersystemic Systemic Risks' (2022), 1.

responses.[250] It is, therefore, important to identify the most distinctive risk profiles surrounding AI systems, in order to design a framework capable of offering meaningful protection for fundamental rights.

For example, the risk of algorithmic bias in biometric categorisation, and the risk of societal manipulation, may be situated within the category of 'systemic risks',[251] given their emerging context, which is complex, uncertain, and ambiguous.[252] Such risks threaten not only individuals but also the wellbeing of society, democracy, equality, and the rule of law. As the UN Special Rapporteur on Extreme Poverty and Human Rights, Philip Alston, cautioned in 2019, there is a grave risk of 'stumbling zombie-like into a digital welfare dystopia'.[253] He underlined that, although new technologies are often presented as tools to increase efficiency and enhance citizens' welfare, in practice they are frequently employed by governments to monitor populations and reduce welfare budgets.[254] Against this backdrop, recognising the systemic dimension of risks associated with AI systems is of paramount importance for the design of an effective risk governance framework. Yet, despite these warnings, the AI Act appears limited in its capacity to fully capture and address such systemic risks.[255]

In sum, the AI Act does not yet provide a clear and comprehensive legal framework for the identification and categorisation of risks. By relying on relatively simplistic risk categories that do not fully reflect the *complexity* of AI systems, it leaves room for gaps in accountability, and may fall short of offering sufficient safeguards for fundamental rights.

[250] V Heyvaert, 'Governing Intersystemic Systemic Risks' (2022).

[251] V Galaz et al, 'Artificial Intelligence, Systemic Risks, and Sustainability' (2021) 67 *Technology in Society* 101741, 4 (discussing algorithmic bias in the context of systemic risks and sustainability).

[252] The concept of 'systemic risk' was first developed by WR Cline in *International Debt: Systemic Risk and Policy Response* (Institute for International Economics/MIT Press, 1984). The notion gained wider prominence with the OECD report 'Emerging Systemic Risks in the 21st Century: An Agenda for Action' (2003), available at oecd.org/futures/globalprospects/37944611.pdf. In the academic literature, O Renn has provided a clear framework, describing systemic risks as 'characterized by high complexity, trans-boundary effects, stochastic relationships, and nonlinear cause-effect patterns with tipping points and often associated with less public attention than they deserve': O Renn, 'New Challenges for Risk Analysis: Systemic Risks' (2021) 24(1) *Journal of Risk Research* 127–33. An illustrative example in the context of AI systems is provided by D Abu Elyounes, 'Why the Resignation of the Dutch Government Is a Good Reminder of How Important It Is to Monitor and Regulate Algorithms' (Harvard Berkman Klein Center, 10 February 2021), available at medium.com/berkman-klein-center/why-the-resignation-of-the-dutch-government-is-a-good-reminder-of-how-important-it-is-to-monitor-2c599c1e0100.

[253] United Nations, 'World Stumbling Zombie-Like into a Digital Welfare Dystopia, Warns UN Human Rights Expert' (press release, 17 October 2019), available at ohchr.org/en/press-releases/2019/10/world-stumbling-zombie-digital-welfare-dystopia-warns-un-human-rights-expert?LangID=E&NewsID=25156 (noting that Big Tech operates in an almost human-rights-free zone, which is particularly problematic when the private sector takes a leading role in designing, constructing, and even operating significant parts of the digital welfare state).

[254] United Nations (2019) (n 253).

[255] Within the final AI Act, the 'systemic risk' category is limited to the high-impact capabilities of general-purpose AI models. See Recital 110 of the AI Act (n 2).

3.5. Discussion: A Call for a Rights-Based Approach

As discussed in the previous chapter, AI systems used in the public sector possess the quality of *publicness*, as they operate within the public sphere (the 'space of appearance'),[256] are infused in power relations, and have a normative impact on individual autonomy. This quality of publicness is grounded in three key principles: *accessibility*, *exposure*, and *consideration*.[257] Accordingly, whenever AI systems are deployed in the public sector it is essential to ensure the accountability of public authorities, so that their use remains consistent with democratic values and the protection of fundamental rights.[258]

In this regard, a rights-based approach appears particularly promising, due to the inherent *ex post* function it entails. Fundamental and human rights perform both *ex ante* and *ex post* functions. While their *ex ante* function guides the decision-making of public authorities, steering them towards legitimate decisions, their *ex post* function enables individuals to hold those authorities accountable once the relevant actions have occurred. This second function is closely related to the notion of accountability, insofar as it is oriented towards the retrospective assessment of state conduct. In this sense, fundamental and human rights provide a 'peculiar language' for individuals to ensure accountability of public authorities. Drawing inspiration from Alexy's 'special case thesis' *(Sonderfallthese)*,[259] they represent a 'particular practical discourse' having an authoritative, institutional character, unlike general practical discourse. Moreover, rights are not only concerned with the limitation of power but also with the adequate protection of the individual's autonomy, where the duties of justification and accountability emerge when it is first being interfered with.[260]

Overly technocratic and bureaucratic legal approaches – particularly those that result in 'privatising public power' or 'publicising private power'[261] in the context of essential requirements and oversight mechanisms – risk constraining the

[256] H Arendt, *The Human Condition* (The University of Chicago Press, 1998).

[257] B Kingsbury and N Maisley, 'Infrastructures and Laws: Publics and Publicness' (Institute for International Law and Justice, NYU School of Law, Working Paper 2021/3, 2021).

[258] 'When you cannot avoid living side by side with all others, you ought to leave the state of nature and proceed with them into a rightful condition.' See I Kant, *The Metaphysics of Morals* (M Gregor trans, Cambridge University Press, 1996) 86.

[259] Alexy, *Theorie der juristischen Argumentation* (1991).

[260] K Möller, 'Lüth and the Objective System of Values: From "Limited Government" towards an Autonomy-Based Conception of Constitutional Rights' in S Choudhry, M Hailbronner, and M Kumm (eds), *Global Canons in an Age of Contestation: Debating Foundational Texts of Constitutional Democracy and Human Rights* (Oxford University Press, 2024l online edn, Oxford Academic, 15 May 2024), https://doi.org/10.1093/9780191956942.003.0014; K Möller, 'Justifying the Culture of Justification' (2019) 17 International Journal of Constitutional Law 1078.

[261] I sincerely thank my colleague and friend, Francisco de Abreu Duarte, for sharing his insights, which helped me to refine my thinking on this point. See his commentary on the 'privatisation of public power' and the 'publicisation of corporate power' in F de Abreu Duarte, 'The Internet Is for Porn! (But Is It?) – The Digital Equilibrium Hypothesis' (*Digital Constitutionalist*, 2022), available at digi-con.org/the-internet-is-for-porn-but-is-it-the-digital-equilibrium-hypothesis/.

development of a fundamental and human rights discourse in emerging domains. As the AI Act has demonstrated, such approaches may place rights-based considerations in the background and make it more difficult for them to take root where they are most urgently needed.[262]

Thus, such an approach tends to overlook the *publicness* of AI systems deployed in the public sector, and may also complicate, and at times obstruct, the accountability of public authorities. This means that, in effect, legislation enables public actors to delegate to private entities an excessive margin of discretion over matters concerning fundamental and human rights – a level of discretion that public authorities themselves would not be permitted to exercise. Furthermore, as Hofmann rightly underlines regarding the increasing role of standardisation in the EU's regulatory approach to digitalisation, 'where private and semi-private standardisation bodies are co-opted to fill a legislative void, the standardisation procedures become a highlighted issue of public interest'.[263]

Moreover, the analysis above has shown that public actors often fail to provide adequate guidance on how such discretion should be exercised. The absence of a meaningful rights-based approach carries the risk that oversight mechanisms will be reduced to purely technical 'tick-box' exercises,[264] thereby undermining their ability to offer meaningful protection for fundamental and human rights.

This dynamic leaves individuals within a 'rightless' framework, where the 'rule of technology'[265] prevails, making it extremely difficult to challenge the status quo or resist oppressive digital public practices.[266] In such a context, Frankensteinian

[262] It should be noted that the *ex post* function of rights also demonstrates that a rights-based approach is fundamentally distinct from a risk-based approach. As U Beck emphasises, the focus of risk lies not in the present or the past, but in the future. Consequently, a risk-oriented approach may be inherently inadequate for the notion of accountability, since accountability is concerned not with potential future harms or current conditions, but with responsibility for past actions. In this respect, experience has shown that the European risk regulation regime has been systematised primarily through the case law of the CJEU, which is necessarily rooted in past decisions. This implies that the accountability dimension of a risk-oriented approach can only be realised in its mature and settled stage, whereas in its initial phase it leaves individuals and society in a state of uncertainty. See K Purnhagen, *The Politics of Systematization in EU Product Safety Regulation: Market, State, Collectivity, and Integration* (Springer, 2013); and U Beck, *Risk Society: Towards a New Modernity* (Sage Publications, 1992).

[263] HCH Hofmann, 'New Regulatory Approaches under the EU's Legislation on Digitalisation: Introduction to the Special Edition of the EJRR "Charting the Landscape of Automation of Regulatory Decision-Making"' (2025) 16 *European Journal of Risk Regulation* 4.

[264] The term 'technical tick-box exercises' has been addressed by N Smuha et al to critique the proposed AI Act, highlighting the risk of reducing compliance to formalistic assessments that fail to safeguard fundamental rights: Smuha et al, 'How the EU Can Achieve Legally Trustworthy AI' (2021). This pattern may be reconsidered as a form of 'economic colonisation of law', a concept referring to technocratic laws that rely excessively on market-based approaches, thereby undermining the effective exercise of fundamental rights. The expression first appeared in a different context: N Lellis and R Dutra, 'Programmatic Crisis and Moralization of the Politics: A Proposal to Define the Bolsonarism from the Experience with the Covid-19 Pandemic' (2020) 4 *International Journal of Latin American Religions* 335–59.

[265] For the term 'rule of technology', see Brownsword and Yeung, *Regulating Technologies: Legal Futures, Regulatory Frames and Technological Fixes* (2008).

[266] Moreover, the centrality of technocratic requirements and reviews in the AI Act highlights its divergence from the GDPR, which is grounded in 'data subject rights', such as the rights to be informed

applications of AI systems and their accompanying 'Frankenlaws',[267] which are backed by legal rules that go beyond rhetorical or science-fictional references, confuse the issues surrounding AI systems and destabilise the legal order. However, the rule of law as an institutional *ideal* bearing an inherent value cannot be reduced to a rule of an instrument, or 'rule of men' (*stricto sensu* version as domination), or 'rule by law'.[268]

The principal reason behind the adoption of such an approach appears to lie in its concern for safeguarding the functioning of the internal market. Indeed, the AI Act explicitly highlights the facilitation of investment and innovation in AI, as well as the smooth functioning of the internal market to prevent fragmentation, among its specific objectives.[269] Within this economic rationale, however, there emerges an over-reliance on market-based mechanisms – particularly self-assessment procedures – for the governance of fundamental and human rights, as well as other non-pecuniary interests.

The questions then arises, is a rights-based approach fundamentally in tension with the wellbeing of the EU market, or, more specifically, are fundamental and human rights incompatible with the goals pursued by public authorities? Here, Dworkin offers a useful distinction between rights and goals. First, he defines collective goals as follows: 'collective goals encourage trade-off benefits and burdens within a community in order to produce some overall benefit for the community as a whole'.[270] Second, according to his thesis, rights can be discovered through arguments that

about the collection of personal data, to access information, to rectification, to be forgotten, and to safeguards relating to automated decision-making and profiling. It is important to note that personal data protection and AI regulation are fundamentally distinct domains. For a comparison between the AI Act and the GDPR, see V Papakonstantinou and P De Hert, 'EU Lawmaking in the Artificial Intelligent Age: Act-ification, GDPR Mimesis, and Regulatory Brutality' (*European Law Blog*, 8 July 2021), available at europeanlawblog.eu/2021/07/08/eu-lawmaking-in-the-artificial-intelligent-age-act-ification-gdpr-mimesis-and-regulatory-brutality/ (arguing that the AI Act Proposal follows the GDPR model in two forms: structurally, in its supervision and enforcement framework, and case-specifically, in its certification mechanisms; but emphasising that data processing is a special activity, while AI regulation has a far broader scope encompassing all instances of AI in human life).

[267] L Dossey, 'Neurolaw or Frankenlaw? The Thought Police Have Arrived' (2010) 6(5) *Explore (NY)* 275–86.

[268] G Palombella, 'The Rule of Law as an Institutional Ideal' (2010) 9(1) *Comparative Sociology* 10 (arguing that the rule of men in *stricto sensu* as domination 'emerges where no positive laws or legal devices are institutionally available, that are suitable to cope with this dominating feature'). See also AL Goodhart, 'The Rule of Law and Absolute Sovereignty' (1958) 106(7) *University of Pennsylvania Law Review* 947 ('I am not speaking about rule by law which can be the most efficient instrument in the enforcement of tyrannical rule: I am speaking about rule under the law which is the essential foundation of liberty. The two are totally distinct.'). See further Section 4.4.4 of this chapter for a detailed discussion on the rule of law.

[269] In the AI Act Proposal, the Commission defined four specific objectives in 2021: '(i) ensure that AI systems placed on the Union market and used are safe and respect existing law on fundamental rights and Union values; (ii) ensure legal certainty to facilitate investment and innovation in AI; (iii) enhance governance and effective enforcement of existing law on fundamental rights and safety requirements applicable to AI systems; (iv) facilitate the development of a single market for lawful, safe and trustworthy AI applications and prevent market fragmentation'. See the AI Act Proposal (n 39).

[270] R Dworkin, *Taking Rights Seriously* (Harvard University Press, 1978) 90–91.

justify a claim, and they have 'a certain threshold against collective goals in general'.[271] This distinction confirms that a degree of tension exists between rights and goals. However, a rights-based approach, with its 'peculiar language', prevents the abuse of power and ensures the reasonable realisation of public purposes. It puts the dynamics of public goals into a qualified judgement. As Rawls underlines in his groundbreaking work *A Theory of Justice*:

> The principles of right, and so of justice, put limits on which satisfactions have value; they impose restrictions on what are reasonable conceptions of one's good. In drawing up plans and in deciding on aspirations men are to take these constraints into account. Hence in justice as fairness one does not take men's propensities and inclinations as given, whatever they are, and then seek the best way to fulfil them. Rather, their desires and aspirations are restricted from the outset by the principles of justice which specify the boundaries that men's systems of ends must respect. We can express this by saying that in justice as fairness the concept of right is prior to that of the good. A just social system defines the scope within which individuals must develop their aims, and it provides a framework of rights and opportunities and the means of satisfaction within and by the use of which these ends may be equitably pursued. The priority of justice is accounted for, in part, by holding that the interests requiring the violation of justice have no value. Having no merit in the first place, they cannot override its claims.[272]

In this light, the precedence of rights cannot be regarded as being in opposition to the goals of public institutions; on the contrary, it provides the very framework of reasonable argumentation for what constitutes the 'good' or the legitimate action of the state.[273] In this sense, fundamental and human rights give effect to the right to justification and accountability precisely through their endorsement on *reasonableness*.[274] As Palombella observes from the perspective of political action, 'in Rawls' construction, justice takes precedence and helps to shape the *admissible* prospects of action towards the good'.[275]

[271] R Dworkin, *Taking Rights Seriously* (1978), 92.

[272] J Rawls, *A Theory of Justice* (Harvard University Press, 1971) 31. For a critique of this idea in the context of the family, see MJ Sandel, *Liberalism and the Limits of Justice* (Cambridge University Press, 1982); and SM Okin, *Justice, Gender, and the Family* (Basic Books, 1989) (arguing that the family is not characterised by the circumstances of justice, but by nobler virtues).

[273] M Kumm, 'The Idea of Socratic Contestation and the Right to Justification: The Point of Rights-Based Proportionality Review' (2010) 4 *Law and Ethics of Human Rights* 141, 168–70 (discussing that a right-based proportionality test is considered as a test of reasonableness).

[274] K Möller, 'Lüth and the Objective System of Values' (2022).

[275] G Palombella, 'The Rule of Law and Its Core' in G Palombella and N Walker (eds), *Relocating the Rule of Law* (Hart Publishers, 2009) 13 (citing also Kant's 'Critique of Practical Reason') (emphasis added). See also I Kant, *Critique of Practical Reason* (M Gregor and A Reath trans, Cambridge Text in the History of Philosophy, 2015) 54 ('instead of the concept of the good as an object determining and making possible the moral law, it is on the contrary the moral law that first determines and makes possible the concept of the good, insofar as it deserves this name absolutely … They [philosophers] should first have searched for a law that determined the will a priori and immediately, and only then determined the object conformable to the will.').

Therefore, it is necessary to move beyond an overly economic and technocratic reasoning.[276] Regulations on AI should not reinforce the growing dominance of market forces, whether at the local or the global level. Otherwise, such an approach could lead to hegemonic legal approaches or a hegemonic free-trade imperative. From the perspective of the rule of law, regulation of AI systems must reflect the power of law, not the law of power. Indeed, the hegemonic market-based approach that reflects the law of the power was deemed not acceptable, as we observed in the two CJEU cases *Schrems I* and *Schrems II*. Those cases have demonstrated that European data strategy following such an approach is not welcomed by the CJEU.[277]

Moreover, the rights-based approach will also provide the necessary ground for the meaningful emergence of three 'generations' of digital human rights: (i) the radical reinterpretation of existing rights; (ii) the articulation of new rights; and (iii) the recognition of new right- and duty-holders.[278] Within this tripartite division, the first generation of digital human rights involves a recalibration of existing human rights. It follows the premises of the 'normative equivalency paradigm', according to which the 'same rights that people have offline must also be protected online'.[279] A notable example is the right to privacy, which possesses significant potential to address novel challenges posed by AI systems. The second generation is characterised by the formulation of entirely new rights, arising both from (i) the limitations of existing frameworks in safeguarding the interests of individuals, and (ii) the emergence of unprecedented needs and concerns that find no counterpart in the offline environment.[280] Examples of such digital human rights may include the right to human decision,[281] the right of access to the Internet, or the right to mental integrity. The third generation focuses on refining our understanding of right-holders, such as newly emerging online personae, as well as duty-bearers, including the direct human rights obligations of technology companies.

Within the second generation, a right to a human decision holds particular significance. Tasioulas defends this right through process-oriented arguments,

[276] 'the facts suggest that market-driven politics can lead to a remarkably rapid erosion of democratically determined collective values and institutions': C Leys, *Market-Driven Politics: Neoliberal Democracy and the Public Interest* (Verso, 2001) 4. See also M Sagoff, *Price, Principle, and the Environment* (Cambridge University Press, 2004) 4 ('market allocation has to be balanced with political deliberation with respect to social policies that involve moral and aesthetic judgment').

[277] M Zalnieriute, 'Data Transfers After Schrems II: The EU–US Disagreements over Data Privacy and National Security' (2022) 55(1) *Vanderbilt Journal of Transnational Law* 1–48, also published as University of New South Wales Law Research Series (discussing that the EU is not a monolithic block on data protection issues).

[278] D Dror-Shpoliansky and Y Shany, 'It's the End of the (Offline) World as We Know It: From Human Rights to Digital Human Rights – A Proposed Typology' (2021) 32(4) *The European Journal of International Law* 1249–82.

[279] D Dror-Shpoliansky and Y Shany, 'It's the End of the (Offline) World as We Know It' (2021).

[280] D Dror-Shpoliansky and Y Shany, 'It's the End of the (Offline) World as We Know It' (2021).

[281] J Tasioulas, 'A Right to Human Decision' Draft Paper (2023), available at academia.edu/116775511/A_Human_Right_to_a_Human_Decision.

specifically those of *explainability*, *answerability*, and *solidarity*.[282] His emphasis on process not only underpins the justification of this right but also invites a critical stance towards the highly technocratic procedures embedded within the law itself. This orientation further raises the question of whether risks to fundamental and human rights can genuinely be identified and addressed through technocratic processes alone. Indeed, overly economic or technocratic reasoning, which risks reducing the engagement between rights and risks to a superficial level, may also hinder the meaningful emergence of these three generations and their critical evaluation. This dynamic may create a 'missing dialogue' between rights and risks, and raises the question of how, and by whom, this silence will be translated into speech. A further factor contributing to the oversimplification of the relationship between rights and risks is the limited public awareness of technological interferences with fundamental and human rights. As I have examined in greater detail elsewhere, the highly complex and often incomprehensible architecture of AI systems significantly constrains the capacity of individuals to act against their misuse, thereby placing them in a predominantly passive position with regard to human rights claims.[283]

Furthermore, the sustainable deployment of AI systems in public services and policies depends on the strength of their 'social licence to operate';[284] that is, the extent to which individuals perceive their use as legitimate, trustworthy, and reliable. In this regard, a rights-based approach is indispensable, as it safeguards the credibility and legitimacy not only of the emerging body of AI law but also of the proper functioning of the internal market.[285]

However, given the fundamental characteristics of AI systems examined in chapter two, a rights-based approach alone is not sufficient to address the challenges they pose. The *inter-systemic, social, complex*, and *dynamic* dimensions of AI require the adoption of an inter-legal approach. AI systems operating in

[282] See J Tasioulas, 'A Right to Human Decision' Draft Paper (2023).

[283] E Biber, 'A Challenge for a Primavera Digitale: The Phantom Influence of Artificial Intelligence Systems' (International Journal of Constitutional Law Blog, ICONnect, New York University School of Law, 3 February 2026) available at: https://www.iconnectblog.com/a-challenge-for-a-primavera-digitale-the-phantom-influence-of-artificial-intelligence-systems/(focusing on the Arendtian understanding of human rights, holding that human rights emerge from the 'capacity to act' or 'right to action').

[284] G Demuijnck and B Fasterling, 'The Social License to Operate' (2016) 136 *Journal of Business Ethics* 675–85.

[285] It is important to note that, from a European private law perspective, MW Hesselink advances a similar approach after examining political theories relating to contracts contrary to public policy or good morals. He suggests that the EU Charter could provide guidance in formulating minimum standards for 'contractual immorality in a morally properly functioning internal market': MW Hesselink, *Justifying Contract in Europe – Political Philosophies of European Contract Law* (Oxford University Press, 2021) 390. See also MW Hesselink, 'Reconstituting the Code of Capital: Could a Progressive European Code of Private Law Help Us Reduce Inequality and Regain Democratic Control?' (2022), paper presented at the conference 'Tracing the Nature, Place, and Effects of EU Private Law in (Re) shaping Global Markets and Orders' (University of Helsinki, online, 16–17 September 2021), and at the EUI Law Faculty Seminar (16 March 2022), available at papers.ssrn.com/sol3/papers.cfm?abstract_id=4075004 (arguing that a European code of private law should consist of fundamental principles rather than detailed rules, since creative lawyers will invariably find ways to circumvent detailed regulation to protect capital).

pluralist public areas characterised by overlapping publics and legal orders – such as in the field of migration and border control management – cannot be adequately regulated and adjudicated solely through a rights-based lens. Rather, they demand an inclusive reasoning that interweaves rights-based protections with inter-legal insights. Therefore, drawing on the theory of inter-legality, this book proposes a 'rights-based inter-legal approach' to strengthen the legal position of individuals and the public, and to reinforce the rule of law in the face of potential misuses of AI systems by public authorities. In doing so, both the regulation and adjudication of AI will be better placed to realise their intended objectives. Accordingly, the next chapter turns to the theory of inter-legality as the theoretical foundation for this proposal.

4

Steering the Pendulum Towards the Rule of Law

A Rights-Based Inter-Legal Approach

4.1. General Overview

Given the fundamental characteristics of the AI systems examined in chapter two, a rights-based approach alone proves insufficient to address the challenges arising from their public use. The *inter-systemic*, *social*, *complex*, and *dynamic* nature of these systems necessitates an inter-legal approach. The justification for such an approach operates across five levels, progressing from a general to a more specific perspective. This chapter begins by examining the notion of inter-legality and its relationship to concepts widely discussed in international law and political administration theory, including monism, dualism, pluralism, regime complex, polycentrism, and global law. It then identifies three fundamental characteristics of inter-legality: (i) the simultaneous emergence of diverse legalities; (ii) a shift in focus from contestations to functions; and (iii) the emergence of a 'law of the case' from composite interweaving norms.

Following a rigorous analysis of the three fundamental features, the chapter turns to doctrinal mechanisms already proposed by legal scholars for safeguarding fundamental rights and freedoms in the digital environment. In this regard, it examines the theory of the horizontal application of fundamental rights; digital constitutionalism; rights; and the rule of law. At a more specific and concrete level, the chapter then demonstrates how the perspective of inter-legality is particularly relevant to AI systems employed by public authorities, advancing the argument that such systems are *inter-legal by default*. Finally, it illustrates the application of a 'rights-based inter-legal approach' to a concrete case through three steps: (i) adopting the vantage point of the affair – the case at hand – under scrutiny; (ii) identifying the relevant normativities governing the case; and (iii) considering the demands of justice that arise from it.[1] The chapter concludes with final remarks.

[1] A previous version of section 4.6. of this chapter ('Application of the Theory of Inter-Legality') was published in the *Italian Law Journal* (open access): E Biber, 'Inter-Legality and Surveillance Technologies' (2021) 2 *Italian Law Journal*, available at theitalianlawjournal.it/biber/. The version included in this book has been revised.

4.2. What does Inter-Legality Stand for?

The first book on the theory of inter-legality was published at the beginning of 2019, by Cambridge University Press: *The Challenge of Inter-Legality*.[2] In this book, Palombella and Klabbers revisited the concept of inter-legality, which was first introduced by Portuguese sociologist Boaventura de Sousa Santos almost 40 years ago.[3] The central aim of the authors was to reintroduce the concept of inter-legality as a legal idea rather than a sociological phenomenon. As Walker observes, inter-legality, with its own legal content, emerges from the interpenetration of legal orders and provides a new normative dimension to the understanding of legal pluralism on a global scale.[4]

A proper engagement with the notion requires careful consideration of the modern legal landscape. The contemporary world is marked by a higher degree of complexity than in the past, and this complexity significantly affects the legal sphere by multiplying the legalities that govern specific issues. A single matter may now be regulated simultaneously by diverse legalities in different *formats*, including state-centred law, transnational regulatory frameworks, *jus gentium* (understood as general principles of law), *jus cogens* norms, and common legal traditions.[5] Indeed, the significant proliferation of jurisgenerative entities beyond the state has been examined in legal scholarship under the emerging field of 'global administrative law'.[6] These diverse legalities, however, are neither unified nor inclined towards harmonisation. As Palombella and Klabbers explain, rather than producing unified or harmonised frameworks, the evolution of legal governance has compelled these layers of legality to become interwoven.[7] Moreover, the state-based character of legalities does not prevent them from intertwining, despite their geo-territorial claims to sovereign power: 'An array of legal "software", self-contained legal regimes pierce the veil of State systems.'[8]

The intertwining of legalities diminishes the role of state law as the dominant icon of the legal world.[9] Interestingly, this development has not been sufficiently

[2] J Klabbers and G Palombella (eds), *The Challenge of Inter-Legality* (Cambridge University Press, 2019).

[3] B de Sousa Santos, 'Law: A Map of Misreading. Towards a Postmodern Conception of Law' (1987) 14(3) *Journal of Law and Society* 279–302, 288 ('as a result of interaction and intersection among legal spaces one cannot properly speak of law and legality but rather of interlaw and interlegality').

[4] N Walker, 'Legalising Inter-Legality' (2022) 1 *European Law Open* 216–27.

[5] G Palombella, '"Formats" of Law and Their Intertwining' in Klabbers and Palombella (eds), *The Challenge of Inter-Legality* (2019) 23–41. See also G Palombella, 'Inter-Legality: On Interconnectedness and "External Sources"' (2021) 7(2) *Italian Law Journal* 943–59. See also E Chiti, 'Administrative Inter-Legality – A Hypothesis' (2021) 7(2) *Italian Law Journal* 985–1002; A Di Martino, 'The Importance of Being a Case – Collapsing of the Law upon the Case in Inter-Legal Situations' (2021) 7(2) *Italian Law Journal* 961–84.

[6] B Kingsbury, N Krisch, and RB Stewart, 'The Emergence of Global Administrative Law' (2005) 68 *Law and Contemporary Problems* 15–62 (identifying some patterns of commonality and connection between diverse national, international, and transnational legal settings).

[7] Palombella, 'Inter-Legality: On Interconnectedness and "External Sources"' (2021), 943.

[8] Palombella, 'Inter-Legality: On Interconnectedness and "External Sources"' (2021), 943.

[9] Palombella, 'Inter-Legality: On Interconnectedness and "External Sources"' (2021), 944. It is important to note that an estimated 80–90% of disputes in the Global South are handled outside the

addressed by legal theorists,[10] whose primary focus has often remained on the 'genetic configuration of law', grounded in its own grammar, language, and 'anatomic' morphology.[11] As William Twining has highlighted,

> Contemporary legal theory needs to tackle issues relating to legal traditions, non-state law, legal pluralism, multiculturalism, human rights, transnational justice, diffusion of law, problems of comparison and generalization, and our collective ignorance of other legal traditions and cultures. Until recently, hardly any of these topics were dreamt of in Hart's legal philosophy or those of most of his followers.[12]

Traditional doctrines concerning the relationship between international and domestic law – namely, monism[13] and dualism[14] – have also proven inadequate for analysing today's complex legal environment. Scholars have argued that these frameworks are unable even to capture how international law functions within states, in practice.[15] To clarify this limitation, it is therefore essential to outline the basic assumptions underlying the two doctrines.

The theoretical foundations of monism and dualism have been debated in legal scholarship since the emergence of international law in Europe and beyond.[16] Monism was first articulated by early Catholic natural lawyers, who conceived of the supreme order as both divine and natural. For these scholars, the legal order was unified, such that the laws of the state could not exist independently from (natural) international law.[17]

state justice and security system; see P Albrecht and HM Kyed, 'Justice and Security: When the State Isn't the Main Provider' (2010) *Danish Institute for International Studies, Policy Brief* (Copenhagen), available at pure.diis.dk/ws/files/811082/PB_Justice_and_Security_web.pdf.

[10] W Twining, 'Schauer on Hart' (2006) 119 *Harvard Law Review Forum* 122.

[11] Palombella, 'Inter-Legality: On Interconnectedness and "External Sources"' (2021), 943–59. Besides missing the opportunity to appreciate what an inter-legal approach can offer, such an understanding also hinders the development of a nuanced legal interpretation that is responsive to the specific social context.

[12] Twining, 'Schauer on Hart' (2006), 122; Palombella, 'Inter-Legality: On Interconnectedness and "External Sources"' (2021), 944–59. See also J Waldron, 'No Barking: Legal Pluralism and the Contrast between Hart's Jurisprudence and Fuller's' in P Cane (ed), *The Hart–Fuller Debate 50 Years On* (Australian National University College of Law, 2008) (arguing that international law, stare decisis, and legal pluralism have barely been touched on in legal theory since 1958).

[13] See a comprehensive study on legal monism in P Gragl, *Legal Monism: Law, Philosophy, and Politics* (Oxford University Press, 2018).

[14] The doctrines of monism and dualism have been extensively discussed in international law scholarship. See B Çalı, 'Beyond Monism and Dualism' in B Çalı, *The Authority of International Law: Obedience, Respect, Rebuttal* (Oxford University Press, 2015) 129 (arguing that monism and dualism do not offer stable or clear guidance to domestic judges on the authority claims of international law).

[15] See a basic discussion on monism and dualism in M Chiam, 'Monism and Dualism in International Law' (2021) *Oxford Bibliographies*, available at oxfordbibliographies.com/view/document/obo-9780199796953/obo-9780199796953-0168.xml.

[16] B Çalı, 'Beyond Monism and Dualism' in B Çalı, *The Authority of International Law: Obedience, Respect, Rebuttal* (Oxford University Press, 2015) 137. See also A von Bogdandy, 'Pluralism, Direct Effect, and the Ultimate Say: On the Relationship Between International and Domestic Constitutional Law' (2008) 6(3–4) *International Journal of Constitutional Law* 399 ('The relationship between the norms of international law and those of domestic law is still understood in terms of concepts developed one hundred years ago: monism and dualism.').

[17] See Çalı, 'Beyond Monism and Dualism' (2015), 138.

Dualism, by contrast, is grounded in the supremacy of the state's will. In this view, international law *(äußeres Staatsrecht)*[18] does not arise from the will of the state and, therefore, cannot form part of a sovereign state's legal order. Instead, it exists in a separate legal realm, external to the domestic system and in constant need of domestication by the sovereign in order to be recognised by domestic courts.[19] In other words, international law may enter legal reasoning or decision-making at the state level only through incorporation by a public authority via domestic legislation. In such cases, the domestic judge is not, strictly speaking, applying international law, but, rather, domestic law.[20]

Both doctrines, however, operate by translating one legality into the other, thereby domesticating the *inter-systemic* dimension into the familiar rationale of a single legal system. In doing so, they fail to acknowledge the plurality of legal orders. Legal pluralism thus emerges as a corrective, seeking to address this deficiency by revising and extending the limitations of monism and dualism.[21]

Legal pluralism, however, does not move beyond the mere recognition of a plurality of legal systems. It offers no legal mechanisms for addressing the relations among these systems.[22] Within a pluralist framework, such relations can only be managed through political instruments. Since political actors are under no legal duty to initiate negotiations concerning inter-systemic relations, legal pluralism ultimately leaves 'no legal way out', so to speak.[23] In this sense, it fails to engage with the porous structure of law that allows diverse legalities to interweave. It is precisely this point that an inter-legal rationale seeks to emphasise.

International law *(ius gentium)*,[24] moreover, does not adequately capture the complexity of modern legal orders or the relationships among them. *Ius gentium*

[18] A Zorn, *Grundzüge des Völkerrechts* (Nabu Press, 2010).

[19] See Çalı, 'Beyond Monism and Dualism' (2015), 138.

[20] See Çalı, 'Beyond Monism and Dualism' (2015), 139.

[21] DW Kennedy, 'One, Two, Three, Many Legal Orders: Legal Pluralism and the Cosmopolitan Dream' (2007) 31 *New York University Review of Law and Social Change* 641. See also SE Merry, 'Legal Pluralism' (1988) 22 *Law and Society Review* 869, 870 (defining legal pluralism as 'a situation in which two or more legal systems coexist in the same social field'). See also G Swenson, 'Legal Pluralism in Theory and Practice' (2018) 20 *International Studies Review* 438–62 (arguing that it is not merely enough to recognise that legal pluralism exists – scholars must understand how it actually functions; and presenting four new legal pluralism archetypes, namely combative, competitive, co-operative and complementary). See also L Benton and R Ross (eds), *Legal Pluralism and Empires 1500–1850* (New York University Press, 2013).

[22] Palombella, 'Inter-Legality: On Interconnectedness and "External Sources"' (2021), 943–59.

[23] Palombella, 'Inter-Legality: On Interconnectedness and "External Sources"' (2021), 943–59.

[24] Will and reason constitute the two ideologically opposed pillars of legality. These pillars become visible in the examination of the foundations of ius gentium, understood as what is shared across diverse legal orders and peoples. As Jeremy Waldron observes, it embodies 'common answers to common problems'. He illustrates these two pillars through the example of *ius gentium*: first, it may be recognised through consensus; second, it may be recognised through reason, reflecting the scientific character of law, and marked by moral and supplementary soundness. In this respect, the two constructions of legality cannot be disentangled, despite their apparent ideological opposition. See J Waldron, 'Foreign Law and the Modern Jus Gentium' (2005) 119 *Harvard Law Review* 129, 133 ('I shall use the Latin phrase "ius gentium" to refer to the law of nations in the more comprehensive sense – a body of law purporting to represent what various domestic legal systems share in the way of common answers to common problems.').

primarily provides a format 'where "commonalities" are put to the forefront: we can learn from similarities, project transplants, and support our choices by reference to their reform, or adopt some normative ideas as criteria of validity of legal norms, as in international law'.[25] This means that *ius gentium* cannot, in itself, fully address either the structure or the substantive content of a legal order; it speaks only to what is common to humanity. Overlooking this crucial limitation risks obscuring the essential connection between law and the social communities in which it is embedded.[26]

Private international law employs the tool of 'conflict of laws' to determine the applicable law in relations that span different legalities involving natural persons, companies, and other legal entities within private law contexts. Yet this framework remains confined to the rationale of a single legal system, since it ultimately revolves around the application of a particular state's laws. As Neil Walker observes, 'The conflict of laws, even at the level of theoretical representation, came more to resemble a parochial form of boundary-maintenance separately sponsored by each domestic legal order according to its own standards of fairness and propriety'.[27]

In political science and public administration literature, the overlapping of international and national institutions and agreements has been analysed through the concepts of 'regime complex' and 'polycentrism'. Although both are beyond the primary scope of this book, two relevant observations merit emphasis. First, a regime complex, defined as a 'loosely coupled set of regimes',[28] does not impose obligations on institutions to engage in mandatory collaboration; relationships among institutions may develop even in the absence of such obligations. Second, polycentrism, defined as 'many centers of decision-making which are formally independent of each other',[29] likewise fails to provide an inter-legal approach, as these centres remain free, autonomous, and abstractly separate, even when functioning in relation to one another.[30]

From the perspective of global law, it is important to recognise that, despite the efforts of global constitutionalists, global law has not developed into a unified and

[25] Palombella, '"Formats" of Law and Their Intertwining' (2019), 30.

[26] Palombella, '"Formats" of Law and Their Intertwining' (2019), 30.

[27] N Walker, 'Seven Pieces of Global Law' in N Walker, *Intimations of Global Law* (Cambridge University Press, 2015) 105.

[28] JS Nye, 'The Regime Complex for Managing Global Cyber Activities' (2014) *Harvard Kennedy School, Belfer Center for Science and International Affairs* 5, available at belfercenter.org/sites/default/files/legacy/files/global-cyber-final-web.pdf. See a detailed definition in A Orsini, J-F Morin, and O Young, 'Regime Complexes: A Buzz, a Boom, or a Boost for Global Governance' (2013) 19 Global Governance 27–39 ('a network of three or more international regimes that relate to a common subject matter; exhibit overlapping membership; and generate substantive, normative or operative interactions recognised as potentially problematic whether or not they are managed effectively').

[29] V Ostrom, CM Tiebout, and R Warren, 'The Organization of Government in Metropolitan Areas: A Theoretical Inquiry' (1961) 55(4) *American Political Science Review* 831–42.

[30] P Parolari, 'L'interlegalità Come Metodo? La Decisione Giudiziale negli Spazi Giuridici Ibridi' in E Chiti, A Di Martino, and G Palombella (eds), *L'età della Interlegalità* (Il Mulino, 2022) 119–35.

structured legal space.[31] Legal systems continue to prioritise the implementation of their own norms, and to maintain jurisdictional boundaries as gatekeepers,[32] rather than embracing 'global' frameworks.[33] Such approaches overlook the importance of contextual considerations, and, in particular, they fail to engage with issues that lie precisely in between legal systems.

It becomes apparent that scholarly attention must move beyond the perspectives discussed above, towards a 'full consideration of the reasons stemming from the diverse legal perspectives involved'.[34] Within this framework, the concept of inter-legality will be further elaborated in the following section, through two guiding metaphors: 'hardware' and 'software'.

4.2.1. Into the 'Machine' of Inter-Legality: From 'Hardware' to Qualified Legal 'Software'[35]

To understand the theory of inter-legality, the concept of law may be considered in two ways, namely as 'hardware' and 'software' systems.[36] The 'hardware' understanding of law refers to a stable and structured system rooted in the state,[37] grounded in the grammatical understanding of law that guarantees its basic existence. The 'software' conception, by contrast, refers to the presence of multiple heterogeneous and external legal normativities that lack any all-harmonising or pre-given framework. Palombella characterises this complex legal situation as an 'array of legal software', encompassing diverse normative entities such as international law, the plurality of regulatory regimes, transnational rule of law and justice, and dialogue among legal orders.[38] This perspective necessitates a departure from a purely stable and structured conception of law.

Although these regimes may appear self-contained, they can in fact be interconnected in countless ways, even within a single case. Within this constellation,

[31] Palombella, '"Formats" of Law and Their Intertwining' (2019).

[32] F Snyder, 'The Gatekeepers: The European Courts and WTO' (2003) 40 *Common Market Law Review* 367.

[33] E Biber, 'Concretisation of Constitutional Norms Referring to the Protection of Private Life in the Individual Application Case-Law' (LLM thesis, Koç University Law School, Istanbul, 2017), available at tez.yok.gov.tr/UlusalTezMerkezi/tezSorguSonucYeni.jsp.

[34] Palombella, 'Inter-Legality: On Interconnectedness and "External Sources"' (2021), 952.

[35] The words machine, hardware and software are not used here in their technical meanings; rather, the purpose is to explain inter-legality through these metaphors. The two metaphors of hardware and software have been employed by G Palombella in 'Global Threads: Weaving the Rule of Law and the Balance of Legal Software' in P Carrozza, F Fontanelli, and G Martinico (eds), *Shaping Rule of Law through Dialogue: International and Supranational Experiences* (Europa Law Publishing, 2009). See also Palombella, 'Inter-Legality: On Interconnectedness and "External Sources"' (2021), 943–59.

[36] G Palombella, 'Global Threads: Weaving the Rule of Law and the Balance of Legal Software' in G Palombella (ed), *Shaping Rule of Law through Dialogue – International and Supranational Experiences* (European Law Publishing, 2010); See also Palombella, 'Inter-Legality: On Interconnectedness and "External Sources"' (2021), 943–59.

[37] See the theoretical discussion on this issue in J Raz, *The Concept of a Legal System: An Introduction to the Theory of a Legal System*, 2nd edn (Clarendon Press, 2012).

[38] Palombella, 'Inter-Legality: On Interconnectedness and "External Sources"' (2021), 943–59.

inter-legality engages with the latter, 'software', understanding of law while transforming the former, 'hardware', conception into 'a working machine', thereby preventing it from falling into obsolescence.[39] In this respect, it is crucial to recognise that global issues shaped by such legal 'software' are generated by diverse and uncoordinated entities operating at state, regional, international, and supranational levels. These regimes embody distinctive rationalities and encompass highly complex regulatory domains, ranging from the environment to security, from business to health, and from the law of war to energy.

Over time, the vast proliferation of distinctive rationalities regulating both public and private matters has blurred the very distinction between public and private law.[40] This development has become particularly obvious with the deployment of AI systems. As explained in chapter two of this book, certain AI systems hold significant promise for the future of crime detection.[41] Yet, given the private power embedded in the programming of such systems, even core state functions such as policing and incarceration – traditionally regarded as activities beyond the scope of multinational corporations and global governance[42] – may be, at least in part, delegated to private actors.

As more regulatory entities disrupt settled legal systems and weaken the traditional dichotomy between public and private law, legal reasoning increasingly relies on the 'software' understanding of law to cope with inter-legal issues.[43] Much like a form of bricolage, legal reasoning draws upon 'relevant' normativities that are not necessarily fused or unified.[44] As Palombella observes, 'extra-state regimes' jurisgenerative outputs get presumptive primacy over local idiosyncratic interests'.[45] In the context of AI systems, for example, state authorities often lack the capacity to prevent international non-governmental organisations from defining ethical requirements and principles to which compliance is expected.[46] Indeed, AI is poised to become one of the most prominent subjects of national and international debate in the twenty-first

[39] Palombella, 'Inter-Legality: On Interconnectedness and "External Sources"' (2021), 943–59.

[40] J Resnik, 'Globalization(s), Privatization(s), Constitutionalization and Statization: Icons and Experiences of Sovereignty in the 21st Century' (2013) 11 *International Journal of Constitutional Law* 162.

[41] A Završnik, 'Criminal Justice, Artificial Intelligence Systems and Human Rights' (2020) 20 *ERA Forum* 567–83.

[42] See Resnik, 'Globalization(s), Privatization(s), Constitutionalization and Statization' (2013).

[43] This can be observed in legal scholarship on judicial dialogue, defined as the 'communication between various judicial authorities', and in references to foreign judgments. See E Karska and K Karski, 'Judicial Dialogue in Human Rights' (2019) 21 *International Community Law* Review 391–99.

[44] For the use of the metaphor 'bricolage' in a legal context, see M Tushnet, 'The Possibilities of Comparative Constitutional Law' (1999) 108 *Yale Law Journal* 1285–86. See also C Lévi-Strauss, *The Savage Mind* (University of Chicago Press, 1966) 17–18.

[45] Palombella, 'Inter-Legality: On Interconnectedness and "External Sources"' (2021), 947.

[46] J Fjeld et al, 'Principled Artificial Intelligence: Mapping Consensus in Ethical and Rights-Based Approaches to Principles for AI' (2020) *Berkman Klein Center for Internet & Society*, available at dash.harvard.edu/handle/1/42160420 (analysing 36 AI principles documents and highlighting eight key themes: privacy; accountability; safety and security; transparency and explainability; fairness and non-discrimination; human control of technology; professional responsibility; and promotion of human values).

century. The initiative 'GlobalPolicy.AI', established to navigate the international AI governance framework, already involves eight international, regional, and transnational partners working to develop guidelines for ethical, rights-respecting, and socially beneficial AI.[47] In this sense, it is clear that:

> in many ways regulations crosscut legal borders and in fact work as part of the 'law' to be applied inside a legal system, without the exit choice being an option. The overwhelming software affects the hardware, then, without being invited to do so.[48]

Therefore, it is necessary to understand the fundamental characteristics of this new social and legal phenomenon in order to propose considerable solutions to *inter-systemic*, *dynamic*, *social*, and *complex* issues, as well as to the overlapping of self-related normativities.

4.3. The Fundamental Characteristics of Inter-Legality

For the sake of analytical clarity, the perspective of inter-legality may be characterised through three fundamental dimensions: (i) the simultaneous emergence of diverse legalities; (ii) a shift in focus from contestation to functions; and (iii) the emergence of a *law of the case* derived from composite interweaving norms. The following sections elaborate on these defining characteristics.

4.3.1. The Simultaneous Emergence of Diverse Legalities

To understand the circumstances of inter-legality, it is essential to recognise the simultaneous emergence, within a single case, of diverse structures, patterns, or 'formats' of legality, each rooted in different historical periods.[49] In other words, although legalities may originate in distinct historical contexts, this does not prevent them from exercising normative power over a legal fact simultaneously. Whenever they are applicable or relevant, they concurrently have a say in a specific case. This demonstrates that the concrete organisations and characteristics of legality – often shaped by historical periods – inform our conceptions of law.[50] The central issue here is not whether one should privilege the most recent or most 'mature' legality, but rather the recognition of their capacity to emerge

[47] See the platform's website at globalpolicy.ai/en/. As of September 2021, the platform had eight partners: the Council of Europe, the European Commission, the European Agency for Fundamental Rights, the Inter-American Development Bank, the OECD and the OECD Artificial Intelligence Policy Observatory, the United Nations, UNESCO, and the World Bank Group.

[48] Palombella, 'Inter-Legality: On Interconnectedness and "External Sources"' (2021), 947.

[49] Palombella, '"Formats" of Law and Their Intertwining' (2019), 23.

[50] Palombella, '"Formats" of Law and Their Intertwining' (2019).

simultaneously in a single case. These concurrently applicable legalities regulate diverse domains of human activity at both national and supranational levels.

State-based efforts have often sought to unify diverse legalities governing the 'external' world under the common framework of international or inter-state law. Such attempts, however, tend to underestimate the significance of differences. As Palombella observes, one of the shortcomings of the 'recurrent attempts at the constitutionalisation of international law is in fact the desire to keep the new global administrative law format within the narrower boundaries of inter-state law'.[51] It is, ultimately, futile to impose a single paradigm in a world where multiple legal factors simultaneously interact, and may follow ideal-type logics and natures regardless of their historical origins. The contemporary legal landscape is more complex than in the past: vertical legalities overlap and jurisgenerative authorities 'exceed and pierce the states'.[52] Thus, the mere existence of national law does not render a state isolated from other legal systems. In the face of increasing social complexity, no legal system – whether labelled 'unified' or 'global' – can be conceived of as independent, isolated, or self-contained.

Furthermore, an inter-legal understanding represents 'what ought to be',[53] in light of the rule of law's requirement to take into account diverse needs and ends, thereby 'prevent[ing] the law from turning into a sheer tool of domination'.[54] Palombella, accordingly, emphasises that 'the understanding of inter-legality can thus be better supported by the understanding of the *formats* of law that have become ideal-type components: through them, inter-legality makes sense as inter-formats as well'.[55] In other words, to grasp what an inter-legal perspective entails – or 'what ought to be' from the vantage point of the case – each relevant format of law and its interaction with other formats must be examined. In this sense, law may be conceived of as different 'geometric figures', each bearing depth despite sharing the same fabric, namely norms.[56]

It should be noted that a universality of shared rationales of law may indeed exist among polities, orders, governments, and peoples. However, as Palombella clearly explains, such universality can only 'come after', and such a horizontal continuity

> cannot be used to prevent enquiries upon law's *depth*, connotations that must be studied in order to understand different answers to questions about what the law is, how it works, and what it does (and eventually why it does so).[57]

[51] Palombella, '"Formats" of Law and Their Intertwining' (2019), 23. He defines global administrative law as 'a flat layer of horizontal law crossing frontiers and organizing diverse fields of human action on a supranational scale'.

[52] Palombella, '"Formats" of Law and Their Intertwining' (2019), 24.

[53] See 'Oughtness' in R Alexy, *A Theory of Constitutional Rights* (Oxford University Press, 2004).

[54] G Palombella, 'The Rule of Law at Home and Abroad' (2016) 8 *Hague Journal on the Rule of Law* 1.

[55] Palombella, '"Formats" of Law and Their Intertwining' (2019), 24. He explains four different legalities to explain the present transformations of contemporary law: law as esprit, *ius gentium*, medieval law, and global administrative law.

[56] Palombella, '"Formats" of Law and Their Intertwining' (2019), 24.

[57] Palombella, '"Formats" of Law and Their Intertwining' (2019), 26.

Indeed, 'law's depth' refers to its geo-territorial idiosyncratic richness. A swift search for similarities, or an attempt to eliminate diversity and disagreement, risks obscuring this crucial dimension.[58] It is therefore necessary, as a first step, to interrogate the differences among the legalities relevant to the issue at hand, in order to benefit from the richness inherent in each.[59] Such an approach makes it possible to analyse each 'geometric figure' or the 'esprit' of law, not in a superficial or merely symbolic sense, but in light of fundamental questions concerning *what ought to be*.

It is important to recognise that, in the context of new technologies, the geo-territorial features of legalities have been partially challenged. Whereas, in the past, the traditional coupling of people and territory was primarily disrupted through migration,[60] the most recent dynamic phenomenon decoupling people from territory is the rise of advanced technologies – including AI systems – which are continuously fed by data collected at both national and supranational levels. This development demonstrates that inter-legality will remain a highly relevant concept in both today's and tomorrow's digital and legal landscapes.

4.3.2. A Shift in Focus from Contestations to Functions

Contestations between different legal systems, or within a single system, have long been a subject of legal scholarship (eg constitutional courts versus supreme courts, transitional courts versus constitutional courts, or even disputes between international courts).[61] The inter-legal approach, however, does not concentrate on such contests or seek to arbitrate them. Instead, it engages with the concrete functionality of the relevant legal systems within the specific context of a case.[62] In this sense, it is a prescriptive approach that challenges assumptions of jurisdictional self-sufficiency; it offers a new path aimed at uncovering the full contexts and underlying reasons drawn from the diverse legalities regulating the matter at hand.[63]

[58] In fact, even when many legal doctrines appear similar, their transformations and interpretations diverge significantly. G Teubner illustrates this point with the example of the concept of good faith. Although the doctrine of good faith was exported from EU law (European Consumer Protection Directive 1994) into British contract law, its meaning has become unpredictable. He therefore suggests using the term 'legal irritants' (rather than 'legal transplants') for such exported doctrines, as they carry an evolutionary dynamic that produces fundamental changes in both their internal and external contexts. See G Teubner, 'Legal Irritants: Good Faith in British Law or How Unifying Law Ends Up in New Divergences' (1998) 61 *Modern Law Review* 11 ('I think that in spite of all benign intentions towards an "Ever Closer Union", attempts at unifying European contract law will result in new cleavages.').

[59] Palombella, '"Formats" of Law and Their Intertwining' (2019), 26–27.

[60] Palombella, '"Formats" of Law and Their Intertwining' (2019), 27.

[61] L Garlicki, 'Constitutional Courts versus Supreme Courts' (2007) 5(1) *International Journal of Constitutional Law* 44–68.

[62] J Klabbers and G Palombella, 'Introduction: Situating Inter-Legality' in Klabbers and Palombella (eds), The Challenge of Inter-Legality (2019), 1–20.

[63] Klabbers and Palombella, 'Introduction: Situating Inter-Legality' (n 62), 1–20; Palombella, 'Inter-Legality: On Interconnectedness and "External Sources"' (2021), 943–59.

In this process, the functional aim of each relevant legal system to deliver justice – or to avoid injustice – is assessed in terms of its practical (dys)functionality. It is important to emphasise that inter-legality does not seek to provide a comprehensive conceptualisation of justice. Rather, it responds to the demands of justice by requiring due consideration of all the normativities arising from the case, while referring only to the fundamental obligation of fairness.[64] In this sense, inter-legality operates as a generative approach that interrogates the reasons underlying the plurality of legalities governing the case.[65]

4.3.3. The Emergence of a *Law of the Case* Derived from Composite Interweaving Norms

By directing attention to (dys)functionality rather than to conflicts between diverse legalities, the 'law of the case' can emerge in an inter-legal sense. This function-oriented perspective on legalities marginalises questions of primacy among different legal orders. In other words, it sets aside unreasonable formal priorities that risk unduly neglecting the interconnections at stake.[66]

The *law of the case*, moreover, cannot be reduced to any single contributing legality. Within the 'inter-legal machine', each legality, with its own rationale, is generative. Together they weave a normative spiral, contributing to the emergence of the composite law of the case through 'an effect of the interpenetration of legal orders'.[67] In this sense, the 'law of the case' constitutes a 'holistic fabric' grounded in the legal arrangements relevant to the specific context. It provides a clear judicial path for resolving the issues at hand, offering more just solutions based on inclusive rather than exclusionary reasoning.[68] As Palombella emphasises, a monist, substantive, global order of law remains far removed from such a context.[69]

4.4. Inter-Legality and Related Theoretical Perspectives in the Context of AI Systems

From a conceptual and theoretical standpoint, the question of inter-legality necessitates an examination of the doctrinal mechanisms proposed by legal scholars

[64] Klabbers and Palombella, 'Introduction: Situating Inter-Legality' (n 62), 1–20; Palombella, 'Inter-Legality: On Interconnectedness and "External Sources"' (2021), 943–59.

[65] Klabbers and Palombella, 'Introduction: Situating Inter-Legality' (n 62), 1–20; Palombella, 'Inter-Legality: On Interconnectedness and "External Sources"' (2021), 943–59.

[66] Palombella, 'Inter-Legality: On Interconnectedness and "External Sources"' (2021), 943–59.

[67] See an interesting review of the perspective of inter-legality, emphasising that the phenomenon refers to 'an effect of the interpenetration of legal orders', in N Walker, 'Legalising Inter-Legality' (2022).

[68] E Biber and N Hogic, 'Online States and Inter-Legality' in Palombella, Chiti, and Di Martino (eds), *L'età della Interlegalità* 367.

[69] Palombella, 'Inter-Legality: On Interconnectedness and "External Sources"' (2021), 959.

in the context of AI systems, aimed at safeguarding the rights and freedoms of individuals in the digital environment. Accordingly, this section addresses the theory of the horizontal application of fundamental rights; digital constitutionalism; rights; and the rule of law.

4.4.1. Inter-Legality and the Theory of Horizontal Effect of Fundamental Rights

The growing power of private entities in programming and reviewing AI systems has produced a paradigmatic shift whereby private actors can also contribute to violations of fundamental rights and the undermining of democratic standards. It is, therefore, crucial to re-emphasise the influence of private power in the design and oversight of such systems, particularly in light of the provisions set out in the AI Act.[70]

According to the AI Act, most reviews are subject to internal 'conformity assessment procedures' (CAP) carried out by providers. CAP is a mechanism adapted from EU product safety law.[71] As explained in chapter three, this means that providers themselves will be responsible for self-assessing the compliance of high-risk AI systems with the essential requirements.[72] Only high-risk AI systems used for real-time remote biometric identification in publicly accessible spaces for a law enforcement purpose are subject to prior authorisation by a judicial authority or an independent administrative authority.[73]

With this exception noted, within the broader framework of high-risk AI systems, private power plays a significant role in the protection of fundamental rights – even where such systems are deployed by public authorities. This recognition is reflected in the European Declaration on Digital Rights and Principles for the Digital Decade, in which the European Commission explicitly referred to private actors as 'businesses':

> The EU vision for digital transformation puts people at the centre, empowers individuals and fosters *innovative businesses* … The Declaration aims to explain shared political intentions. Not only does it recall … it should also serve as a reference point for *businesses* and other relevant actors when developing and deploying new technologies.[74]

[70] Regulation (EU) 2024/1689 of the European Parliament and of the Council of 13 June 2024 laying down harmonised rules on artificial intelligence and amending Regulations (EC) No 300/2008, (EU) No 167/2013, (EU) No 168/2013, (EU) 2018/858, (EU) 2018/1139 and (EU) 2019/2144 and Directives 2014/90/EU, (EU) 2016/797 and (EU) 2020/1828 (Artificial Intelligence Act), OJ L 1689, 12 July 2024.

[71] For a basic explanation and a flow chart on the CAP, see European Commission, 'The "Blue Guide" on the implementation of EU product rules 2016,' 65, 68, available at ec.europa.eu/docsroom/documents/18027/.

[72] See a detailed analysis of the AI Act in Chapter 3 of this book.

[73] Art 5(3) of the AI Act (n 70).

[74] European Commission, 'European Declaration on Digital Rights and Principles for the Digital Decade' COM(2022) 28 final, Brussels, 26 January 2022.

This implies that public power can no longer be regarded as the sole source of concern in safeguarding fundamental rights and democratic values.[75] A new orbit of potential infringement has emerged, rooted in private power. This development challenges the conventional understanding of constitutional law and necessitates a reconsideration of the relationship between constitutional law and private law.

The relationship between constitutional law and private law can be clarified through the theory of horizontal effect *(Drittwirkung)*.[76] According to German legal theorist Alexy, to understand the horizontal effect of constitutional rights, a legal system can be considered from two perspectives, namely the norm-oriented perspective and the perspective based on positions and relations. While the norm-oriented perspective includes the possibility of abstracting out from positions and relations, the perspective based on positions and relations has the power to draw distinctions.[77] From the latter standpoint, Alexy explains that constitutional rights norms have an influence on the relations between citizens because there are cases of rights against the judiciary in private law matters. Therefore, constitutional rights norms have a 'radiating effect' on the entire legal system, meaning that

> constitutional rights norms do not simply contain defensive rights of the individual against the state, but at the same time they embody an objective order of values, which applies to all areas of law as a basic constitutional decision, and which provides guidelines and impulses for the legislature, administration and judiciary.[78]

He explains the 'radiation thesis' by relying on the objective side of constitutional rights principles[79] on the basis of threefold abstraction, namely abstraction from the right-holder (beneficiary), from the addressee (the subject), and from the specific characteristics of the object. In the case of freedom of expression, for instance, if (x) has the right to free expression against a state (s), then (s) has a duty to (x) in respect of free expression. Abstracting from the right-holder (x), the subject (s), and the specific characteristics of the object (here, refraining from state interference), this threefold analysis, according to him, turns the right of

[75] O Pollicino and G De Gregorio, 'Constitutional Law in the Algorithmic Society' in H-W Micklitz et al (eds), *Constitutional Challenges in the Algorithmic Society* (Cambridge University Press, 2022) 6.

[76] S Walkila, *Horizontal Effect of Fundamental Rights in EU Law* (European Law Publishing, 2016).

[77] Alexy, *A Theory of Constitutional Rights* (2004), 351–52.

[78] BVerfGE 39, 1 (41), in Alexy, *A Theory of Constitutional Rights* (2004), 351–52.

[79] He replaces the concept of an 'objective order of values' with principles, reformulating the BVerfGE's value theory as a theory of principles. See also some interesting research on the judgment, arguing that the claim about the 'objective system of values' *(Objektive Wertordnung)* makes the judgment a rightful part of a *global* canon on human rights, in K Möller, 'Lüth and the "Objective System of Values": From "Limited Government" towards an Autonomy-based Conception of Constitutional Rights' in S Choudhry, M Hailbronner, and M Kumm (eds), *Global Canons in an Age of Contestation: Debating Foundational Texts of Constitutional Democracy and Human Rights* (Oxford University Press, 2024; Oxford Academic, 15 May 2024), https://doi.org/10.1093/9780191956942.003.0014). See also A Sajo and R Uitz, *The Constitution in Private Relations: Expanding Constitutionalism* (Eleven International Publishing, 2005).

(x) against the state into pure good *(Gesolltsein)* of freedom of expression.[80] In the continuation of his analysis, he refers to this side of constitutional rights principles as 'principles at the highest level of abstraction'.[81]

Ultimately, this understanding of the objective side of constitutional rights *(objektive Wertordnung)* lays the groundwork for the theory of horizontal effect: constitutional rights influence the interpretation of private law as 'value-decisions' or 'evaluating guiding norms'; in other words, as *objective principles at the highest level of abstraction*.[82] There are two avenues where this influence can be observed: the concretisation of private law general clauses *(Generalklauseln)* as 'points of entry' *(Einbruchstellen)* and the interpretation of private law norms requiring justification beyond the literal meaning of the law can both reveal this influence. This influence is perfectly defined in the famous *Lüth* judgment of the BVerfGE:

> As a constitutional requirement, the judge must consider whether the substantive private law provisions to be applied by him are influenced by constitutional rights in the way described; if they are, he must have regard for the modification of private law arising in this way when interpretating and applying these provisions.[83]

However, within the EU there remains resistance to recognising the horizontal effects of EU provisions that are not expressly addressed to individuals.[84] The provisions of the EU Charter, moreover, are primarily binding on Member States and EU institutions, and they often appear too imprecise and abstract to enable private parties to determine in advance whether their systems comply with these provisions.[85] In addition, although the AI Act imposes specific legal requirements on AI providers, it does not clearly establish that the obligation to respect

[80] Alexy, *A Theory of Constitutional Rights* (2004), 353–54.

[81] It is worth noting that, according to Alexy, the adoption of these principles has both advantages and disadvantages. On the one hand, their flexibility provides a starting point for doctrinal justification of constitutional requirements across all areas of law. On the other hand, their vagueness invites ambiguous forms of legal reasoning.

[82] Alexy, *A Theory of Constitutional Rights* (2004), 355.

[83] BVerfGE 7, 198 (206). See the key considerations of the decision at bundesverfassungsgericht.de/SharedDocs/Entscheidungen/EN/1958/01/rs19580115_1bvr040051en.html. Alexy identifies three theories describing the horizontal effect: one indirect, one direct, and one mediated by rights against state. The first – the theory of indirect horizontal effect – addresses what has just been outlined so far, highlighting that constitutional rights are objective principles. The second – the theory of direct effect or absolute effect – holds that subjective private rights of the individual flow directly from constitutional rights; in this sense, constitutional rights can create or modify existing private norms. The third theory is more radical: because the state made the private law systems available and enforceable, it is already a participant in potential infringements of constitutional rights interests by other citizens. Therefore, the state must be responsible even though infringements are conducted by private actors. See also D Grimm, 'Fundamental Rights in the Interpretation of the German Constitutional Court' in D Grimm, *Constitutionalism: Past, Present, and Future* (Oxford University Press, 2016) 173–75 (interpreting the *Lüth* judgment of the BVerfGE as a 'modernisation of the whole legal order without legislative amendments' in Germany). See also P Quint, 'Free Speech and Private Law in German Constitutional Theory' (1989) 48(2) *Maryland Law Review* 247 (discussing the difference between the American state action doctrine and the German doctrine elaborated in the *Lüth* judgment).

[84] D Leczykiewicz, 'Horizontal Application of the Charter of Fundamental Rights' (2013) 4 *European Law Review* 483.

[85] D Leczykiewicz, 'Horizontal Application of the Charter of Fundamental Rights' (2013), 483.

fundamental rights applies to private AI providers in a direct and unmediated manner.[86]

An inter-legal approach may provide a more effective response to such resistance and uncertainty. Rather than focusing on the horizontal applicability of norms – whether derived from supranational or national orders – or on the controversies concerning whether rights were intended to bind private parties, an inter-legal perspective adopts a functional approach. Its first step is to examine the relevance of a particular legal order in the concrete case. In the context of AI systems, fundamental and human rights acquire particular relevance when such systems are deployed by public actors.[87] These are the systems that monitor the public and make decisions regarding public issues. Accordingly, fundamental and human rights lie at the core of their use and may be addressed with high public significance by courts, often outweighing the commercial interests of private companies.[88] Furthermore, the imposition of rights obligations on private actors is particularly crucial, given the asymmetry of power between individuals subjected to these systems and the private companies that possess the resources and expertise to design and deploy them.

Such an approach does not exclude the application of private law norms; rather, they are subject to fair consideration whenever they are relevant to the case at hand. In this way, the horizontal application of rights is prevented from becoming a problematic issue. It is also important to emphasise that this approach has the capacity to cultivate an appropriate balance between liberalism and public intervention, as well as between social justice and the free market.

4.4.2. Inter-Legality and Digital Constitutionalism

Modern constitutions aim to limit the power of governments in order to protect individuals' fundamental and human rights.[89] With their immense capacity

[86] N Smuha et al, 'How the EU Can Achieve Legally Trustworthy AI: A Response to the European Commission's Proposal for an Artificial Intelligence Act' (2021) LEADS Law, University of Birmingham for a Legal, Ethical and Accountable Digital Society, 5 August 2021, 9, available at papers.ssrn.com/sol3/papers.cfm?abstract_id=3899991.

[87] The relevance of fundamental and human rights can clearly be observed in the decisions of Facebook's private court, the so-called 'Oversight Board', which frequently refers to international human rights law, even in cases involving the use of AI by private entities. The first decisions of the Oversight Board, issued in January 2021, are instructive in this regard, as they invoke Arts 19 and 20 of the International Covenant on Civil and Political Rights (ICCPR), as well as the United Nations Human Rights Committee. See Oversight Board, *Case Decision 2020-003-FB-UA* (28 January 2021), available at oversightboard.com/decision/FB-QBJDASCV/.

[88] Regarding the significance of value theory of fundamental rights, and its distinction from the liberal theory of fundamental rights, see a brief comment in B Rusteberg, 'Theorie, Interpretation und Dogmatik der Grundrechte bei Ernst-Wolfgang Böckenförde' (*Verfassungsblog*, 6 May 2019), available at verfassungsblog.de/theorie-interpretation-und-dogmatik-der-grundrechte-bei-ernst-wolfgang-boeckenfoerde/ (arguing that, while the liberal understanding conceives fundamental rights as subjective defensive rights, the value-based understanding conceives them as objective norms).

[89] JHH Weiler and M Wind, *European Constitutionalism Beyond the State* (Cambridge University Press, 2003) 16; JHH Weiler, 'The Transformation of Europe' (1991) 100 *Yale Law Journal* 2403.

to organise digital content and process vast amounts of data, online platforms have accelerated the expansion of their discretionary power into matters of public law. The EU's response to this development has been described as 'digital constitutionalism',[90] with its central focus on limiting the exercise of digital power.[91] As Suzor emphasises, this concept may be defined as rethinking 'how the exercise of power ought to be limited (made legitimate) in the digital age'.[92] In this sense, within the EU, digital constitutionalism has emerged as a legal response to the transformation of economic freedom into the disproportionate, quasi-public power of online platforms.[93]

A major challenge to digital constitutionalism lies in the triangular relationship between the state, the market, and the individual, which creates a puzzling context for the protection of fundamental rights and freedoms. Within the EU, one response to this challenge has been the 'concretisation' *(Konkretisierung)* of Articles 7 and 8 of the EU Charter by the CJEU. In other words, the Court has 'translated' conventional fundamental rights into *digital* fundamental rights by scrutinising algorithmic activities and data-driven practices. This jurisprudence has given rise to far-reaching 'codifications' of digital rights. The most prominent example could be the *Google Spain* judgment, which established the 'right to be forgotten online'.[94] Additional significant developments include the 'right not to be subject to a decision based solely on automated processing' or the 'right to obtain human intervention',[95] as established by the GDPR. A crucial driver behind this expansion has been the adoption of the EU Charter, following the 2009 Lisbon Treaty.[96] The Charter has not only broadened the scope of rights protection in the digital domain, but has also substantially enhanced the CJEU's authority in fundamental rights adjudication, to the extent that the Court

[90] G De Gregorio, 'The Rise of Digital Constitutionalism in the European Union' (2021) 19 *International Journal of Constitutional* Law 41–70 (analysing the path and the reasons for the change in the EU from a liberal constitutionalist approach to a digital constitutionalist approach); G De Gregorio, *Digital Constitutionalism in Europe: Reframing Rights and Powers in the Algorithmic Society* (Cambridge University Press, 2022). See also E Celeste, 'Digital Constitutionalism: A New Systematic Theorization' (2019) 33(1) *International Review of Law, Computers and Technology* 76–99; See also E Biber and N Hogic, 'Online States and Inter-Legality' (2022); E Biber, 'Digital Constitutionalism in Europe: Exploring a Constellation of Legalities' in G De Gregorio, O Pollicino, and P Valcke (eds), *The Oxford Handbook of Digital Constitutionalism* (OUP, 2025); E Biber, 'Book Review: Digital Constitutionalism in Europe: Reframing Rights and Powers in the Algorithmic Society (Cambridge Studies in European Law and Policy): by De Gregorio, G. (2022). Cambridge: Cambridge University Press. £95' (2022) 37(3) *International Review of Law, Computers & Technology* 341–44.

[91] C Padovani and M Santaniello, 'Digital Constitutionalism: Fundamental Rights and Power Limitation in the Internet Eco-System' (2018) 80 *International Communication Gazette* 2.

[92] N Suzor, 'Digital Constitutionalism: Using the Rule of Law to Evaluate the Legitimacy of Governance by Platforms' (2018) 4(3) *Social Media and Society* 4.

[93] De Gregorio, 'The Rise of Digital Constitutionalism in the European Union' (2021).

[94] Case C-131/12 *Google Spain SL and Google Inc v Agencia Española de Protección de Datos (AEPD) and Mario Costeja González* [2014] ECLI:EU:C:2014:317, 13 May 2014.

[95] Art 22 GDPR. See also J Tasioulas, 'A Right to Human Decision' Draft Paper (2023), available at academia.edu/116775511/A_Human_Right_to_a_Human_Decision.

[96] Charter of Fundamental Rights of the European Union [2012] OJ C 326/391.

has been described as functioning, in important respects, as a 'human rights tribunal'.[97]

However, despite the activist role of the CJEU in safeguarding fundamental rights in the digital sphere, digital constitutionalism does not adequately account for the *inter-systemic* nature of the challenges posed by AI systems. For example, it overlooks the Court's self-referential and isolated style, which has been observed in its jurisprudence.[98] Recent studies indicate that the CJEU now makes fewer references to both the ECHR and the case law of the ECtHR than it did in earlier years.[99] Some commentators have further emphasised that:

> The ECJ's [CJEU] silence about the – actual and possible – roles of the European Court of Human Rights is particularly disturbing and … it might be recalled that one court – albeit … the ECJ – might not always be enough for safeguarding the rule of law.[100]

This means that, although digital constitutionalism in the EU adheres to 'rights constitutionalism',[101] thereby reinforcing the protection of fundamental rights through 'codification' in the case law of the CJEU, and EU legislation, it does not sufficiently consider the inter-legal character of rights – an aspect that could enable a more balanced and comprehensive consideration of all relevant legal perspectives.

The distinctiveness nature of the concept is also reflected in its growing emphasis[102] on the 'Brussels Effect',[103] which highlights the EU's capacity to

[97] G De Búrca, 'After the EU Charter of Fundamental Rights: The Court of Justice as a Human Rights Adjudicator?' (2013) 20(2) *Maastricht Journal of European and Comparative Law* 168.

[98] De Búrca, 'After the EU Charter of Fundamental Rights' (2013) ('the three years since the Charter came into force reveals that the CJEU is referring even less now to the ECHR than it did before, and even more rarely to the case law of the Court of Human Rights'). It is important to note that European legality was not conceived as a complex legal universe. As the CJEU stated, European legality achieved integration through an 'autonomous legal order'. See Case 26/62 *Van Gend en Loos* ECLI:EU:C:1963:1 and Case 6/64 *Costa v ENEL* ECLI:EU:C:1964:66 ('By contrast with ordinary international treaties the EEC Treaty has created its own legal system which, on the entry into force of the Treaty, became an integral part of the legal systems of the Member States and which their courts are bound to apply.'). See also Palombella, '"Formats" of Law and Their Intertwining' (2019), 30–31.

[99] G De Búrca, 'After the EU Charter of Fundamental Rights' (2013). It is important to note that a strong reliance on a single legal perspective may lead not only to the overlooking of contextual considerations but also to inconsistent or variable assessments of legal concepts. See H Ruiz Fabri, 'Is There a Case – Legally and Politically – for Direct Effect of WTO Obligations?' (2014) 25 *European Journal of International Law* 162 ('it appears that the ECJ is locked in its own reasoning about direct effect, cannot renounce its power, but just restrain itself on an ad hoc basis and therefore remain ambivalent in its reasoning and at risk of being criticized as inconsistent or activist. If this is so, it is because, as has been shown, direct effect is itself an ambivalent tool which can be used either as a sword to open legal orders or as a shield to keep them closed, and the Court uses it both ways.').

[100] C Dupré, 'Individuals and Judges in Defense of the Rule of Law' (*Verfassungsblog*, 28 July 2018), available at verfassungsblog.de/individuals-and-judges-in-defense-of-the-rule-of-law/.

[101] A Chilton and M Versteeg, *How Constitutional Rights Matter* (Oxford University Press, 2020) 79.

[102] G De Gregorio, 'The Declaration on European Digital Rights and Principles: A First Analysis from Digital Constitutionalism' (*The Digital Constitutionalist*, 2022), available at digi-con.org/the-declaration-on-european-digital-rights-and-principles-a-first-analysis-from-digital-constitutionalism/.

[103] A Bradford, *The Brussels Effect: How the European Union Rules the World* (Oxford University Press, 2020).

shape global dynamics, while placing relatively less focus on the EU's commitment to the rule of law. Such a focus may risk overlooking the explicit reference to 'Europeans' in the Declaration on European Digital Rights and Principles, described as the 'expression of the consolidation of digital constitutionalism'.[104] Indeed, despite the fact that Chapter I of the Declaration is titled 'putting people at the centre of the digital transformation', its content is framed exclusively around 'Europeans'.[105]

In the context of AI systems, such an approach seems incomplete, as these technologies are already being deployed in the monitoring and control of EU borders, with particular implications for third-country nationals.[106] This practice risks undermining the EU's very commitment to protecting fundamental rights, democracy, and the rule of law. Accordingly, the Union's constitutional efforts to limit the exercise of digital power should evolve towards more inclusive legal perspectives when addressing the challenges posed by AI systems.

4.4.3. Inter-Legality and Fundamental and Human Rights

The most dynamic subjects of inter-legality are fundamental and human rights, as they are regulated at national and supranational levels. The degree of porosity and interconnection at this level is particularly pronounced, since fundamental and human rights are recognised across numerous legal systems and demand a high level of protection.[107] This makes the field of fundamental and human rights law a more suitable vehicle for establishing an inter-legal foundation than many other areas of law.[108]

[104] De Gregorio, 'The Declaration on European Digital Rights and Principles' (2022).
[105] The full content of Chapter I is as follows: 'People are at the centre of the digital transformation in the European Union. Technology should serve and benefit all Europeans and empower them to pursue their aspirations, in full security and respect of their fundamental rights. We commit to: strengthening the democratic framework for a digital transformation that benefits everyone and improves the lives of all Europeans; taking necessary measures to ensure that the values of the Union and the rights of individuals as recognised by Union law are respected online as well as offline; fostering responsible and diligent action by all digital actors, public and private, for a safe and secure digital environment; actively promoting this vision of the digital transformation, also in our international relations.' See European Commission, 'European Declaration on Digital Rights and Principles for the Digital Decade' (n 74).
[106] See, for instance, the project at iborderctrl.eu/The-project ('The main objective is to enable faster and thorough border control for third-country nationals crossing the land borders of EU Member States (MS), with technologies that adapt to the future development of Schengen border management.').
[107] Palombella, 'Inter-Legality: On Interconnectedness and "External Sources"' (2021) ('rights are capturing inter-legality concerns, due to their mixed belonging in different legalities').
[108] Palombella, 'Inter-Legality: On Interconnectedness and "External Sources"' (2021). The relationship between rights and inter-legality is most clearly demonstrated at the conclusion of this section, which focuses on the application of the theory.

The most well-known case illustrating the relevance of rights to an inter-legal approach is the *Kadi* judgment[109] of the CJEU.[110] The case has been described as the 'most visible and interesting case'[111] of the Court in the field of external relations in recent years. The basic facts are as follows: Kadi was identified by the UN Security Council as a possible supporter of al-Qaeda, and his name was placed on a blacklist of al-Qaeda affiliates. As a consequence, the Security Council imposed sanctions against him, including the freezing of his assets. The EU subsequently transposed this sanction through a regulation, which Kadi challenged before the EU Courts.[112]

The CJEU reviewed the EU regulation transposing the UN resolution that sanctioned Kadi by freezing his assets. The Court emphasised that such a review did not amount to a review of the UN Security Council measures themselves.[113] Instead, relying on the foundational principles of the EU legal order – namely, the protection of fundamental rights – the Court held that Kadi's rights to an effective judicial remedy and to property had been violated, as he had not been informed of the reasons for his inclusion on the blacklist of al-Qaeda affiliates.[114]

This outcome reflects the Court's adoption of a 'dualist' approach, grounded in the rationale that what occurs within one legal order (the EU) does not interfere with the functioning of the international legal order. The cost of this position, however, was the disregard of Article 103 of the UN Charter, which establishes the obligation to implement United Nations Security Council (UNSC) resolutions.[115]

From an inter-legal point of view, Palombella interprets this situation as follows:

> The logic of the two legalities being like two separate circles, was clearly contrasting against the reality, and the case at stake, in its concrete structure, proved the interconnection between the Security goal on one side and the protection of fundamental rights in the EU, on the other. The balancing and comprehensive consideration of the two sides would have been a more credible and better justified reasoning.[116]

In this sense, fundamental and human rights law highlights two key issues that justify an inter-legal approach. First, it illustrates the complexity of overlapping

[109] Joined Cases C-402/05 P and C-415/05 P *Yassin Abdullah Kadi and Al Barakaat International Foundation v Council and Commission* ECLI:EU:C:2008:461 *(Kadi Judgment).*

[110] Palombella and Klabbers analyse the judgment in detail in their principal works on inter-legality.

[111] J Kokott and C Sobotta, 'The Kadi Case – Constitutional Core Values and International Law – Finding the Balance?' (2012) 23 *European Journal of International Law* 1015–24.

[112] *Kadi Judgment* (n 109).

[113] *Kadi Judgment* (n 109).

[114] *Kadi Judgment* (n 109).

[115] Art 103 of the UN Charter provides: 'In the event of a conflict between the obligations of the Members of the United Nations under the present Charter and their obligations under any other international agreement, their obligations under the present Charter shall prevail.'

[116] Palombella, 'Inter-Legality: On Interconnectedness and "External Sources"' (2021).

legal systems, owing to the mixed belonging of rights to different legalities – a status rooted in the universal understanding of human rights. This perspective maintains that the justification of human rights rests on valuable features of human beings, such as the protection of minorities and the universality of rights. The main claim of this approach is that human rights are grounded in our humanity, and by virtue of this quality they are possessed by all human beings.[117] As such, they have been deemed universal.[118]

Nonetheless, the protection of rights must be guaranteed within national contexts, shaped by their own cultures of justification and interpretation. The ECtHR employs the doctrine of the margin of appreciation as a primary tool to exercise deference to domestic understandings of human rights.[119] However, where a consensus is established among the Contracting States,[120] or where a relevant state fails the proportionality test,[121] no margin of appreciation can be granted. The discretionary use of the doctrine has been debated by legal scholars on reasonable grounds, with some describing it as a 'slippery concept'.[122] Owing to its close connection with domestic legal orders, the doctrine illustrates two crucial points concerning the relationship between human rights and inter-legality. First, it provides a valuable setting for understanding what an inter-legal approach entails, namely a perspective interwoven across both domestic and international orders. Moreover, the very need for such a doctrine underscores the strong capacity of rights to capture inter-legal issues. Furthermore, this complexity extends not only to the human rights obligations of public authorities

[117] J Tasioulas, 'On the Foundations of Human Rights' in R Cruft, SM Liao, and M Renzo (eds), *Philosophical Foundations of Human Rights* (Oxford University Press, 2015) 45. According to the anti-foundationalist understanding of human rights, their existence depends on social practices. This view denies 'extra-contextual, ahistorical, and non-situational' grounds of human rights. For a defence of the anti-foundationalist approach – arguing that it better accounts for the margin of appreciation and European consensus, which determine the normative content of human rights on the basis of contingent social practices – see B Tripkovic, 'A New Philosophy for the Margin of Appreciation and European Consensus' (2021) 42(1) *Oxford Journal of Legal Studies* 207–34. By contrast, the foundationalist understanding of human rights allows social practices to play a role in grounding rights only insofar as such a role derives from more fundamental moral grounds. See also S Fish, *Doing What Comes Naturally: Change, Rhetoric, and the Practice of Theory in Literary and Legal Studies* (Duke University Press, 1989) 344.

[118] It is important to note that the ECtHR has played a significant role in shaping one of the most elaborate systems of human rights protection in the world, as the analysis in Chapter 1 has demonstrated within the context of emerging advanced technologies.

[119] Art 1 of Protocol 15 of the Convention provides: 'At the end of the preamble to the Convention, a new recital shall be added, which shall read as follows: "Affirming that the High Contracting Parties, in accordance with the principle of subsidiarity, have the primary responsibility to secure the rights and freedoms defined in this Convention and the Protocols thereto, and that in doing so they enjoy a margin of appreciation, subject to the supervisory jurisdiction of the European Court of Human Rights established by this Convention."'.

[120] See a perfect example on the application of the margin of appreciation in *Evans v United Kingdom* App no 6339/05 (ECtHR, 10 April 2007).

[121] *Evans v United Kingdom* (n 120).

[122] R O'Connell, *European Principles of Interpretation and Application in Law, Democracy, and the European Court of Human Rights* (Cambridge University Press, 2020) 79.

but also to the obligations of private actors, through the horizontal effect of constitutional rights.[123]

Second, this level of complexity requires a qualified legal assessment that takes into account a balanced and comprehensive consideration of all *relevant* legal perspectives. It shifts attention away from the question of which legality must prevail and instead towards identifying the most functional interpretative choice – one that preserves the core meaning of the right(s) at stake[124] and prevents injustice.

4.4.4. Inter-Legality and the Rule of Law

Legal scholars have increasingly reflected on new technologies, to develop strategies that ensure compatibility with the rule of law, human rights, and human dignity. Addressing the challenges posed by these technologies requires reimagining both legal approaches and the rule of law itself as a constraint on the arbitrary exercise of power, as well as reconsidering the future of traditional domains, such as criminal law, tort law, and contract law.[125] This is a demanding task, since solutions must be devised in a new and partly 'unknown' environment shaped by the epistemic difficulties of emerging technologies, including AI systems. Yet the epistemic nature of the problem does not justify the existence of 'free zones' in which the rule of law ceases to apply in the digital sphere. On the contrary, it may compel modern law and its mechanisms to reinvent themselves. As Hildebrandt warns, if we fail to meet this challenge, the consequences will be serious:

> If we do not learn how to uphold and extend the legality that protects individual persons against arbitrary or unfair state interventions, the law will lose its hold on our imagination. It may fold back into a tool to train, discipline or influence people whose behaviours are measured and calculated to be nudged into compliance, or, the law will be replaced by techno-regulation, whether or not that is labelled as law.[126]

In other words, it is only legality – when adequately extended and comprehended – that can protect the individual against arbitrariness. The main question to be addressed here is, *how can we comprehend legality within the new environment created by advanced technologies?* This question invites reflection on the concept of the rule of law[127] at a more granular level.

[123] E Frantziou, *The Horizontal Effect of Fundamental Rights in the European Union: A Constitutional Analysis* (Oxford University Press, 2019).

[124] Palombella, 'Inter-Legality: On Interconnectedness and "External Sources"' (2021).

[125] R Brownsword, *Law, Technology and Society, Re-imaging the Regulatory Environment* (Routledge, 2019).

[126] M Hildebrandt, *Smart Technologies and the End(s) of Law* (Edward Elgar, 2015) 17.

[127] Brownsword, *Law, Technology and Society* (2019), 111. He argues that the central idea of the rule of law is that 'it is an ideal that sets its face against both arbitrary governance and irresponsible citizens'.

The rule of law[128] is often regarded as an *ideal*[129] that addresses a 'peculiar relationship' between two essential domains of Western law: *jurisdictio* and *gubernaculum* – justice and sovereignty.[130] In practice, this relationship is reflected in political institutions, sources of law, and even social practices, all of which aim to maintain a reasonable balance between these domains.[131] The ongoing debate surrounding this balance oscillates between the 'good' and the 'right', in search of an answer to the question of whether the rule of law should primarily serve to protect the 'right' or to produce the 'good'.[132] These two dimensions highlight the dual character of the rule of law: the relationship between *jurisdictio* and *gubernaculum* underscores its institutional dimension, while the tension between the 'good' and the 'right' generates its philosophical aspect.

As Palombella argues, the framework of the rule of law, 'cornered' by relational institutional concepts (*jurisdictio* and *gubernaculum*) and relational philosophical concepts (the right and the good), demonstrates its *normative* capacity to exceed its 'local' boundaries[133] and to operate

The actions of the former must always conform to legal rules, while the latter – citizens – must respect the rules and decisions thereby established. In this context, Brownsword observes that, 'whether acting offline or online, no one is above the law, and the rule of law signifies that the law rules'. In other words, the rule of law remains relevant in every context, including those shaped by non-normative instruments.

[128] The concept of the rule of law has its fundamental roots in the notion of the *Rechtsstaat* in German public law doctrine. In the nineteenth century, Robert von Mohl – considered the first author to introduce the concept – emphasised that the *Rechtsstaat* has no other purpose than 'to regulate the coexistence of the people in such a way that each of its members is supported and fostered in the freest and most comprehensive exercise and employment of all their faculties'. See R von Mohl, *Die deutsche Polizei-Wissenschaft nach den Grundsätzen des Rechtsstaates*, vol I, 2nd edn (Tübingen, 1844) 8. He identified five forms of the state, namely: (i) theocratic; (ii) despotic; (iii) patrimonial; (iv) patriarchal; and (v) Rechtsstaat (at 5). The entire volume is available at Münchener Digitalisierungszentrum at digitale-sammlungen.de/de/view/bsb10766998?page=34.

[129] J Meierhenrich and M Loughlin (eds), *The Cambridge Companion to the Rule of Law* (Cambridge University Press, 2021). See also S Ranchordás, 'The International Rule of Law Time After Time: Temporary Institutions Between Change and Continuity' in M Ambrus and RA Wessel (eds), *Netherlands Yearbook of International Law: Between Pragmatism and Predictability: Temporariness in International Law* (TMC Asser Press, 2014) 67.

[130] G Palombella, 'The Rule of Law and Its Core' in G Palombella and N Walker (eds), *Relocating the Rule of Law* (Hart Publishing, 2009); G Palombella, 'The Rule of Law as an Institutional Ideal' (2010) 9(1) *Comparative Sociology* 10; Palombella, 'Global Threads: Weaving the Rule of Law and the Balance of Legal Software' (2010); G Palombella, 'The EU's Sense of the Rule of Law and the Issue of Its Oversight' (2014) EUI Working Papers RSCAS 2014/125; G Palombella, 'The Rule of Law beyond the State: Failures, Promises and Theory' (2009) 7(3) *International Journal of Constitutional Law* 442–67; G Palombella, 'The Rule of Law in Global Governance – Its Normative Construction, Function and Import' (2010) Institute for International Law and Justice Colloquium, New York University School of Law; D Kochenov, 'The Missing EU Rule of Law' in C Closa and D Kochenov (eds), *Reinforcing Rule of Law Oversight in the European Union* (Cambridge University Press, 2016).

[131] Palombella, 'The Rule of Law and Its Core' (2009).

[132] Palombella, 'The Rule of Law and Its Core' (2009). On this philosophical ground, he argues that, due to this aspect of the rule of law, the concept cannot be reduced to a particular institutional setting. See also Palombella, 'The Rule of Law as an Institutional Ideal' (2010) (stating that the rule of law concerns questions of justice, the problem of liberty, non-domination, the balance between the right and the good, and the validity of law).

[133] This can be interpreted as the 'rule of law effect', which I have reserved for discussion elsewhere.

within a wider context beyond the state.[134] In other words, through both its institutional and philosophical dimensions, the rule of law assumes an inherent normative power that resists restriction to a 'single directing mind'.[135] More specifically, the institutional dimension of the rule of law – grounded in respect for the individuality of human beings – extends its scope beyond territorial manifestations, encompassing 'the founding revolutionary charts of modernity, constitutional documents, [and] the statutes of contemporary supranational organizations'.[136] Its philosophical dimension, at the same time, refers to the preservation of the tension between the right and the good through institutional devices, demanding 'the non-disposability of justice *(jurisdictio)* by the rule of the sovereign'.[137]

An inter-legal approach, in this sense, aligns with the rule of law through its emphasis on the simultaneous emergence of diverse legalities, the shift of focus from contestation to functions, and the emergence of the 'law of the case' from composite interweaving norms, as explained above. In other words, it engages with the rule of law in its fundamental dimension – as an *ideal* – rather than as 'a form representing the State'.[138] Thus, an inter-legal perspective arises not only from the nature of the subject matter but also from the outer layers that extend beyond the state, thereby forming the *core* of the rule of law.[139]

4.5. Artificial Intelligence is Inter-Legal by Default

Legal issues surrounding artificial intelligence are, by default, inter-legal and 'global'. In other words, questions raised by AI systems – particularly in areas such as biometrics and social benefits – cannot be effectively addressed by isolated national regulatory or administrative systems. There are at least five reasons why

[134] Palombella, 'The Rule of Law and Its Core' (2009).

[135] It should be noted that, in authoritarian states where women's perspectives are disregarded, an inclusive approach – one that invites a plurality of legal perspectives or, as Palombella observes, a 'broader understanding of social normativity' – is of particular importance. See also K O'Donovan, 'Engendering Justice: Women's Perspective and the Rule of Law' (1989) 39 *University of Toronto Law Journal* 127.

[136] Palombella, 'The Rule of Law and Its Core' (2009), 12. In another article, he argues that the couple between the right and the good can also be characterised by 'enhancing the connection of this requisite balance-relation with the non-domination feature'. See Palombella, 'The Rule of Law as an Institutional Ideal' (2010), 19.

[137] Palombella, 'The Rule of Law and Its Core' (2009), 16.

[138] Palombella, 'The Rule of Law and Its Core' (2009) ('if we look at the rule of law as a form representing the State, we would be making a big mistake').

[139] Palombella, 'The Rule of Law and Its Core' (2009) (citing Sartori: 'the rule of law does not postulate the State, but an autonomous law, external to the State: the common law, the case-law, in sum the judge made and jurists' law. Therefore, there is a 'rule of law' without the State: and more precisely it does not require the State to monopolize the production of law', in G Sartori, 'Nota sul rapporto tra Stato di dritto e Stato di giustizia' (1964) in *Rivista internazionale di filosofia del dritto* 310). It may be argued that, in this sense, an inter-legal approach constitutes an essential requirement of the rule of law.

an inter-legal approach is especially relevant to the challenges posed by AI. The following reasoning builds on the fundamental characteristics of AI systems used by public authorities, as identified in chapter two of this book.

First, AI systems deployed in the public sector are institutionally and interdisciplinarily *inter-systemic*, engaging a wide range of disciplines and institutions. From an institutional perspective, the 'GlobalPolicy.AI'[140] platform provides a concrete illustration of the *inter-systemic* dimension of AI systems and highlights the necessity of an inter-legal approach. Its primary objective is to facilitate co-operation among intergovernmental organisations, and to assist policymakers in navigating the international AI governance framework by providing access to relevant tools and best practices. The platform is distinctive in that it functions as a one-stop resource for both AI policy experts and the public. As of September 2021, it included eight partners: the Council of Europe, the European Commission, the European Agency for Fundamental Rights, the Inter-American Development Bank, the OECD and the OECD Artificial Intelligence Policy Observatory (OECD.AI), the UN, UNESCO, and the World Bank Group.

The platform pursues two main objectives, defined as follows: 'to provide information about each organisation's work on AI, thereby helping policy makers and the wider public navigate the international AI governance landscape and access relevant resources', and 'to strengthen co-operation between the different organizations, leveraging each other's work and making progress together towards common goals'.[141] Among its key priorities, the platform explicitly identifies the alignment of AI with human rights and democracy.[142]

At first glance, the GlobalPolicy.AI platform offers a compelling illustration of interwoven regulatory settings, as it brings together eight distinct organisations focused on the singular issue of AI governance. The platform also demonstrates the transboundary nature of AI, comparable to global challenges such as security or climate change. By calling for co-operation and the pursuit of common goals that concern all people and humanity, it explicitly frames AI as a 'global' issue.

Striving to develop common goals for AI through this platform naturally creates a fertile ecosystem for inter-legality, since at the descriptive level 'inter-legality captures the crossing threads of originally separate regulators as well as legalities'.[143] Each of the participating intergovernmental organisations has published statements, reports, communications, and guidelines examining the societal, ethical, legal, and economic impacts of AI on individuals and the environment, and all have affirmed that they regard AI as a common concern. Accordingly, AI – so extensively characterised as a global phenomenon – cannot be treated as merely a 'national' issue. Put differently, the rapidly expanding proliferation of extra-state

[140] See the platform's website at globalpolicy.ai/en/.

[141] GlobalPolicy.AI (n 140).

[142] The platform identifies three key areas. The other two are 'responsible development and use of trustworthy AI' and 'AI to advance the sustainable development goals' (n 140).

[143] G Palombella, 'Exploring the Rationale of Inter-Legality' (2022) 1 *Rivista di filosofia del diritto* 9.

regimes and international organisations addressing AI has generated an ecosystem in which 'two or more legal systems coexist in the same social field'.[144]

Second, positioning AI as a solution to other major challenges renders it materially interconnected with broader global concerns. This framing underscores the interdisciplinary, *inter-systemic* dimension of AI systems. For example, it would be naïve to regulate AI-driven surveillance technologies, such as biometric identification or categorisation systems, without considering their implications for global security. Axelrod and Keohane capture this dynamic through the notion of 'issue-linkage': 'Most issues are linked to other issues. This means that games being played on different issues – different "chessboards," in Stanley Hoffmann's wording – affect one another. Connections between games become important when issues are linked.'[145] Furthermore, the UN has emphasised the role AI may play in addressing global challenges. On 15 September 2021, the UN High Commissioner for Human Rights, Michelle Bachelet, stressed this potential:

> Artificial intelligence can be a force for good, helping societies overcome some of the great challenges of our times. But AI technologies can have negative, even catastrophic, effects if they are used without sufficient regard to how they affect people's human rights.[146]

Third, AI systems used in the public sector are *dynamic* in terms of both development and adoption. Since closed legal systems are not able to capture such a dynamic field and the changes it causes in the society,[147] an inter-legal approach is highly necessary. Such dynamism requires up-to-date approaches. In this sense, an inter-legal approach is promising, as it has always remained dynamic by excluding the monopoly or hegemony of a single legal order.

Fourth, as discussed in chapters two and three, AI systems used in the public sector are marked by *complexity*. This complexity arises from three interrelated dimensions: (a) their reliance on black-box mechanisms that obscure internal decision-making processes; (b) the use of heterogeneous terminology that complicates identification and classification; and (c) the integration of diverse techniques and applications. Moreover, such systems are inherently *social*, in that (a) they mediate and facilitate key aspects of the functioning of social institutions and structures, (b) they recognise and respond to the social components of their environment, (c) they structure interactions between individuals and the system through processes of identification, categorisation, and detection, and (d) they weave broader social contexts by aggregating and interpreting individual data within collective frameworks.

[144] See Merry, 'Legal Pluralism', 870 (defining legal pluralism as 'a situation in which two or more legal systems coexist in the same social field').

[145] R Axelrod and RO Keohane, 'Achieving Cooperation under Anarchy: Strategies and Institutions' (1985) 38(1) *World Politics* 239.

[146] United Nations, 'Urgent Action Needed over Artificial Intelligence Risks to Human Rights' (*UN News*, 2021), available at news.un.org/en/story/2021/09/1099972.

[147] Palombella, 'Exploring the Rationale of Inter-Legality' (2022), 4.

The main claim advanced by legal scholars is that the challenges posed by AI systems have not yet been adequately addressed, leaving existing regimes insufficient to cope with them. This underlines the necessity of an inter-legal approach, as opposed to reliance on closed legal systems that are unlikely to resolve the problems at hand. In addition to national, international, regional, and even 'global' initiatives regulating new technologies – particularly AI – these technologies themselves contribute an additional layer to the complex regulatory context through private regulations, often reinforced by the 'invisible handshake'.[148] Yet it must be recognised that external sources or extra-state normativities face an inherent problem: they are deprived of democratic legitimacy. This lack of democratic and substantive legitimacy may undermine their effectiveness, rendering them dysfunctional in relation to the legal systems they are intended to address.[149]

In this sense, AI issues introduce additional layers of complexity and require a reconsideration of the dynamics of the regulatory context. It is foreseeable that such a broad and interconnected field will inevitably test the limits and scope of existing legal regimes. Inter-legality, however, directs us to identify the *law of the case* within the interwoven legal texture.[150] This composite legal practice may prove more demanding than applying rules sourced from a single legal system. Nevertheless, an inter-legal approach is indispensable for addressing the challenges posed by AI systems.

Fifth, the inadequacy of law in addressing AI risks creating a kind of 'lawless' space. Unlike other approaches, inter-legality is able to respond to such a gap of lawfulness, precisely because it functions as a bridge between legal systems by uncovering the connections among them. From an inter-legal perspective, the diversity of jurisgenerative entities, regimes, and orders collectively contributes to bridging this gap, thereby transforming composite law into a governing force capable of addressing the issue at stake.[151]

This reasoning demonstrates that *AI is inter-legal by default* and, therefore, necessitates an inter-legal approach. Such an approach ensures that the *inter-systemic*, *complex*, *dynamic*, and *social* issues surrounding AI are not left unsettled. As Habermas observes,

> the point is to protect areas of life that are functionally dependent on social integration through values, norms and consensus formation; and to protect them from falling prey to the system imperatives of economic and administrative subsystems that grow with dynamics of their own. And finally to defend them from becoming converted, through the steering medium of the law, to a principle of socialization which is, for them, dysfunctional.[152]

[148] M Birnhack and N Elkin-Koren, 'The Invisible Handshake: The Reemergence of the State in the Digital Environment' (2003) *Virginia Journal of Law and Technology* 1–57.

[149] Palombella, 'Inter-Legality: On Interconnectedness and "External Sources"' (2021). See also Palombella, 'Exploring the Rationale of Inter-Legality' (2022), 12.

[150] Palombella, 'Inter-Legality: On Interconnectedness and "External Sources"' (2021).

[151] Palombella, 'Exploring the Rationale of Inter-Legality' (2022), 12.

[152] J Habermas, 'Law as Medium and Law as Institution' in G Teubner (ed), *Dilemmas of Law in the Welfare State* (De Gruyter, 1986) 220.

4.6. Application of the Theory of Inter-Legality

This section seeks to clarify the application of a 'rights-based inter-legal approach' to a concrete case involving advanced surveillance technologies, through three steps: (i) adopting the vantage point of the affair – the case at hand – under scrutiny; (ii) identifying the relevant normativities governing the case; and (iii) considering the demands of justice that arise from it.[153]

4.6.1. A Rights-Based Inter-Legal Approach in the Surveillance Judgment of the BVerfG

On 19 May 2020, the German Federal Constitutional Court (BVerfG) delivered a landmark ruling, holding that the surveillance of telecommunications involving non-German individuals located outside German territory violates the German Constitution.[154] In its judgment, the court conducted a constitutional review *(Rechtssatzverfassungsbeschwerde)* on specific provisions of the Federal Intelligence Service Act,[155] which authorised German authorities to collect and process communication data exchanged between non-German nationals abroad.[156] The complainants – a group of journalists and NGOs – argued that these provisions of the Act (BND Act) violated the fundamental rights to privacy and the freedom of press.[157]

The German government contended that it was not bound by the Basic Law when conducting surveillance activities targeting foreign individuals outside German territory.[158] The Federal Constitutional Court, however, held that this position was inconsistent with Articles 5 and 10 of the Basic Law, which safeguard freedom of expression of the press, as well as the privacy of communications. The

[153] The previous version of this section of the book was published in the *Italian Law Journal* (open access): E Biber, 'Inter-Legality and Surveillance Technologies' (2021) *Italian Law Journal*, available at theitalianlawjournal.it/biber/. The version included in this book has been revised and reconsidered.

[154] BVerfG, 19 May 2020, 1 BvR 2835/17. Direct citations in this section refer to the official English translation of the judgment, as published on the website of the BVerfG, available at bundesverfassungsgericht.de/SharedDocs/Entscheidungen/EN/2020/05/-rs20200519_1bvr283517en.html. For other important judgments of the BVerfG assessing the constitutionality of surveillance regulations, see BVerfG 20 April 2016, 1 BvR 966/09 – 1 BvR 1140/09; BVerfG 14 July 1999, 1 BvR 2226/94 – 1 BvR 2420/95 – 1 BvR 2437/95.

[155] Gesetz über den Bundesnachrichtendienst – BNDG of 20 December 1990.

[156] The constitutional complaint mainly challenged §§ 6,7 and §§ 13 to 15 BNDG. See in n 154 and n 155.

[157] See n 154, para 33. Arts 5(1), second sentence, and 10(1). Art 5(1): 'Jeder hat das Recht, seine Meinung in Wort, Schrift und Bild frei zu äußern und zu verbreiten und sich aus allgemein zugänglichen Quellen ungehindert zu unterrichten. Die Pressefreiheit und die Freiheit der Berichterstattung durch Rundfunk und Film werden gewährleistet. Eine Zensur findet nicht statt.'; Art 10(1): 'Das Briefgeheimnis sowie das Post- und Fernmeldegeheimnis sind unverletzlich.'

[158] See n 154.

court further required the legislator to revise the existing statutory framework to ensure compliance with constitutional safeguards by 31 December 2021.[159]

The court's reasoning gives rise to several significant questions from the perspective of both international and European human rights law. Foremost among these is whether the German Federal Government remains bound by the provisions of the Basic Law when interfering with the rights of non-German individuals outside German territory. Drawing on international human rights law, the court answered this question in the affirmative, advancing three principal arguments in support of the government's accountability on foreign soil. These arguments were grounded primarily in the interpretation of paragraphs 2 and 3 of Article 1 of the Basic Law.[160]

Indeed, pursuant to Article 1(3) of the Basic Law, the court affirmed that German authorities are comprehensively bound by the fundamental rights enshrined in the German Constitution, and this obligation is not limited to territory of the Federal Republic *(Staatsgebiet)* or to the German people *(Staatsvolk)*.[161] In this regard, by referring to the history of the Basic Law and employing a teleological interpretation, the court underscored that the Constitution is designed to ensure a comprehensive reading of the fundamental rights, grounded in the principle of human dignity.[162]

Secondly, with reference to Article 1(2) and the Preamble, the court held that the Basic Law recognises inviolable and inalienable human rights as the foundation of every community, and as essential to peace and justice in the world.[163] Accordingly, the fundamental rights guaranteed under the Basic Law must be situated within the broader context of international human rights protections. This line of reasoning requires that fundamental rights of the Basic Law must be interpreted in the context of Germany's obligations under international law.[164]

Finally, the court observed that recent technological developments and their applications necessitate a comprehensive interpretation of Article 1(3) of the Basic Law – one that accounts for the novel threats posed to fundamental rights and the resulting shifts in powers.[165] On this basis, the court highlighted that German authorities remain bound by international human rights obligations irrespective of territorial boundaries, particularly in the context of technologies that enable cross-border services.[166] In other words, the court underscored that a comprehensive

[159] See n 154.

[160] Art 1(2): 'Das Deutsche Volk bekennt sich darum zu unverletzlichen und unveräußerlichen Menschenrechten als Grundlage jeder menschlichen Gemeinschaft, des Friedens und der Gerechtigkeit in der Welt.'; Art 1(3): 'Die nachfolgenden Grundrechte binden Gesetzgebung, vollziehende Gewalt und Rechtsprechung als unmittelbar geltendes Recht'.

[161] n 154, paras 87–89.

[162] n 154, para 89.

[163] n 154, para 94.

[164] n 154, paras 94–95.

[165] n 154, para 105.

[166] n 154, para 105.

and purposive reading of the Basic Law is especially imperative in light of emerging technologies, which extend the reach of state authority into third countries.

The judgment offers a significant example of a rights-based inter-legal reasoning. Therefore, this section of the book aims at analysing the judgment through a three-step framework: (i) adopting the vantage point of the affair – the case at hand – under scrutiny; (ii) identifying the relevant normativities governing the case; and (iii) considering the demands of justice that arise from it.[167] The first step reflects the theory of inter-legality, specifically its insight that diverse legalities may emerge simultaneously and interact within a single dispute. The second and third steps shift the focus from contestation to function and trace how a 'law of the case' crystallises from the interweaving of composite norms.

The purpose of developing this three-step analysis is to equip judges with an analytical framework through which to apply the perspective of inter-legality in conjunction with a rights-based inter-legal approach. Figure 4.1 below illustrates the three foundational pillars of the concept.[168]

Figure 4.1 Inter-Legal Reasoning

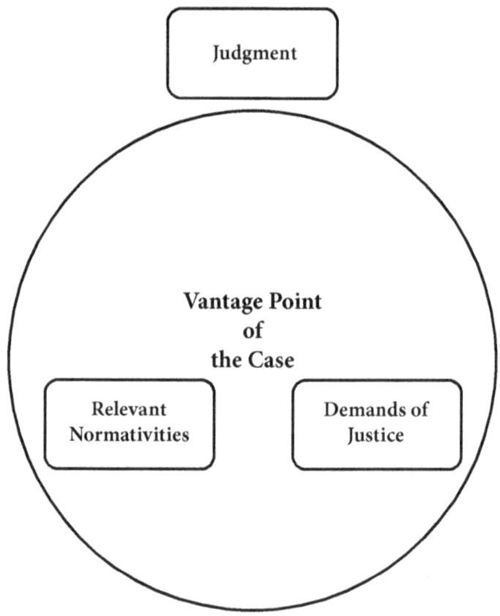

It should be emphasised that no hierarchical relationship exists among the three steps of the framework; rather, they interact with one another and operate in a dynamic mutually guiding manner. Nevertheless, the *Vantage Point of the Case* is the most essential step of inter-legality[169] – situated at the centre of the circle – and

[167] Klabbers and Palombella, 'Introduction: Situating Inter-Legality' (2019), 1–20. See also Palombella, 'Theory, Realities, and Promises of Inter-Legality: A Manifesto' (2019) in Klabbers and Palombella, *The Challenge of Inter-Legality*, 363–90.

[168] The chart is the original contribution of the author.

[169] Klabbers and Palombella, 'Introduction: Situating Inter-Legality' (2019), 2 ('the shift toward the construction of law from the angle of the case is essential to an inter-legality approach').

therefore constitutes the appropriate point of departure for the analysis. As the pillar of *Demands of Justice* requires a reconnoitre of the *Relevant Normativities*, it necessarily forms the final phase of the inquiry. The analysis then concludes with a set of overarching remarks on the implications of the case.

4.6.1.1. Adopting the Vantage Point of the Affair under Scrutiny

The concept of inter-legality fundamentally focuses on the vantage point of the case.[170] In this regard, Palombella underscores the importance of the angle of the case at stake as follows:

> One that seeks to reach the layer controlling the case in its deepest fundus, i.e. the place where, one would say with Wittgenstein, 'I have reached bedrock, and my spade is turned.' To be required to think of law in terms of inter-connectedness, among many normativities.[171]

To fully appreciate the standpoint of the case, it is necessary to outline the practice of strategic surveillance conducted by the Federal Intelligence Service, which may be summarised in five steps: (i) accessing telecommunication data through the interception of signals from telecommunications networks; (ii) diverting data or employing other interception methods that initiate a multi-step, fully automated process of sorting and analysis, followed by the filtering of data (the so-called DAFIS filtering mechanism); (iii) collecting and storing all traffic data remaining after the application of the filtering mechanism, without the use of selectors;[172] (iv) manually screening the data to assess its relevance for the Federal Intelligence Service; (v) co-operating with other intelligence services.[173] Among these steps, the filtering system is particularly contentious. Although the Federal Intelligence Service applies certain parameters designed to identify data connected to individuals within Germany or to German citizens, 'it is unknown how many telecommunication processes are falsely categorized as purely foreign telecommunications' due to the use of intermediary services located abroad or the use of hot spots.[174] This problematic aspect of the filtering mechanism partly arises from the technological features of the surveillance process itself.

In this context, the court engaged in a detailed examination of the characteristics of the advanced surveillance technologies and highlighted their fundamental differences from traditional forms of surveillance employed in the past:

> In the past, the only purpose of gathering foreign intelligence was the early detection of dangers to avert armed attacks on German territory; measures directly targeting individuals were limited to a small group of persons, as a result of both the technical

[170] See n 62.
[171] Gianluigi Palombella, 'Theory, Realities, and Promises of Inter-Legality A Manifesto' (2019), 380.
[172] It is a computer-based analysis through cross-checking and other methods. See n 154, para 21.
[173] n 154, paras 16–26.
[174] n 154, para 19.

> possibilities and the intelligence interest at the time (cf. BVerfGE 67, 157 <178>). Given today's possibilities of communication and the accompanying internationalisation, potential impending dangers (*drohende Gefahren*) originating from abroad have multiplied. Information technology makes it possible to communicate directly across borders, regardless of physical distance, and to coordinate without any delay.[175]

Furthermore, the court emphasised that, in light of new technological developments, restricting the application of fundamental rights to national borders would expose individuals to vulnerability and risk, causing the protection of fundamental rights to fall behind the rapid pace of ongoing internationalisation:

> In light of such developments, an understanding of fundamental rights according to which their protection ended at national borders would deprive holders of fundamental rights of all protection and would result in fundamental rights protection lagging behind the realities of internationalisation [...]. It could undermine fundamental rights protection in an increasingly important area that is characterised by intrusive state action and where – in the field of security law – fundamental rights are especially significant in general. By contrast, in binding the state as the relevant actor, Art. 1(3) GG accounts for such novel risks and helps bring them into the general framework of the rule of law that is created by the Basic Law.[176]

According to the BVerfG, the international dimension of modern communications, which operate both within states and across national borders, obscures the traditional distinction between the domestic and the foreign.[177] This interpretation indicates that the court conceptualises the *vantage point of the case* as *virtual*, situated in the technological context of cross-border services. In other words, these technologies, by rendering time and space effectively irrelevant, virtualise the vantage point of the case and present courts with disputes that cannot be confined to national borders. Within this framework, an inter-legal approach assumes particular significance, as the cross-border nature of such communications generates a space that intensifies interactions between legal systems. The dynamic and unpredictable character of this space further necessitates viewing legal systems as fundamentally interactional rather than as closed and rigidly structured systems.[178] This interactional understanding, in turn, compels the identification of the relevant normativities governing the dispute – the second pillar of the analysis.

[175] n 154, para 107.
[176] n 154, para 110.
[177] n 154, para 109.
[178] See WW van der Burg, *The Dynamics of Law and Morality: A Pluralist Account of Legal Interactionism* (Ashgate, 2014) 10, for a discussion of product versus practice models of law. According to S Taekema, the product model of law generates a systemic conception of legal order, while the practice model of law addresses an interactional legal order. See also S Taekema, 'Between or Beyond Legal Orders? Questioning the Concept of Legal Order' in Klabbers and Palombella, *The Challenge of Inter-Legality* (2019), 69–88.

4.6.1.2. Identifying the Relevant Normativities Governing the Case

Inter-legality does not simply describe the plural co-existence of distinct legalities operating in parallel; it reflects the reality of their 'unavoidable interconnectedness'.[179] An inter-legal approach underlines that no single legality or regime can function effectively in isolation. As Palombella observes, 'their functional isolation is a myth'.[180] As a result, the effectiveness of a given legality can only be enhanced by considering it situated in a dialogue with its 'interlocutors'. For instance, 'The European Convention of Human Rights may well be conceived as a kind of constitutional legality, but its ordering strength depends on the ways "other" legal systems accept and implement its normative clauses.'[181]

Within this framework, as a consequence of the interconnectedness of legalities, an inter-legal approach enables the observer to recognise that these legalities are not merely connected but also interwoven.[182] Disregarding this interwovenness or relying exclusively on a single legality might reduce justice to a mere 'lame verdict'.[183] This implies that the inclusion or consideration of the normative character of each legality is not a matter of choice; rather, where they are interwoven, interconnected, and de facto competing or concurring, it is a necessity.[184] In other words, every relevant legality within a condition of 'legal porosity'[185] – a space where multiple networks of legal orders compel 'constant transition and trespassing'[186] – possesses an objective claim to justice, due to its potential justice-related function.[187] Such a perspective precludes the monopoly or hegemony of any one legal order,[188] and instead invites all relevant legalities to move towards

[179] Palombella, 'Theory, Realities, and Promises of Inter-Legality: A Manifesto' (2019), 366.

[180] Palombella, 'Theory, Realities, and Promises of Inter-Legality: A Manifesto' (2019), 367.

[181] Palombella, 'Theory, Realities, and Promises of Inter-Legality: A Manifesto' (2019), 367. See also W Sadurski, 'Partnering with Strasbourg: Constitutionalism of the European Court of Human Rights, the Accession of Central and East European States to the Council of Europe, and the Idea of Pilot Judgments' (2009) 9 *Human Rights Law Review* 397.

[182] Palombella, 'Theory, Realities, and Promises of Inter-Legality A Manifesto' (2019), 365–68.

[183] Palombella, 'Theory, Realities, and Promises of Inter-Legality A Manifesto' (2019), 386.

[184] Palombella, 'Theory, Realities, and Promises of Inter-Legality A Manifesto' (2019), 363–90.

[185] B de Sousa Santos, 'Law: A Map of Misreading' in B de Sousa Santos, *Toward a New Common Sense: Law, Science and Politics in the Paradigmatic Transition* (Routledge, 1995) 473.

[186] de Sousa Santos (1995), 473.

[187] Palombella emphasises this point, marking a distinction from Santos' idea of inter-legality: 'it is true what Santos wrote that we live "in between". But inter-legality is not just a state of things we can exploit, and profit from contradictions and divergences among separate and mutually irrelevant normative orders. Not as a subjective sociological but as an objective legal notion, inter-legality allows us to consider the law as something different; we should pretend to avail of inter-legality also in a different sense', in Palombella, 'Theory, Realities, and Promises of Inter-Legality A Manifesto' (2019), 378.

[188] The term 'legal hegemony' has been widely debated by legal scholars following the well-known PSPP judgment of the BVerfG (Judgment of the Second Senate of 05 May 2020–2 BvR 859/15 §§ 1-237). According to the BVerfG, the review conducted by the CJEU on the European Central Bank's decisions concerning the Public Sector Purchase Programme did not satisfy the principle of proportionality. For discussions on legal hegemony, see A von Bogdandy, 'German Legal Hegemony' (*Verfassungsblog*, 5 October 2020), available at verfassungsblog.de/german-legal-hegemony/. See

equilibrium, thereby dissolving the tension between them.[189] Crucially, this perspective aligns with the rule of law which requires attention to diverse needs and ends, and 'prevents the law from turning into a sheer tool of domination'.[190] In so doing, it holds the potential to close so-called 'legal black holes'[191] and to address the questions generated by the interconnectedness of legalities, thereby strengthening the culture of justification.[192]

The judgment of the BVerfG clearly engaged with such 'empirical reconnaissance'[193] which takes place in the ecosystem of inter-legality, taking into account interrelatedness of legalities in the context of the case. In other words, the court identified and examined the relevant legalities that together form an ecosystem of inter-legality shaped by the case at hand.

According to the court, the relevant normativities governing the case comprised both the international norms and the German Constitution. This result was derived from the interpretation of paragraphs 2 and 3 of Article 1, which focuses on their 'multifaced nature'. In other words, the court construed the normative text of these provisions in such a way as to recognise that the relevant norms extend beyond a single, system-sourced positive law, and instead draw upon more than one legal order:

> In Art. 1(2) GG, the Basic Law acknowledges inviolable and inalienable human rights as the basis of every community, of peace, and of justice in the world. The Basic Law thus places fundamental rights in the context of international human rights guarantees that seek to provide protection beyond national borders and are afforded to individuals as human beings. Accordingly, Art. 1(2) and Art. 1(3) GG build upon the guarantee of human dignity enshrined in Art. 1(1) GG.[194]

also A von Bogdandy et al, 'German Legal Hegemony' (2020) Max Planck Institute for Comparative Public Law and International Law (MPIL) Research Paper No 2020-43, available at ssrn.com/abstract=3727378.

[189] G Palombella, 'Theory, Realities, and Promises of Inter-Legality A Manifesto' (2019), 381–82.

[190] Palombella, 'The Rule of Law at Home and Abroad' (2016).

[191] A Barak, *The Judge in a Democracy* (Princeton University Press, 2008) 298 (arguing that judicial review eliminates legal black holes). The term 'legal black hole' was coined by J Steyn in 2004. See J Steyn, 'Guantanamo Bay: The Legal Black Hole' (2004) 53(1) *International and Comparative Law Quarterly* 1 ('The most powerful democracy is detaining hundreds of suspected foot soldiers of the Taliban in a legal black hole at the United States naval base at Guantanamo Bay, where they await trial on capital charges by military tribunals.'). In 2006, Dyzenhaus introduced the term 'legal grey holes' to describe 'disguised black holes' that addresses situations in which 'there are some legal constraints on executive action – it is not a lawless void – but the constraints are so insubstantial that they pretty well permit government to do as it pleases'. He further emphasised that such grey holes are worse than legal black holes ('since such grey holes permit government to have its cake and eat it too, to seem to be governing not only by law but in accordance with the rule of law, they and their endorsement by judges and academics might be even more dangerous from the perspective of the substantive conception of the rule of law than true black holes'). See D Dyzenhaus, *The Constitution of Law: Legality in a Time of Emergency* (Cambridge University Press, 2006) 42.

[192] See M Cohen-Eliya and I Porat, 'Proportionality and the Culture of Justification' (2011) 59 *American Journal of Comparative Law* 463–90, for a discussion of the term 'culture of justification' and its relation to the principle of proportionality.

[193] G Palombella, 'Theory, Realities, and Promises of Inter-Legality: A Manifesto' (2019), 382. Palombella uses the term 'reconnaissance' in the sense of both exploration and recognition.

[194] n 154, para 94.

This tension-free and equilibrating reading of the Constitution implicitly adopts the perspective of inter-legality, which moves beyond the 'usual, traditional perspective, a perspective that is limited by the political, legal and cognitive borders of a single self-contained system'.[195] In this respect, inter-legality bears a resemblance to Friedrich Müller's structuring legal theory (SLT), developed at the University of Heidelberg.[196] SLT can be described as a 'post-positivist' theory which holds that legal norms are not identical with the text in which they appear *('Rechtsnorm ist ungleich Normtext')*.[197] Instead, interpretation and application are seen as dynamic processes in which norms have to be actively constructed.[198] From this perspective, both SLT and inter-legality share the view that the norm text alone is insufficient, and that norms must be placed within a wider and more comprehensive framework. In other words, by taking account of the interplay of relevant actors and contextual factors, both perspectives move away from the outdated view that legislation alone, in and of itself, contains the single correct solution to every legal dispute.[199]

Furthermore, this perspective illustrates that the BVerfG is reorienting its approach to international law, at least in the context of surveillance technologies. Some scholars have observed that, for the Federal German Constitutional Court,

> international law does feature only in [the domestic courts'] jurisprudence if and to the extent permitted by [the domestic courts'] domestic law. [Therefore,] [w]hen the Court applies international law or implements international decisions, it does so because domestic law requires it, not because they are organs of the international community.[200]

However, in this judgment, where no strict hierarchy of legalities is established, the court interpreted the Basic Law through the lens of internationalisation, grounding its reasoning in the principle of human dignity as a universal ideal.[201] At the same time, the court highlighted the responsibilities of the German state within a united Europe and the wider international community.[202] Its emphasis on the

[195] Klabbers and Palombella, 'Introduction: Situating Inter-Legality' (2019), 1.

[196] F Müller and R Christensen, *Juristische Methodik* (Dunker & Humblot, 2013) 263. For the basic premises of the theory, see M Klatt, *Making the Law Explicit: The Normativity of Legal Argumentation* (Hart Publishing, 2008) 54–56 ('the text is only a "guideline", as such it has no claim to normativity' … 'the rule is not the beginning, but the product of the process of the application of the law').

[197] See further discussion about the SLT in M Klatt, 'Contemporary Legal Philosophy in Germany' (2007) 93(4) *Archiv für Rechts- und Sozialphilosophie* 519–39.

[198] Klatt, 'Contemporary Legal Philosophy in Germany' (2007), 519–39.

[199] Klatt, 'Contemporary Legal Philosophy in Germany' (2007), 519–39.

[200] A Paulus, 'National Courts and the International Rule of Law – Remarks on the book by André Nollkaemper' (2012) 4 *Jerusalem Review of Legal Studies* 5, 8–9.

[201] See a discussion about the judgment's universalist and international language in M Milanovic, 'Surveillance and Cyber Operations' in M Gibney et al (eds), *Research Handbook on Extraterritorial Human Rights Obligations* (Routledge, 2020) 10–11. See also a broader discussion on the concept of human dignity in German constitutional law in A Barak, 'Human Dignity in German Constitutional Law' in A Barak, *Human Dignity: The Constitutional Value and the Constitutional Right* (Cambridge University Press, 2015) 225–42.

[202] n 154, paras 94–95.

responsibility of the German state towards the protection of fundamental rights also suggests that sovereignty should not be understood merely as something constrained by fundamental rights, but also as a responsibility for the protection of fundamental rights, with the individual placed at the centre.[203] In this sense, sovereignty is reimagined as a form of 'humanised state sovereignty': one that is accountable for the safeguarding of humanity.[204]

Such a reading naturally leads the BVerfG to engage with the relevant case law of the ECtHR. In its reasoning, the court cited the leading decisions concerning the territorial scope of the ECHR.[205] On the basis of these cases, the BVerfG observed that the ECtHR's approach rests largely on the doctrine of 'effective control over territory', and that it remains unclear whether, and to what extent, the Convention protects against surveillance measures undertaken abroad by the Convention States:

> The European Court of Human Rights is mainly guided by the criterion of whether a state exercises effective control over an area outside its own territory; on this basis, it has in many cases affirmed the applicability of Convention rights abroad (cf. in summary ECtHR [GC], Al-Skeini and Others v. the United Kingdom, Judgment of 7 July 2011, no. 55721/07, §§ 132 et seq. with further references; cf. also Aust, Archiv des Völkerrechts 52 <2014>, p. 375 <394 et seq.> with further references). However, there has been no final determination as to whether protection is afforded against surveillance measures carried out by Contracting Parties in other states. In a decision that has not become final yet, the First Section of the European Court of Human Rights measured the implementation of surveillance measures targeting persons abroad against the standards of the Convention without any restrictions and found such measures to be in violation of the Convention. The complainants in this case included foreign nationals who were not present or resident in the state against which the applications were directed (cf. ECtHR, Big Brother Watch and Others v. the United Kingdom, Judgment of 13 September 2018, no. 58170/13 and others, § 271). Similarly, a Swedish foundation challenged strategic foreign surveillance powers under Swedish law that exclude domestic communications. The European Court of Human Rights reviewed these powers without calling into question the Convention's applicability abroad (cf. ECtHR, Centrum för Rättvisa v. Sweden, Judgment of 19 June 2018, no. 35252/08). Both proceedings are now pending before the Grand Chamber.[206]

It is worth noting that in *Bankovic and Others v. Belgium* the ECtHR made clear that

> the Convention is a multi-lateral treaty operating … in an essentially regional context and notably in the legal space of the Contracting States. … The Convention was

[203] A Peters, 'Humanity as the A and Ω of Sovereignty' (2009) 20(3) *European Journal of International Law* 513–44.
[204] Peters, 'Humanity as the A and Ω of Sovereignty', 513–44.
[205] ECtHR, *Al-Skeini and others v United Kingdom*, App No 55721/07, 7 July 2011, para 132; ECtHR, *Big Brother Watch and others v United Kingdom*, App No. 58170/13 et al, 13 September 2018; ECtHR, *Centrum for Rättvisa v Sweden*, App No 35252/08, 19 June 2018.
[206] n 154, paras 97–98.

> not designed to be applied throughout the world, even in respect of the conduct of Contracting States.[207]

However, in the context of foreign surveillance, many human rights scholars have highlighted the inconsistency of the Court's extraterritorial jurisprudence.[208]

They argued that, although the ECtHR has delivered several significant rulings on the matter, the meaning of Article 1 – providing that 'the high Contracting Parties shall secure to everyone within their jurisdiction the rights and freedoms defined in Section I of this Convention' – remains unclear.[209]

Finally, the BVerfG observed that the extraterritorial application of the Basic Law is directed solely at constraining the actions of German state authorities, and therefore does not amount to a violation of the principle of non-intervention under international law:[210]

> The binding effect of fundamental rights does not amount to a violation of the principle of non-intervention or to a restriction of other states' executive or legislative powers. It neither imposes German law on other states, nor does it supplant the fundamental rights of other states. In particular, the binding effect of fundamental rights does not extend German state powers abroad, but limits potential courses of action of German state authority.[211]

Following this reasoning, the court emphasised that Article 53 of the ECHR permits Contracting Parties to provide more extensive protection for fundamental rights, noting that 'the Convention does not rule out further-reaching fundamental rights protection by the Contracting Parties'.[212] This provision of scope of discretion in determining the level of protection enables the court to draw on other relevant legalities in order to meet the demands of justice in the case – marking the third step of our analysis.

[207] ECtHR, *Bankovic and Others v Belgium and Others*, App No 52207/99, 10 May 2001, para 80. See also 'Guide on Article 1 of the European Convention on Human Rights', updated on 31 December 2020, available at echr.coe.int/documents/guide_art_1_eng.pdf.

[208] See a summary of ECtHR case law regarding mass surveillance in 'Mass Surveillance – Factsheet', European Court of Human Rights, Press Unit, May 2021, available at echr.coe.int/documents/fs_mass_surveillance_eng.pdf.

[209] M Milanovic, *Extraterritorial Application of Human Rights Treaties Law, Principles and Policy* (Oxford University Press, 2011); S Miller, 'Revisiting Extraterritorial Jurisdiction: A Territorial Justification for Extraterritorial Jurisdiction under the European Convention' (2009) 20(4) *The European Journal of International Law* 1223–46; M Milanovic, 'Human Rights Treaties and Foreign Surveillance: Privacy in the Digital Age' (2015) 56(1) *Harvard International Law Journal* 81–146. See also ECtHR, 'Extra-territorial jurisdiction of States Parties to the European Convention on Human Rights' (July 2018) European Court of Human Rights Press Unit, available at echr.coe.int/documents/fs_extra-territorial_jurisdiction_eng.pdf.

[210] n 154, paras 101–03.

[211] n 154, para 101.

[212] n 154, para 99. It should be noted that this Article is of particular importance from the perspective of inter-legality. It substantially seconds inter-legal reasoning for two reasons: first, it considers that there might be relevant legalities related to the issue at stake; second, it directs domestic courts to seek just solutions. Art 53 of the ECHR provides: 'nothing in this Convention shall be construed as limiting or derogating from any of the human rights and fundamental freedoms which may be ensured under the laws of any High Contracting Party or under any other agreement to which it is a party'.

4.6.1.3. Considering the Demands of Justice Stemming from the Case

With regard to the third step, guided by the first and second, the court implicitly drew upon the doctrine of 'effective control over rights'. Unlike the doctrines of effective control over territory and over persons, of the ECtHR, this approach – the 'effective control over rights doctrine' that is consistent with a right-based inter-legal approach – turns on the question of whether a state exercises effective control over the enjoyment of the rights.[213] This line of reasoning emerged from the court's reconnaissance of the close relationship between human rights and fundamental rights. In this light, the court considered the German state to be accountable both under the Basic Law and under international conventions, making express reference to the Universal Declaration of Human Rights and the International Covenant on Civil and Political Rights:

> This link between fundamental rights and human rights guarantees is incompatible with the notion that the applicability of the fundamental rights of the Basic Law ends at the national border, which would exempt German public bodies from having to adhere to fundamental rights and human rights when they act abroad vis-à-vis foreigners. Such a notion would run counter to the Basic Law's aim of ensuring that every person is afforded inalienable rights on the basis of international conventions and beyond national borders – including protection from surveillance (cf. Art. 12 of the Universal Declaration of Human Rights, Art. 17(1) of the International Covenant on Civil and Political Rights). Given the realities of internationalised political action and the ever increasing involvement of states beyond their own borders, this would result in a situation where the fundamental rights protection of the Basic Law could not keep up with the expanding scope of action of German state authority and where it might – on the contrary – even be undermined through the interaction of different states. Yet the fact that the state as the politically legitimated and accountable actor is bound by fundamental rights ensures that fundamental rights protection keeps up with an international extension of state activities.[214]

It is important to observe that the court did not establish a definitive doctrinal link between fundamental rights and human rights; rather, it underscored that fundamental rights cannot be regarded as a closed legal regime, given their inherent relationship with human rights. While the court acknowledged a terminological distinction between the two, it emphasised that this distinction 'cannot be used as an argument against the integration of fundamental rights into the

[213] See a discussion on the doctrine of effective control over rights in B Çalı, 'Has "Control Over Rights Doctrine" for Extraterritorial Jurisdiction Come of Age? Karlsruhe too, has spoken, now it's Strasbourg's turn' (*EJIL: Talk!*, 21 July 2020), available at ejiltalk.org/has-control-over-rights-doctrine-for-extra-territorial-jurisdiction-come-of-age-karlsruhe-too-has-spoken-now-its-strasbourgs-turn/. Compare with the debate on the concept of 'preserving legal space' of the ECtHR in M Rojszczak, 'Extraterritorial Bulk Surveillance after the German BND Act Judgment' (2021) 17(1) *European Constitutional Law Review* 53–77 (arguing that the concept would prevent individuals from finding themselves in a 'legal vacuum' in the context of electronic surveillance).

[214] n 154, para 96.

context of universal human rights'.[215] Otherwise, fundamental rights would risk proving inadequate when German public authorities act abroad in relation to non-nationals. In this respect, the link between fundamental rights and human rights is crucial, as it prevents the erosion of fundamental rights through the interaction of different states.[216] In other words, human rights are always of fundamental relevance when questions of domestic fundamental rights arise, and they hold significant potential to provide additional protection for such rights.

Furthermore, the court reasoned that, in light of the realities of internationalised political action, such a universal reading of fundamental rights is unavoidable. This, in turn, entails the legal responsibility of German public authorities at the global level. Consequently, by recognising the link between human rights and fundamental rights, and by drawing upon international human rights law, the court may be seen as implicitly invoking the doctrine of effective control over rights – an approach that reflects a rights-based inter-legal approach.

The doctrine of effective control over rights has been recognised by a number of international institutions. Notably, the UN Human Rights Committee, in its General Comment no 36, expressly observed that:

> In light of article 2 (1) of the Covenant, a State party has an obligation to respect and ensure the rights under article 6 of all persons who are within its territory and all persons subject to its jurisdiction, that is, all persons over whose enjoyment of the right to life it exercises power or effective control. This includes persons located outside any territory effectively controlled by the State whose right to life is nonetheless affected by its military or other activities in a direct and reasonably foreseeable manner (see para. 22 above).[217]

[215] n 154, para 94.

[216] See a discussion on the relation between human rights and fundamental rights in G Palombella, 'From Human Rights to Fundamental Rights: Consequences of a conceptual distinction' (2007) 93(3) *ARSP: Archiv Für Rechts- Und Sozialphilosophie/Archives for Philosophy of Law and Social Philosophy* 396–426 (arguing that human rights are deontological imperatives concerning what we owe to human beings, whereas fundamental rights are tied to those things that contribute to the existence of a society).

[217] UN Human Rights Committee, General Comment No 36, § 63. Art 6 of the ICCPR: '1. Every human being has the inherent right to life. This right shall be protected by law. No one shall be arbitrarily deprived of his life. 2. In countries which have not abolished the death penalty, sentence of death may be imposed only for the most serious crimes in accordance with the law in force at the time of the commission of the crime and not contrary to the provisions of the present Covenant and to the Convention on the Prevention and Punishment of the Crime of Genocide. This penalty can only be carried out pursuant to a final judgement rendered by a competent court. 3. When deprivation of life constitutes the crime of genocide, it is understood that nothing in this article shall authorize any State Party to the present Covenant to derogate in any way from any obligation assumed under the provisions of the Convention on the Prevention and Punishment of the Crime of Genocide. 4. Anyone sentenced to death shall have the right to seek pardon or commutation of the sentence. Amnesty, pardon or commutation of the sentence of death may be granted in all cases. 5. Sentence of death shall not be imposed for crimes committed by persons below eighteen years of age and shall not be carried out on pregnant women. 6. Nothing in this article shall be invoked to delay or to prevent the abolition of capital punishment by any State Party to the present Covenant.'

A comparable approach is evident in the *Report on the Right to Privacy in the Digital Age* of the Office of the United Nations High Commissioner for Human Rights (OHCHR), particularly in the context of digital surveillance:

> [D]igital surveillance therefore may engage a State's human rights obligations if that surveillance involves the State's exercise of power or effective control in relation to digital communications infrastructure, wherever found, for example, through direct tapping or penetration of that infrastructure. Equally, where the State exercises regulatory jurisdiction over a third party that physically controls the data, that State also would have obligations under the Covenant. If a country seeks to assert jurisdiction over the data of private companies as a result of the incorporation of those companies in that country, then human rights protections must be extended to those whose privacy is being interfered with, whether in the country of incorporation or beyond.[218]

In 2017, the Inter-American Court of Human Rights, in its Advisory Opinion on the Environment and Human Rights, likewise affirmed that extraterritorially affected victims fall within the jurisdiction of the state of origin 'when the state of origin exercises effective control over activities carried out that caused the harm and consequent violation of human rights'.[219]

The doctrine has also been advanced by a number of human rights experts in light of the realities surrounding surveillance technologies. They argue that, in the context of communication surveillance, a state's human rights obligations are triggered whenever it interferes with the rights of an individual, irrespective of whether that individual has any connection to the state concerned.[220] Moreover, they argue that the doctrines of effective control over the individual and over territory are ill-suited to the particular nature of communication surveillance, in which state control over both infrastructure and individuals is essentially virtual.[221] As Brunner observes,

> communications surveillance programs most often involve a state's collection and review of data from its own territory, even though the communications may originate and terminate in other states and the rights holders may be beyond the collecting state's jurisdiction. Some types of collection more clearly involve extraterritorial action – e.g., a state's interception of communications traffic via equipment located in its embassies abroad – but the impact on rights occurs in a different manner from the exercise of 'effective control' over persons or territory.[222]

[218] OHCHR, 'Report on the Right to Privacy in the Digital Age' (2014), available at https://digitallibrary.un.org/record/777869?ln=en&v=pdf.

[219] Inter-American Court of Human Rights, *Advisory Opinion on the Environment and Human Rights* (2017) OC-23/17, 15 November, Series A No 23, § 104(h).

[220] P Margulies, 'The NSA in Global Perspective: Surveillance, Human Rights, and International Counterterrorism' (2014) 82 *Fordham Law Review* 2148–52 (arguing that a state exercises 'virtual control' over communications infrastructure when it engages in surveillance activities).

[221] L Brunner, 'Digital Communication and the Evolving Right to Privacy' in MK Land and J Aronson, *New Technologies for Human Rights and Practice* (Cambridge University Press, 2018) 236–39.

[222] L Brunner, 'Digital Communication and the Evolving Right to Privacy' in Land and Aronson, *New Technologies for Human Rights and Practice* (2018) 236–39.

Although the BVerfG did not explicitly invoke the doctrine of effective control over rights, its reliance on international human rights law – principally through general references to Article 12 of the Universal Declaration of Human Rights[223] and Article 17 of the International Covenant on Civil and Political Rights,[224] both of which safeguard the right to privacy – together with its universalist reading of the Constitution, allowed the fundamental rights protected under the Basic Law to extend beyond national borders. This approach enabled the court to respond to the demands of justice arising from the case, thereby advancing to the third step of the present analysis.

4.6.2. Concluding Remarks

The concept of inter-legality has developed in response to recent global transformations. Processes of globalisation and the emergence of transnational challenges have unsettled the state-centred framework of the Westphalian and Hobbesian order.[225] In this transformative, incomplete, or 'suspended' period, states have sought to preserve their authority over a wide range of issues – whether or not these are regulated at the regional or global level – and have endeavoured to maintain their national roles as effectively as possible.[226] Yet, the rise of cross-border concerns, from climate change to security, has increasingly eroded state power.[227] The growing influence of extra-state regimes and international organisations further illustrates the extent to which states have loosened the 'chain of control' in numerous domains.[228]

In this context, institutions such as the World Trade Organization, the EU, the UN Convention on the Law of the Sea, the ECHR, the Codex Alimentarius Commission, the World Intellectual Property Organization, and the International Organization for Standardization shift attention away from the narrowly defined 'public' of states.[229] A striking recent example is the COVID-19 crisis: although first identified regionally in December 2019, it rapidly spread across the globe, leaving no state untouched by its effects.[230] The World Health Organization played

[223] Art 12: 'No one shall be subjected to arbitrary interference with his privacy, family, home or correspondence, nor to attacks upon his honour and reputation. Everyone has the right to the protection of the law against such interference or attacks.'

[224] Art 17(1): '1. No one shall be subjected to arbitrary or unlawful interference with his privacy, family, home or correspondence, nor to unlawful attacks on his honour and reputation.'

[225] Palombella, 'Theory, Realities, and Promises of Inter-Legality: A Manifesto' (2019), 363; JL Dunoff and JP Trachtman (eds), *Ruling the World? Constitutionalism, International Law, and Global Governance* (Cambridge University Press, 2009); M Tushnet, 'The Inevitable Globalisation of Constitutional Law' (2009) 49 *Virginia Journal of International Law* 985.

[226] Palombella, 'Theory, Realities, and Promises of Inter-Legality: A Manifesto' (2019), 363.

[227] Palombella, 'Theory, Realities, and Promises of Inter-Legality: A Manifest' (2019), 363.

[228] Palombella, 'Theory, Realities, and Promises of Inter-Legality: A Manifesto' (2019), 364.

[229] Palombella, 'Theory, Realities, and Promises of Inter-Legality: A Manifesto' (2019), 364–65.

[230] WHO, 'WHO announced COVID-19 outbreak as a pandemic on 11 March 2020', available at euro.who.int/en/health-topics/health-emergencies/coronavirus-covid-19#:~:text=WHO%20announced%20COVID%2D19,on%2011%20March%202020.

an essential role in managing the crisis through the publication of numerous documents and the issuance of guidance.[231] This experience provides a particularly stark illustration that *ordre public* in the twenty-first century cannot be reduced to national interests alone.[232]

The emphasis on 'internationalisation' and the role of advanced technologies in the judgment discussed above demonstrates that the BVerfG has taken this ongoing transition into account. By construing human dignity as a universal ideal, by underscoring the link between fundamental rights and human rights, and by acknowledging the increasingly internationalised nature of political action, the court effectively introduced the German Constitution to its interlocutors. On this basis, it carried out an 'empirical reconnaissance'[233] of the relevant normativities governing the case. Notably, the court extended its reasoning by engaging not only with international human rights regimes but also with the jurisprudence of the ECtHR and relevant international conventions. Strictly speaking, such engagement with 'other legalities' was not a logical necessity, since the court might have arrived at similar conclusions by interpreting the inner rationale of the German Constitution as protecting individuals against the actions of the German state. Yet, by drawing together the composite law of the case – sourced from more than one legal order – the court demonstrated an awareness of 'what is passing by the real substance of the case in-between multiple legalities settings'.[234] Ultimately, this rights-based inter-legal reasoning enabled the court to close 'virtual legal black holes',[235] and thereby to avert injustice.

[231] See the details regarding the crisis in 'WHO, COVID-19', available at euro.who.int/en/health-topics/health-emergencies/coronavirus-covid-19#:~:text=WHO%20announced%20COVID%2D19,on%2011%20March%202020.

[232] WHO, 'WHO Chief Warns Against COVID-19 "Vaccine Nationalism"', available at news.cgtn.com/news/2020-10-26/WHO-chief-warns-against-COVID-19-vaccine-nationalism--UTD8hxtXeE/index.html. See also F Bieber, 'Global Nationalism in Times of the COVID-19 Pandemic' (2020) *Nationalities Papers* (Cambridge University Press) 1–13 (arguing that the COVID-19 crisis risks reinforcing pre-existing national dynamics).

[233] Palombella, 'Theory, Realities, and Promises of Inter-Legality: A Manifesto' (2019), 382. Palombella uses the term 'reconnaissance' in the sense of both exploration and recognition.

[234] Palombella, 'Theory, Realities, and Promises of Inter-Legality: A Manifesto' (2019), 382.

[235] The term 'black holes', coined by Steyn, has inspired me to coin the term 'virtual legal black holes'. See Steyn, 'Guantanamo Bay: The Legal Black Hole' (2004).

5

Conclusion

Inter-Legalising the Pendulum

The European Commission observes that exponential technological advances are 'gradually blur[ring] the lines between the physical, digital, and biological spheres and push[ing] frontiers of what computers are capable of doing'.[1] Although the precise boundaries remain elusive, it is evident that these developments are fundamentally transforming nearly every dimension of society, encompassing fields as varied as politics, the economy, legal frameworks, and cultural production. The transformations brought about by advanced technologies – most notably artificial intelligence (AI) systems – are frequently presented as overwhelmingly positive, particularly in their capacity to stimulate innovation and change. By enabling novel methods for processing unprecedented volumes of data, these technologies have provided new opportunities for governance and economic activity. Within this new paradigm, data and information have become essential assets, fundamentally reconstituting the primary sources of economic and social value[2] in what is increasingly referred to as digital[3] or information capitalism.[4]

It would, of course, be inconceivable for a transformation that permeates nearly every aspect of life not to have an impact on our rights. The emergence of this new configuration has broadened the scope for the enjoyment of fundamental and human rights. Rights which were once understood primarily within the boundaries of physical spaces and traditional institutions are now being redefined and extended through *digital* and *intelligent* environments. Freedom of expression, for instance, has taken on radically new dimensions in the digital sphere, where voices may be amplified across global networks and endowed with the power to reach audiences on a scale that was once unimaginable. Similarly, this digital era has lifted the geographical barriers to entrepreneurship, essentially offering individuals unprecedented opportunities to innovate and participate in economic life.

[1] European Commission, Shaping the Digital Transformation in Europe (Communications Networks, Content & Technology, September 2020), available at digital-strategy.ec.europa.eu/en/news/commission-publishes-analysis-macro-economic-potential-digital-transformation-independent.

[2] Ö Tene and J Polonetsky, 'Big Data for All: Privacy and User Control in the Age of Analytics' (2013) 11 *Northwestern Journal of Technology and Intellectual Property* 239.

[3] D Schiller, *Digital Capitalism: Networking the Global Market System* (MIT Press, 1999).

[4] JE Cohen, *Between Truth and Power: The Legal Construction of Information Capitalism* (Oxford University Press, 2020).

At the same time, this evolution has opened new avenues for governance, fundamentally reshaping how states deliver public services, safeguard public security, and interact with citizens within increasingly complex, intelligent, and interconnected environments.

However, as illustrated in the chapter one of this book, the analysis of the leading judgments of both the ECtHR and the CJEU reveals that new technologies pose significant challenges to the protection of fundamental and human rights. In particular, they test the scope and the application of rights such as the right to data protection, the right to respect for private life, and the right to effective judicial remedy in ways that are both novel and complex. Advanced technologies, by their very design and operation, have introduced novel forms of interference with the enjoyment of fundamental rights and human rights.

This view is proven by the growing use of AI systems by public authorities. These systems already mark a significant turning point in the protection of rights. The issues at stake are no longer confined to data protection and respect for private life; they now extend to a wider range of fundamental and human rights, including non-discrimination, access to justice, the right to access to documents, and even mental integrity. In this sense, AI has the potential to affect rights and freedoms more profoundly than any previous technology.

Public authorities, policymakers, and private entities in the European Union have been increasingly attentive to the potential risks and dangers posed by AI systems. A growing body of reports, communications, statements, and ethics guidelines has been delivered with the purpose of safeguarding fundamental European values and principles from the design phase through to the deployment of such technologies.[5] In this context, Article 2 of the Treaty of the European Union,[6] the EU Charter of Fundamental Rights, and the relevant articles of the GDPR are frequently referenced and incorporated. Core values of the Union – such as human dignity, equality, justice, non-discrimination and non-stigmatization, autonomy and individual responsibility, informed consent, privacy, and social responsibility – are constantly highlighted as guiding principles.

However, as argued in chapter three, the European Union's current reliance on a risk-based approach has required a critical examination, as it risks undermining the protection of fundamental and human rights within the public realm. Against this backdrop, and building on the guiding question of how such rights can be safeguarded in the face of challenges posed by AI systems – particularly in the fields of biometrics and social welfare, within the 'irregular square' captured by the state, the market, extra-state actors, and the individual – this book has discovered the dynamics of a 'rights-based inter-legal approach'.

[5] See Chapter 3 of the book for a discussion on the European approach.

[6] Consolidated Version of the Treaty on European Union [2012] OJ C 326/13. Art 2 of the TEU states that 'The Union is founded on the values of respect for human dignity, freedom, democracy, equality, the rule of law and respect for human rights, including the rights of persons belonging to minorities. These values are common to the Member States in a society in which pluralism, non-discrimination, tolerance, justice, solidarity and equality between women and men prevail.'

The analysis in chapter two established the foundational pillars of this approach. By analysing concrete AI practices in the public sphere, it identified six core characteristics of systems employed by public authorities, with particular focus on the domains of social benefits and biometrics:

(i) AI systems deployed in the public sector are simultaneously institutionally and interdisciplinarily *inter-systemic*, insofar as they operate across multiple institutional settings while drawing upon insights, methods, and techniques from a wide range of disciplines.
(ii) AI systems used in the public sector are inherently *dynamic*, both in terms of their rapid technological development and in their patterns of adoption across different institutional and societal contexts.
(iii) AI systems employed in the public sector are characterised by significant *complexity*. This complexity arises from three interrelated dimensions: (a) their reliance on black-box mechanisms that obscure internal decision-making processes; (b) the use of heterogeneous terminology that complicates identification and classification; and (c) the integration of diverse techniques and applications.
(iv) AI systems used in the public sector are fundamentally *social* in nature. This social dimension is manifested in several ways: (a) they mediate and facilitate key aspects of the functioning of social institutions and structures; (b) they recognise and respond to the social components of their environment; (c) they structure interactions between individuals and the system through processes of identification, categorisation, and detection; and (d) they weave[7] broader social contexts by aggregating and interpreting individual data within collective frameworks.
(v) AI systems used in the public sector possess a *private* dimension, insofar as their development depends heavily on specialised technical expertise that is primarily concentrated within private entities and initiatives.
(vi) AI systems used in the public sector embody the quality of *publicness*. By operating within the public sphere – the 'space of appearance'[8] – they become embedded in existing power relations and exert a normative impact on the autonomy of individuals. The quality of *publicness*, in this sense, requires adherence to three fundamental principles: *accessibility*, *exposure*, and *consideration*.[9]

Building on the *publicness* characteristic of AI systems and a critical analysis of the AI Act, chapter three advanced a rights-based approach, grounded also in the

[7] The term 'weaving' is employed intentionally, rather than 'coding', in order to underscore the social dimension of AI systems and to distinguish it from their purely technical dimension.
[8] H Arendt, *The Human Condition* (University of Chicago Press, 1998) ('everything that appears in public can be seen and heard by everybody and has the widest possible publicity').
[9] B Kingsbury and N Maisley, 'Infrastructures and Laws: Publics and Publicness' (Institute for International Law and Justice, NYU School of Law, Working Paper 2021/3).

accountability dimension emerging from the *ex post* function of fundamental and human rights. It argued that excessively technocratic and bureaucratic legal frameworks risk narrowing the space for a meaningful fundamental and human rights discourse in emerging domains. As the AI Act has demonstrated, such approaches may relegate rights-based considerations to the background, thereby hindering their effective flourishing precisely where they are most needed. In this way, the *publicness* of AI systems deployed in the public sector is often overlooked, while the accountability of public authorities may be complicated or, at times, obstructed. This dynamic leaves individuals within a 'rightless' framework, where the 'rule of technology'[10] prevails, making it extremely difficult to challenge the status quo or resist oppressive digital public practices. A rights-based approach instead, with its 'peculiar language', prevents the abuse of power and ensures the reasonable realisation of public purposes.

However, as the analysis of chapter two demonstrated, the other fundamental characteristics of AI systems reveal that a rights-based approach, while essential, is not by itself sufficient to meet the full range of challenges these technologies present. Their *inter-systemic* nature, *social* embeddedness, *complexity*, and *dynamic* evolution call for a broader and more responsive framework – an inter-legal approach. This book has, therefore, defended such an approach on five principal grounds, seeking to show how it can complement and strengthen rights-based protections in a constructive and balanced manner.

First, AI systems deployed in the public sector are institutionally and interdisciplinarily *inter-systemic*, engaging a wide range of disciplines and institutions. From an institutional perspective, the 'GlobalPolicy.AI'[11] platform provides a concrete illustration of the *inter-systemic* dimension of AI systems and highlights the necessity of an inter-legal approach. Its primary objective is to facilitate co-operation among intergovernmental organisations, and to assist policymakers in navigating the international AI governance framework, by providing access to relevant tools and best practices. The platform is distinctive in that it functions as a one-stop resource for both AI policy experts and the public. As of September 2021, it included eight partners: the Council of Europe, the European Commission, the European Agency for Fundamental Rights, the Inter-American Development Bank, the OECD and the OECD Artificial Intelligence Policy Observatory (OECD.AI), the United Nations, UNESCO, and the World Bank Group.

The platform pursues two main objectives, defined as follows: 'to provide information about each organization's work on AI, thereby helping policy makers and the wider public navigate the international AI governance landscape and access relevant resources', and 'to strengthen co-operation between the different organizations, leveraging each other's work and making progress together towards

[10] For the term 'rule of technology', see R Brownsword and K Yeung, *Regulating Technologies: Legal Futures, Regulatory Frames and Technological Fixes* (Hart Publishing, 2008).

[11] See the platform's website at globalpolicy.ai/en/.

common goals'.[12] Among its key priorities, the platform explicitly identifies the alignment of AI with human rights and democracy.[13]

At first glance, the GlobalPolicy.AI platform offers a compelling illustration of interwoven regulatory settings, as it brings together eight distinct organisations focused on the singular issue of AI governance. The platform also demonstrates the transboundary nature of AI, comparable to global challenges such as security or climate change. By calling for co-operation and the pursuit of common goals that concern all people and humanity, it explicitly frames AI as a 'global' issue.

Striving to develop common goals for AI through this platform naturally creates a fertile ecosystem for inter-legality, since at the descriptive level 'inter-legality captures the crossing threads of originally separate regulators as well as legalities'.[14] Each of the participating intergovernmental organisations has published statements, reports, communications, and guidelines examining the societal, ethical, legal, and economic impacts of AI on individuals and the environment, and all have affirmed that they regard AI as a common concern. Accordingly, AI – so extensively characterised as a global phenomenon – cannot be treated as merely a 'national' issue. Put differently, the rapidly expanding proliferation of extra-state regimes and international organisations addressing AI has generated an ecosystem in which 'two or more legal systems coexist in the same social field'.[15]

Second, positioning AI as a solution to other major challenges renders it materially interconnected with broader global concerns. This framing underscores the interdisciplinary, *inter-systemic* dimension of AI systems. For example, it would be naïve to regulate AI-driven surveillance technologies – such as biometric identification or categorisation systems – without considering their implications for global security. Axelrod and Keohane capture this dynamic through the notion of 'issue-linkage': 'Most issues are linked to other issues. This means that games being played on different issues – different "chessboards," in Stanley Hoffmann's wording – affect one another. Connections between games become important when issues are linked.'[16] Furthermore, the United Nations has emphasised the role AI may play in addressing global challenges. On 15 September 2021, the UN High Commissioner for Human Rights, Michelle Bachelet, stressed this potential:

> Artificial intelligence can be a force for good, helping societies overcome some of the great challenges of our times. But AI technologies can have negative, even catastrophic,

[12] GlobalPolicy.AI (n 11).

[13] The platform identifies three key areas. The other two are 'responsible development and use of trustworthy AI' and 'AI to advance the sustainable development goals' (n 11).

[14] G Palombella, 'Exploring the Rationale of Inter-Legality' (2022) 1 *Rivista di filosofia del diritto* 9.

[15] See SE Merry, 'Legal Pluralism' (1988) 22 *Law & Society Review* 869, 870 (defining legal pluralism as 'a situation in which two or more legal systems coexist in the same social field').

[16] R Axelrod and RO Keohane, 'Achieving Cooperation under Anarchy: Strategies and Institutions' (1985) 38(1) *World Politics* 239.

> effects if they are used without sufficient regard to how they affect people's human rights.[17]

Third, AI systems used in the public sector are *dynamic* in terms of both development and adoption. Since closed legal systems are not able to capture such a dynamic field and the changes it causes in the society,[18] an inter-legal approach is highly necessary. Such dynamism requires up-to-date approaches. In this sense, an inter-legal approach is promising, as it has always remained dynamic by excluding the monopoly or hegemony of a single legal order.

Fourth, as discussed in chapters two and three, AI systems used in the public sector are marked by *complexity*. This complexity arises from three interrelated dimensions: (a) their reliance on black-box mechanisms that obscure internal decision-making processes; (b) the use of heterogeneous terminology that complicates identification and classification; and (c) the integration of diverse techniques and applications. Moreover, such systems are inherently *social*, in that (a) they mediate and facilitate key aspects of the functioning of social institutions and structures, (b) they recognise and respond to the social components of their environment, (c) they structure interactions between individuals and the system through processes of identification, categorisation, and detection, and (d) they weave broader social contexts by aggregating and interpreting individual data within collective frameworks.

The main claim advanced by legal scholars is that the challenges posed by AI systems have not yet been adequately addressed, leaving existing regimes insufficient to cope with them. This underlines the necessity of an inter-legal approach, as opposed to reliance on closed legal systems that are unlikely to resolve the problems at hand. In addition to national, international, regional, and even 'global' initiatives regulating new technologies – particularly AI – these technologies themselves contribute an additional layer to the complex regulatory context through private regulations, often reinforced by the 'invisible handshake'.[19] Yet it must be recognised that external sources or extra-state normativities face an inherent problem: they are deprived of democratic legitimacy. This lack of democratic and substantive legitimacy may undermine their effectiveness, rendering them dysfunctional in relation to the legal systems they are intended to address.[20]

In this sense, AI issues introduce additional layers of complexity and require a reconsideration of the dynamics of the regulatory context. It is foreseeable that such a broad and interconnected field will inevitably test the limits and scope of existing legal regimes. Inter-legality, however, directs us to identify the *law of*

[17] United Nations, 'Urgent Action Needed over Artificial Intelligence Risks to Human Rights' (UN News, 2021), available at news.un.org/en/story/2021/09/1099972.

[18] Palombella, 'Exploring the Rationale of Inter-Legality' (2022), 4.

[19] Michael Birnhack and Niva Elkin-Koren, 'The Invisible Handshake: The Reemergence of the State in the Digital Environment' (2003) *Virginia Journal of Law and Technology* 1–57.

[20] G Palombella, 'Inter-Legality: On Interconnectedness and "External Sources"' (2021) 7(2) *Italian Law Journal* 943–59. See also Palombella, 'Exploring the Rationale of Inter-Legality' (2022), 12.

the case within the interwoven legal texture.[21] This composite legal practice may prove more demanding than applying rules sourced from a single legal system. Nevertheless, an inter-legal approach is indispensable for addressing the challenges posed by AI systems.

Fifth, the inadequacy of law in addressing AI risks creating a kind of 'lawless' space. Unlike other approaches, inter-legality is able to respond to such a gap of lawfulness, precisely because it functions as a bridge between legal systems by uncovering the connections among them. From an inter-legal perspective, the diversity of jurisgenerative entities, regimes, and orders collectively contributes to bridging this gap, thereby transforming composite law into a governing force capable of addressing the issue at stake.[22]

Taken together, these five arguments demonstrate that the AI systems deployed by public authorities in the field of social benefits and biometrics are 'inter-legal by default'. They therefore require an inter-legal approach. In this light, the proposed 'rights-based inter-legal approach' has inter-legalised the 'pendulum', reorienting its trajectory from the rule of technology to the rule of law.

[21] Palombella, 'Inter-Legality: On Interconnectedness and "External Sources"' (2021).
[22] Palombella, 'Exploring the Rationale of Inter-Legality' (2022), 12.

BIBLIOGRAPHY

Books and Academic Articles

Albrecht P and HM Kyed, 'Justice and Security: When the State Isn't the Main Provider' (2010) Danish Institute for International Studies, Policy Brief (Copenhagen), available at pure.diis.dk/ws/files/811082/PB_Justice_and_Security_web.pdf.

Alexy, R, *A Theory of Legal Argumentation*, trans R Adler and N MacCormick (Clarendon Press, 1989).

——, *Theorie der juristischen Argumentation: Die Theorie des rationalen Diskurses als Theorie der juristischen Begründung* (Suhrkamp, 1991) 263.

——, 'The Special Case Thesis' (1999) 12(4) *Ratio Juris* 374 (examining the objections against the 'special case thesis' raised by J Habermas in 1996).

——, *A Theory of Constitutional Rights* (Oxford University Press, 2004).

Alfonseca M et al, 'Superintelligence Cannot Be Contained: Lessons from Computability Theory' (2021) 70 *Journal of Artificial Intelligence Research*, available at jair.org/index.php/jair/article/view/12202.

Allen, C, 'Artificial Life, Artificial Agents, Virtual Realities: Technologies and Autonomous Agency' in L Floridi (ed), *The Cambridge Handbook of Information and Computer Ethics* (Cambridge University Press, 2010).

Alon-Barkat, S and M Busuioc, 'Human–AI Interactions in Public Sector Decision-Making: "Automation Bias" and "Selective Adherence" to Algorithmic Advice' (2022) *Journal of Public Administration Research and Theory* 7–8, available at papers.ssrn.com/sol3/papers.cfm?abstract_id=3794660.

Anderson M and SL Anderson, *Machine Ethics* (Cambridge University Press, 2011).

Andorno, R, 'The Precautionary Principle: A New Legal Standard for a Technological Age' (2004) 1(1) *Journal of International Biotechnology Law* 11–19, available at doi.org/10.1515/jibl.2004.1.1.11.

Angwin, J, J Larson, S Mattu, and L Kirchner. 'Machine Bias' (*ProPublica*, 23 May 2016), available at propublica.org/article/machine-bias-risk-assessments-in-criminal-sentencing.

Anton, DK, 'Treaty Congestion in Contemporary International Environmental Law' in S Alam, JH Bhuiyan, TMR Chowdhury, and EJ Techera (eds), *Routledge Handbook of International Environmental Law* (Routledge, 2012).

Apostolakis, GE, 'How Useful Is Quantitative Risk Assessment?' (2004) 24(3) *Risk Analysis* 516.

Appel, H, N Anand and A Gupta, 'Introduction: Temporality, Politics and the Promise of Infrastructure' in H Appel, N Anand, and A Gupta (eds), *The Promise of Infrastructure* (Duke University Press, 2018).

Archer MS and AM Maccarini (eds), *What Is Essential to Being Human? Can AI Robots Not Share It?* (Routledge, 2021).

Arendt, H. *The Human Condition* (University of Chicago Press, 1998).

Aven T and BS Krohn, 'A New Perspective on How to Understand, Assess and Manage Risk and the Unforeseen' (2014) 121 *Reliability Engineering & System Safety* 1–10.

Aven T and J-E Vinnem, *Risk Management: With Applications from the Offshore Petroleum Industry* (Springer, 2007).

Axelrod R and R O Keohane. 'Achieving Cooperation under Anarchy: Strategies and Institutions', *World Politics* 38 (1985), 1, 239.

Bagheri, A, JD Moreno, and S Semplici, *Global Bioethics: The Impact of the UNESCO International Bioethics Committee* (Springer, 2016).

Balkin, JM, 'The Path of Robotics Law' (2015) 6 *California Law Review* 45–60 Yale Law School, Public Law Research Paper No 536.

Barak, A, *The Judge in a Democracy* (Princeton University Press, 2008) 298.
——, *Proportionality: Constitutional Rights and Their Limitations* (Cambridge University Press, 2012).
——, 'Human Dignity in German Constitutional Law' in A Barak, *Human Dignity: The Constitutional Value and the Constitutional Right* (Cambridge University Press, 2015).
Barfield (ed), W, *The Cambridge Handbook of the Law of Algorithms* (Cambridge University Press, 2021).
Barrett, LF, 'Darwin Was Wrong: Your Expressions Do Not Reveal Your Emotions' (*Scientific American*, 27 April 2022), available at scientificamerican.com/article/darwin-was-wrong-your-facial-expressions-do-not-reveal-your-emotions.
Bassini, M, 'Fundamental Rights and Private Enforcement in the Digital Age' (2019) 25(2) *European Law Journal* 188–97.
Beck, U, *Risk Society: Towards a New Modernity* (Sage Publications, 1992) 34.
Benhabib, S, 'The Embattled Public Sphere: Hannah Arendt, Jürgen Habermas and Beyond' (1997) 90 *Theoria: A Journal of Social and Political Theory* 1–24.
Benton L and R Ross (eds), *Legal Pluralism and Empires 1500–1850* (New York University Press, 2013).
Biber, E, 'Concretisation of Constitutional Norms Referring to the Protection of Private Life in the Individual Application Case-Law' (LLM thesis, Koç University Law School, Istanbul 2017), available at tez.yok.gov.tr/UlusalTezMerkezi/tezSorguSonucYeni.jsp.
——, 'Inter-Legality and Surveillance Technologies' (2021) 2 *Italian Law Journal*, available at theitalianlawjournal.it/biber/.
——, 'Machines Learning the Rule of Law: EU Proposes the World's First Artificial Intelligence Act' (*Verfassungsblog*, 13 July 2021), available at verfassungsblog.de/ai-rol.
——, 'Book Review: Digital Constitutionalism in Europe: Reframing Rights and Powers in the Algorithmic Society (Cambridge Studies in European Law and Policy): by De Gregorio, G. (2022). Cambridge: Cambridge University Press. £95' (2022) 37(3) *International Review of Law, Computers & Technology* 341–44.
——, 'Between Humans and Machines: Judicial Interpretation of the Automated Decision-Making Practices in the EU' in HCH Hofmann and F Pflücke (eds), *Governance of Automated Decision-Making and EU Law* (Oxford University Press, 2024; online edn, Oxford Academic, 16 August 2024).
——, 'A Challenge to a *Primavera Digitale:* The "Phantom Influence" of Artificial Intelligence Systems', Draft Paper (2025), on file with author.
——, 'A Close Reading of the European Commission's Guidelines on Prohibited Artificial Intelligence Practices: A Powerful Reflection of the European Approach to AI' (2025) (2)3 *Journal of AI Law and Regulation* 266–73.
——, 'Digital Constitutionalism in Europe: Exploring a Constellation of Legalities' in G De Gregorio, O Pollicino, and P Valcke (eds), *The Oxford Handbook of Digital Constitutionalism* (OUP, 2025).
——, 'Art. 2 The Principle of Solidarity and Inclusion' in R Ducato, A Strowel, and E Marique (eds), *The Declaration on European Digital Rights and Principles for the Digital Decade: A Commentary with a Legal Design Perspective* (forthcoming).
Biber E and M Capasso, 'The Right to Mental Integrity in the Age of Artificial Intelligence: Cognitive Human Enhancement Technologies' in B Custers and E Fosch-Villaronga (eds), *Law and Artificial Intelligence: Legal, Ethical, and Regulatory Issues of AI* (Information Technology and Law Series, Springer, 2022).
Biber E and N Hogic, 'Online States and Inter-Legality' in G Palombella, E Chiti, and A Di Martino (eds), *L'età della Interlegalità* (Il Mulino, 2022) 367.
Bieber, F, 'Global Nationalism in Times of the COVID-19 Pandemic' (2020) *Nationalities Papers* (Cambridge University Press) 1–13.
Birnhack M and N Elkin-Koren, 'The Invisible Handshake: The Reemergence of the State in the Digital Environment' (2003) 8 *Virginia Journal of Law and Technology* 1–57.
Böckenförde, E-W, 'Grundrechtstheorie und Grundrechtsinterpretation' (1974) 27 *Neue Juristische Wochenschrift (NJW)* 1529–38.

Boehmer-Christiansen, S, 'The Precautionary Principle in Germany: Enabling Government' in T O'Riordan and J Cameron (eds), *Interpreting the Precautionary Principle* (Earthscan, 1994).

Bogdandy A von, 'Pluralism, Direct Effect, and the Ultimate Say: On the Relationship Between International and Domestic Constitutional Law' (2008) 6(3–4) *International Journal of Constitutional Law* 399.

Bogdandy, A von, 'German Legal Hegemony' (*Verfassungsblog*, 5 October 2020), available at verfassungsblog.de/german-legal-hegemony/.

Bogdandy et al, A von, 'German Legal Hegemony' (2020) Max Planck Institute for Comparative Public Law and International Law (MPIL) Research Paper No 2020-43, available at ssrn.com/abstract=3727378.

Bonnefon J-F, *The Car That Knew Too Much: Can a Machine Be Moral?* (MIT Press, 2021).

Bostrom, N, *Superintelligence: Paths, Dangers, Strategies* (Oxford University Press, 2014).

Bowker, GC, K Baker, F Millerand, and D Ribes, 'Toward Information Infrastructure Studies: Ways of Knowing in a Networked Environment' in J Hunsinger et al (eds), *International Handbook of Internet Research* (Springer, 2010).

Bradford, A, *The Brussels Effect: How the European Union Rules the World* (Oxford University Press, 2020).

Brennan, T, W Dieterich, and B Ehret, 'Evaluating the Predictive Validity of the COMPAS Risk and Needs Assessment System' (2009) 36(1) *Criminal Justice and Behavior* 21–40.

Bringsjord, S and NS Govindarajulu, 'Artificial Intelligence' in EN Zalta and U Nodelman (eds), *The Stanford Encyclopedia of Philosophy* (Fall 2024 Edition), UR, available at https://plato.stanford.edu/archives/fall2024/entries/artificial-intelligence/>.

Brkan, M, 'The Essence of Fundamental Rights to Privacy and Data Protection: Finding the Way through the Maze of the CJEU's Constitutional Reasoning', paper presented at the conference 'The Essence of Fundamental Rights in EU Law', Leuven, 17–18 May 2018.

Brownsword, R, *Law, Technology and Society, Re-imaging the Regulatory Environment* (Routledge, 2019).

Brownsword, R and D Beyleveld, *Human Dignity in Bioethics and Biolaw* (Oxford University Press, 2001).

Brownsword, R and M Goodwin, *Law and the Technologies of the Twenty-First Century* (Cambridge University Press, 2012) 46–71.

Brownsword, R and K Yeung, *Regulating Technologies: Legal Futures, Regulatory Frames and Technological Fixes* (Hart Publishing, 2008).

Brunner, L, 'Digital Communication and the Evolving Right to Privacy' in MK Land and J Aronson, *New Technologies for Human Rights and Practice* (Cambridge University Press, 2018).

Bryson JJ and PP Kime, 'Just an Artifact: Why Machines Are Perceived as Moral Agents' in *Proceedings of the 22nd International Joint Conference on Artificial Intelligence (IJCAI 2011)* (Barcelona, 16–22 July 2011).

Bublitz, J-C, 'The Nascent Right to Psychological Integrity and Mental Self-Determination' in A von Arnauld et al (eds), *The Cambridge Handbook of New Human Rights Recognition* (Cambridge University Press, 2020).

Burrell, J, 'How the Machine Thinks: Understanding Opacity in Machine Learning', *Big Data & Society* (January–June 2016) 1.

Çalı, B, 'Beyond Monism and Dualism' in B Çalı, *The Authority of International Law: Obedience, Respect, Rebuttal* (Oxford University Press, 2015).

——, 'Has "Control Over Rights Doctrine" for Extraterritorial Jurisdiction Come of Age? Karlsruhe too, has spoken, now it's Strasbourg's turn' (*EJIL: Talk!*, 21 July 2020), available at ejiltalk.org/has-control-over-rights-doctrine-for-extra-territorial-jurisdiction-come-of-age-karlsruhe-too-has-spoken-now-its-strasbourgs-turn/.

Camerer, CF, 'Behavioral Economics and Artificial Intelligence', paper presented at the NBER Conference (2017), available at governance40.com/wp-content/uploads/2018/12/Camerer.pdf.

Cardoso, T, 'Ottawa's Use of AI for Immigration a "High-Risk Laboratory": Report' (*The Globe and Mail*, 25 September 2018), available at theglobeandmail.com/politics/article-ottawas-use-of-ai-for-immigration-a-high-risk-laboratory-report/.

Cassirer, E, *An Essay on Man: An Introduction to a Philosophy of Human Culture* (Doubleday Anchor Books, 1944), 43.

Cassirer, E, 'A Clue to the Nature of Man: the Symbol' (*Yale University Blog*, 16 June 2021), available at blog.yalebooks.com/2021/06/16/a-clue-to-the-nature-of-man-the-symbol.

Castells, M, *The Information Age: Economy, Society and Culture, Volume I: The Rise of the Network Society*, 2nd edn (Wiley-Blackwell, 2010) 21.

Cave, S, K Dihal, and S Dillon, *AI Narratives: A History of Imaginative Thinking about Intelligent Machines* (Oxford University Press, 2020).

Celeste, E, 'Digital Constitutionalism: A New Systematic Theorization' (2019) 33(1) *International Review of Law, Computers and Technology* 76–99.

Channon, M, L McCormick, and K Noussia, *The Law and Autonomous Vehicles* (Informa Law from Routledge, 2019).

Chiam, M, 'Monism and Dualism in International Law' (2021) *Oxford Bibliographies*, available at oxfordbibliographies.com/view/document/obo-9780199796953/obo-9780199796953-0168.xml.

Chilton A and M Versteeg, *How Constitutional Rights Matter* (Oxford University Press, 2020) 79.

Chiti, E, 'Administrative Inter-Legality – A Hypothesis' (2021) 7(2) *Italian Law Journal* 985–1002.

Cihon, P, 'Standards for AI Governance: International Standards to Enable Global Coordination in AI Research & Development', Technical Report, Centre for the Governance of AI, Future of Humanity Institute, University of Oxford (2019), available at fhi.ox.ac.uk/wp-content/uploads/Standards_-FHI-Technical-Report.pdf.

Cihon, P, M Maas, and L Kemp, 'Fragmentation and the Future: Investigating Architectures for International AI Governance' (2020) 11(5) *Global Policy* 545.

Cline, WR, *International Debt: Systemic Risk and Policy Response* (Institute for International Economics/ MIT Press, 1984).

Cockfield, AJ, 'Towards a Law and Technology Theory' (2004) 30(3) *Manitoba Law Journal* 383.

Coeckelbergh, M, *Human Being @ Risk: Enhancement, Technology, and the Evaluation of Vulnerability Transformations* (Springer, 2013) 27.

Coeckelbergh, M, *Green Leviathan or the Poetics of Political Liberty: Navigating Freedom in the Age of Climate Change and Artificial Intelligence* (Routledge, 2021).

Cohen, JE, *Between Truth and Power: The Legal Construction of Information Capitalism* (Oxford University Press, 2020).

Cohen-Eliya, M and I Porat, 'Proportionality and the Culture of Justification' (2011) 59 *American Journal of Comparative Law* 463–90.

Cole, D, 'The Chinese Room Argument' in EN Zalta and U Nodelman (eds), *The Stanford Encyclopedia of Philosophy* (Winter 2024 Edition), available at https://plato.stanford.edu/archives/win2024/entries/chinese-room/.

Collingridge, D, *The Social Control of Technology* (St Martin's Press, 1980) 19.

Covello V and FW Allen, *Seven Cardinal Rules of Risk Communication* (US Environmental Protection Agency, Office of Policy Analysis, 1988), available at archive.epa.gov/publicinvolvement/web/pdf/risk.pdf.

Covello, VT, 'Risk Communication: An Emerging Area of Health Communication Research' (1992) 15(1) *Communication Yearbook* 359.

Covello, VT, D von Winterfeldt, and P Slovic, 'Communicating Risk Information to the Public' in JC Davies, VT Covello, and FW Allen (eds), *Risk Communication* (Conservation Foundation, 1987).

Crawford, K, *Atlas of AI: Power, Politics and the Planetary Cost of Artificial Intelligence* (Yale University Press, 2021) 116–19.

De Azevedo Cunha, MV, NN Gomes, L Lixinski, and LT Féteira, *New Technologies and Human Rights: Challenges to Regulation* (Routledge, 2013).

De Búrca, G, 'After the EU Charter of Fundamental Rights: The Court of Justice as a Human Rights Adjudicator?' (2013) 20(2) *Maastricht Journal of European and Comparative Law* 168.
De Gregorio, G, 'The Rise of Digital Constitutionalism in the European Union' (2021) 19 *International Journal of Constitutional Law* 41–70.
De Gregorio, G, *Digital Constitutionalism in Europe: Reframing Rights and Powers in the Algorithmic Society* (Cambridge University Press, 2022).
De Gregorio, G and P Dunn, 'The European Risk-Based Approaches: Connecting Constitutional Dots in the Digital Age' (2022) 59(2) *Common Market Law Review* 473–500.
Decker, M and M Gutmann, 'Robo- and Informationethics: Some Introducing Remarks' in AM Esser, A Grunwald, and M Gutmann (eds), *Robo- and Informationethics: Some Fundamentals, Hermeneutics and Anthropology*, vol 3 (Lit Verlag, 2012).
Demuijnck, G and B Fasterling, 'The Social License to Operate' (2016) 136 *Journal of Business Ethics* 675–85.
Di Martino, A, 'The Importance of Being a Case – Collapsing of the Law upon the Case in Inter-Legal Situations' (2021) 7(2) *Italian Law Journal* 961–84.
Dignum, V, 'Relational Artificial Intelligence' (2022) arXiv:2202.07446, available at arxiv.org/abs/2202.07446.
Dinneen, N. 'Precautionary Discourse: Thinking Through the Distinction Between the Precautionary Principle and the Precautionary Approach in Theory and Practice' (2013) 32(1) *Politics and the Life Sciences* 2–21.
Dizikes P, 'Explained: Knightian Uncertainty – The Economic Crisis Has Revived an Old Philosophical Idea About Risk and Uncertainty. But What Is It, Exactly?' (*MIT News Office*, 2 June 2010), available at news.mit.edu/2010/explained-knightian-0602#:~:text=Therefore%2C%20according%20to%20Knight%2C%20risk,odds%20in%20the%20first%20place.
Doorn N and SO Hansson, 'Factors and Margins of Safety' in N Möller et al (eds), *Handbook of Safety Principles* (Wiley, 2018) 100.
Dossey, L, 'Neurolaw or Frankenlaw? The Thought Police Have Arrived' (2010) 6(5) *Explore (NY)* 275–86.
Dowd, R, *The Birth of Digital Human Rights* (Palgrave Macmillan, 2022) 240.
Drahos, P (ed), *Regulatory Theory: Foundations and Applications* (Australian National University Press, 2017).
Dror-Shpoliansky D and Y Shany, 'It's the End of the (Offline) World as We Know It: From Human Rights to Digital Human Rights – A Proposed Typology' (2021) 32(4) *The European Journal of International Law* 1249–82.
Dunoff JL and JP Trachtman (eds), *Ruling the World? Constitutionalism, International Law, and Global Governance* (Cambridge University Press, 2009).
Dworkin, R, *Taking Rights Seriously* (Harvard University Press, 1978) 90–91.
Dworkin, R, *Life's Dominion* (HarperCollins, 1993) 7.
Dyzenhaus, D, *The Constitution of Law: Legality in a Time of Emergency* (Cambridge University Press, 2006) 42.
Easterbrook, FH, 'Cyberspace and the Law of the Horse' (1996) *University of Chicago Legal Forum* 207–16.
Edwards, P, 'We Have Been Assimilated: Some Principles for Thinking About Algorithmic Systems' (Working Conference on Information Systems and Organizations (IS&O), San Francisco, CA, 2018) 19–27.
Ekmekci, PE and B Arda, *Artificial Intelligence and Bioethics* (Springer, 2020).
Fabbrini F and E Celeste, 'The Right to be Forgotten in the Digital Age: The Challenges of Data Protection Beyond Borders' (2020) 21 *German Law Journal* 55–65.
Farrand, B, 'Regulatory Capitalism, Decentered Enforcement, and Its Legal Consequences for Digital Expression: The Use of Copyright Law to Restrict Freedom of Speech Online' (2013) 10(4) *Journal of Information Technology and Politics* 404–22.
Feintuck, M, 'Precautionary Maybe, but What's the Principle? The Precautionary Principle, the Regulation of Risk, and the Public Domain' (2005) 32(3) *Journal of Law and Society* 392.

Feuillet-Liger, B and K Orfali, *The Reality of Human Dignity in Law and Bioethics: Comparative Perspectives* (Springer, 2018).

Fish, S, *Doing What Comes Naturally: Change, Rhetoric, and the Practice of Theory in Literary and Legal Studies* (Duke University Press, 1989) 344.

Fisher, E, 'Precaution, Precaution Everywhere: Developing a "Common Understanding" of the Precautionary Principle in the European Community' (2002) 9(1) *Maastricht Journal of European and Comparative Law* 18.

Fjeld J et al, 'Principled Artificial Intelligence: Mapping Consensus in Ethical and Rights-Based Approaches to Principles for AI', Berkman Klein Center for Internet & Society at Harvard University, 15 January 2020, available at dash.harvard.edu/server/api/core/bitstreams/c8d686a8-49e8-4128-969c-cb4a5f2ee145/content.

Flage, R, 'Maintenance Optimization and Its Relation to Safety' in N Möller et al (eds), *Handbook of Safety Principles* (Wiley, 2018).

Floridi, L, 'A Look into the Future Impact of ICT on our Lives' (2007), 9–10, available at ssrn.com/abstract=3844463.

—— (ed), *The Cambridge Handbook of Information and Computer Ethics* (Cambridge University Press, 2010).

——, 'Translating Principles into Practices of Digital Ethics: Five Risks of Being Unethical' (2019) 32 *Philosophy & Technology* 185–93.

Floridi L and JW Sanders, 'On the Morality of Artificial Intelligence' (2004) 14 *Minds and Machines* 351.

Fossa, F, '"I Don't Trust You, You Faker!" On Trust, Reliance, and Artificial Agency' (2019) 39 *Teoria* 63–80.

Frantziou, E, *The Horizontal Effect of Fundamental Rights in the European Union: A Constitutional Analysis* (Oxford University Press, 2019).

Funk, M and B Irrgang. *Robotics in Germany and Japan: Philosophical and Technical Perspectives*, Dresdner Studien zur Philosophie der Technologie, vol 5 (Peter Lang, 2014).

Galaz et al, V, 'Artificial Intelligence, Systemic Risks, and Sustainability' (2021) 67 *Technology in Society* 101741, 4.

Garcia, EV, 'Multilateralism and Artificial Intelligence: What Role for the United Nations?' in M Tinnirello (ed), *The Global Politics of Artificial Intelligence* (2006).

Garlicki, L, 'Constitutional Courts versus Supreme Courts' (2007) 5(1) *International Journal of Constitutional Law* 44–68.

Garrido, A, 'Mathematics and Artificial Intelligence, Two Branches of the Same Tree' (2010) 2 *Procedia – Social and Behavioral Sciences* 1133–36.

Gentner, D, KJ Holyoak, and BN Kokinov (eds), *The Analogical Mind: Perspectives from Cognitive Science* (Bradford, 2001).

Gilmore, G, 'Legal Realism: Its Cause and Its Cure' (1961) 70 *Yale Law Journal* 1038.

Goklany, IM, *The Precautionary Principle: A Critical Appraisal of Environmental Risk Assessment* (Cato Institute, 2001).

González et al, JL, 'Integral Monitoring System in Cases of Gender Violence: VioGén System' (2018) 4(1) *Behavior & Law Journal* 29–40.

Gowans, C, 'Moral Relativism' in EN Zalta (ed), *Stanford Encyclopedia of Philosophy* (first published 2004, substantive revision 2019, Stanford University), available at plato.stanford.edu/entries/moral-relativism/.

Gragl, P, *Legal Monism: Law, Philosophy, and Politics* (Oxford University Press, 2018).

Green, B, 'The Flaws of Policies Requiring Human Oversight of Government Algorithms' (2022) 45 *Computer Law & Security Review* 1–22.

Green, B and A Kak, 'The False Comfort of Human Oversight as an Antidote to AI Harm' (*Future Tense*, 15 June 2021), available at slate.com/technology/2021/06/human-oversight-artificial-intelligence-laws.html.

Grimm, D, 'Fundamental Rights in the Interpretation of German Constitutional Court' in *Constitutionalism: Past, Present, and Future* (Oxford University Press, 2016) 167–69.

Gutmann, M, B Rathgeber, and T Syed, 'Action and Autonomy: A Hidden Dilemma in Artificial Autonomous Systems' in M Decker and M Gutmann (eds), *Robo- and Informationethics: Some Fundamentals, Hermeneutics and Anthropology*, vol 3 (Lit Verlag, 2012).

Häberle, P, *Europäische Rechtskultur: Versuch einer Annäherung in zwölf Schritten* (Nomos Verlagsgesellschaft, 1994) 72.

Habermas, J, 'Law as Medium and Law as Institution' in G Teubner (ed), *Dilemmas of Law in the Welfare State* (De Gruyter, 1986).

——, *The Structural Transformation of the Public Sphere: An Inquiry into a Category of Bourgeois Society* (trans by Thomas Burger with the assistance of Frederick Lawrence, MIT Press, 1989).

——, *Between Facts and Norms: Contributions to a Discourse Theory of Law and Democracy* (MIT Press, 1996) 204, 206.

——, *Ein neuer Strukturwandel der Öffentlichkeit und die deliberative Politik* (Suhrkamp, 2022) 54.

Habermas, J, S Lennox, and F Lennox, 'The Public Sphere: An Encyclopedia Article (1964)' (1974) 3 *New German Critique* 49–55.

Hamet, P and J Tremblay, 'Artificial Intelligence in Medicine' (2017) 69 *Metabolism – Clinical and Experimental* 36–40.

Harari, YN, *Homo Deus: A Brief History of Tomorrow* (Harper, 2016).

Harremoes, P et al (eds), *The Precautionary Principle in the 20th Century: Late Lessons from Early Warnings* (European Environment Agency Earthscan, 2002) 209.

Head, BW and J Alford, 'Wicked Problems: Implications for Public Policy and Management' (2015) 47(6) *Administration & Society* 711–39.

Hesselink, MW, *Justifying Contract in Europe – Political Philosophies of European Contract Law* (Oxford University Press, 2021) 390.

——, 'Reconstituting the Code of Capital: Could a Progressive European Code of Private Law Help Us Reduce Inequality and Regain Democratic Control?' (2022), paper presented at the conference 'Tracing the Nature, Place, and Effects of EU Private Law in (Re)shaping Global Markets and Orders', University of Helsinki, online, 16–17 September 2021), and at the EUI Law Faculty Seminar (16 March 2022), available at papers.ssrn.com/sol3/papers.cfm?abstract_id=4075004.

Heyvaert, V, 'Governing Intersystemic Systemic Risks: Lessons from Covid and Climate Change' (2022) *Modern Law Review* 1–30.

Hildebrandt, M, 'The Dawn of a Critical Transparency Right for the Profiling Era' in J Bus et al (eds), *Digital Enlightenment Yearbook* (IOS Press, 2012) 41.

——, *Smart Technologies and the End(s) of Law* (Edward Elgar, 2015).

——, 'Closure: On Ethics, Code and Law' in *Law for Computer Scientists and Other Folk* (Oxford University Press, 2020).

——, 'Smart Technologies' (2020) 9(4) *Internet Policy Review* 2.

——, 'The Artificial Intelligence of European Union Law' (2020) 21(1) *German Law Journal* 74.

——, 'Global Competition and Convergence of AI Law' in JM Smith, J Husa, C Valcke, M Barreto, and T de Mendonca (eds), *Elgar Encyclopaedia of Comparative Law* (Edward Elgar, 2022).

Hildebrandt M and K O'Hara (eds), *Life and the Law in the Era of Data-Driven Agency* (Edward Elgar, 2020).

Hofmann, HCH, 'New Regulatory Approaches under the EU's Legislation on Digitalisation: Introduction to the Special Edition of the EJRR "Charting the Landscape of Automation of Regulatory Decision-Making" (2025) 16 European Journal of Risk Regulation 4.

Hofstadter, D, 'Epilogue: Analogy as the Core of Human Cognition' in D Gentner, KJ Holyoak, and BN Kokinov (eds), *The Analogical Mind: Perspectives from Cognitive Science* (Bradford, 2001).

Hood, C, H Rothstein, and R Baldwin, *The Government of Risk: Understanding Risk Regulation Regimes* (Oxford University Press, 2001).

Joerges, C and J Neyer, 'Politics, Risk Management, World Trade Organization Governance and the Limits of Legalization' (2003) 30(3) *Science and Public Policy* 220.

Jonas, H. *The Imperative of Responsibility: In Search of Ethics for the Technological Age*, trans H Jonas with the collaboration of D Herr (Chicago, IL: University of Chicago Press, 1984).

——, *Das Prinzip Verantwortung: Versuch einer Ethik für die Technologische Zivilisation*, 5th edn (Suhrkamp, 2003).

Jongepier, F and M Klenk. *The Philosophy of Online Manipulation* (Routledge, 2022).

Kaminski, ME and G Malgieri, 'Impacted Stakeholder Participation in AI and Data Governance' (2025) 27(1) *Yale Journal of Law & Technology* 265.

Kamper, C, 'Kafkaesque AI? Legal Decision-Making in the Area of Machine Learning' (2020) 24(2) *University of San Francisco Intellectual Property and Technology Law Journal* 251.

Kant, I, *The Metaphysics of Morals* (M Gregor tr, Cambridge University Press, 1996).

——, *The Metaphysics of Morals* (Cambridge University Press, 2005).

——, *Critique of Practical Reason* (M Gregor and A Reath trs, Cambridge Text in the History of Philosophy, 2015).

Karska, E and K Karski, 'Judicial Dialogue in Human Rights' (2019) 21 *International Community Law Review* 391–99.

Kaun, A, 'Suing the Algorithm: The Mundanization of Automated Decision-Making in Public Services through Litigation' (2021) *Information, Communication & Society* 1–17.

Kennedy, DW, 'One, Two, Three, Many Legal Orders: Legal Pluralism and the Cosmopolitan Dream' (2007) 31 *New York University Review of Law and Social Change* 641.

Kierkegaard, S and P Kierkegaard, 'Danger to Public Health: Medical Devices, Toxicity, Virus and Fraud' (2013) 29(1) *Computer Law & Security Review* 14.

Kingsbury, B, 'International Law and Inter-Public Law' (2009) 49 *Nomos: Moral Universalism and Pluralism* 167–204.

Kingsbury, B, N Krisch, and RB Stewart, 'The Emergence of Global Administrative Law' (2005) 68 *Law and Contemporary Problems* 15–62.

Kingsbury, B and N Maisley, 'Infrastructures and Laws: Publics and Publicness' (Institute for International Law and Justice, NYU School of Law, Working Paper 2021/3, 2021).

Klabbers, J and G Palombella, 'Introduction: Situating Inter-Legality' in J Klabbers and G Palombella (eds), *The Challenge of Inter-Legality* (Cambridge University Press, 2019).

—— (eds), *The Challenge of Inter-Legality* (Cambridge University Press, 2019).

Klang, M and A Murray (eds), *Human Rights in the Digital Age* (Cavendish, 2005).

Klatt, M, 'Contemporary Legal Philosophy in Germany' (2007) 93(4) *Archiv für Rechts- und Sozialphilosophie* 519–39.

——, *Making the Law Explicit: The Normativity of Legal Argumentation* (Hart Publishing, 2008).

——, 'Robert Alexy's Philosophy of Law as System' in M Klatt (ed), *Institutionalized Reason: The Jurisprudence of Robert Alexy* (Oxford University Press, 2012) 4–5.

Klonick, K, 'The New Governors: The People, Rules, and Processes Governing Online Speech' (2017) 131 *Harvard Law Review* 1599–1603.

Knight, FH, *Risk, Uncertainty and Profit* (Houghton Mifflin Company, 1921) 516.

Kochenov, D, 'The Missing EU Rule of Law' in C Closa and D Kochenov (eds), *Reinforcing Rule of Law Oversight in the European Union* (Cambridge University Press, 2016).

Kokott, J and C Sobotta, 'The Kadi Case – Constitutional Core Values and International Law – Finding the Balance?' (2012) 23 *European Journal of International Law* 1015–24.

Kumm, M, 'The Idea of Socratic Contestation and the Right to Justification: The Point of Rights-Based Proportionality Review' (2010) 4 *Law and Ethics of Human Rights* 141.

——, 'The Cosmopolitan Turn in Constitutionalism: An Integrated Conception of Public Law' (2013) 20 *Indiana Journal of Global Legal Studies* 609.

Kuner, C, LA Bygrave, and L Drechsler (eds), *GDPR: A Commentary* (Oxford University Press, 2020).

Land, MK and JD Aronson, *New Technologies for Human Rights Law and Practice* (Cambridge University Press, 2018).

Leczykiewicz, D, 'Horizontal Application of the Charter of Fundamental Rights' (2013) 4 *European Law Review* 483.

Lee, K and M Fanguy, 'Online Exam Proctoring Technologies: Educational Innovation and Deterioration?' (2022) *British Journal of Educational Technology* 1–16.

Leenes, R, et al, 'Regulatory Challenges of Robotics: Some Guidelines for Addressing Legal and Ethical Issues' (2017) 9(1) *Law, Innovation and Technology* 1–44.
Lellis, N and R Dutra, 'Programmatic Crisis and Moralization of the Politics: A Proposal to Define the Bolsonarism from the Experience with the Covid-19 Pandemic' (2020) 4 *International Journal of Latin American Religions* 335–59.
Lessig, L, *Code and Other Laws of Cyberspace* (Basic Books, 1999).
Lévi-Strauss, C, *The Savage Mind* (University of Chicago Press, 1966).
Leys, C, *Market-Driven Politics: Neoliberal Democracy and the Public Interest* (Verso, 2001) 4.
Lin, P, K Abney, and GA Bekey, *Robot Ethics: The Ethical and Social Implications of Robotics* (MIT Press, 2014).
Lind, K, 'Central Authorities Slow to React as Sweden's Cities Embrace Automation of Welfare Management' (2020), available at algorithmwatch.org/en/trelleborg-sweden-algorithm/.
Lomas, N, 'Orwellian AI Lie Detector Project Challenged in EU Court' (*TechCrunch*, 5 February 2021), available at techcrunch.com/2021/02/05/orwellian-ai-lie-detector-project-challenged-in-eu-court.
Manheim, KM and L Kaplan, 'Artificial Intelligence: Risks to Privacy and Democracy' (2019) 21 *Yale Journal of Law and Technology* 106.
Mantelero, A, *Beyond Data: Human Rights, Ethical and Social Impact Assessment in AI* (Information Technology and Law Series, vol 36, Asser Press Springer, 2022).
Margulies P, 'The NSA in Global Perspective: Surveillance, Human Rights, and International Counterterrorism' (2014) 82 *Fordham Law Review* 2148–52.
Marshall, J, *Personal Freedom through Human Rights Law? Autonomy, Identity and Integrity under the European Convention on Human Rights* (Martinus Nijhoff, 2009).
Marten, D and H-J Papier, *Handbuch der Grundrechte in Deutschland und Europa*, vol IV: *Grundrechte in Deutschland – Einzelgrundrechte I*, 1st edn (CF Müller, 2011).
McCarthy, J, M Minsky, N Rochester, and CE Shannon, 'Proposal for the Dartmouth Summer Research Project on Artificial Intelligence', 31 August 1955, reprinted in (2006) 27(4) *AI Magazine*.
McCorduck, P, *Machines Who Think: A Personal Inquiry into the History and Prospects of Artificial Intelligence* (AK Peters, 2004).
McCrudden, C, 'Human Dignity and Judicial Interpretation of Human Rights' (2008) 19(4) *European Journal of International Law* 654–724.
Mathur, A, G Acar, MJ Friedman, E Lucherini, J Mayer, M Chetty, and A Narayanan, 'Dark Patterns at Scale: Findings from a Crawl of 11K Shopping Websites', *Proceedings of the ACM on Human-Computer Interaction* 3(CSCW), Art 81 (2019), available at arxiv.org/abs/1907.07032.
Meierhenrich, J and M Loughlin (eds), *The Cambridge Companion to the Rule of Law* (Cambridge University Press, 2021).
Merry, SE, 'Legal Pluralism' (1988) 22 *Law & Society Review* 869, 870.
Meyer, B, 'John McCarthy' (2011), available at cacm.acm.org/blogs/blog-cacm/138907-john-mccarthy/fulltext.
Milanovic, M, *Extraterritorial Application of Human Rights Treaties Law, Principles and Policy* (Oxford University Press, 2011).
——, 'Human Rights Treaties and Foreign Surveillance: Privacy in the Digital Age' (2015) 56(1) *Harvard International Law Journal* 81–146
——, 'Surveillance and Cyber Operations' in M Gibney et al (eds), *Research Handbook on Extraterritorial Human Rights Obligations* (Routledge, 2020).
Miller, S, 'Revisiting Extraterritorial Jurisdiction: A Territorial Justification for Extraterritorial Jurisdiction under the European Convention' (2009) 20(4) *European Journal of International Law* 1223–46.
Mittelstadt, B, 'Principles Alone Cannot Guarantee Ethical AI' (2019) 1(11) *Nature Machine Intelligence* 501.
Möller, K, 'Justifying the Culture of Justification' (2019) 17 *International Journal of Constitutional Law* 1078.

——, 'Lüth and the "Objective System of Values": From "Limited Government" towards an Autonomy-based Conception of Constitutional Rights' in *Global Canons in an Age of Contestation: Debating Foundational Texts of Constitutional Democracy and Human Rights* (Oxford University Press, 2024; online edn, Oxford Academic, 15 May 2024), https://doi.org/10.1093/9780191956942.003.0014.

Morin, A, 'Characteristics of an Effective Internal Dialogue in the Acquisition of Self-Information' (1995) 15 *Imagination, Cognition and Personality* 45–58.

Müller, F, 'Arbeitsmethoden des Verfassungsrechts' in *Enzyklopädie der Geisteswissenschaftlichen Arbeitsmethoden* (R Oldenburg Verlag, 1971) 123–90.

Müller, F and R Christensen, *Juristische Methodik* (Dunker & Humblot, 2013).

——, *Juristische Methodik: Band I – Grundlegung für die Arbeitsmethoden der Rechtspraxis*, 11th edn (Dunker & Humblot, 2013).

Müller, VC, 'Ethics of Artificial Intelligence and Robotics' in *Stanford Encyclopedia of Philosophy* (2018), available at plato.stanford.edu/entries/ethics-ai.

Murphy, T and G Ó Cuinn, 'Work in Progress: New Technologies and the European Court of Human Rights' (2010) 10 *Human Rights Law Review* 601–38.

Narayanan, A and S Kapoor, *AI Snake Oil: What Artificial Intelligence Can Do, What It Can't, and How to Tell the Difference* (Princeton University Press, 2024).

Nemitz, P, 'Constitutional Democracy and Technology in the Age of Artificial Intelligence' (2018) 376(2133) *Philosophical Transactions of the Royal Society A: Mathematical, Physical and Engineering Sciences* 4.

Neyland, D, 'Bearing Accountable Witness to the Ethical Algorithmic System' (2016) 41 *Science, Technology & Human Values* 50.

Nilsson, NJ, *The Quest for Artificial Intelligence: A History of Ideas and Achievements* (Cambridge University Press, 2010), available at ai.stanford.edu/~nilsson/QAI/qai.pdf.

Nordström, M, 'AI under Great Uncertainty: Implications and Decision Strategies for Public Policy' (2021) *AI & Society*, available at doi.org/10.1007/s00146-021-01263-4.

Nye, JS, 'The Regime Complex for Managing Global Cyber Activities' (2014) *Harvard Kennedy School, Belfer Center for Science and International Affairs* 5, available at belfercenter.org/sites/default/files/legacy/files/global-cyber-final-web.pdf.

Nyholm, S, J Danaher, and BD Earp, 'The Technological Future of Love' in N McKeever, A Grahle, and J Saunders (eds), *Love: Past, Present, and Future* (Routledge, 2022).

O'Connell, R, *European Principles of Interpretation and Application in Law, Democracy, and the European Court of Human Rights* (Cambridge University Press, 2020) 79.

O'Donovan K, 'Engendering Justice: Women's Perspective and the Rule of Law' (1989) 39 *University of Toronto Law Journal* 127.

Okin, SM, *Justice, Gender, and the Family* (Basic Books, 1989).

Orsini, A, J-F Morin, and O Young, 'Regime Complexes: A Buzz, a Boom, or a Boost for Global Governance' (2013) 19 *Global Governance* 27–39.

Ostrom, V, CM Tiebout, and R Warren, 'The Organization of Government in Metropolitan Areas: A Theoretical Inquiry' (1961) 55(4) *American Political Science Review* 831–42.

Padovani, C and M Santaniello, 'Digital Constitutionalism: Fundamental Rights and Power Limitation in the Internet Eco-System' (2018) 80(4) *International Communication Gazette* 295–301.

Pagallo, U, *The Laws of Robots: Crimes, Contracts, and Torts* (Law, Governance and Technology Series, vol 10, Springer, 2013).

Palazzo, G, F Krings, and U Hoffrage. 'Ethical Blindness' (2012) 109 *Journal of Business Ethics* 325.

Palenchar, MJ and RL Heath, 'Strategic Risk Communication: Adding Value to Society' (2007) 33(2) *Public Relations Review* 120–29.

Palmerini, E and E Stradella (eds), *Law and Technology: The Challenge of Regulating Technological Development* (Pisa University Press, 2013).

Palombella, G, 'From Human Rights to Fundamental Rights: Consequences of a conceptual distinction' (2007) 93(3) *ARSP: Archiv Für Rechts- Und Sozialphilosophie/Archives for Philosophy of Law and Social Philosophy* 396–426.

——, 'Global Threads: Weaving the Rule of Law and the Balance of Legal Software' in P Carrozza, F Fontanelli, and G Martinico (ed), *Shaping Rule of Law through Dialogue: International and Supranational Experiences* (Europa Law Publishing, 2009).
——, 'The Rule of Law and Its Core' in G Palombella and N Walker (eds), *Relocating the Rule of* (Hart Publishing, 2009).
——, 'The Rule of Law beyond the State: Failures, Promises and Theory' (2009) 7(3) *International Journal of Constitutional Law* 442–67.
—— (ed), *Shaping Rule of Law through Dialogue – International and Supranational Experiences* (European Law Publishing, 2010).
——, 'The Rule of Law as an Institutional Ideal' (2010) 9(1) *Comparative Sociology* 10.
——, 'The Rule of Law in Global Governance – Its Normative Construction, Function and Import' (2010) Institute for International Law and Justice Colloquium, New York University School of Law.
——, 'The EU's Sense of the Rule of Law and the Issue of Its Oversight' (2014) EUI Working Papers RSCAS 2014/125.
——, 'The Rule of Law at Home and Abroad' (2016) 8 *Hague Journal on Rule of Law* 1.
——, '"Formats" of Law and Their Intertwining' in J Klabbers and G Palombella (eds), *The Challenge of Inter-Legality* (Cambridge University Press, 2019).
——, 'Theory, Realities, and Promises of Inter-Legality: A Manifesto' in J Klabbers and G Palombella (eds), *The Challenge of Inter-Legality* (Cambridge University Press, 2019).
——, 'Access to Justice: Dynamic, Foundational, and Generative' (2021) 34(2) *Ratio Juris* 121–38.
——, 'Fundamental Rights: From Limits to Common Goals' (2021, on file with author) 3.
——, 'Inter-Legality: On Interconnectedness and "External Sources"' (2021) 7(2) *Italian Law Journal* 943–59.
——, 'Some Reflections upon Access to Justice in the Transnational Setting, as a "Right to Law"' in JE David et al (eds), *Strengthening Human Rights Protection* (Cambridge University Press, 2021).
——, 'Exploring the Rationale of Inter-Legality' (2022) 1 *Rivista di filosofia del diritto* 9.
Palombella, G and N Walker (eds), *Relocating the Rule of Law* (Hart Publishing, 2009).
Parizeau, M-H, 'The Tension between Autonomy and Dignity' in P Kemp, J Rentorff, and NM Johansen (eds), *Bioethics and Biolaw, vol. II: Four Ethical Principles* (Rhodos International Science and Art Publishers and Centre for Ethics and Law, 2000).
Parolari, P, 'L'interlegalità Come Metodo? La Decisione Giudiziale negli Spazi Giuridici Ibridi' in E Chiti, A Di Martino, and G Palombella (eds), *L'età della Interlegalità* (Il Mulino, 2022).
Pasquale, F, *The Black Box Society: The Secret Algorithms That Control Money and Information* (Harvard University Press, 2015).
Paulus, A, 'National Courts and the International Rule of Law – Remarks on the book by André Nollkaemper' (2012) 4 *Jerusalem Review of Legal Studies* 5.
Perrault, R, et al, Stanford Human-Centered Artificial Intelligence, 'Artificial Intelligence Index 2019 Annual Report' (2019), available at hai.stanford.edu/sites/default/files/ai_index_2019_report.pdf.
Peters, A, 'Humanity as the A and Ω of Sovereignty' (2009) 20(3) *European Journal of International Law* 513–44.
Petit, N and J De Cooman, 'Models of Law and Regulation for AI', EUI Working Paper RSCAS 2020/63, Robert Schuman Centre for Advanced Studies (2020), 1–21.
Pipitone, A and A Chella, 'What Robots Want? Hearing the Inner Voice of a Robot' (2021) 24 *iScience* 102371, 1.
Pistor, K, *The Code of Capital: How the Law Creates Wealth and Inequality* (Princeton University Press, 2019).
Plato, *The Republic*, Book 4 435a–436c, ed by GRF Ferrari, trans by T Griffith (Cambridge University Press, 2000) 131.
Pollicino, O, 'Diabolical Persistence: Thoughts on the *Schrems II* Decision' (*MediaLaws – Commenti Forum*, 24 December 2020), available at medialaws.eu/rivista/diabolical-persistence-thoughts-on-the-schrems-ii-decision.

Pollicino, O and G De Gregorio, 'Constitutional Law in the Algorithmic Society' in H-W Micklitz et al (eds), *Constitutional Challenges in the Algorithmic Society* (Cambridge University Press, 2022).
Pollicino, O and G Romeo (eds), *The Internet and Constitutional Law: The Protection of Fundamental Rights and Constitutional Adjudication in Europe* (Routledge, 2016).
Preston, J and M Bishop (eds), *Views into the Chinese Room: New Essays on Searle and Artificial Intelligence* (Oxford University Press, 2002).
Purnhagen, K, *The Politics of Systematization in EU Product Safety Regulation: Market, State, Collectivity, and Integration* (Springer, 2013).
Quint, P, 'Free Speech and Private Law in German Constitutional Theory' (1989) 48(2) *Maryland Law Review* 247.
Rai, A, 'Explainable AI: From Black Box to Glass Box' (2020) 48 *Journal of the Academy of Marketing Science* 137–41.
Ranchordás, S, 'The International Rule of Law Time After Time: Temporary Institutions Between Change and Continuity' in M Ambrus and RA Wessel (eds), *Netherlands Yearbook of International Law: Between Pragmatism and Predictability: Temporariness in International Law* (TMC Asser Press, 2014) 67.
——, 'Empathy in the Digital Administrative State' (2022) 71 *Duke Law Journal* 1341–89.
Raso, FA, H Hilligoss, V Krishnamurthy, C Bavitz, and L Kim, 'Artificial Intelligence & Human Rights: Opportunities & Risks', Berkman Klein Center for Internet & Society at Harvard University, 25 September 2018, available at cyber.harvard.edu/sites/default/files/2018-09/2018-09_AIHumanRightsSmall.pdf?subscribe=Download+the+Report.
Rawls, J, *A Theory of Justice* (Harvard University Press, 1971) 31.
Raz, J, 'On the Nature of Rights' (1984) XCIII *Mind* 194–214.
——, *The Concept of a Legal System: An Introduction to the Theory of a Legal System*, 2nd edn (Clarendon Press, 2012).
Reidenberg, JR, 'States and Internet Enforcement' (2004) *University of Ottawa Law & Technology Journal* 213.
Renn, O, 'New Challenges for Risk Analysis: Systemic Risks' (2021) 24(1) *Journal of Risk Research* 127–33.
Resnik, J, 'Globalization(s), Privatization(s), Constitutionalization and Statization: Icons and Experiences of Sovereignty in the 21st Century' (2013) 11 *International Journal of Constitutional Law* 162.
Roberts, H and L Floridi, 'The EU and the US: Two Different Approaches to AI Governance' (Oxford Internet Institute, 2021), available at oii.ox.ac.uk/news-events/news/the-eu-and-the-us-two-different-approaches-to-ai-governance/.
Robila, M and SA Robila, 'Applications of Artificial Intelligence Methodologies to Behavioral and Social Sciences' (2020) 29 *Journal of Child and Family Studies* 2957.
Rojszczak, M, 'Extraterritorial Bulk Surveillance after the German BND Act Judgment' (2021) 17(1) *European Constitutional Law Review* 53–77.
Ruggiu, D, 'Implementing a Responsible Research and Innovation Framework for Human Enhancement According to Human Rights: The Right to Bodily Integrity and the Rise of "Enhanced Societies"' (2018) 10(1) *Law, Innovation and Technology* 1–40.
Ruiz Fabri, H, 'Is There a Case – Legally and Politically – for Direct Effect of WTO Obligations?' (2014) 25 *European Journal of International Law* 162.
Russell, SJ and P Norvig, *Artificial Intelligence: A Modern Approach*, 3rd edn (Pearson, 2010).
Sadurski, W, 'Partnering with Strasbourg: Constitutionalism of the European Court of Human Rights, the Accession of Central and East European States to the Council of Europe, and the Idea of Pilot Judgments' (2009) 9 *Human Rights Law Review* 397.
Sagoff, M, *Price, Principle, and the Environment* (Cambridge University Press, 2004) 4.
Sajo, A and R Uitz, *The Constitution in Private Relations: Expanding Constitutionalism* (Eleven International Publishing, 2005).
Sánchez-Monedero, J and L Dencik, 'The Politics of Deceptive Borders: "Biomarkers of Deceit" and the Case of iBorderCtrl' (2022) 25(3) *Information, Communication & Society* 414.

Sandel, MJ, *Liberalism and the Limits of Justice* (Cambridge University Press, 1982)
Sartori, G, 'Nota sul rapporto tra Stato di diritto e Stato di giustizia' (1964) in *Rivista internazionale di filosofia del dritto* 310.
Scantamburlo, T, A Charlesworth, and N Cristianini, 'Machine Decisions and Human Consequences' in K Yeung and M Lodge (eds), *Algorithmic Regulation* (Oxford University Press, 2019).
Schiller, D, *Digital Capitalism: Networking the Global Market System* (MIT Press, 1999).
Schuett, J, 'A Legal Definition of AI' (2019) arXiv:1909.01095, available at arxiv.org/abs/1909.01095.
Searle, JR, 'Minds, Brains, and Programs' (1980) 3 *Behavioral and Brain Sciences* 417–57.
——, 'Is the Brain's Mind a Computer Program?' (*Scientific American*, January 1990) 26.
——, *The Mystery of Consciousness* (New York Review Books, 1997).
Slavin, K, 'How Algorithms Shape Our World', TED Global, 2011, available at ted.com/talks/kevin_slavin_how_algorithms_shape_our_world.
Smolan S, *The Human Face of Big Data* (PBS Documentary, 24 February 2016).
Smuha, N, 'From a "Race to AI" to a "Race to AI Regulation": Regulatory Competition for Artificial Intelligence' (2021) 13(1) *Law, Innovation and Technology* 57–84.
Smuha, N, E Ahmed-Rengers, A Harkens, W Li, J MacLaren, R Piselli, and K Yeung, 'How the EU Can Achieve Legally Trustworthy AI: A Response to the European Commission's Proposal for an Artificial Intelligence Act', LEADS Law, University of Birmingham – Legal, Ethical and Accountable Digital Society, 5 August 2021, 9, available at papers.ssrn.com/sol3/papers.cfm?abstract_id=3899991.
Snyder, F, 'The Gatekeepers: The European Courts and WTO' (2003) 40 *Common Market Law Review* 367.
Sousa Santos, B de, 'Law: A Map of Misreading. Towards a Postmodern Conception of Law' (1987) 14(3) *Journal of Law and Society* 279–302.
——, 'Law: A Map of Misreading' in B de Sousa Santos, *Toward a New Common Sense: Law, Science and Politics in the Paradigmatic Transition* (Routledge, 1995).
Spano, R, 'The Rule of Law as the Lodestar of the European Convention on Human Rights: The Strasbourg Court and the Independence of the Judiciary' (2021) 27 *European Law Journal* 211–27.
Stewart, RB, 'Environmental Regulatory Decision Making Under Uncertainty' (2001) *University College London Symposium on the Law & Economics of Environmental Policy* 20, available at ucl.ac.uk/cserge/Stewart.pdf.
Steyn, J, 'Guantanamo Bay: The Legal Black Hole' (2004) 53(1) *International and Comparative Law Quarterly* 1.
Stone, P, R Brooks, E Brynjolfsson, R Calo, O Etzioni, G Hager, J Hirschberg, S Kalyanakrishnan, E Kamar, S Kraus, K Leyton-Brown, D Parkes, W Press, A Lee, J Shah, M Tambe, and A Teller, 'Artificial Intelligence and Life in 2030: One Hundred Year Study on Artificial Intelligence' (Stanford University, September 2016), available at ai10020201023.sites.stanford.edu/sites/g/files/sbiybj18871/files/media/file/ai100report10032016fnl_singles.pdf.
Sunstein, CR, 'Beyond the Precautionary Principle' (2002) University of Chicago, John M Olin Law & Economics Working Paper No 149, 2.
——, 'The Paralyzing Principle' (Winter 2002–2003) 25(4) *Regulation* 32–37.
——, *Laws of Fear Beyond the Precautionary Principle* (Cambridge University Press, 2005).
Surowiecki J, 'What Does Breaking Up Big Tech Really Mean?' (*MIT Technology Review*, 30 June 2021), available at technologyreview.com/2021/06/30/1026502/big-tech-breakup-monopoly-antitrust.
Susser, D, B Roessler, and H Nissenbaum, 'Technology, Autonomy, and Manipulation' (2019) 8(2) *Internet Policy Review*, available at policyreview.info/articles/analysis/technology-autonomy-and-manipulation.
Suzor, N, 'Digital Constitutionalism: Using the Rule of Law to Evaluate the Legitimacy of Governance by Platforms' (2018) 4(3) *Social Media and Society* 4.
Swenson, G, 'Legal Pluralism in Theory and Practice' (2018) 20 *International Studies Review* 438–62.
Taekema, S, 'Between or Beyond Legal Orders? Questioning the Concept of Legal Order' in J Klabbers and G Palombella (eds), *The Challenge of Inter-Legality* (Cambridge University Press, 2019).
Tamanaha, BZ, *On the Rule of Law: History, Politics, Theory* (Cambridge University Press, 2012).

Tang, X, X Li, Y Ding, M Song, and Y Bu, 'The Pace of Artificial Intelligence Innovations: Speed, Talent, and Trial-and-Error' (2020) 14(4) *Journal of Informetrics* Article 101094, doi.org/10.1016/j.joi.2020.101094.

Tasioulas, J, 'Consequences of Ethical Relativism' (1998) 6(2) *European Journal of Philosophy* 156–71.

——, 'On the Foundations of Human Rights' in R Cruft, SM Liao, and M Renzo (eds), *Philosophical Foundations of Human Rights* (Oxford University Press, 2015).

——, 'Artificial Intelligence, Humanistic Ethics' (2022) 151(2) *Dædalus: Journal of the American Academy of Arts & Sciences* 232.

——, 'A Right to Human Decision' Draft Paper (2023), available at academia.edu/116775511/A_Human_Right_to_a_Human_Decision.

——, 'Work and Play in the Shadow of AI' in D Edmonds (ed), *AI Morality* (Oxford University Press, 2024).

Tene, Ö and J Polonetsky, 'Big Data for All: Privacy and User Control in the Age of Analytics' (2013) 11 *Northwestern Journal of Technology and Intellectual Property* 239.

Teubner, G, 'Legal Irritants: Good Faith in British Law or How Unifying Law Ends Up in New Divergences' (1998) 61 *Modern Law Review* 11.

Thompson, N, 'When Tech Knows You Better Than You Know Yourself' (*Wired*, 4 October 2018), available at wired.com/story/artificial-intelligence-yuval-noah-harari-tristan-harris.

Thomson, JJ, 'The Trolley Problem' (1995) 94(6) *Yale Law Journal* 1395–415.

Tokamani, P, 'Persuasive Technology and Human Rights' (LLM thesis, Tilburg University, 2016), available at arno.uvt.nl/show.cgi?fid=142041.

Tripkovic, B, 'A New Philosophy for the Margin of Appreciation and European Consensus' (2021) 42(1) *Oxford Journal of Legal Studies* 207–34.

Trouwborst, A, *Evolution and Status of the Precautionary Principle in International Law* (Springer, 2002).

Turilli, M and L Floridi, 'The Ethics of Information Transparency' (2015) 11 *Ethics and Information Technology* 105.

Turing, AM, 'Computing Machinery and Intelligence' (1950) 59(236) *Mind* 433–60.

Tushnet, M, 'The Possibilities of Comparative Constitutional Law' (1999) 108 *Yale Law Journal* 1285–286.

——, 'The Inevitable Globalisation of Constitutional Law' (2009) 49 *Virginia Journal of International Law* 985.

Twining, W, 'Schauer on Hart' (2006) 119 *Harvard Law Review Forum* 122.

Uschold, M, 'The Importance of Distinguishing between Terms and Concepts' (*Semantic Arts*, 22 August 2013), available at semanticarts.com/the-importance-of-distinguishing-between-terms-and-concepts.

Uschold, M and M Gruninger, 'Ontologies: Principles, Methods and Applications' (1996) 11 *Knowledge Engineering Review* 93–136.

Vallor, S, 'Artificial Intelligence and the Ethics of Self-Learning Robots' in P Lin, K Abney, and R Jenkins (eds), *Robot Ethics 2.0: From Autonomous Cars to Artificial Intelligence* (Oxford University Press, 2017).

Van der Burg, WW, *The Dynamics of Law and Morality: A Pluralist Account of Legal Interactionism* (Ashgate, 2014) 10.

Van Kolfschooten, H, 'EU Regulation of Artificial Intelligence: Challenges for Patients' Rights' (2022) 59 *Common Market Law Review* 106.

Veale, M and F Zuiderveen Borgesius, 'Demystifying the Draft EU Artificial Intelligence Act' (2021), available at arxiv.org/abs/2107.03721v1.

Véliz, C, *Privacy is Power: Why and How You Should Take Back Control of Your Data* (Bantam Press, 2020).

Versteeg, M and A Chilton, *How Constitutional Rights Matter* (Oxford University Press, 2020) 79.

Von Mohl, R, *Die deutsche Polizei-Wissenschaft nach den Grundsätzen des Rechtsstaates*, vol I, 2nd edn (Tübingen 1844); the entire volume is available at Münchener Digitalisierungszentrum at digitale-sammlungen.de/de/view/bsb10766998?page=34.
Vos, E, 'Antibiotics, the Precautionary Principle and the Court of First Instance: Cases T-13/99 *Pfizer Animal Health SA v Council of the European Union* and T-70/99 *Alpharma Inc v Council of the European Union*' (2004) 11(2) *Maastricht Journal of European and Comparative Law* 187–200.
Wagner, B, 'Ethics as an Escape from Regulation: From Ethics-Washing to Ethics-Shopping?' in E Bayamlioglu, I Baraliuc, LAW Janssens, and M Hildebrandt (eds), *Being Profiled: Cogitas ergo sum - 10 Years of Profiling the European Citizen* (Amsterdam University Press, 2019) 84–89, doi:10.1515/9789048550180-016.
Wagner, B, M Kettemann, and K Vieth (eds), *Research Handbook on Human Rights and Digital Technology: Global Politics, Law and International Relations* (Edward Elgar, 2019).
Waldron, J, 'Foreign Law and the Modern Jus Gentium' (2005) 119 *Harvard Law Review* 129, 133.
——, 'No Barking: Legal Pluralism and the Contrast between Hart's Jurisprudence and Fuller's' in P Cane (ed), *The Hart–Fuller Debate 50 Years On* (Australian National University College of Law, 2008).
Walker, N, 'Seven Pieces of Global Law' in N Walker, *Intimations of Global Law* (Cambridge University Press, 2015).
——, 'Legalising Inter-Legality' (2022) 1 *European Law Open* 216–27.
Walkila, S, *Horizontal Effect of Fundamental Rights in EU Law* (European Law Publishing, 2016).
Wallach, W and C Allen, *Moral Machines: Teaching Robots Right from Wrong* (Oxford University Press, 2008).
Wallach, W and GE Marchant, 'Toward the Agile and Comprehensive International Governance of AI and Robotics' (2019) 107(3) *Proceedings of the IEEE* 505.
Weiler, JHH, 'The Transformation of Europe' (1991) 100 *Yale Law Journal* 2403.
Weiler, JHH and M Wind, *European Constitutionalism Beyond the State* (Cambridge University Press, 2003) 16.
Weizenbaum, J, *Computer Power and Human Reason: From Judgment to Calculation* (The MIT, WH Freeman and Company New York, 1976).
Whitman, JQ, 'On Nazi Honor and New European Dignity' in C Joerges and NS Ghaleigh (eds), *Darker Legacies of Law in Europe: The Shadow of National Socialism and Fascism over Europe and Its Legal Traditions* (Hart Publishing, 2003).
Whittaker, M, et al, 'AI Now Report 2018' (AI Now Institute, December 2018), available at ainowinstitute.org/AI_Now_2018_Report.pdf.
Wischmeyer, T and T Rademacher (eds), *Regulating Artificial Intelligence* (Springer, 2020).
Wright, D and J Copas, 'Prediction Scores for Risk Assessment' in R Baldwin (ed), *Law and Uncertainty: Risks and Legal Processes* (Kluwer Law International, 1997).
Yeung, K, *Securing Compliance: A Principled Framework* (Hart Publishing, 2004).
——, *Regulating Technologies: Legal Futures, Regulatory Frames and Technological Fixes* (Hart Publishing, 2008).
Zalnieriute, M, 'Data Transfers After Schrems II: The EU–US Disagreements over Data Privacy and National Security' (2022) 55(1) *Vanderbilt Journal of Transnational Law* 1–48, also published as University of New South Wales Law Research Series.
Završnik, A, 'Criminal Justice, Artificial Intelligence Systems and Human Rights' (2020) 20 *ERA Forum* 567–83.
Zhang, D, S Mishra, E Brynjolfsson, J Etchemendy, D Ganguli, B Grosz, T Lyons, J Manyika, JC Niebles, M Sellitto, Y Shoham, J Clark, and R Perrault, 'The AI Index 2021 Annual Report', AI Index Steering Committee, Human-Centered AI Institute, Stanford University (Stanford, CA, March 2021).
Zorn, A, *Grundzüge des Völkerrechts* (Nabu Press, 2010).
Zuboff, S, *The Age of Surveillance Capitalism: The Fight for a Human Future at the New Frontier of Power* (Profile Books, 2019).

Online Sources, Reports, Blog Posts, and Newspaper Articles

Abu Elyounes, D, 'Why the Resignation of the Dutch Government Is a Good Reminder of How Important It Is to Monitor and Regulate Algorithms' (Harvard Berkman Klein Center, 10 February 2021), available at medium.com/berkman-klein-center/why-the-resignation-of-the-dutch-government-is-a-good-reminder-of-how-important-it-is-to-monitor-2c599c1e0100.

Access Now, 'An EU Artificial Intelligence Act for Fundamental Rights: A Civil Society Statement' (2021), available at accessnow.org/cms/assets/uploads/2021/11/joint-statement-EU-AIA.pdf.

Ada Lovelace Institute, 'People, Risks, and the Unique Requirements of AI: 18 Recommendations to Strengthen the EU AI Act', Policy Briefing (2022), available at adalovelaceinstitute.org/wp-content/uploads/2022/03/Policy-briefing-People-risk-and-the-unique-requirements-of-AI-18-recommendations-to-strengthen-the-EU-AI-Act.pdf.

AlgorithmWatch, 'Automating Society Report 2020' (2020), available at automatingsociety.algorithmwatch.org/wp-content/uploads/2020/12/Automating-Society-Report-2020.pdf.

Anderson, R, 'The Panopticon is Already Here' (*The Atlantic*, September 2020), available at theatlantic.com/magazine/archive/2020/09/china-ai-surveillance/614197/.

Baynes, C, 'Government "Deported 7,000 Foreign Students after Falsely Accusing Them of Cheating in English Language Tests"' (*The Independent*, 14 June 2019), available at independent.co.uk/news/uk/politics/home-office-mistakenly-deported-thousands-foreign-students-cheating-language-tests-theresa-may-windrush-a8331906.html.

Berthet, A, 'Why Do Emerging AI Guidelines Emphasize "Ethics" over Human Rights?' (*Open Global Rights*, 10 July 2019), available at openglobalrights.org/why-do-emerging-ai-guidelines-emphasize-ethics-over-human-rights.

Carmichael, J, 'Google Knows You Better than Yourself' (*The Atlantic*, 19 August 2014), available at theatlantic.com/technology/archive/2014/08/google-knows-you-better-than-you-know-yourself/378608/.

Cave, S, 'To Save Us from a Kafkaesque Future, We Must Democratise AI', *The Guardian* (4 Jaunary 2019), available at theguardian.com/commentisfree/2019/jan/04/future-democratise-ai-artificial-intelligence-power.

Center for AI and Digital Policy, 'Artificial Intelligence and Democratic Values Index' (Washington DC, 2022), available at caidp.org/reports/aidv-2021/.

Cornell Law School, 'Black Letter Law', Cornell Law School Legal Information Institute, available law.cornell.edu/wex/black_letter_law.

Costa, E and D Halpern, 'The Behavioural Science of Online Harm and Manipulation, and What to Do About It – An Exploratory Paper to Spark Ideas and Debate' (The Behavioural Insight Team, 2019), available at bi.team/publications/the-behavioural-science-of-online-harm-and-manipulation-and-what-to-do-about-it.

Council of Europe, 'Datavisualisation', available at coe.int/en/web/artificial-intelligence/national-initiatives.

Council of the European Union, 'EU restrictive measures in response to the crisis in Ukraine', available at consilium.europa.eu/en/policies/sanctions/restrictive-measures-ukraine-crisis.

Council of Europe and the Italian Chairmanship of the Committee of Ministers co-organised the 'High-Level Segment – Inaugural Meeting of the Committee on Artificial Intelligence (CAI)' in Rome, to elaborate an appropriate legal framework on AI based on the Council of Europe's standards on human rights, democracy and the rule of law, available at coe.int/en/web/artificial-intelligence/-/inaugural-meeting-of-the-committee-on-artificial-intelligence-cai-.

Dave, P, 'Exclusive: Google Blocks RT, Sputnik from Play App Store in Europe' (*Reuters*, 2 March 2022), available at reuters.com/technology/exclusive-google-blocks-rt-sputnik-play-app-store-europe-2022-03-02.

De Abreu Duarte, F, 'The Internet Is for Porn! (But Is It?) – The Digital Equilibrium Hypothesis' (2022) *Digital Constitutionalist*, available at digi-con.org/the-internet-is-for-porn-but-is-it-the-digital-equilibrium-hypothesis/.

De Gregorio, G, 'The Declaration on European Digital Rights and Principles: A First Analysis from Digital Constitutionalism' (2022) *The Digital Constitutionalist*, available at digi-con.org/the-declaration-on-european-digital-rights-and-principles-a-first-analysis-from-digital-constitutionalism/.

Debate: China's Social Credit System (*Verfassungsblog*, 28 June 2019), available at verfassungsblog.de/category/debates/chinas-social-credit-system/.

Deutsch D, 'Philosophy That Will Be the Key That Unlocks Artificial Intelligence' (*The Guardian*, 3 October 2012), available at theguardian.com/science/2012/oct/03/philosophy-artificial-intelligence.

Dupré, C, 'Individuals and Judges in Defense of the Rule of Law' (*Verfassungsblog*, 28 July 2018), available at verfassungsblog.de/individuals-and-judges-in-defense-of-the-rule-of-law/.

Edelman, 'Trust Barometer 2022', available at edelman.com/trust/2022-trust-barometer.

El Mundo, 'Las asesinadas que denunciaron se valoraron como "riesgo bajo o nulo"' (9 December 2014), available at elmundo.es/espana/2014/12/09/54861553ca4741734b8b457e.html.

Electronic Privacy Information Center, 'AI in the Criminal Justice System', available at epic.org/issues/ai/ai-in-the-criminal-justice-system/.

Encyclopaedia Britannica, 'al-Jazari', available at britannica.com/biography/al-Jazari.

EPO, 'EPO Refuses DABUS Patent Applications Designating a Machine Inventor' (20 December 2019), available at epo.org/news-events/news/2019/20191220.html.

European Commission, Press Corner, 'Leading the Digital Decade', 1 June 2021, available at ec.europa.eu/commission/presscorner/detail/en/speech_21_2804.

European University Institute, 'The Digital Services Act (DSA): Views of the Cathedral' (2022), available at eui.eu/events?id=547317.

FRA, *Bringing Rights to Life: The Fundamental Rights Landscape of the European Union* (Publications Office of the European Union, 2012), available at fra.europa.eu/sites/default/files/fra-2012-bringing-rights-to-life_en.pdf.

Grover, N, 'Study Explores Inner Life of AI with Robot That Thinks Out Loud' (*The Guardian*, 21 April 2021), available at amp.theguardian.com/technology/2021/apr/21/study-inner-life-ai-robot-thinks-out-loud?__twitter_impression=true.

Hoepman, J-H, 'The European Declaration on Digital Rights Puts People in the Firing Line of the Digital Transformation' (6 March 2022), available at blog.xot.nl/2022/03/06/the-european-declaration-on-digital-rights-puts-people-in-the-firing-line-of-the-digital-transformation/index.html.

IEEE, 'Artificial Intelligence and Machine Learning, 5G and IoT Will Be the Most Important Technologies in 2021, According to New IEEE Study' (19 November 2020), available at ieee.org/about/news/2020/survey-chief-information-officers-and-chief-technology-officers.html.

Interview with a computer scientist at the Technical University of Munich, available at tum.de/en/about-tum/news/press-releases/details/33313.

Investopedia, 'Spillover Effect', available at investopedia.com/terms/s/spillover-effect.asp.

Ioannidis, N and O Gkotsopoulou, 'The Palimpsest of Conformity Assessment in the Proposed Artificial Intelligence Act: A Critical Exploration of Related Terminology' (*European Law Blog*, 2 July 2021), available at europeanlawblog.eu/2021/07/02/the-palimpsest-of-conformity-assessment-in-the-proposed-artificial-intelligence-act-a-critical-exploration-of-related-terminology/.

Kissinger, HA, 'How the Enlightenment Ends: Philosophically, Intellectually – in Every Way – Human Society Is Unprepared for the Rise of Artificial Intelligence' (*The Atlantic*, June 2018), available at theatlantic.com/magazine/archive/2018/06/henry-kissinger-ai-could-mean-the-end-of-human-history/559124.

Krupiy, T, 'Why the Proposed Artificial Intelligence Regulation Does Not Deliver on the Promise to Protect Individuals from Harm' (*European Law Blog*, 23 July 2021), available at europeanlawblog.eu/2021/07/23/why-the-proposed-artificial-intelligence-regulation-does-not-deliver-on-the-promise-to-protect-individuals-from-harm/.

Lyceum Project Philosophers Panel, 'White Paper on Aristotelian AI Ethics', available at youtube.com/watch?v=trVqxqToknQ&t=1965s.

Malgieri, G and M Ienca, 'The EU Regulates AI but Forgets to Protect Our Mind' (*European Law Blog*, 7 July 2021), available at europeanlawblog.eu/2021/07/07/the-eu-regulates-ai-but-forgets-to-protect-our-mind/.

Massachusetts Institute of Technology (MIT), 'Moral Machine Experiment', available at moralmachine.net/.

Munoz, JM, 'Chile: Right to Free Will Needs Definition' (*Nature*, 29 October 2019), available at nature.com/articles/d41586-019-03295-9.

Nemitz, P and E Gräf, 'Artificial Intelligence Must Be Used According to the Law, or Not at All' (*Verfassungsblog*, 28 March 2022), available at verfassungsblog.de/roa-artificial-intelligence-must-be-used-according-to-the-law/.

NeuroRights Foundation, 'Mission', available at neurorightsfoundation.org/mission.

New York Times, 'Kennan Now Backs an Agency in UN on World Pollution', 3 March 1972, available at nytimes.com/1972/03/03/archives/kennan-now-backs-an-agency-in-un-on-world-pollution.html.

New York Times Magazine, 'The Year in Ideas: A to Z' (9 December 2001), available at nytimes.com/2001/12/09/magazine/the-year-in-ideas-a-to-z-precautionary-principle.html.

OECD Report, 'Emerging Systemic Risks in the 21st Century: An Agenda for Action' (2003), available at oecd.org/futures/globalprospects/37944611.pdf.

Papakonstantinou, V and P De Hert, 'EU Lawmaking in the Artificial Intelligent Age: Act-ification, GDPR Mimesis, and Regulatory Brutality' (*European Law Blog*, 8 July 2021), available at europeanlawblog.eu/2021/07/08/eu-lawmaking-in-the-artificial-intelligent-age-act-ification-gdpr-mimesis-and-regulatory-brutality/.

Puri, A, 'Rule of Law, AI, and the "Individual"' (*Verfassungsblog*, 3 April 2022), available at verfassungsblog.de/roa-individual/.

Rotenberg, M, 'Time to Assess National AI Policies', Communications of the ACM (2020), available at cacm.acm.org/blogs/blog-cacm/248921-time-to-assess-national-ai-policies/fulltext.

Rusteberg, B, 'Theorie, Interpretation und Dogmatik der Grundrechte bei Ernst-Wolfgang Böckenförde' (*Verfassungsblog*, 6 May 2019), available at verfassungsblog.de/theorie-interpretation-und-dogmatik-der-grundrechte-bei-ernst-wolfgang-boeckenfoerde/.

Schaake, M, 'Big Tech Faces Moral Reckoning in Ukraine' (*Financial Times*, 7 March 2022), available at ft.com/content/d35c5e95-e0cb-4350-9dbd-e971e7070b63.

Society for Risk Analysis, 'Risk Analysis Introduction', available at sra.org/risk-analysis-introduction/.

SoftBank Robotics, 'Pepper', available at softbankrobotics.com/emea/en/pepper.

United Nations, 'World Charter for Nature' (28 October 1982), available at refworld.org/docid/3b00f22a10.html.

——, 'Rio Declaration on Environment and Development' in 'Report of the United Nations Conference on Environment and Development' (12 August 1992), available at un.org/en/development/desa/population/migration/generalassembly/docs/globalcompact/A_CONF.151_26_Vol.I_Declaration.pdf.

——, 'World Stumbling Zombie-Like into a Digital Welfare Dystopia, Warns UN Human Rights Expert' (Press Release, 17 October 2019), available at ohchr.org/en/press-releases/2019/10/world-stumbling-zombie-digital-welfare-dystopia-warns-un-human-rights-expert?LangID=E&NewsID=25156.

——, 'Urgent Action Needed over Artificial Intelligence Risks to Human Rights' (UN News, 15 September 2021), available at news.un.org/en/story/2021/09/1099972.

Weiner, E, 'Renaissance Florence Was a Better Model for Innovation than Silicon Valley Is' (*Harvard Business Review*, 25 January 2016), available at hbr.org/2016/01/renaissance-florence-was-a-better-model-for-innovation-than-silicon-valley-is.

World Economic Forum, 'Edelman Trust Barometer: Cycle of Distrust Threatens Action on Global Challenges' (2022), available at weforum.org/agenda/2022/01/edelman-trust-barometer-2022-report/.

World Health Organization, 'WHO Chief Warns Against COVID-19 "Vaccine Nationalism"', available at news.cgtn.com/news/2020-10-26/WHO-chief-warns-against-COVID-19-vaccine-nationalism--UTD8hxtXeE/index.html.

——, 'COVID-19', available at euro.who.int/en/health-topics/health-emergencies/coronavirus-covid-19#:~:text=WHO%20announced%20COVID%2D19,on%2011%20March%202020.
——, 'Communication and Community Engagement', available at who.int/emergencies/risk-communications.
——, 'WHO Announced COVID-19 Outbreak as a Pandemic on 11 March 2020', available at euro.who.int/en/health-topics/health-emergencies.
World Wide Web Foundation, 'Policy Brief W20 Argentina: Artificial Intelligence – Open Questions about Gender Inclusion' (2018), available at webfoundation.org/docs/2018/06/AI-Gender.pdf.
Wright, R, 'Home Office Told Thousands of Foreign Students to Leave UK in Error' (*Financial Times*, 6 May 2018), available at ft.com/content/2ae9b7d2-4d0c-11e8-8a8e-22951a2d8493.
Yong, E, 'A Popular Algorithm Is No Better at Predicting Crimes Than Random People' (*The Atlantic*, 17 January 2018), available at theatlantic.com/technology/archive/2018/01/equivant-compas-algorithm/550646.

Projects and International Platforms

'AVATAR', an automated lie detector and deception detection technology based on eye tracking, available at discernscience.com/avatar/.
CEN-CENELEC, available at cencenelec.eu/.
Global Policy.AI Platform, available at globalpolicy.ai/en.
IborderCtrl Project, iborderctrl.eu/The-project.
Lyceum Project, J Ober, and J Tasioulas, 'AI Ethics with Aristotle White Paper' (17 June 2024), available at oxford-aiethics.ox.ac.uk/lyceum-project-ai-ethics-aristotle-white-paper.
N-EXTLAW, co-ordinated by M Bartl, available at nonextractivefuture.eu/the-project/.
Reclaim You Face, available at reclaimyourface.eu/.
Sienna Project, available at sienna-project.eu/.
Sienna Project, 'D2.4: Ethical Analysis of Human Genetics and Genomics' (2019), available at enodo.org/record/4068016.
UK Parliament, 'The UK's smart border technology to detect deception', available at post.parliament.uk/research-briefings/post-pn-375/.

Artificial Intelligence and Science Fiction, Art and Literature

A Space Odyssey, directed by Stanley Kubrick. UK/US: 1968.
al-Jazari, Ibn al-Razzaz, *The Book of Knowledge of Ingenious Mechanical Devices (Kitab fi Ma'rifat al-Hiyal al-Handasiyya)*, trans and annotated by DR Hill (D Reidel Publishing Company, 1974).
Bär, S, *Artificial Intelligence in Greek and Roman Epic* (Bloomsbury, 2024).
Biblioteca Ambrosiana, *Codex Atlanticus: The Largest Existing Collection of Writings and Drawings by Leonardo da Vinci* (Milan), available at codex-atlanticus.ambrosiana.it/#/.
Blade Runner, directed by Ridley Scott. US/Hong Kong: 1982.
Cambiano, G, 'Automaton' (1994) 25 *Studi Storici* 613–33.
Čapek, K, *R.U.R. (Rossum's Universal Robots)* (1921).
Drachmann, AG, *The Mechanical Technology of Greek and Roman Antiquity* (University of Wisconsin Press, 1963).
Eco, U, *Il pendolo di Foucault* (Bompiani, 2014).
Ex Machina, directed by Alex Garland. US: 2014.

Freeth T et al, 'A Model of the Cosmos in the ancient Greek Antikythera Mechanism' (2021) 11 *Scientific Reports* 5821, available at doi.org/10.1038/s41598-021-84310-w.
Her, directed by Spike Jonze. US: 2013.
HUM∀NS, created by Sam Vincent and Jonathan Brackley. UK/US: 2015.
I, Robot, directed by Alex Proyas. US/Germany: 2004.
Interstellar, directed by Christopher Nolan. US: 2014.
Kafka, F, *The Trial*, trans M Mitchell (Oxford World's Classics, 2009).
Kiecol, D, *Leonardo* (Koenemann, 2023).
Landels, JG, *Engineering in the Ancient World* (Chatto & Windus, 1978).
Midnight at the Pera Palace. The series is based on the book by C King, *Midnight at the Pera Palace: The Birth of Modern Istanbul* (WW Norton & Company, 2015). It is available at netflix.com/title/81212136.
Pedretti C (ed), *Leonardo da Vinci: Fragments at Windsor Castle from the Codex Atlanticus* (Phaidon, 1957), 39–40, no 12705.
Rhodius, A, *The Argonautica*, with an English trans by RC Seaton, MA (William Heineman/GP Putnam's Sons, 1912) Book IV, 407.
Richter, JP, *Scritti Letterari di Leonardo da Vinci (The Literary Works of Leonardo da Vinci)* (S Low, Marston, Searle & Rivington, 1883), available at archive.org/details/literaryworksofl02leon/page/n3/mode/2up, 289.
Shelley, M, *Frankenstein* (1818).
Stephens, E, 'The Mechanical Turk: A Short History of "Artificial Artificial Intelligence"' (2023) 31(1) *Cultural Studies* 65–87.
Stross, C, *Saturn's Children* (2008).
Tregillis, I, *The Mechanical* (2015).
Westworld, created by Jonathan Nolan and Lisa Joy. HBO, US: 2016.

INDEX

www.ingramcontent.com/pod-product-compliance
Ingram Content Group UK Ltd.
Pitfield, Milton Keynes, MK11 3LW, UK
UKHW021811130926
475425UK00008B/90

9 781509 979011